American Law from a
Catholic Perspective

Catholic Social Thought

This series focuses on Catholic social thought and its application to current social, political, economic, and cultural issues. The titles in this series are written and edited by members of the Society of Catholic Social Scientists. They survey and analyze Catholic approaches to politics, sociology, law, economics, history, and other disciplines. Within these broad themes, authors explore the Church's role and influence in contemporary society. The Society of Catholic Social Scientists was formed in 1992 to rejuvenate a distinctively Catholic scholarship in the social sciences.

Titles in the Series

The Public Order and the Sacred Order, by Stephen M. Krason, 2009.
Bioethics, Law, and Human Life Issues, by D. Brian Scarnecchia, 2010.
Pope Pius XII on the Economic Order, by Rupert J. Ederer, 2011.
Economics As If God Matters, by Rupert J. Ederer, 2011.
Toward the Common Good, edited by Robert F. Gorman, 2011.
Sociology and Catholic Social Teaching, edited by Stephen R. Sharkey, 2012.
Child Abuse, Family Rights, and the Child Protective System, edited by Stephen M. Krason, 2013.
Catholicism and Historical Narrative: A Catholic Engagement with Historical Scholarship, edited by Kevin Schmiesing, 2014.
The Crisis of Religious Liberty, edited by Stephen M. Krason, 2014.
American Law from a Catholic Perspective: Through a Clearer Lens, edited by Ronald J. Rychlak, 2015.

American Law from a Catholic Perspective

Through a Clearer Lens

Edited by Ronald J. Rychlak

ROWMAN & LITTLEFIELD
Lanham • Boulder • New York • London

Published by Rowman & Littlefield
A wholly owned subsidiary of The Rowman & Littlefield Publishing Group, Inc.
4501 Forbes Boulevard, Suite 200, Lanham, Maryland 20706
www.rowman.com

Unit A, Whitacre Mews, 26-34 Stannary Street, London SE11 4AB

British Library Cataloguing in Publication Information Available

Library of Congress Cataloging-in-Publication Data
The hardback edition of this book was previously cataloged by the Library of Congress as follows:

American law from a Catholic perspective : through a clearer lens / Edited by Ronald J. Rychlak.
p. cm. — (Catholic social thought)
Includes bibliographical references and index.
ISBN 978-0-8108-8917-0 (cloth : alk. paper)
ISBN 978-1-4422-6168-6 (pbk.: alk. paper)
ISBN 978-0-8108-8918-7 (ebook)
1. Law—Religious aspects—United States. 2. Catholic Church—Doctrines. 3. Church and state—United States. I. Rychlak, Ronald J., editor.
KF358.A44 2015
261.5—dc23
2014039700

∞ ™ The paper used in this publication meets the minimum requirements of American National Standard for Information Sciences Permanence of Paper for Printed Library Materials, ANSI/NISO Z39.48-1992.

Printed in the United States of America

To my daughter Susanna:
Two Ss, two Ns, and two As
But only one you!

Contents

Foreword

Gerard V. Bradley

What should one expect to learn from a volume about American law from a Catholic perspective?

In one respect, not much: the roster of distinctively Catholic *laws* in American history is short. The list includes the priest-penitent testimonial privilege, which seems to have been first articulated in this country in the 1813 New York case of *People v. Phillips* (a criminal prosecution in which Jesuit Fr. Anthony Kohlmann was called as a witness). It also includes the novel legal form we call "corporation sole," which was created across American jurisdictions in the mid-nineteenth century to make Church property holdings safe from lay trustees' revolts. (The prevailing rule had vested Church ownership in boards of laypersons and was itself an artifact of our Protestant heritage.)

These and very few other American laws are distinctively Catholic, by dint of debt to what Catholics hold by way of doctrine but which other Christians do not. Differences between Catholics and the various Protestant groupings in matters of doctrine, as well as on modes of worship and form of church governance, were and are substantial. But they have been muted substantially by the limited relevance of these ecclesiastical matters to any sound account of the political common good. And they have been rendered invisible, in a way, by the First Amendment. Properly interpreted, that cardinal provision prohibits laws which presuppose the truth (or falsity) of any church's position on doctrine, liturgy, and church authority.

Considered not in view of their distinctive doctrines but as a particular political constituency, Catholics have contributed mightily, of course, to the making and enforcing of America's laws. How could it be otherwise? They have long constituted a quarter or so of the population; America is a democracy, and Catholicism is not politically quietist. But the laws with decisive

Catholic fingerprints on them are surprisingly few. They include the rules governing the state's relationship with nonpublic schools (for these schools have been mostly Catholic); the early stages of the law pertaining to organized labor (for Catholics predominate some of those nascent unions); "morals" laws (about divorce, contraception, censorship) after World War II; and the anti-abortion movement after *Roe v. Wade.* Catholics are presently (2014) in the forefront of resistance to the Obama Administration's "contraceptive" mandate. They have formidable Protestant allies in that fight.

Some other areas of American law owe their origins and meaning in large part to the *presence* of Catholics in America. Among these is church-state law, including provisions of state constitutions since the founding and the interpretation of the federal Constitution since World War II. These provisions can only be fully accounted for by treating them partly as attempts to stymie Catholic culture-forming power. Spasms of anti-Catholicism pockmark American history. Up to and into the twentieth century these paroxysms owed to Protestant disapproval of Catholicism as an abhorrent religious system, one suffused by superstition, displacement of individual conscience by priestly authority, and further marred by an alleged dual political allegiance. More recently the distinctive religious features of the faith have become matters of indifference, and the Pope is solely a spiritual leader. Now it is their witness to the moral truth which most distinguishes America's Catholics from their countrymen.

The pre-Vatican II emphasis in Church teachings favoring a Catholic confessional state fueled some of Americans' anti-Catholicism, even though it was stillborn on these shores. One could scour the most detailed accounts of American history and come up empty looking for a Catholic prelate or politician or who either denied that teaching in principle *or* who favored it as an American practice. It is not curious, then, that in today's challenging environment Church leaders (possibly without exception) ground their claims against government incursions upon *law*, especially the First Amendment, and not upon the *truth.* As the Council Fathers wrote in *Dignitatis Humanae*, "The freedom of the Church is the fundamental principle in what concerns the relations between the Church and governments and the whole civil order," an "independence which is necessary for the fulfillment of her divine mission" (*Dignitatis Humanae*, ¶13).

All things considered, Catholics' distinctive influence on the content of America's laws has been disproportionately, and surprisingly, modest. The main narrative arc here has instead been Catholics' embrace of our nation's political institutions and their adoption of its ambient political ethos and culture. There has never been a "Catholic" political party in America. Nor has there been an enduring, countercultural "Catholic" critique of prevailing economic forms and practices. The original solidaristic emphases of Catholic-dominated labor organizations, for example, soon gave way to a trade union mentality. The superb chapter in this volume by Breen and Strang on the failure of any distinctively Catholic legal education to get aloft in America is both a reflection of this assimilation and a minor cause of it. Those who attended Catholic law schools were trained to think in ways scarcely distinguishable from their peers.

This widespread assimilation of America's Catholics is understandable (up to a point), and not entirely to be regretted. For the moral scope of any public authority's actions is the common good, which in turn is anchored by the human good, *simpliciter*, and sound moral norms. The natural law is, in other words, the foundation of sound civil law; revealed propositions and strictly ecclesiastical practices hardly register on even a well-ordered political society's radar. And, although it has been a term seldom used by non-Catholic Americans, *natural law* doing business as "common" or "biblical" or "traditional" morality was the framework with which America's Protestants and Jews approached matters of law and politics. Catholics could and usually did make common cause with these other God-fearing people on matters affecting their common life as Americans.

It is therefore no mystery why an audible Catholic voice about laws emerged only after the second world war. For it was then that American Protestantism was fully beset by modern skepticism, especially on moral questions, and a corollary loss of grip on the meaning and nature of civil law. The outstanding chapter herein on legal philosophy by Robert George shows that, while there is not a single Catholic legal philosophy, there are many which are compatible with the faith and thus that there is, perhaps, a family of Catholic positions. A sound legal philosophy is grounded, in other words, in natural law. After WWII, America's Protestants (and many others) lost that ground. And this distinctively Catholic voice was largely extinguished by 1970, not because of a Protestant *resourcement*, but due to the post-Vatican II Catholics' loss of that ground, too.

What then should one expect to learn from a volume about American law from a Catholic perspective? Not much in the form of a descriptive history, save insofar as that history provides the material content for a rich and illuminating moral evaluative framework. One would rightly expect from such a volume a treasure-house for anyone interested in a distinctly Catholic normative perspective on a law. One should expect a critical guide to the moral evaluation of laws.

This excellent volume delivers it.

The moral evaluative perspective which unfolds in succeeding pages illumines, justifies, and (where appropriate) critiques America's laws. The chapters correspond to conventional legal categories and thus the catalogue of major courses at any American law school: torts, property, family law, corporations, intellectual property, constitutional law, immigration, labor law, and the like. These subject-matter chapters are complemented by Michael

Ariens's account of Catholicism in the intellectual discipline of legal history. And the volume concludes with more synthetic chapters on human rights and Catholic social teaching (by William Saunders) and on bioethics (by Hadley Arkes).

This volume is relentlessly critical. But that is not to say that it is full of criticism. There is much to celebrate in the story of American laws. A great deal—though far from all—of the legal developments described in these pages lives up to the requirements of critical morality. Even when the enacted laws so qualify, however, the essays here contribute to our understanding of the point and justification of those laws. For example, the right sort of environmental laws could be established due to an exaggerated sense of the sacredness of nature, a fetishism which sometimes approaches idolatry. Or they could be grounded upon a properly Catholic understanding of stewardship. Lucia Silecchia's chapter on environmental law helps the reader to sort out these streams of thought. Capital punishment, for an additional example, has been limited in American law for several reasons, mostly having to do with allegedly ineradicable flaws in our system of criminal adjudication and the speculative quality of claims that it is necessary to deter those tempted to commit certain heinous crimes. The Church's emerging teaching in favor of abolition, however, is rooted in a strict moral norm against intentionally killing *anyone.* Dorie Klein's essay comparing Catholic social teaching on the death penalty with Eighth Amendment jurisprudence leads the reader into this important argument.

I should like to add to this valuable collection a few examples of the sometime subtle casuistry which a fully Catholic perspective on law requires. Put differently, here are some illustrations of how deeply into the sinews of practical, everyday lawyering, of lawmaking, and of legal scholarship the truths of Catholic faith penetrate and work their formative influences.

The universal Catechism allows that some persons have no "right" to the truth and may be told lies. That probably is supported by a preponderance of authority in the tradition. But I would defend the "minority" view, which is compatible with the Catechism (which does *not* say that anyone is ever *obliged* to lie): lying is always wrong.

Now, people lie when they assert a proposition as true which they believe to be false. I taught trial advocacy to law students for twenty-seven years, the fruits of a misspent young adulthood as a trial lawyer. The questions that arose in that class about truthfulness include these: When do trial lawyers assert propositions? Do trial lawyers lie when they cross-examine a witness in a way that suggests some part of the witness's story is false—a part that the lawyer knows to be true? How about closing argument? Can the entire trial exercise be considered a performance, in which lawyers are understood to play parts, so that the norm against lying is inapposite? That sounds a bit like our adversarial system, and a lot like the average trial lawyer's understanding of it. But, if so, how can trials be defended as a proper means of dispute resolutions? Trials resolve claims of right, which are aspects of justice. But justice has to do with the truth about what happened.

The Catholic scholar must be alert to the relevance of truths of the faith to legal issues. Right-to-die (that is, assisted suicide) judicial opinions typically implicate three such truths. Almost any such opinion will assert or at least presuppose the truth of the following three claims. The first is that persons who refuse medical treatment because they prefer to die, and so rid themselves of pain and indignity, do not commit suicide. These persons "simply let nature take its course." But this is false. The second claim (usually presupposed) is a false metaphysical dualism, the mistaken view that the body is the instrument of the "person," much as a car is related to its driver. The third false claim is that opposition to the right to die rests upon "sectarian" or "theological" doctrine, not on a "rational basis."

The Catholic lawyer, lawmaker, legal scholar must resist any action theory which does not, as these opinions do not, allow us to see how our Lord was a martyr, not a suicide. The Catholic must reject all dualistic accounts of the person and affirm that the person is a dynamic unity of body and spirit. Dualism denies that unity, and so undermines the faith lives of Christians who can no longer understand the dignity of bodiliness and find it difficult to take seriously many aspects of faith—Jesus in the Eucharist, the virgin birth, resurrection of the body, original sin, and so on. Finally, Catholics must utterly reject the authority—even the competence—of courts to tell them what is knowable by reason and what is knowable only by and through revelation.

Preface

Ronald J. Rychlak

I am very proud to be associated with this book. The contributors are some of the most brilliant Catholic legal thinkers in the United States today. Some are close friends, others are people I have long admired, and several fall into both categories. I learned a great deal from the reading that I did during the editing process, and I am convinced that this is a book to which I will frequently return throughout my career.

I would first like to thank the Society of Catholic Social Scientists for presenting me with this opportunity. The Society was founded in 1992 by people who were concerned that the role of faith and Catholic social teaching was not being considered by the modern social sciences. The Society challenged this secularized approach to the social sciences by combining academic analysis with true fidelity to the Magisterium.

American Law from a Catholic Perspective: Through a Clearer Lens brings that same approach to American law, combining insightful legal analysis with Catholic social teachings that are true to the Magisterium. Given the stature of the authors and the quality of the chapters, this book is already an important addition to the Society's body of work.

I would like to thank the contributors. I identified top Catholic writers in various areas of law, and I set out to get those people to write for the book. Most of them readily agreed; I only had to beg a few. Importantly, most were pretty good about meeting deadlines. Alas, like most lawyers, many were less inclined to follow length limits. In general, however, the papers were so strong that even with harsh editing I could not in good faith take them down to the originally suggested length.

Speaking of editing, my wife Claire deserves at least as much credit as I do. She did all of the formatting, all the layout, and also did at least one round of editing on each paper. She has experience in these matters. She has edited my writing for more than twenty-five years and during that time she has prevented numerous (sometimes embarrassing) errors from going out under my name. Her work on this project, however, was above and beyond the call of duty. Without her, I would not have been able to complete this project. I do not know how to pay her back, but I assume that she will have some suggestions.

Chapter One

Religion and Roman Catholicism in American Legal History

Michael Ariens

[L]aw, as a systematization of social relations at a given level, cannot be understood without an analysis of the sexual orientations, the moral and religious beliefs, the economic production and the military forces that characterize a given society at a given moment, and are expressed in associations of individuals and in conflicts. . . . [W]hat is no longer conceivable is that history of law should be autonomous; for by its very nature it is a formulation of human relations rooted in manifold human activities. [1]

This chapter takes a twofold approach: It first lists and describes the main texts in American legal history and evaluates them in light of the presence or absence of discussions of religion, Christianity, and Catholic Christianity. It then offers a contrapuntal sketch of American legal history, a sketch that attempts to envision whether, and if so, how, the lived experience of Roman Catholics in America affects our understanding of American legal history. Narrative overarching histories of American law only lightly touch upon Catholicism. Two relatively new compendiums do a better job of discussing the relation between law and religion, though both are written at a broad level of generality. This sketch in a minor key is offered to provide the reader a more capacious understanding of American legal history, one that touches upon issues of religion, and in particular, Roman Catholicism.

THE SCHOLARSHIP OF AMERICAN LEGAL HISTORY

American legal history is both a traditional subject and a relative newcomer to the curriculum of the law school and to academic legal scholarship. Antebellum legal educators such as Joseph Story, David Hoffman, and others

1

made both the science of law and its history a focal point in the education of lawyers. In the late nineteenth century, scholars grouped together as a "school" known as historical jurisprudence studied the history of law, most often English legal history, to examine and explain concepts of law, including American law.[2] The most famous example of such writing, of course, was *The Common Law* (1881) by Oliver Wendell Holmes, Jr. But by the early twentieth century, historical jurisprudence was marginalized in the modern law school, and legal academics diminished the attention given to the history of law in favor of the study of common-law doctrine. Just a few law schools offered any legal history course from the late nineteenth century through the middle of the twentieth century.[3] American law schools explicitly limited the scope of legal education to the study of legal doctrine, though the definition of doctrine encompassed legislative and administrative materials by the 1950s. It was not until 1970 that the first in "a series of appointments by elite law schools of persons interested in legal history scholarship" was made.[4] From 1970 to the present, the study of legal history by legal academics has exploded, and most American law schools now offer one or more courses on legal history, particularly American legal history.

In the first two decades of the twentieth century, few scholarly writings on American legal history existed. Those American legal scholars who continued to write on matters of legal history remained largely tied to a strand of historical jurisprudence, focusing either on English legal history or English legal history as influencing the development of American law. For example, between 1907 and 1909, a three-volume compendium titled *Select Essays in Anglo-American History* was published. The essays emphasized "Anglo" rather than "American" history. They were designed to provide the reader with a sense of the English foundations of American law, not to investigate American sources of American law. A large number of essays traced the English development of various American common-law legal doctrines, and several discussed the history of English legal institutions, including courts and the legal profession. Several early twentieth century scholars published articles or books organizing the history of common-law doctrines. One of the most skilled efforts was John Henry Wigmore's four-volume survey of the law of evidence, *A Treatise on the Anglo-American System of Evidence in Trials at Common Law* (1904–1905). Wigmore's massive treatise not only stated current evidence law in English-speaking countries, he gave the reader the historical and jurisprudential context of its development and suggested improvements in the law. Wigmore's *Treatise* was designed for practicing lawyers, and most legal history, as exemplified in Wigmore's *Treatise*, was work undertaken in the service of explaining current law. In 1908, Harvard Law School Professor Charles Warren wrote a two-volume history of the Harvard Law School, and a few years later his *A History of the American Bar* (1911) was published. This scholarship was a very large step above so-called bench and bar histories of the same period, which uncritically lauded past lawyers and judges from a particular state or locality. In general, American legal history in the first half of the twentieth century was largely "internalist" history. An internalist study focused on the development of laws and legal institutions, in particular legal systems. Very little found within these writings included any examination of the influences of society on legal developments, such as whether, and if so how, social changes affected legal doctrine.

This changed with the publication of J. Willard Hurst's *The Growth of the Law: The Law Makers* (1950). Hurst's book was a significant accomplishment and a major milestone in writing on American legal history.[5] It was not a study of the influence of English legal history on American law, but a study of American law through American historical sources. Further, Hurst provided a viewpoint: "primarily that of a professional interest in law as an instrument of social values."[6] Hurst published a number of other first-rate works on legal history during his long and influential life, and his viewpoint, to study law as an instrument rather than as an end, influenced American legal history scholarship for over a generation. In some respects it still echoes today. The "law and society" approach was an "externalist" approach to legal history, an approach consciously distinct from its predecessor.

Hurst was followed, in time and spirit, by Lawrence Friedman in *Contract Law in America: A Social and Economic Case Study* (1965) and *A History of American Law* (1973). The latter was, as Friedman wrote in his preface, "the first attempt to do anything remotely like a general history, a survey of the development of American law, including some treatment of substance, procedure, and legal institutions."[7] Friedman's general history took the reader to the end of the nineteenth century. Three decades later, he wrote a companion book, *American Law in the Twentieth Century* (2002). Friedman has been and remains an important and prolific scholar. Possibly even more so than Hurst, Friedman rejects the autonomy of law from society. In his *History* he noted his effort to write "a *social* history of American law."[8] Similarly, Kermit L. Hall in *The Magic Mirror: Law in American History* (1989) described it as a "book about the history of American legal culture and the law in action."[9] All three, in greater or lesser measure, were, as Hall wrote, attempting "to elucidate the interaction of law and society as revealed over time. . . ."[10] One criticism of this approach was that law was always the dependent variable, and society the independent variable.

Morton Horwitz's *The Transformation of American Law, 1780–1860* (1977) and *The Transformation of American Law, 1870–1960: The Crisis of Legal Orthodoxy* (1992) both followed and departed in some ways from the Hurst/Friedman paradigm. In Horwitz's view in 1977, "Law is autonomous to the extent that ideas are autonomous, at least in the short run."[11] By the time of *Transformation II*, Horwitz gave "cultural factors somewhat more explanatory weight, although I continue to insist that the development of law cannot be understood independently of social context."[12]

Between the time of the publication of the first and second *Transformation* books, legal historians began to write against the dominant strain of historiography, progressive historiography, championed by Charles Beard in *An Economic Interpretation of the Constitution* (1913) and other works. Beard's thesis saw "conflict" between groups with differing interests. Thus, *Economic Interpretation* argued that persons owning property urged adoption of a Constitution that protected their interests against those of the mass of people who owned no land. Horwitz's 1977 *Transformation I* was a critical example of that clash of interests prevalent in progressive historiography. In addition to the turn away from progressivism, Peter Novick's *That Noble Dream: The "Objectivity Question" and the American Historical Profession* (1988) investigated the problem of the "record" and the writer, the difficulty of trying to tell something more than just a "story," or providing more than just an "entertainment."[13] *Transformation II* was influenced by these historiographical turns, but did not wholly depart from Horwitz's initial approach.[14]

The most recent history of American law is the first of three volumes by G. Edward White, *Law in American History, Volume I: From the Colonial Years Through the Civil War* (2012). White found both "internalist" history and Friedman's (and thus the progressive) view that law mirrored society too limiting, and instead chose a third way, one that allows "historians to read legal materials from the past simultaneously as intraprofessional documents and historical artifacts."[15]

In addition to those narrative histories are two books of "Cases and Materials" on American legal history. Stephen Presser and Jamil Zainaldin first published *Law and American History: Cases and Materials* in 1980. Hall, William Wiecek, and Paul Finkelman's *American Legal History: Cases and Materials* was first published in 1991. Both remain in print in subsequent editions, the former in its eighth edition (2013) and the latter in its fourth edition (2010, with James W. Ely, Jr., replacing Wiecek beginning with the third edition).[16]

Two American legal history reference works also have been published. *The Cambridge History of Law in America* (2008) consists of three volumes; the one-volume *A Companion to American Legal History* was published in 2013.

Finally, two American law journals focus on legal history, though not just American legal history. The *American Journal of Legal History* began publishing in 1957 and *Law and History Review* in 1983. Both were products, in at least some respect, of the American Society of Legal History, which itself was formally created in 1956.

CATHOLICISM IN AMERICAN LEGAL HISTORY SCHOLARSHIP

The emergence of a number of books focused on the broad study of American legal history allows one to evaluate the treatment in such works of religion, Christianity, and Catholic Christianity, in descending level of generality. In general, relatively little of the narrative histories discusses the influence of religion on legal developments, much less the intersection of Roman Catholicism with the history of American law. The case books are somewhat better, and the chapters on law and religion in the compendiums provide more substantial coverage, though some gaps remain.

Hurst made scattered but repeated references to tensions attributable to differences among Americans "in religion, race, color, and social class" with which lawmakers were necessarily concerned. Hurst's broad statement reached a specific level of generality regarding Roman Catholicism only once. In reference to one consequence of the Massachusetts Constitutional Convention of 1917, Hurst discussed the fact of "a ban on state aid to sectarian (that is, Roman Catholic) institutions." Hurst concluded that this ban was not the reason for the convention, but simply one of its two major consequences.

Friedman's 1973 *History* and both of Horwitz's *Transformations* offered very little in terms of any discussion of religion, much less Roman Catholicism. For example, in Friedman's 1973 *History*, only one index entry exists for "church and state" (no index entry exists for "religion," "Christianity," or "Catholic," or "Roman Catholic"). That entry leads the reader to a brief discussion (less than one paragraph) of the Free Exercise cases involving Jehovah's Witnesses in the 1940s and the Establishment Clause cases of the early 1960s concerning Bible reading and prayers in the public schools. This brief statement is found in Friedman's *Epilogue*, as his 1973 *History* ends at the beginning of the twentieth century. Horwitz's 1978 *Transformation* has no index item regarding religion, and his 1992 *Transformation* has one on "Catholicism." That reference leads one to the following: "While one school of thought, mainly Catholic, sought to blame moral relativism for the spread of a 'might makes right' philosophy, others wished to show instead that an absolutist mindset was actually more conducive to the growth of totalitarianism." White's *Law in American History* includes few references to either religion or Catholicism. He notes the religious discord in England and Scotland as generating emigration to the American colonies from there, and the Quebec Act of 1774, which gave Catholics, most of whom traced their ancestry to France, freedom of religious worship.

Friedman's 1992 *American Law* was more expansive on law and religion, though his discussions are relatively modest. Friedman includes a four-page survey each of *Religion and the Law: A Case Study* and *Religion and the Law*. He begins, "America also was and is an intensely religious country."[17]

The case study is the 1925 Scopes trial, which is studied briefly and some-what inaccurately. The section transitions to a story of religious pluralism in America and to one of Friedman's favorite subjects, the rise of expressive individualism in twentieth century America. In his second short study, Fried-man discusses the rise of Catholic elementary and high schools, *Pierce v. Society of Sisters* (1925) (very briefly), and the "hardy" staying power of *Everson v. Board of Education* (1947) and later Establishment Clause cases concerning religious matters in public education. This staying power, he concludes, is a result of an American embrace of "plural equality."

Friedman includes additional references to Catholicism, usually related to social issues such as abortion, divorce, and adoption, as well as one reference to "anti-Catholicism," which notes the second rise of the Ku Klux Klan in the 1920s. A similar approach is taken in Hall's *Magic Mirror*. Most references to Roman Catholicism are linked to social issues. One statement found in Hall but in none of the other works is a discussion of the integration from the late nineteenth century on of Catholics and Jews into the American legal profession. A second helpful addition in Hall is his discussion of the impor-tance of Christianity in the development of legal institutions in colonial America. Hall writes, "Despite its divisiveness, religion was also a unifying force in the colonial experience. Post-Reformation Protestant thought pro-claimed the existence of fixed standards of justice, based on Divine Reason that was superior to man-made law."

The two "Cases and Materials" books are significantly more generous in their treatment of religion than the narrative legal histories. The Hall, Finkel-man, and Ely case book gives the reader a very good sense of the importance of religion in the development of the American colonies and its laws. It also includes a section on the laws that ended religious establishments in the revolutionary and early national period. It discusses the transformation of the nation between 1850 and 1924 from "a nation largely populated by Protes-tants of Anglo-Saxon and northern European origin" to a country in which the immigration of "[m]illions of Catholics and Jews destroyed the Protestant hegemony of an earlier age." The book also includes two modern religious liberty cases, one involving prayer in public schools and the other concerning state regulation of peyote possessed for a religious use. This last material is less helpful, for it is provided with little context.

Like Hall, Finkelman, and Ely, Presser and Zainaldin's *Law and Juris-prudence* also includes a school prayer case (*Lee v. Weisman* [1992]). Unlike them, Presser and Zainaldin do not include any discussion of law and religion as such. Instead, in the notes following *Lee v. Weisman*, Presser and Zainal-din remind the student-reader of the eighteenth-century belief in a "divinely-inspired natural law," and discuss the republican view that "there could be no law without morality and no morality without religion." They also offer a brief mention of Father Francis E. Lucey's rejection in the 1930s of legal realism as antidemocratic.

Both American legal history reference works include chapters on "law and religion." The 2013 *Companion*, a one-volume work, has a fifteen-page chapter providing an overview of the history and historiography of law and religion. Its author, Steven K. Green, gives a fair assessment of the historical issues of law and religion and explains the variety of disciplines from which these histories have been written. Green's overview is relatively brief, and he ignores some issues and skims others. The three-volume *Cambridge History* takes an interesting and possibly revealing approach. Both Volume I, which extends from 1580 to 1815, and Volume II, which spans from 1789 to 1920, include a chapter on law and religion. The chapter in Volume I is a lengthy, thorough study, joined by a lengthy bibliographical essay. It is a learned essay explaining the importance of understanding how differences in Protestantism in the regions and particular colonies affected social and legal developments in those particular places. (It also notes the brief period in which Maryland was a Roman Catholic colony, a period that ended by the beginning of the eighteenth century.) The essay also makes the important point that, to a great extent in colonial America, "America's Protestant culture still defined itself by opposition to Catholicism—a fact of lasting historical significance." Volume II looks at law and religion in the long nineteenth century (1789–1920). It explains that early national period writings "embracing democratic principles in religion as well as politics" means "Roman Catholicism was the primary object of such attacks." The author, Sarah Barringer Gordon, accepts at least in part the relationship between antipathy toward Catholicism and "separation of church and state": "Thus in a world defined in part by anti-Catholicism, separation of church and state took root and flourished." (Green is much more skeptical of this assertion.) She also discusses anti-Catholicism in the failed federal and successful state Blaine amendments, which constitutionally banned state aid to religious institutions, most particularly, Roman Catholic elementary and high schools. Additionally, she is clear-eyed in noting that mid- and late-nineteenth century "secularization" efforts (such as justifying Sunday blue laws on secular "day of rest" rather than religious "Ten Commandments" grounds) may have been based in some part on "virulent anti-Catholicism," but such prejudice existed against other religions as well, such as Mormonism. She helpfully includes other justifications for the secularization thesis, as well as the argument that the thesis itself is wrong.

These two excellent essays make it more puzzling that no such chapter is found in Volume III, which dates from 1920 to the present. The references to religion in Volume III are few and unenlightening. The index to Volume III lists three references to Catholics, each found in a separate essay. Two concern Catholicism and Hollywood movie censorship by the Hays Office,

which seems highly disproportionate to other possible topics. The only relevant reference to Catholics is a brief discussion of Catholic critics of third-
generation rights talk based on Catholic social thought. The Ku Klux Klan is
mentioned in Volume III only in connection to the issue of race, not religion.
The Scopes trial (again, mentioned in Volume II but not in Volume III), the
importance of religion in the civil rights movement (Martin Luther King, Jr.,
is mentioned only twice), the emerging acceptance of Jews and Catholics in
law and politics in post–World War II America, the rise of evangelicals in
politics and law beginning in the late 1970s, the nearly constant effort of the
Supreme Court to interpret the Religion Clauses from *Everson v. Board of
Education* (1947) and the Jehovah's Witnesses cases (*Cantwell v. Connecticut* [1940] and others) to the present, and the decline in the Supreme Court of
Protestants the concomitant rise of Catholics and Jews are all left unmen-
tioned. It is as if the editors decided the secularization thesis was clearly
proven, despite the cautions made by Barringer Gordon in Volume II. It is a
disappointing effort.

CATHOLICISM IN AMERICAN LEGAL HISTORY

Legal and social developments in the colonial and early national period were
profoundly influenced by Protestantism, but it is also generally accepted that
the *de facto* Protestant establishment ended in the 1920s. The post–World
War II "integration" of Catholics and Jews, including the popularity of Will
Herberg's *Protestant-Catholic-Jew* (1955) and the election of John F. Kennedy as president in 1960, signaled another shift in American culture, as did
the joining of evangelicals and Catholics on a number of social issues in the
aftermath of *Roe v. Wade* (1973).

American Protestantism was shaped in part by anti-Catholicism, which
provides a window into some minor chords in American legal history. By
looking at several issues of legal history during these three eras, one discov-
ers evidence of subtle shifts in American legal history and legal thought.
These events and issues may give the reader a different light on the contours
of American legal history.

In the early national period, five states constitutionally limited public
office to Protestants. Some states initially amended such restrictions to require one be a "Christian," which allowed Catholics but not Jews to serve in
public office. Though Massachusetts eliminated its religious test restriction
in 1820, public office in New Hampshire was not open to Catholics or Jews
until 1876. For the dominant Protestant culture, the few numbers of Jews and
Catholics made it easy for lawmakers to ignore an issue of political equality.
A related issue for Catholics was the priest-penitent evidentiary privilege.
The first American case on the topic was *People v. Phillips* (1813), decided

by New York City Mayor DeWitt Clinton in his additional capacity as a judge. Clinton held that the privilege was protected by both the common law and as a matter of constitutional law. A few years later, a Massachusetts court refused to recognize the privilege. In 1828, the New York legislature adopted the first statute recognizing the privilege of a priest not to disclose a confession made to him "in the course of discipline," but the rise of this privilege was slow. Only four states had such a privilege by 1850, only half by 1900, and just two-thirds by the early 1970s, when the Federal Rules of Evidence were crafted. This history indicates the relation between political power and minority status. In the early nineteenth century, Catholics were a minority group (and often identified with another minority group, Irish immigrants), and the slow adoption of the privilege in other states suggests that the minority status of Catholics lessened or obviated any need for legal recognition of the priest-penitent privilege. A study of DeWitt Clinton's solicitousness in *Phillips* provides some evidence for this proposition. Clinton's easy acceptance of the privilege was due in part to his desire to serve his political interests, as Catholics were an emerging electoral bloc in New York City. Clinton had shown his devotion to Catholics as a political body as early as 1806, when he led the effort to eliminate the state's religious test for political office, allowing Catholics to serve. These events may be used to illustrate early understandings of civil rights and minority groups, and more broadly to assess the meanings of democratization in the antebellum United States.

A second antebellum legal issue was whether one could make a bequest in a will for the benefit of a religious body. In a Virginia case, *Gallego's Executors v. Attorney General* (1832), the court held void a bequest of $4,000 to the Roman Catholic congregation in Richmond. That is because no Roman Catholic congregation existed as a matter of law. The bequest was thus invalid as a matter of common law and in equity. *Gallego's Executors* is not only a case of "democratization" (that is, the church is the membership, or congregation, and that changes constantly because persons opt out and in of membership) but a case of intransigence and fear. The common law and equity provisions were written in England to diminish the Roman Catholic Church, and the court's adoption of those rules suggests how little some legal ideas changed in the transmission of law. The opinion was also fearful of the Catholic Church: "The history of the papal see, and the religious houses under its dominion, is but a history of the cupidity of monks and devotees, veiled under the sacred garb of our holy religion." Virginia is just one of a number of states that barred the incorporation of churches and assumed that control of church property was left in the hands of elected trustees, which was contrary to Roman Catholic canon law. In general, states did not alter their laws to fit the needs of different religious organizations; they required those organizations to meet the requirements of the law. This eventually led to the problematic church property cases of the 1960s and 1970s, which used a "democratic" understanding for Protestant denominations that used a different model.

This suspicion of Catholicism was found in social events of the time as well. In 1834, an anti-Catholic riot occurred outside of Boston, in which a convent was burned down. A decade later, anti-Catholic riots took place in Philadelphia. In 1842, the local Roman Catholic Bishop, Francis Kentrick, complained that Catholic schoolchildren were required to read from the Protestant Bible in the common schools. The local Board of Controllers allowed children to read from their own Bible. By March 1844, nativists claimed this decision was an effort to ban the Bible in the schools, and riots claiming the lives of thirteen people and injuries to fifty more took place in May and July. Anti-Catholic riots were just one reason why riots took place at alarming levels in the 1830s and, to a lesser extent, later. Ideas of community and individualism (coined by Tocqueville in his study of Americans in the early 1830s), of the rule of law and Judge Lynch (coined in 1835), of the death of republican virtue and the rise of democratic liberalism may all be discussed in light of the presence of this modest number of Catholics. Additionally, the nativist fear that the Protestant Bible might be banned in the common school illustrated the antebellum belief "Christianity is a part of the common law," espoused by Joseph Story and rejected by Thomas Jefferson.

The Bible-reading controversy had just begun. An early case was *Donahoe v. Richards* (1854), decided in Maine. The court rejected the claim of religious conscience by a Catholic schoolchild, who wanted to read from the Catholic Bible. *Donahoe* was decided just before the anti-Catholic Know-Nothing Party took brief political power in several states, a reaction to the arrival of nearly a million Irish, many Catholic, fleeing the Potato Famine. Post–Civil War cases were ordinarily resolved like *Donahoe*, though it may be useful to assess the reasons why two cases concluded otherwise. Was it greater political power of Catholics in those communities that led to this result, a "modern" sense of nonestablishment, or some other reason? Bible-reading cases also allow one to view claims of "separation of church and state" in light of anti-Catholic bias, which may show that the "constitutional religious freedom of Americans developed in accord with popular expectations—that minority rights were redefined to satisfy majority perceptions of them."[18] As noted above, this is a contested idea that allows one to think about the shaping of constitutional thought and history and how American legal history may be understood in light of Protestant–Catholic interactions in addition to republican virtue politics–democratic liberalism politics. More particularly, the Bible-reading cases helped lead to the creation of the parochial school system, which generated a different set of legal issues in the post–Civil War era that generated a majority rule–minority rights legal dispute.

The Blaine Amendment was proposed in late 1875. It banned states from using state funds for religious instruction and was intended to ban aid to Catholic schools. Though it failed to pass Congress, it was proposed from 1875 to 1907, and several Western states were required to include a Blaine amendment to achieve statehood. Three-quarters of state constitutions include a Blaine amendment.

The number of Catholics rose during the last half of the nineteenth century from about 5 percent to 16 percent of the population. Most states, by court decision, legislation, or school board directive, allowed use of the Protestant Bible in the common school from *Donahoe* through the middle of the twentieth century. State Blaine amendments banned using public funds for parochial schools during this time. The result was the instantiation of a separate Catholic educational structure. This structure was the subject of a whole series of cases in the post–World War II era, most memorably *Lemon v. Kurtzman* (1971), which can be used to discuss modern constitutional law and the rise of balancing tests instead of rule, a consequence of legal realism.

The rise of legal realism in the 1930s presented an additional opportunity. Why did Catholic natural law thought appear so marginal among non-Catholic legal academics, and was the revival of natural law thinking after World War II attributable to anything other than revulsion toward Hitler? Edward Purcell's *The Crisis of Democratic Theory* (1973) offers some excellent background. Horwitz's brief statement quoted above indicated the paucity of thinking in narrative histories about how and why legal realism was opposed, either generally (by Lon Fuller and other "secular" natural law thinkers) or by Catholic legal scholars, all of whom were teaching in Catholic law schools.

Catholic law schools, as part of Catholic universities, have historically provided a pathway to the legal profession for Catholic immigrants and their sons (and, sometimes, daughters). Given the rigors of a written bar examination and the competition found in a market-based legal services economy, have Catholic law schools provided a distinctive legal education to their students? Further, can Catholic lawyers demonstrate a distinctive value to the mores of the American legal profession? The rise in the 1980s of what is known as the "religious lawyering" movement can trace its roots to Catholic legal scholars, most particularly Thomas Shaffer, but this is a new path of developing history. The readers of this book will determine the course of any continued progress in Catholic legal history.

CONCLUSION

The legal history of American Roman Catholics and Catholic ideas has largely eluded general narratives of the history of American law. This chapter suggests some historical events concerning the Catholic experience in America that may offer the reader a new way to think about American law, but more work needs to be done on alternate paths of American legal thought, and the influence of Catholic legal thought.

NOTES

1. A. D. Momigliano, "The Consequences of New Trends in the History of Ancient Law," *Studies in Historiography* (Harper, 1966), 239, 240–41, *quoted in* Robert W. Gordon, *J. Willard Hurst and the Common Law Tradition in American Legal Historiography*, 10 Law & Soc'y Rev. 9 (1975).

2. See generally David Rabban, *Law's History: American Legal Thought and the Transatlantic Turn to History* (Cambridge University Press, 2013).

3. Joan Sidney Howland, *A History of Legal History Courses Offered in American Law Schools*, 53 Am. J. Leg. Hist. 363, 367 (2013).

4. G. Edward White, *Reflections on the "Republican Revival": Interdisciplinary Scholarship in the Legal Academy*, 6 Yale J. L. & Humanities 1, 17 n. 33 (1994) (noting hiring of Morton Horwitz by Harvard Law School); see also Stephen B. Presser and Jamil S. Zainaldin, *Law and Jurisprudence in American History: Cases and Materials* (Thomson West, 2006) (noting hiring by University of Chicago Law School of nonlawyer historian Stanley Katz in 1970).

5. The reemergence of legal history was foreshadowed by two law review articles: Willard Hurst, *Legal History: A Research Program*, 1942 Wis. L. Rev. 323; and D. J. Boorstin, *Tradition and Method in Legal History*, 54 Harv. L. Rev. 424 (1941).

6. J. Willard Hurst, *The Growth of the Law: The Law Makers* (Little, Brown & Co., 1950), v.

7. Lawrence M. Friedman, *A History of American Law*, 2nd ed. (Simon & Schuster, 1985), 11.

8. Friedman, *History of American Law*, 12.

9. Kermit L. Hall, *The Magic Mirror: Law in American History* (Oxford University Press, 1989), vii.

10. Hall, *The Magic Mirror*, vii.

11. Morton J. Horwitz, *The Transformation of American Law, 1780–1860* (Harvard University Press, 1977), xiii.

12. Morton J. Horwitz, *The Transformation of American Law, 1870–1960: The Crisis of Legal Orthodoxy* (Oxford University Press, 1992), vii.

13. Peter Novick, *That Noble Dream: The "Objectivity Question" and the American Historical Profession* (Cambridge University Press, 1988).

14. See G. Edward White, *The Lost Origins of American Judicial Review*, 78 Geo. Wash. L. Rev. 1145, 1146–51 (2010). Much else can be said about Horwitz's shift, but not within current space constraints.

15. G. Edward White, *Law in American History, Volume I: From the Colonial Years Through the Civil War* (Oxford University Press, 2012), 9.

16. Stephen Presser and Jamil Zainaldin, *Law and American History: Cases and Materials* (West Publishing Co., 1980); Kermit L. Hall, Paul Finkelman, and James W. Ely, Jr., *American Legal History: Cases and Materials* (Oxford University Press, 2010).

17. Friedman, *History of American Law*, 506.

18. Philip Hamburger, *Separation of Church and State* (Harvard University Press, 2004), 483.

Chapter Two

The Ethics of Lawyers and Judges

Perspectives from Catholic Social Teaching

Robert A. Destro

> The Rules of Professional Conduct are rules of reason. They should be interpreted with reference to the purposes of legal representation and the law itself.
> —ABA Model Rules of Professional Conduct, *Scope*, 14

> In a jurisprudence of mitzvoth, the loaded, evocative edge is at the assignment of responsibility. . . .
> —Robert M. Cover, *Obligation: A Jewish Jurisprudence of the Social Order*,
> 5 J. L. & Rel. 65 (1987)

> All the Christian faithful, and especially bishops, are to strive diligently to avoid litigation among the people of God as much as possible, without prejudice to justice, and to resolve litigation peacefully as soon as possible.
> —Code of Canon Law, 1446 §1

There is no such thing as a lawyer without a client. The roles of the lawyer—and, hence, the boundaries of acceptable professional conduct—are defined by the duties the lawyer undertakes on behalf of the client. A person who is otherwise qualified to practice law does not really become a lawyer until the moment that he/she undertakes to advise or represent a client, and the client accepts. So too with a judge, who swears or affirms that he/she "will administer justice without respect to persons, and do equal right to the poor and to the rich, and . . . will faithfully and impartially discharge and perform all the duties incumbent upon me . . . under the Constitution and laws of the United States."[1] A corrupt or biased judge is, by this measure, no judge at all.

Because duty is the foundation of all professional relationships, the task at hand is to explore the ways in which Catholic social teaching ("CST") can guide American lawyers' understanding of the duties they undertake when they represent their clients, when they serve as prosecutors, or when they ascend to the bench. This chapter focuses only on the ethics of judging and provides a brief comparison between the process orientation of the Code of Judicial Conduct for United States Judges[2] and the more substantive orientation of Catholic social teaching.

The observations in this chapter apply with equal force to *all* discussions of professional ethics—not just those that bind the legal profession. Though professions may differ in the ways in which they parse the duties that define the professional relationship (e.g., lawyer-client, judge-litigant, doctor-patient, social worker-client, priest-penitent, etc.), *every* profession's definitions of "good practice," "professionalism," and "professional conduct" are based on the degree to which the professional has complied with the duties that define the relationship.

"Good practice," "professionalism," and "professional conduct" are also defined—to a large degree—by simply "following the rules" of professional conduct. Michael Davis of the Illinois Institute of Technology's Center for the Study of Ethics in the Professions observes that "following 'the rules,' while not all there is to professional ethics, is generally enough for responsible conduct (or, at least, is so when the profession's code of ethics is reasonably well-written, as most are)."[3]

> If rules were merely verbal entities, as nonsense syllables are, learning them would amount to nothing more than memorizing formulas. Such rote learning is (as Whitbeck says) not worth the attention of a college course. But rules, especially the rules of professional ethics, are more than nonsense syllables. They mean something. That meaning is not merely linguistic (like the meaning of most puns) or merely propositional (like the meaning of a scientific law). What rules generally mean, and what rules of professional ethics always mean, are acts required, allowed, or forbidden. Rules are guides to conduct (and, so, also standards for evaluating conduct). No one has learned a rule of professional ethics (in any robust sense of "learned a rule") who has not understood it as a guide to conduct, indeed, who does not have a pretty good idea how to guide her conduct by the rule. Those who learn the rules of professional ethics without understanding how they guide conduct have taken only a small step toward learning them.[4]

The observations in this chapter are anchored to the specific rules of professional conduct governing judges, in the law governing judicial conduct, in the Code of Canon Law governing judges, and in the principles of Catholic social teaching that are relevant to the duties judges have as they execute their judicial role. Since the ultimate audience for this book is (or should be) Catholic lawyers and judges, the goal is to demonstrate that the task of reading rules of professional conduct *in light of* Catholic social teaching is not simply a means of "restating existing legal obligations, [it] is [rather] to set a new standard of care, one higher than existed before."[5]

THE RULES IN CONTEXT: CATHOLIC SOCIAL TEACHING AS AN ETHICAL FRAMEWORK

Before launching into an examination of the specific ethics rules governing the behavior of federal judges, it is useful to explain "Catholic Social Teaching." In an address entitled "Catholic Social Teaching and American Legal Practice," the late Avery Cardinal Dulles, S.J., provided the following description:

> Over the centuries, and especially in the past 150 years, the Catholic Church has built up a body of social teaching that is intended to contribute to the formation of a society marked by peace, concord, and justice toward all. This body of teaching, based on reason and revelation, has been refined through dialogue with Greek philosophy and Roman law, as well as the experience of the Church throughout two millennia, in interaction with many cultures in Europe, the Americas, and other continents. It seems safe to say that no other institution has developed a body of social teaching rivaling that of the Catholic Church, in depth, coherence, and completeness. Unlike the Church's strictly doctrinal teaching, which is addressed specifically to believers, Catholic social teaching is directed to all persons of good will, including those of any or no religion. It presupposes only that its addressees are interested in building a just and peaceful society on earth.[6]

The first compilation of that vast body of work, *Compendium of the Social Doctrine of the Church*, was completed on June 29, 2004.[7] Its purpose was to produce an authoritative collection of materials in which the Church would "speak 'the words that are hers' with regard to questions concerning life in society" and provide a compilation that would "systematically present the foundations of Catholic social doctrine."[8] More recent documents, published in the ten years since publication of the *Compendium*, include encyclicals by Pope Benedict XVI and Pope Francis,[9] as well as their homilies, letters, and speeches[10]; the pronouncements of the United States Conference of Catholic Bishops and its counterparts around the world[11]; and the reflections of those who examine the anthropological and moral principles on which the Catholic natural law tradition is based. Writing in 2003, Saint Pope John Paul II suggested that the nature of the legal profession is such that

> it behooves lawyers, all law-makers, legal historians and legislators themselves always to have, as St. Leo the Great asked of them, a deep "love of justice" (*Sermon on the Passion*, 59), and to try always to base their reflections and practice on the anthropological and moral principles which put man at the centre of the elaboration of laws and of legal practice.[12]

Speaking to a visiting delegation from the International Academy of Trial Lawyers in 1989, Saint Pope John Paul II observed that "lawyers . . . are committed to the resolution of conflicts and the pursuit of justice through legal and rational means," and confirmed the nearly universal (if unexpressed)[13] view of most lawyers that our "work is indispensable for the construction of a truly humane and harmonious social order. . . ."[14] This is true, said the Pontiff, if (and only if) lawyers understand that "all the branches of law are an eminent service to individuals and society."[15]

Among the many themes in the corpus of Catholic social teaching that speak to the fundamental obligations that lawyers owe to their clients, to the system of justice, and to themselves, the following are most directly relevant to the life and work of lawyers and the important role they play in society.

1. The dignity of the human person: "A just society can become a reality only when it is based on the respect of the transcendent dignity of the human person,"[16] understood and valued as "an intelligent and conscious being, capable of reflecting on himself and therefore of being aware of himself and his actions."[17]

2. The priority of the common good: *"*Just as the moral actions of an individual are accomplished in doing what is good, so too the actions of a society attain their full stature when they bring about the common good."[18] It is therefore "the duty of the state"—and of the lawyers who formulate, interpret, and enforce its policies—to ensure by their actions "the coherency, unity and organization of the civil society of which it is an expression."[19]

3. Solidarity as both a moral virtue that demands recognition of "the interdependence between individuals and peoples,"[20] *and as a social principle* that becomes the measure by which we can determine the need for the "creation or appropriate modification of laws, market regulations, and juridical systems."[21]

4. The principle of subsidiarity, which affirms the inherent dignity and natural rights of communities formed by individuals for a common purpose, and which, by definition, rejects "various reductionist conceptions of the human person"[22] that would view the client as either "an absolute individual being, built up by himself and on himself, as if his characteristic traits depended on no one else but himself," or "as a mere cell of an organism that is inclined at most to grant it recognition in its functional role within the overall system."[23]

5. The universal destination of goods requires that the poor, the marginalized, and in all cases those whose living conditions interfere with their proper growth should be the focus of particular concern.[24]

THROUGH A CLEARER LENS: THE LAWYER AS JUDGE

The Preamble to the American Bar Association's Model Rules of Professional Conduct begins with a statement of the important roles that lawyers undertake on behalf of their clients and society: [1] A lawyer, as a member of the legal profession, is a representative of clients, an officer of the legal system and a public citizen having special responsibility for the quality of justice. [25]

The Preamble to the ABA's Model Code of Judicial Conduct contains a similar admonition:

> [1] An independent, fair and impartial judiciary is indispensable to our system of justice. The United States legal system is based upon the principle that an independent, impartial, and competent judiciary, composed of men and women of integrity, will interpret and apply the law that governs our society. Thus, the judiciary plays a central role in preserving the principles of justice and the rule of law. Inherent in all the Rules contained in this Code are the precepts that judges, individually and collectively, must respect and honor the judicial office as a public trust and strive to maintain and enhance confidence in the legal system. [26]

For me, the most important phrase in these excerpts is in the Preamble to the Model Rules of Professional Conduct: "having special responsibility for the quality of justice." If there is to be a meaningful discussion of the ethical obligations of lawyers and judges, we need to know *which* lawyers bear that "special responsibility for the quality of justice": *All of them*, whatever their role, or the subset of lawyers who are operating in their role as "public citizens"?

In order to discern the most natural reading of the Preamble to the Model Rules, we must engage in a bit of statutory construction. We must take the words as we find them and read them together as a whole in light of their intended purpose.

Reading the Preamble as a whole, we find that the text differentiates among the "representational functions" described by paragraph [1], the "non-representational roles" described in paragraph [3], and the "official" functions described in paragraph [2]. In this reading, a "*special* responsibility for the *quality* of justice" arises only when the lawyer is acting as "a public citizen":

A lawyer, as a member of the legal profession, is:

1. a representative of clients (when serving as an advisor, advocate, negotiator, or evaluator) [27]
2. an officer of the legal system, and
3. a public citizen having special responsibility for the quality of justice (when serving in a non-representational role, such as third-party neu-

tral, an advocate for prison reform, a member of the business community, or any other non-practicing capacity).[28]

Reading the Preamble in light of the *entire* Model Rules of Professional Conduct, however, produces a more striking possibility: that is, that *every* lawyer *always* has "a special responsibility for the quality of justice."[29]

I can hear the objections already. One is statutory: A fair reading of the text and structure of the Model Rules in light of their history cannot support that proposition. The other is ethical: A lawyer's duty is to her client *alone*.[30]

The point here is simple: Acting together in the courts, lawyers and judges "interpret and apply the law that governs our society." It only stands to reason that those who, by virtue of their training, experience, and position, play such a critical role in administering the law *should* have a "special responsibility for the quality of justice."

Expressed in this manner, the initial paragraph of the Preamble would be *understood* to make the following statement of principle:

> As a member of the legal profession, a lawyer has a "special responsibility for the quality of justice" in [*all* cases, including when] serving as:
>
> 1. a representative of clients [e.g., advisor, advocate, negotiator, or evaluator]
> 2. an officer of the legal system, *or*
> 3. a public citizen [when serving in a non-representational role, such as third-party neutral, a member of the business community, or other any non-practicing capacity, including as a private citizen.]

There is little doubt that assigning a "special responsibility" for the *quality* of justice to every lawyer, notwithstanding the role being played, raises significant questions about how this "quality of justice" obligation affects the other obligations assumed by lawyer in the role that she is playing at the time (e.g., advisor, advocate, judge, law professor). Answering these questions is one of the more urgent tasks facing the legal profession.

This is where looking at the obligations of lawyers *in light of* Catholic social teaching is helpful. We need to see whether it would help us to formulate a "restate[ment of] existing legal obligations, [and] to set a new standard of care, one higher than existed before."[31]

In the sections that follow, I attempt that "restatement" of the existing legal obligations of a judge, and attempt to show that, when read in light of the principles of CST, the relevant codes of professional conduct *already* require that higher standard of care.

The Lawyer as Judge: Ethics and the Code of Judicial Conduct

This analysis begins with the rules governing the conduct of lawyers who become judges for a very simple reason: The role of the judge (or Justice) is *to do justice* in *every case.* Or is it?

Consider again, the words of the oath of office required of all federal judges:

> Each justice or judge of the United States shall take the following oath or affirmation before performing the duties of his office: "I, XXX XXX, do solemnly swear (or affirm) that I will administer justice without respect to persons, and do equal right to the poor and to the rich, and that I will faithfully and impartially discharge and perform all the duties incumbent upon me as XXX under the Constitution and laws of the United States. So help me God."[32]

A close reading of the judicial oath says a good bit about the obligations of the judicial role. Its components are 1) to administer justice; 2) without respect to persons; 3) to do equal right to the poor and to the rich; and 4) to faithfully and impartially discharge all the duties assigned to a judge under the Constitution and laws of the United States.

If viewed purely through the lens of the applicable rules of judicial conduct—here, the Code of Conduct for United States Judges[33]—we begin to get a sense what each of these components means. The "administration of justice without respect to persons" includes faithful execution of all "adjudicative" and "administrative" responsibilities in a "patient, dignified, respectful, and courteous manner" that respects "every person who has a legal interest in a proceeding, and that person's lawyer," as well as "jurors, witnesses, lawyers, and others with whom the judge deals in an official capacity."[34] "[I]mpartially discharg[ing] all the duties assigned to a judge under the Constitution and laws of the United States" is, if understood purely by reference to the specific prohibitions of the Code, largely a command that the judicial *process* be conducted in an environment where the proceedings are formal, balanced, fully transparent, and untainted by any conceivable appearance of bias or conflict of interest.[35]

It is only when we get to the command that the judge "do equal right to the poor and to the rich" that the process orientation of the Code of Conduct for American judges and Justices becomes painfully apparent. To the extent that the clause commands that the judge afford an identical *process* to the poor and the rich, the clause adds nothing of substance to our understanding of the obligations of the judge.[36] She must treat *all* persons coming before her court with dignity and respect.

If, however, the "equal right to the poor and to the rich" clause has substantive content *beyond* "process equality," it must be found somewhere *outside* the Code of Conduct for United States Judges: that is, in the Constitution and laws of the United States, or in legal traditions that draw explicitly on the teachings of scripture that do impose such obligations.

The New Lens: Catholic Social Teaching on the Duties of a Judge

The examination of the duties of a judge viewed through the lens of Catholic social teaching begins with a short story told by United States District Court Judge Joseph F. Anderson of South Carolina. In the course of a speech lamenting the demise of the civil jury trial, Judge Anderson reported on a remark he "overheard at a recent judicial conference," and observed that

> . . . [O]ne of my colleagues on the federal bench commented that he had not tried a single civil case in the preceding calendar year. Some had been pruned from the docket with orders granting summary judgment or motions to dismiss, and the rest were put to bed with successful ADR tactics—mediation before an appointed mediator or bare-knuckled settlement conference with the judge. That judge concluded his glowing self-assessment with the observation, "After all, we're in the dispute resolution business."
>
> The oath that we Article III judges take when we assume the bench says nothing about dispute resolution. Instead, the oath commands that we "will administer justice . . . and do equal right to the poor and the rich . . . ."[37]

In Judge Anderson's view, the objective of a "real trial" is "to arrive at the truth, vindicate rights, and to do justice."[38] In an Alternative Dispute Resolution ("ADR") proceeding, by contrast, "every claim is assumed to have some value; where true justice is considered too expensive or an unattainable abstraction."[39]

Consider, now, the approach embodied in Canon 1446 of the Code of Canon Law:

> §1. All the Christian faithful, and especially bishops, are to strive diligently to avoid litigation among the people of God as much as possible, without prejudice to justice, and to resolve litigation peacefully as soon as possible.
>
> §2. Whenever the judge perceives some hope of a favorable outcome at the start of litigation or even at any other time, the judge is not to neglect to encourage and assist the parties to collaborate in seeking an equitable solution to the controversy and to indicate to them suitable means to this end, even by using reputable persons for mediation.
>
> §3. If the litigation concerns the private good of the parties, the judge is to discern whether the controversy can be concluded advantageously by an agreement or the judgment of arbitrators according to the norm of cann. 1713–1716 (which, in order to prevent judicial contentions, permits the judge to refer the case to one or more arbitrators).

There is no lament here when a trial ("judicial contention") is either settled or referred for arbitration. What explains the difference in approach?

The answer is relatively simple: Judge Anderson's story speaks volumes because it provides a fleeting glimpse of how one federal judge conceives his role—and, hence, his obligations as a federal judge. If Article III judges are not in the business of "dispute resolution," the judge has no independent obligation to be a *doer* of justice. In this view, federal judges are *administrators* of justice—impartial referees. As we shall see shortly, both the rich *and* the poor suffer under such a crabbed interpretation of the judicial role.

Canon Law takes the opposite approach. The judge is most definitely "in the dispute resolution business" because his duty is "to strive diligently to avoid litigation among the people of God as much as possible, without prejudice to justice."[40] So, too, do the Hebrew Bible[41] and Shari'a.[42]

In order to understand why this is so, we must return to the principles of CST enshrined in the *Compendium*:

1. Lawsuits are, by definition, "contentious." To the extent that the *priority of the Common Good* means anything, it is the duty *of the state—* and of the lawyers who formulate, interpret, and enforce its policies— to ensure by their actions "the coherency, unity and organization of the civil society of which it is an expression."[43] A judge must, therefore, have the authority to seek mediators and, in case of impasse, to refer the matter for ADR, *whether the litigators want to proceed with the trial or not.*

2. Lawsuits are brutal, time consuming, and expensive. To the extent that we take seriously the argument that "[a] just society can become a reality only when it is based on the respect of the transcendent dignity of the human person,"[44] the judge cannot simply be an impartial referee. A robust understanding of "the transcendent dignity of the human person" requires that the *judge* take and keep control of the trial so that the transcendent dignity of the persons involved in the dispute is respected at every point in the proceeding.[45]

3. Lawsuits leave deep scars, especially when the winning party is thought by the other as having gamed the system. *Solidarity as a moral virtue*, by contrast, demands recognition of "the interdependence between individuals and peoples," *and as a social principle*, it becomes the measure by which we can determine whether there is a need for the "modification of laws, market regulations, and juridical systems,"[46] including the Code of Judicial Conduct.

4. Lawsuits represent a *failure* of the negotiating process, in that a "contentious" proceeding is the result of the parties being either unable or unwilling to resolve their dispute amicably. To the extent that we take the principle of *subsidiarity* seriously, the judge is obligated under

Canon 1141(2) to force negotiations or arbitration whenever he or she "perceives some hope of a favorable outcome at the start of litigation or even at any other time. . . ."

5. Lawsuits are expensive and are generally beyond the means of persons of limited means. They are impossible for the poor. To the extent that we take seriously the *universal destination of goods*, we must pay special attention to the way in which our adversarial legal system imposes crushing burdens on "the poor, the marginalized and in all cases those whose living conditions interfere with their proper growth."[47] ADR proceedings (mediation or arbitration) are the *preferred* dispute resolution mechanisms in such cases because they are less expensive and strive to preserve the relationships among the parties.

CONCLUSION

The goal of this chapter is to demonstrate that reading the rules of professional conduct *in light of* Catholic social teaching is not simply a means of "restating existing legal obligations, [it] is [rather] to set a new standard of care, one higher than existed before."[48] We could, of course, wait for the Supreme Court of the United States to rule that the poor are entitled to free legal advice and counsel whenever they need it, but given the Court's record on the subject thus far, I would not hold my breath. Nor would I wait for the states either.

To the extent that progress needs to be made in improving the plight of those trapped in the gears of the legal system, we must consider retraining— and reorienting—the judges themselves. In an extremely thoughtful, and thought-provoking, speech the Honorable Joan B. Gottschall of the United States District Court for the Northern District of Illinois suggested that commentators

> . . . usually paid little attention to the place where I believe ethical and/or religious views play the greatest role: in judges' determination of the facts of a controversy. Here, trial court judges have an enormously important role to play: in the facts we make part of the evidentiary record—whether by our evidentiary rulings or by our power to call for and hear evidence the parties might not otherwise present to us—and in the facts we choose to emphasize in our decisions. In these ways, by our substantial power to shape the evidentiary record, and in our largely unreviewable power to decide what evidence should be believed or credited as salient or determinative, our most important values—whether their source is ethical, religious, or political—have a frequently dispositive impact on the outcome. Indeed, as every practicing lawyer knows, the facts the lawyers prove and the facts the judge finds frequently compel the disposition of the case.[49]

Offering judges a short course on Catholic social teaching would not be popular, and, in some states, it is doubtful that a continuing legal education program coordinator would even approve such a course for credit. (It would not be "legal" enough.) Nonetheless, the remarks of thoughtful lawyers like Judge Gottschall and the many others suggest that there is a need to try.

NOTES

1. 28 U.S.C. § 453 (Oaths of Justices and Judges). *Compare*, Ohio Rev. Code § 3.23 (2014) ("that I will administer justice without respect to persons, and will faithfully and impartially discharge and perform all the duties incumbent upon me [as a judge] according to the best of my ability and understanding").

2. The Code of Conduct for United States Judges [hereinafter CCUSJ] available at http://www.uscourts.gov/RulesAndPolicies/CodesOfConduct/CodeConductUnitedStatesJudges.aspx (accessed April 1, 2014). The Code was initially adopted by the Judicial Conference of the United States on April 5, 1973. See Judicial Conference of the United States (1971), "Communication from the Chief Justice of the United States transmitting the Proceedings of the Judicial Conference of the United States, April 5–6, 1973, House Doc. No. 93-103 (93rd Cong., 1st Sess., May 21, 1973) at 9-11, at http://www.uscourts.gov/uscourts/FederalCourts/judconf/proceedings/1973-04.pdf (accessed April 1, 2014).

3. Michael Davis, "Professional Responsibility: Just Following the Rules," 18, no. 1 *Business & Professional Ethics Journal* (Spring 1999): 65.

4. Davis, "Professional Responsibility" at 67–68 and n. 3 (footnote omitted), *referencing* Caroline Whitbeck, *Ethics in Engineering Practice and Research* (Cambridge University Press, 1998).

5. Davis, "Professional Responsibility" at 75.

6. Avery Cardinal Dulles, S. J., *Catholic Social Teaching and American Legal Practice*, 30 Fordham Urban L. J. 277, 279 (2002) (footnote omitted). *See* Harold J. Berman, *The Interaction of Law and Religion* (Abingdon Press, 1974), 49–76.

7. Pontifical Council for Justice and Peace, *Compendium of the Social Doctrine of the Church* (USCCB Communications, 2005) [hereinafter *Compendium*].

8. Letter to His Eminence Cardinal Renato Raffaele Martino from Cardinal Angelo Sodano, Secretary of State, June 29, 2004, ¶1.

9. See, e.g., Pope Francis, *Lumen fidei* ("The Light of Faith"), June 29, 2013, ¶3: In the process, faith came to be associated with darkness. There were those who tried to save faith by making room for it alongside the light of reason. Such room would open up wherever the light of reason could not penetrate, wherever certainty was no longer possible. Faith was thus understood either as a leap in the dark, to be taken in the absence of light, driven by blind emotion, or as a subjective light, capable perhaps of warming the heart and bringing personal consolation, but not something which could be proposed to others as an objective and shared light which points the way.

10. See, e.g., Pope Francis, Morning Meditation in the Chapel of the *Domus Sanctae Marthae*, "Disciples of the Lord and Not of Ideology," Thursday, October 17, 2013 (commenting on Luke 11:47–54), which recounts the Lord's warning to the doctors of the law: "Woe to you lawyers! For you have taken away the key of knowledge; you did not enter yourselves, and you hindered those who were entering").

11. See, e.g., Homily of Cardinal Seán O'Malley, Mission for Migrants, Mass on the Border in Nogales, Arizona, April 1, 2014 (commenting on the famous question posed to Jesus by a scholar of the law in Luke 10:25–29: "Who is my neighbor?"); Permanent Council of the Canadian Conference of Catholic Bishops, Pastoral Letter on Freedom of Conscience, Monday, May 14, 2012.

12. *Message of John Paul II to Bishop Lucien Fruchaud of Saint-Brieuc and Tréguier for the 700th Anniversary of the Birth of St. Ivo Hélory [St. Ives] of Brittany*, May 13, 2003.

13. Mary Ann Glendon has observed that "in the Law Day rhetoric of bar association officials, exhortations to uphold the rule of law have given way to self-serving portrayals of lawyers as vindicators of an ever-expanding array of claims and rights." Mary Ann Glendon, *A Nation Under Lawyers: How the Crisis in the Legal Profession Is Transforming American Society* (Harvard University Press, 1996) at 5.

14. *Address of His Holiness John Paul II, to the Members of the International Academy of Trial Lawyers*, Castel Gandlofo, September 22, 1989.

15. *Message of John Paul II to Bishop Lucien Fruchaud, supra* note 12.

16. *Compendium,* ¶132.

17. *Compendium,* ¶131.

18. *Compendium,* ¶164.

19. *Compendium,* ¶168.

20. *Compendium,* ¶193.

21. *Compendium,* ¶186.

> Just as it is gravely wrong to take from individuals what they can accomplish by their own initiative and industry and give it to the community, so also it is an injustice and at the same time a grave evil and disturbance of right order to assign to a greater and higher association what lesser and subordinate organizations can do. For every social activity ought of its very nature to furnish help to the members of the body social, and never destroy and absorb them.

> Pius XI, *Quadragesimo Anno,* ¶79 (1931); *cf.* John Paul II, Encyclical Letter *Centesimus Annus,* ¶48 (1991); *Catechism of the Catholic Church,* ¶1883.

22. *Compendium,* ¶124.

23. *Compendium,* ¶125.

24. *Compendium,* ¶182.

25. American Bar Association, Model Rules of Professional Conduct [hereinafter ABA Model Rules]. ABA Model Rules, Preamble ¶1 (brackets and numbering supplied).

26. American Bar Association, Model Code of Judicial Conduct (2011), Preamble ¶1.

27. See ABA Model Rules, Preamble ¶2.

28. ABA Model Rules, Preamble ¶3.

29. See, e.g., ABA Model Rules, Rule 1.14, Comment 5 (Clients with diminished capacity; need to take protective action when the client is "at risk of substantial physical, financial or other harm unless action is taken"); Rule 2.1 [Advisor] (In rendering advice, a lawyer may refer not only to law but to other considerations such as moral, economic, social and political facts, that may be relevant to the client's situation); ABA Standards for the Prosecution Function 3-1.2 (c): "The duty of the prosecutor is to seek justice, not merely to convict."

30. ABA Model Rules 1.6, 1.7 (conflict of interest).

31. Davis, "Professional Responsibility," *supra* note 3 at 75.

32. 28 U.S.C. § 453 (Oaths of Justices and Judges). *Compare*, Ohio Rev. Code § 3.23 (2014) ("that I will administer justice without respect to persons, and will faithfully and impartially discharge and perform all the duties incumbent upon me [as a judge] according to the best of my ability and understanding").

33. The Code of Conduct for United States Judges [hereinafter CCUSJ].

34. CCUSJ, Canon 3(A) (Adjudicative Responsibilities). These include (1) "be[ing] faithful to, maintain[ing] professional competence in the law"; (2) "hear[ing] and decid[ing] matters assigned, unless disqualified . . ." and (6) "dispose promptly of the business of the court." CCUSJ, Canon 3(B) (Administrative Responsibilities); CCUSJ, Canon 3(A)(3); CCUSJ, Canon 3(A) (2–3).

35. 28 U.S.C. § 455 (requiring disqualification when a judge's impartiality "might reasonably be questioned"); *Caperton v. A.T. Massey Coal Co.*, 556 U.S. 868, 129 S. Ct. 2252 (2009) (Due Process Clause of the Fourteenth Amendment requires recusal when "the probability of actual bias on the part of the judge or decisionmaker is too high to be constitutionally tolerable.") See generally, Charles Gardner Geyh, *Federal Judicial Center, Judicial Disqualifica-*

tion: An Analysis of Federal Law, Second Edition (Federal Judicial Center, 2010); CCUSJ, Canon 2 (avoidance of impropriety and appearance of impropriety); Canon 3(B)(1) ("partisan interests, public clamor, or fear of criticism"); (B)(2) (control of the courtroom environment); (B)(4) (no *ex parte* communications); (B)(6) (avoid public commentary); (C) (grounds for disqualification); Canon 5 (avoidance of political activity).

36. See, e.g., *Patterson v. McLean Credit Union*, 485 U.S. 617, 618 (1988) (*per curiam*) (no special consideration for civil rights plaintiffs); *Kern v. TXO Corp.*, 738 F.2d 968 (8th Cir., 1984) (dismissal without prejudice should have been conditioned on plaintiff's payment of costs and attorney fees, even though plaintiff was an individual and defendant was a large corporation); *United States v. VandeBreak*, 679 F.3d 1030, 1042 (8th Cir., 2012) (Beam, J., dissenting) (complaining that the District Court's calculation of the sentence imposed on the defendants had been improperly influenced by its view that "both were already wealthy, multi-millionaire businessmen").

37. Joseph F. Anderson, Jr., *Where Have You Gone, Spot Mozingo? A Trial Judge's Lament over the Demise of the Civil Jury Trial*, 4 Fed. Cts. L. Rev. 99, 107–8 (2010).

38. Anderson, *Where Have You Gone?* at 107.

39. Anderson, *Where Have You Gone?* quoting an "avowed opponent of mandatory ADR, Arkansas Federal Judge Thomas Eisele." See G. Thomas Eisele, "The Case Against Mandatory Court-Annexed ADR Programs," 75 *Judicature*, June/July 1991, at 34, 36:

> [ADR programs] . . . are clearly different in kind and in basic philosophy. In real trials, the objective is to arrive at the truth, vindicate rights, and to do justice. The evidence presented at a real trial is all important. . . . Not so with ADRs. They operate in a different atmosphere: where fault, guilt or innocence, right or wrong are not central to the process; where one-tenth of a loaf is better than none; . . . where the evidence is de-emphasized; where every claim is assumed to have some value; where true justice is considered too expensive or an unattainable abstraction.

40. Code of Canon Law, c. 1446 § 1.

41. Isaiah 11:3–4:

> And his delight shall be in the fear of the LORD; and he shall not judge after the sight of his eyes, neither decide after the hearing of his ears; But with righteousness shall he judge the poor, and decide with equity for the meek of the land; and he shall smite the land with the rod of his mouth, and with the breath of his lips shall he slay the wicked.

> Isaiah 1:17: Learn to do well; seek justice, relieve the oppressed, judge the fatherless, plead for the widow.

42. Qur'an:

> 95:8 Is not God the most just of judges?

> 4:58 BEHOLD, God bids you to deliver all that you have been entrusted with unto those who are entitled thereto, and whenever you judge between people, to judge with justice. Verily, most excellent is what God exhorts you to do: verily, God is all-hearing, all-seeing!

> 26:83 O my Sustainer! Endow me with the ability to judge [between right and wrong], and make me one with the righteous.

> 38:22 As they came upon David, and he shrank back in fear from them, they said: "Fear not! [We are but] two litigants. One of us has wronged the other: so judge thou between us with justice, and deviate not from what is right, and show [both of] us the way to rectitude.

43. *Compendium,* ¶168.

44. *Compendium,* ¶131.

45. *Estelle v. Williams,* 425 U.S. 501 (1976) is a good example of this problem. Writing for the Court, the late Chief Justice Warren Burger held that, while a state judge may not compel an accused person to stand trial before a jury while dressed in prison garb, his failure to make a timely objection waived his objection. Justices Brennan and Marshall dissented, arguing:

> The Court's statement that "[t]he defendant's clothing is so likely to be a continuing influence throughout the trial that . . . an unacceptable risk is presented of impermissible factors" affecting the jurors' judgment, thus presenting the possibility of all unjustified verdict of guilt, *ante* at 425 U.S. 505, concedes that respondent's trial in identifiable prison garb constituted a denial of due process of law.

The dissenting Justices noted further that:

> Respondent appeared at trial wearing a white T-shirt with "Harris County Jail" stenciled across the back, oversized white dungarees that had "Harris County Jail" stenciled down the legs, and shower thongs. Both of the principal witnesses for the State at respondent's trial referred to him as the person sitting in the "uniform." Record on Appeal in Tex. Ct. of Crim. App. 108, 141 (No.73-3854).
>
> 425 U.S. at 515–16 & n. 1.

46. *Compendium,* ¶193.

47. *Compendium,* ¶182.

48. Davis, "Professional Responsibility," *supra* note 3 at 75.

49. Hon. Joan B. Gottschall, *Factfinding as a Spiritual Discipline,* 4 U. St. Thomas L. J., 325 (2006).

Chapter Three

A Brief History of American Catholic Legal Education

The Arc of an Uncertain Identity

John M. Breen and Lee J. Strang

INTRODUCTION

The first Catholic law school in the United States was founded in 1869. Today twenty-nine American law schools operate under Catholic auspices. The history of American Catholic legal education is a story of great success and tremendous failure—success as legal education and failure as education that is discernibly Catholic.

In this chapter, we first describe the founding of Catholic law schools in the United States. The purpose of these schools was to facilitate the upward social mobility of Catholic immigrants and their children, while lending prestige and financial resources to their host universities. Second, we recount a brief period where several leading Catholic legal scholars urged Catholic law schools to become, for the first time, distinctively Catholic—an effort that was largely unsuccessful. Third, we detail the period, from approximately 1965 to 1990, where the unself-conscious Catholic identity of these schools became ever more attenuated. Fourth, we explore the post-1990 movement of some Catholic law schools to become more intentionally Catholic. We close with a tentative prescription for those Catholic law faculties, deans, and university leaders who wish to make their law schools genuinely and robustly Catholic.

ORIGINS AND CHARACTERISTICS OF AMERICAN CATHOLIC LEGAL EDUCATION

Catholic legal education in the United States began in 1869 with the founding of Notre Dame Law School. By 1935 there were twenty law schools affiliated with a Catholic college or university.[1]

Catholic colleges and universities founded or acquired law schools primarily for three reasons. First, these schools were a means of facilitating the upward mobility of American Catholics. In the nineteenth and early twentieth centuries, most of the Catholic population in the United States was made up of successive waves of immigrants, largely drawn from the poor and working classes. Legal education was a relatively inexpensive mechanism that Church-affiliated colleges and universities could employ to provide American Catholics with a means of social and economic advancement.

Second, from the start, Catholic colleges and universities suffered from a chronic lack of resources and a lack of academic credibility that was both actual and perceived. They saw adding law schools as a way of increasing both while making only a modest investment.[2] Catholic law schools frequently hired only one or two full-time faculty. Practicing lawyers serving as adjuncts taught many of the school's classes, often free of charge. Most Catholic law schools began as evening schools in office space rented in the business district of their host cities. The addition of a law school boosted Catholic university revenue because, especially in urban areas, there were young, working men who wished to advance and who had the incentive and money to pay law school tuition.

Relatedly, adding a law school boosted the academic standing of Catholic institutions by enabling them to better mimic their more prestigious secular and Protestant peers.[3] A major change in American higher education in the late nineteenth century was the adoption of the German university model[4] in which the various disciplines focused on discrete subject matters, each with its own methods and standards. Adding law schools was an easy, low cost, way for Catholic colleges to move in this direction.

Third, in a handful of instances, Catholic universities founded law schools to meet the needs of the local bar. Typically, a group of practicing attorneys—usually, though not always, Catholic—would approach the local Catholic college and ask it to open a law school to provide the means for men to become lawyers and facilitate economic growth in the area.

A fourth and quite distant motivation for founding Catholic law schools was the goal of articulating a distinctively Catholic perspective on law. This was the dominant goal in only one instance. The American bishops created the Catholic University of America ("CUA") to be an academically rigorous graduate school for American Catholics. One component of this vision included graduate legal education from a distinctively Catholic perspective.[5]

Outside of CUA, however, the most prominent—and frequently the only—evidence of a Catholic philosophy of law at Catholic law schools was the presence of a solitary jurisprudence course taught from the natural law perspective, usually by a nonlawyer priest serving on the faculty.

Although the origins of these schools did not include a self-conscious articulation and exposition of law and justice from a Catholic point of view, most Catholic law schools were nevertheless culturally Catholic, many of them deeply so. Nearly all the faculty at these schools, and the vast majority of students were Catholic, so the schools themselves reflected a common way of life and looking at the world. The school calendar observed a number of religious feasts; the academic year commenced with Mass; there was usually at least one cleric on staff; students formed religious-themed student groups and participated in school-sponsored retreats and communion breakfasts; and the aesthetic environment of the school included crucifixes and images of Catholic saints related to law.

Beyond these cultural markers of identity, Catholic legal education was not self-consciously Catholic or otherwise distinctive. Instead, Catholic law schools mimicked their secular peers in their course offerings, teaching methods, professional norms, and practices. The goals for these schools at this time were to secure their foundation, receive accreditation, and fit in. Being distinctively Catholic simply was not part of this equation.

AN UNFRUITFUL ATTEMPT AT SELF-CONSCIOUS CATHOLIC LEGAL EDUCATION

In the 1930s–1940s, a number of leading Catholic legal academics critically examined the status of Catholic legal education and concluded that, while these schools faithfully replicated the courses and methods of instruction found in their secular peers, they were not meaningfully Catholic. To remedy this situation, Brendan F. Brown, dean at CUA's Columbus School of Law; James Thomas Connor, dean of Loyola University New Orleans School of Law; and William F. Clarke, dean of DePaul University College of Law set forth the first, serious, sustained proposal for Catholic law schools to be distinctively and self-consciously Catholic.

A number of factors contributed to their critical assessment and proposal for reform. The Great Depression challenged the economic stability of the global market economy, which, coupled with the rise of nondemocratic political arrangements—Fascism in Europe and Marxism in the Soviet Union—challenged America's liberal democracy. The rise of legal realism in American law schools called into question the moral and metaphysical premises upon which the legal order in the West had been established for millennia. Together, these factors led these Catholic legal academics to conclude that a distinctively Catholic voice needed to be heard in the legal academy and in American society more generally.

The reform proposal put forward by these scholars largely built upon the worldwide Neo-Scholastic movement then reaching its apex.[6] This movement—a revival in the thought of St. Thomas Aquinas, and to a lesser extent other medieval scholastic thinkers—began in the mid-nineteenth century. It was given enormous prestige by Pope Leo XIII in his encyclical, *Aeterni Patris*, in which he urged the Church's teachers to "endeavor to implant the doctrine of Thomas Aquinas in the minds of students, and set forth clearly his solidity and excellence over others."[7] The revival was so successful that, by the early twentieth century, Neo-Thomism had become *the* defining feature of Catholic higher education—a comprehensive worldview touching upon all disciplines.

Leaders in Catholic legal education, like Brown, Clarke, and Connor, identified the contemporary threats to a correct understanding of law as totalitarianism abroad and legal realism at home.[8] Other prominent Catholic legal scholars, such as Walter B. Kennedy at Fordham, Miriam Theresa Rooney at CUA, and Francis E. Lucey, S.J., the longtime law school regent at Georgetown, all engaged in debates in scholarly journals, making use of Thomism to challenge the "newer jurisprudence."[9] By examining the law through a Thomistic lens, they argued that Catholic law schools possessed the intellectual capacity to secure the correct foundations of law in theory and in practice. The cure for these modern ailments was a thorough study of the natural law and the establishment of "a legal culture under the influence of a neo-scholastic philosophy."[10]

The reform proposal to make Catholic law schools distinctly Catholic did not, however, achieve success. A host of factors account for this failure, many of which represent a reversal of the circumstances that inspired the proposal in the first instance: the end of the Great Depression and the advent of post-war prosperity; the defeat of Fascism in Europe and the implicit acknowledgement of the authority of natural law at Nuremberg and in the Universal Declaration of Human Rights[11]; and the decline of legal realism as a vibrant movement in the academy.[12]

Other reasons for the failure related to the proposal itself. The proposal called for a significant change from the original purposes that had inspired Catholic legal education. Few faculty at Catholic law schools were engaged in a culture of scholarship and most were not equipped to articulate and apply Thomistic natural law theory in their classes or written work because of their inadequate training in the subject. In addition, some perceived the proposal as religious and theological in nature, and so unsuited to professional education.

The failure of the reform movement also followed from the fragmentation of Neo-Scholasticism into rival schools of thought.[13] Neo-Scholasticism had provided the reformers with the analytical tools necessary to make the reform proposal coherent and plausible.[14] Without the stable, intellectual architecture provided by Neo-Scholasticism, the proposal lost its energy and coherence and ceased to serve as a viable program for reform.

CULTURAL UPHEAVAL, VATICAN II, AND THE FURTHER ATTENUATION OF CATHOLIC IDENTITY

American Catholic legal education continued in its traditional pattern until the late-1960s. With the exception of some outward signs and practices acknowledging an ostensible religious affiliation, Catholic law schools were near–carbon copies of their non-Catholic counterparts. Beginning in the late-1960s, however, even this stable—though thin—facet of Catholic identity began to give way.

The 1960s were a turbulent time in the United States. No traditional institution, structure, or way of life was left unmarred, and Catholic law schools were no exception. The cultural turmoil and social upheaval of the era was defined by the Vietnam War and the public protests and general distrust of government it inspired; the sexual revolution and "women's liberation"; and the civil rights movement and the struggle to overcome historic racism. At the same time, dramatic changes were taking place within the Catholic Church in the wake of the Second Vatican Council, which met from 1962 to 1965. The Council brought about enormous changes in the Church's liturgical life[15] and it fostered new interest in the study of sacred scripture,[16] ecumenism,[17] and inter-religious dialogue.[18] It introduced new ways of thinking about religious freedom and the proper relation between church and state.[19] It articulated the Church's self-understanding and her relationship with the world at large in new ways.[20] It also stimulated Catholic interest in new approaches to philosophy beyond the bounds of Thomism. When combined with the other societal convulsions of the day, Vatican II "produced nothing less than a spiritual earthquake in the American church."[21] Many Catholics then felt free to question not only political but also ecclesiastical authority, and, in the process, Catholicism became a deeply contested concept.

In time, the initial excitement generated by the Council gave way to the reality that not all change was for the better. While most American Catholics welcomed celebrating the liturgy in the vernacular, weekly Mass attendance dropped precipitously. Thousands of men and women left the priesthood and religious life, and new vocations plummeted.[22] Fewer parents sent their children to Catholic primary and secondary schools, causing schools to close.[23] The publication of Pope Paul VI's 1968 encyclical letter, *Humanae Vitae*,[24] reaffirming the Church's historic teaching against contraception, was greeted with public dissent by some priests, theologians, and lay people. [25] The fact that there were no real consequences for the dissenters only reinforced the idea that the meaning of Catholicism was protean and manipulable, that one could pick and choose among the doctrines of the Church, yet still remain Catholic. [26] In the wake of the Council, "[s]o many spiritual and religious landmarks were suddenly swept away that the average Catholic was left in a state of complete bewilderment." [27]

Combined with the pressures of cultural change, this fracturing of the American Catholic consensus also influenced the development of American Catholic universities. In the *Land O' Lakes Statement*, issued in 1967, the representatives of several leading Catholic universities declared their independence from "authority of whatever kind, lay or clerical, external to the academic community itself." [28] From 1968 to 1975, nearly every American Catholic college and university underwent a reorganization formally separating from the religious orders that founded them and transferring the ownership and control of these institutions to largely lay boards of trustees. [29]

This historic move had three key components, each of which contributed to Catholic higher education's secularization. First, university presidents wanted the freedom to act as real chief executives, without having to answer to the agendas and priorities of the provincials within their respective religious orders. Second, these institutions sought independence from church governance. Perhaps more importantly, they sought to rid themselves of the perception of church control, which they regarded as an impediment to the rise of their academic reputations among their secular peers. Third, many Catholic universities were experiencing severe financial difficulties in the early 1960s. To ensure their survival they sought to gain access to a variety of newly created sources of government aid. To be eligible for these funds, the legal advice that the university presidents obtained recommended a process of secularization: not only in the formal separation of the university from its founding religious order, but in the university's hiring practices, in its affiliation with other Catholic schools, in the religious appearance of its campus and classrooms, and even in the content of its theology classes. [30]

Legal education was also undergoing enormous change. Inspired by law-as-a-vehicle-for-change as witnessed in the movements for civil rights, women's rights, and environmentalism, and a desire to avoid service in Vietnam, the number of American law students doubled from 1965 to 1975. Catholic law schools shared in this dramatic expansion of student enrollment. However, many of the students attending Catholic law schools were no longer Catholic, and many that were lacked the catechesis of earlier generations.

To meet this increase in student body, the size of law school faculties likewise expanded. However, this unprecedented growth occurred at a time when Catholic higher education, like the Church in general, had lost the ability to state with confidence the source and meaning of its identity. A desire to "engage the world"—a prominent theme in Vatican II—led to hiring law faculty without regard for, and in some cases, precisely *because* they did not understand or possess an interest in the school's Catholic mission. The already faint traces of Catholic philosophy in the curriculum (the once common mandatory jurisprudence course) were done away with or replaced with classes taught from a non-Catholic perspective. Clinical legal education became popular in America's law schools during this time, and Catholic law schools followed this trend sponsoring clinics where students learned the basics of legal representation while serving the poor and disadvantaged. These clinics were, however, begun for pedagogical reasons and not out of a devotion to Catholic mission.[31] To make matters worse, the prior cultural Catholicism that had distinguished Catholic legal education, collapsed as well. Catholic student groups, such as the St. Thomas More Society, withered away, and other Catholic practices, such as Mass and crucifixes in law school classrooms, disappeared.

While no school was exempt from these forces, some weathered the storm better than others. In particular, Notre Dame Law School maintained a definite Catholic identity in its curriculum, student body, and cultural life. The key to this success was the university's charge that to maintain its Catholic identity the number of faculty who are "committed Catholics" must "predominate"—a point taken up in earnest by the law school in its hiring practices.[32]

A SECOND CHANCE FOR SELF-CONSCIOUS CATHOLIC LEGAL EDUCATION: 1990–PRESENT

Beginning in the mid-1980s, a number of events and trends in the Church moved the American Catholic conversation toward a renewed consensus and away from the pluralism and confusion that characterized the immediate post-conciliar period. *The Ratzinger Report* published in 1985, the 1985 Extraordinary Synod of Bishops, and the 1986 removal of Father Charles Curran from Catholic University all signaled that the scope of legitimate conceptions of Catholicism was narrowing.

The start of this renewal began in 1978 when the College of Cardinals elected Karol Wojtyla to serve as Pope. A man of courage, charisma, conviction, and great personal holiness, John Paul II inspired many disillusioned Catholics and younger people with his vibrant orthodoxy and deep Christian humanism. One especially significant, early decision in his pontificate was the selection Joseph Ratzinger to serve as prefect of the Congregation for the Doctrine of the Faith. In 1985, Ratzinger agreed to a book-length interview with Italian journalist Vittorio Messori, published as *The Ratzinger Report*. In the interview, Ratzinger acknowledged that the implementation of Vatican

II had been "problematic." The Council documents, he said, had often been misinterpreted resulting in "many abuses in the post-conciliar period," misleading the faithful and impairing the Church's evangelical mission.[33]

Ratzinger's comments helped frame the discussion at the Extraordinary Synod of Bishops convoked by the Pope later in 1985.[34] The Synod rejected the "partial and selective reading" and "superficial interpretation" of Vatican II that sought to elevate the "spirit of the Council" above the conciliar texts and that saw the Council as marking a decisive break with the Christian past. Instead, the Synod insisted that the authoritative conciliar texts "be understood in continuity with the great tradition of the Church."[35] The Synod also recommended that a "catechism or compendium of all Catholic doctrine" be prepared that might serve as "a point of reference" for the faithful in their knowledge of the faith.[36] Work began on such a text shortly thereafter and, in 1992, the Holy See published the *Catechism of the Catholic Church*, which John Paul II commended as "a sure norm for teaching the faith and thus a valid and legitimate instrument for ecclesial communion."[37]

These and other efforts aimed at returning Catholics to the essence of the faith and restoring a sense of stability began to bear fruit in many ways, including some related to legal education. First, the Church witnessed a revival of orthodoxy among a subset of the new generation of American Catholics, including some legal educators. These men and women came of age when the negative effects of the radical pluralism of the Church of the 1960s to 1970s became evident. Second, many Catholics began to grasp the implications of the collapse of a broader Catholic subculture that took place following World War II with the growing affluence of American Catholics who abandoned their ethnic, parish-centered urban neighborhoods in favor of the suburbs.[38] This loss was augmented by the confusion that took place following Vatican II. For the first time in a generation, many perceived the crucial need for Catholic, culture-preserving institutions, including universities and law schools. Third, *Roe v. Wade* prompted a reexamination of the foundations of law and the need for institutions to articulate a correct understanding of a just legal order.[39] The abortion license created in *Roe* challenged the legitimacy of contemporary law and legal institutions at their root. Catholics saw the need for law schools to critique the abortion license and to set forth an alternate conception of law premised on the dignity of every human life.[40]

Through the mid-1980s, Catholic educators continued to explore the boundaries of Catholic identity. Indeed, while the Church's bishops took up Pope John Paul II's call for authentic renewal based on the work of the Council, many theology faculties at Catholic universities became centers of institutionalized dissent.[41] However, in 1986 the Holy See removed Father Charles Curran from his position on the pontifically chartered theology faculty at Catholic University of America for his writings promoting views on marriage, sexuality, and abortion contrary to the Church's teaching.[42] Although the case dragged on in the civil courts for several years, CUA was ultimately victorious, and this victory dramatically signaled a new resolve on the part of church authorities to ensure the authenticity of Catholic identity in the university setting.[43]

At the same time, a new conversation was taking place between university presidents and authorities in Rome. The Holy See was preparing a document on Catholic higher education and it sought the input of university officials. The ultimate product of these conversations was the apostolic constitution *Ex Corde Ecclesiae* issued by Pope John Paul II in 1990.[44] Among its more salient features the document insisted that Catholic universities publicly declare their identity as such and that "Catholic teaching and discipline . . . influence all university activities."[45] The university's Catholic identity was to be confirmed through a juridical relation with the local church and maintained through a majority of Catholic faculty.[46]

The presidents had been reluctant conversation partners in the Holy See's work to ensure the Catholic character of Catholic universities, first by all but overtly rejecting earlier drafts of the document,[47] and, when those efforts proved unsuccessful, by lobbying the American bishops to draft a set of norms that would maintain the status quo.[48] This latter effort also proved unsuccessful in that the bishops ultimately acceded to the Roman position.[49] To date, however, the reform sought by *Ex Corde Ecclesiae* has not been realized, due to a lack of interest on the part of bishops, faculty, and university administrators. Apart from the establishment of a number of centers and institutes dedicated to Catholic "mission" or "heritage," Catholic university campuses look much the same today as they did prior to *Ex Corde.*[50]

The document, and the process which generated it, were, however, successful in one important respect. It halted the trajectory of Catholic universities toward the fate of their Protestant counterparts where historic and ceremonial vestiges of a once-meaningful religious identity were all that remained.[51] It prompted a reconsideration of Catholic identity that otherwise would not have taken place.

In the context of Catholic legal education, the effect of *Ex Corde* was to put the topic of Catholic identity squarely on the table for conversation. Whereas prior to *Ex Corde*, discussions regarding a law school's identity as a Catholic institution were infrequent and strictly internal, Catholic identity in legal education became the subject of a robust, public conversation featured in numerous law review articles and several published symposia.[52] Even those hostile to a meaningful Catholic mission were reluctant to publicly recommend a complete abandonment of the school's historic identity,[53] so the discussion quickly focused not on *whether* but on *how* the school would be Catholic.[54] In this way, *Ex Corde* and the conversation it inspired prevented—or at least forestalled for the time being—the slow death of Catholic identity due to neglect and the inertia of a process of secularization already well advanced.[55]

The discussion prompted by *Ex Corde Ecclesiae* also led to the founding of two new, distinctively Catholic law schools, and the attempted revitalization of some existing schools. Ave Maria School of Law and the University of St. Thomas School of Law were each founded in 1999.[56] The inspiration, organization, operation, and aspirational goals of each school reflected an overt commitment to a distinctive Catholic identity.

At roughly the same time, a handful of Catholic law schools attempted to reinvigorate their dormant Catholic identity. The most significant example was Villanova University School of Law. Under the leadership of Dean Mark Sargent from 1997 to 2009, Villanova partially succeeded in reviving its Catholic identity by organizing an annual conference on Catholic social thought and founding a new journal dedicated to the topic by establishing the Scarpa Chair in Catholic Legal Studies and hosting an annual conference organized by the chairholder, and by hiring a number of faculty dedicated to the school's Catholic mission.[57]

THE FUTURE OF CATHOLIC LEGAL EDUCATION: PROSPECTS FOR REFORM

The vast majority of Catholic law schools today find themselves in a precarious position with regard to their Catholic identity. In some respects, this position is no different than it has been through most of their history. There are, however, at least four significant differences from the time in which the earlier proposal for reform was put forth in the 1930s, 1940s, and today— differences that would make any contemporary effort to reform Catholic legal education all the more difficult.

First, the environment for legal education today is highly competitive for attracting qualified students and generating a sufficient level of income to maintain a school's facilities, programs, and support for scholarship. In this climate of increased competition and increased emphasis on learning the practical skills of lawyering,[58] the pressure is for Catholic law schools to do what they have done in the past—follow the lead of their non-Catholic counterparts and fit in. Although the opportunity to be distinctive is plainly present, choosing such an alternate approach requires not only conviction as to its outward appeal and innate value, but courage to see the project through in the face of opposition and derision, from colleagues in the legal academy,[59] from one's own faculty, and from others in the Catholic community.[60]

Second, schools today know that Catholic identity means *something*. With few exceptions, however, they are unwilling publicly to say what this identity is beyond the platitudes of a handful of well-chosen slogans. This may be due to a lack of consensus among faculty and administrators or because the anemic brand of Catholic identity found in most schools today *is* the consensus, and reticence serves the interests of those who subscribe to it. Having an honest conversation about a school's Catholic identity can be exceedingly difficult. Still, if such conversations were to take place they would do so in the wake of *Ex Corde Ecclesiae* and the extensive commentary it has generated. While these materials might facilitate this dialogue by serving as the locus of discussion, they would also likely make the conversation more difficult since the starting place for *Ex Corde* is far beyond where all but a tiny minority of American Catholic law schools find themselves today.

Third, throughout their history, Catholic law school faculties have been reluctant to see their schools embrace a robust sense of mission that would distinguish them from their secular peers. Nevertheless, the reluctance today is ideological rather than practical in nature, and far more entrenched than in the past. From the founding era through the 1950s, opposition to efforts to make Catholic law schools more identifiably Catholic was based on institutional inertia and a fear that such an emphasis would threaten the integrity of the school and its reputation as a place of rigorous professional study and training. Today, by contrast, many faculty do not wish to be associated with a law school that is conspicuously and unapologetically Catholic. Because of its stance with respect to the most neuralgic issues of the day (e.g., sexuality, same-sex marriage, abortion, and contraception), many in the legal academy view the Church as an oppressive, antiquated, and patriarchal institution. Each of these issues has a legal dimension and would receive serious attention in an authentically Catholic law school in a way that many faculty would find objectionable. By contrast, if the Catholic identity of a school remains confined to the decorative aspects of graduation ceremonies and a nod in the direction of a generalized concern for the poor and "social justice," most faculty are content to reserve their objections in favor of the school's historic ties, while others hold their noses and cash their paychecks.

Fourth, in the first half of the twentieth century, Neo-Scholasticism readily presented itself as "a theoretical rationale for the existence of Catholic colleges and universities as a distinctive element in American higher education."[61] Catholic legal educators in the 1930s and 1940s similarly looked to Neo-Scholasticism as the source of an intellectual architecture that would revitalize their institutions.

The temptation today would be to look for a relatively discrete body of thought that could organize and structure Catholic law schools and distinguish them from their non-Catholic counterparts. Although Thomism remains a vital field of study, it hardly seems poised to regain the position of preeminence it once held in Catholic intellectual life. Even if it did, the practical challenges of building a law faculty equipped to integrate Thomism within the study of law present in the 1940s are even more acute today. Catholic social teaching, the other major candidate for such a body of thought, suffers from other deficiencies.[62] Catholic social teaching's capacious scope, its lack of concrete answers to specific social problems, its susceptibility to manipulation and facile engagement, and its scriptural and other theological roots, call into question its capacity to serve in this role.[63]

Still, to fulfill its Catholic mission, a Catholic law school may wish to emphasize some body of thought that serves as its animating principle—an intellectual architecture that organizes, structures, and informs the school's curriculum, pedagogy, and scholarly pursuits. To serve in this capacity, a body of thought needs to possess at least the following six characteristics: (1) sufficient richness of intellectual resources; (2) aptitude for legal questions; (3) adequate determinacy; (4) intellectual respectability; (5) consistency with Catholic theological and philosophical commitments; and (6) a sufficient number of personnel trained or trainable in the body of thought.

The first characteristic requires that a body of thought have the necessary contingent of concepts, arguments, and forms of analyses to meet the demands of organizing legal education. Legal education has many facets, both theoretical and practical, so that an organizing body of thought must be able to account for and justify these facets in a satisfactory way. For instance, any plausible candidate must provide an adequate account of the concept and virtue of justice, the focal point of law.[64]

The second characteristic is that the proposed body of thought must include, within the subjects of its purview, law and legal issues. There are many bodies of thought that have little or nothing to say about law as such. Only those that have the capacity to answer the most important legal issues, and most legal issues, would be viable candidates.

The third characteristic is that a body of thought must provide determinate answers, to some adequate degree, to many legal questions, especially those that are fundamental. A body of thought need not be entirely determinate in its answers to all legal issues; however, viable candidates must narrow the range of acceptable answers in a way that is both comprehensive and coherent.

Intellectual respectability is the fourth characteristic and it has two components: first, the body of thought must have the characteristics of other respectable bodies of thought, such as internal coherence, having worked out major issues, and professional recognition; and second, it must substantively be worthy of respect. The first component, in practice, means that a viable candidate has been the subject of years of reflection and argumentation among its adherents, otherwise, intellectual competitors will (rightly) dismiss it. The second component means that the substantive answers proposed by a body of thought are plausible.

The fifth characteristic ensures that a body of thought organizing a Catholic law school fits Catholicism. To serve as the organizing principle behind a Catholic law school, a body of thought must be consistent with Catholicism's philosophical and theological commitments. A plausible candidate need not expressly affirm the doctrine of the Trinity or the Real Presence of Christ in the Eucharist, but it cannot contradict the Church's theological doctrines on these and other matters.

Lastly, the body of thought must have enough people trained in it to adequately organize and staff Catholic legal education or, at the very least, have the capability of being taught to an adequate number of people. If few American lawyers are well versed in a particular body of thought, and if they cannot be adequately trained in it, then it may face insurmountable obstacles as a locus of identity in Catholic legal education.

Finally, we believe that if a law school wants to fulfill its mission by providing a Catholic perspective on law within the legal academy it must have faculty who embrace this mission. It seems obvious, that to be Catholic, a law school must have a Catholic faculty. Surely, as *Ex Corde Ecclesiae* provides, the majority of faculty at a Catholic academic institution must be Catholic.[65] That does not mean that a Catholic law school may not hire non-Catholics, nor does it mean that a law school adequately ensures the integrity of its mission by hiring faculty who identify as Catholic. Adherence to the school's mission counts for more than outward religious affiliation, and an individual claiming to be Catholic may in fact be deeply hostile to a Catholic perspective on law and legal issues. To this end, the following negative criterion is necessary to secure a law school's Catholic identity: A faculty candidate should be deemed unacceptable if his or her current or proposed scholarship or public advocacy would undermine the common good by seeking to advance the ethical licitness, cultural acceptability, or legal protection of any action that is intrinsically evil or gravely immoral. Such a negative criterion would preclude a Catholic law school from hiring candidates who write in favor of abortion, contraception, same-sex marriage, polygamy, prostitution, and the use of torture, and against religious freedom and the rights of conscience. To ensure the competent training of their students, the faculty at Catholic law schools would still introduce students to the strengths and weaknesses of the arguments marshaled in favor of these positions. By not hiring faculty who publicly advocate in favor of these views, however, Catholic law schools would avoid giving institutional support to those who stand against the Catholic Church in the public square.

NOTES

1. See John M. Breen and Lee J. Strang, *The Road Not Taken: Catholic Legal Education at the Middle of the Twentieth Century*, 51 Am. J. Legal Hist. 553, 637 (2011) (appendix listing

keys dates for Catholic law schools). The appendix to the article contains an error in that it lists Duquesne University School of Law as being founded in 1878. Duquesne University was founded in that year but the Law School was founded in 1911. See "Duquesne University School of Law: History—A Higher Calling," available at http://www.duq.edu/academics/ schools/law/about-the-school-of-law/history. Even before Notre Dame, St. Louis University established the first law school in the United States under Catholic auspices in 1843. However, the school ceased operations in 1847 following the death of Judge Richard Buckner, and it did not resume operations again until 1908. See Edward J. Power, *A History of Catholic Higher Education in the United States* (Bruce Pub. Co., 1958), 223. Some texts mistakenly date the beginning of St. Louis University School of Law to 1842. John F. Dunsford, *St. Louis—Pioneer Catholic Law School*, 3 Cath. Law. 237 (1957); "St. Louis University School of Law; School of Law History," available at http://www.slu.edu/school-of-law-home/about-us/history.

2. This was unlike, for example, the relatively high investment necessary for a medical school. This different financial calculus partially explains why there are only five Catholic medical schools in the United States, compared to approximately six times as many law schools. See Power, *supra* note 1 at 243–53 (describing the different histories of Catholic medical and law schools and attributing the different number of each to cost, among other factors).

3. See Philip Gleason, *Contending with Modernity: Catholic Higher Education in the Twentieth Century* (Oxford University Press, 1995), 95–102 (describing the addition of professional schools as "a response to both the galloping professionalization of" American life "and to the mobility aspirations of American Catholics").

4. See George M. Marsden, *The Soul of the American University: From Protestant Establishment to Established Nonbelief* (Oxford University Press, 1994), 103–10 (describing the awe in which elite American university personnel held German universities and how they modeled American universities after the German model); see also Marsden at 155.

5. See Joseph Nuesse, *The Thrust of Legal Education at the Catholic University of America, 1895–1954*, 35 Cath. U. L. Rev. 33 (1985).

6. For surveys of the origins, growth, and ultimate fragmentation of Neo-Scholasticism, see Gerald A. McCool, S.J., *Nineteenth-Century Scholasticism: The Search for a Unitary Method* (Fordham University Press, 1977); Gerald A. McCool, *The Neo-Thomists* (Marquette University Press, 1994).

7. Pope Leo XIII, *Aeterni Patris*, ¶31 (1879).

8. James Thomas Connor, *Some Catholic Law School Objectives*, 36 Cath. Educ. Rev. 161, 165 (March 1938).

9. See, e.g., Francis E. Lucey, S.J., *Natural Law and American Legal Realism: Their Respective Contributions to a Theory of Law in a Democratic Society*, 30 Geo. L. J. 493 (1942); Walter B. Kennedy, *Principles or Facts?* 4 Fordham L. Rev. 53 (1935); Miriam Theresa Rooney, *Lawlessness, Law, and Sanction* (Catholic University of America Press, 1937).

10. Brendan F. Brown, *Jurisprudential Aims of Church Law Schools in the United States, A Survey*, 13 Notre Dame Law 163, 167 (1938).

11. Rodger D. Citron, *The Nuremberg Trials and American Jurisprudence: The Decline of Legal Realism, the Revival of Natural Law, and the Development of Legal Process Theory*, Mich. St. L. Rev. 385 (2006); Mary Ann Glendon, *Foundations of Human Rights: The Unfinished Business*, 44 Am. J. Juris. 1 (1999).

12. Breen and Strang, *The Road Not Taken, supra* note 1, at 629–30.

13. McCool, *Nineteenth-Century Scholasticism, supra* note 6.

14. Undergraduate faculties at many Catholic colleges and universities chafed under the hegemony of Thomism imposed from above as a rigid template for all thought. Gleason, *Contending with Modernity, supra* note 3 at 287–98.

15. Vatican Council II, *Sacrosanctum Concilium* (Constitution on the Sacred Liturgy, 1963).

16. Vatican Council II, *Dei Verbum* (Dogmatic Constitution on Divine Revelation, 1965).

17. Vatican Council II, *Unitatis Redintegratio* (Decree on Ecumenism, 1964).

18. Vatican Council II, *Nostra Aetate* (Declaration on the Relationship of the Church to Non-Christian Religions, 1965).

19. Vatican Council II, *Dignitatis Humanae* (Declaration on Religious Freedom, 1965).

20. Vatican Council II, *Lumen Gentium* (Dogmatic Constitution on the Church, 1964). Vatican Council II, *Gaudium et Spes* (1965).

21. Gleason, *Contending with Modernity, supra* note 3 at 305.

22. James Hitchcock, "The Empty Cloister," in James Hitchcock, *The Decline and Fall of Radical Catholicism* (Image Books, 1971); Avery Cardinal Dulles, "Passionate Uncertainty," *First Things* (April 2002) (reviewing Peter McDonough and Eugene C. Bianchi, *Passionate Uncertainty: Inside the American Jesuits* [2002]).

23. Peter Steinfels, *A People Adrift: The Crisis of the Roman Catholic Church in America* (Simon & Schuster, 2003), 29–31.

24. Pope Paul VI, *Humanae Vitae* (1968).

25. Janet E. Smith, *Humanae Vitae–A Generation Later* (Catholic University of America Press, 1991), 161–93.

26. Ralph M. McInerny, *What Went Wrong with Vatican II: The Catholic Crisis Explained* (Sophia Institute Press, 1998); George Weigel, *The Courage to Be Catholic: Crisis, Reform and the Future of the Church* (Basic Books, 2002), 57–86.

27. Thomas Bokenkotter, *A Concise History Of The Catholic Church* (Doubleday, 1990), 368.

28. "Land O' Lakes Statement on the Nature of the Contemporary Catholic University," (1967) *reprinted in American Catholic Higher Education: Essential Documents, 1967–1990,* ed. Alice Gallin, O.S.U. (University of Notre Dame Press, 1992), 7–16 [hereinafter *Essential Documents*].

29. James Tunstead Burtchaell, *The Dying of the Light: The Disengagement of Colleges and Universities from Their Christian Churches* (Eerdmans Pub. Co., 1998), 705–16 (summarizing the author's detailed study of this movement in the preceding pages).

30. Burtchaell, *The Dying of the Light* at 597–602.

31. In the years that followed Catholic law schools would point to these clinics as proof of their Catholic identity understood as a firm commitment to "social justice," the content of which was never well defined. See John M. Breen, *Justice and Jesuit Legal Education: A Critique,* 36 Loyola U. Chicago L. J. 383 (2005).

32. "Report of the Committee on University Priorities" (1973), *reprinted in Notre Dame Magazine* (December 1973) at 13. Similar language has appeared in every Notre Dame strategic plan since the first COUP Report in 1973. See, e.g., "A Strategic Plan–Notre Dame 2010: Fulfilling the Promise," § II.1.C (2003) ("It remains our goal that dedicated and committed Catholics predominate in number among the faculty . . .").

33. Joseph Cardinal Ratzinger and Vittorio Messori, *The Ratzinger Report* (Ignatius Press, 1985), 29–31.

34. See George Weigel, *Witness to Hope: The Biography of John Paul II* (Harper Perennial, 2005), 502–3.

35. *The Final Report of the 1985 Extraordinary Synod,* § I.4 and § I.5.

36. *The Final Report of the 1985 Extraordinary Synod,* § III.5.

37. Pope John Paul II, *Fidei Depositium,* ¶3 (Apostolic Constitution, 1992).

38. See Russell Shaw, *American Church: The Remarkable Rise, Meteoric Fall, and Uncertain Future of Catholicism in America* (Ignatius Press, 2013) (describing the early-to-mid-nineteenth century American Catholic subculture and arguing for its revival). Jay P. Dolan, *In Search of an American Catholicism: A History of Religion and Culture in Tension* (Oxford University Press, 2002), 180–89; Philip Gleason, *Keeping the Faith: American Catholicism Past and Present* (University of Notre Dame Press, 1987), 58–81; Charles R. Morris, *American Catholic: The Saints and Sinners Who Built America's Most Powerful Church* (Vintage, 1997), 255–81.

39. *Roe v. Wade,* 410 U.S. 113 (1973).

40. See, e.g., Robert M. Byrne, *An American Tragedy: The Supreme Court on Abortion,* 41 Fordham L. Rev. 807 (1973); Robert A. Destro, *Abortion and the Constitution: The Need for a Life-Protective Amendment,* 63 Cal. L. Rev. 1250 (1975); John T. Noonan, Jr., *The Root and*

Branch of Roe v. Wade, 63 Neb. L. Rev. 668 (1984); Gerard V. Bradley, *Life's Dominion: A Review Essay*, 69 Notre Dame L. Rev. 329 (1993); John M. Breen and Michael A. Scaperlanda, *Never Get Out'a the Boat: Stenberg v. Carhart and the Future of American Law*, 39 Conn. L. Rev. 1 (2006).

41. George A. Kelly, *The Battle for the American Church* (Doubleday, 1979).

42. See letter to Father Charles Curran from Joseph Cardinal Ratzinger, Prefect, Congregation for the Doctrine of the Faith, July 25, 1986, available at http://www.vatican.va/roman_curia/congregations/cfaith/documents/rc_con_cfaith_doc_19860725_carlo-curran_en.html (accessed March 13, 2014).

43. *Curran v. The Catholic University of America*, No. 1562–87 (D.C. Super. Ct. Feb. 28, 1989), 117 Daily Wash. L. Rptr. 653 (April 3, 1989). For an account of this dispute that favors Curran, see Larry Witham, *Curran vs. Catholic University: A Study of Authority and Freedom in Conflict* (Edington-Rand, 1991).

44. Pope John Paul II, *Ex Corde Ecclesiae* (Apostolic Constitution, 1990).

45. *Ex Corde Ecclesiae*, art. 2.

46. *Ex Corde Ecclesiae*, arts. 4.4 and 5. The document also provided that Catholic theologians were to teach by virtue of "a mandate received from the church . . . [and] are to be faithful to the magisterium." *Ex Corde Ecclesiae*, art. 4.3.

47. Examples of these efforts can be found in *Essential Documents*, *supra* note 28 at 259–322, 381–83.

48. James T. Burtchaell, C.S.C., *Out of the Heartburn of the Church*, 25 J. College & U. L. 653 (1999).

49. United States Conference of Catholic Bishops, *The Application of Ex Corde Ecclesiae for the United States* (2000), available at http://www.usccb.org/beliefs-and-teachings/how-we-teach/catholic-education/higher-education/the-application-for-ex-corde-ecclesiae-for-the-united-states.cfm (accessed March 13, 2014).

50. Examples of Catholic institutions within what is supposed to be a Catholic institution include the Center for Catholic Studies at the University of St. Thomas, http://www.stthomas.edu/cathstudies/; Hank Center for Catholic Intellectual Heritage at Loyola University Chicago, http://www.luc.edu/ccih/; Institute of Catholic Studies at John Carroll University, http://sites.jcu.edu/catholic/; and Joan and Ralph Lane Center for Catholic Studies and Social Thought at the University of San Francisco, http://www.usfca.edu/lanecenter/.

51. See Marsden, *Soul of the American University*, *supra* note 4; Burtchaell, *supra* note 29.

52. The Religiously Affiliated Law Schools held a symposium on *The Ideal of a Catholic Law School*, and it was published by Marquette Law Review: Michael J. Perry, *The Idea of a Catholic University*, 78 Marq. L. Rev. 325 (1995); Thomas L. Shaffer, *Why Does the Church Have Law Schools?* 78 Marq. L. Rev. 401 (1995); Christopher Wolfe, *The Ideal of a (Catholic) Law School*, 78 Marq. L. Rev. 487 (1995).

53. *But see* Daniel Gordon, *Ex Corde Ecclesiae: The Conflict Created for American Catholic Law Schools*, 34 Gonz. L. Rev. 125 (1999); Leonard Pertnoy and Daniel Gordon, *Would Alan Dershowitz Be Hired to Teach Law at a Catholic Law School? Catholicizing, Neo-Brandeising, and an American Constitutional Policy Response*, 23 Seattle U. L. Rev. 355 (1999).

54. Mark A. Sargent, *An Alternative to the Sectarian Vision: The Role of the Dean in an Inclusive Catholic Law School*, 33 U. Tol. L. Rev. 171, 180 (2001) (distinguishing the question of "how" versus "whether" a school should be Catholic and distinguishing what he calls an "exclusive" and "sectarian" model from an "inclusive" model); Mark Tushnet, "Catholic Legal Education at a National Law School: Reflections on the Georgetown Experience," in *Georgetown at Two Hundred: Faculty Reflections on the University's Future*, ed. William. C. Madden (Georgetown University Press, 1990), 321, 325–32 (setting forth four models whereby a national law school might be "Catholic" but concluding that if such a school succeeds in attaining national status its identity as Catholic will "be at best subsidiary").

55. For brief but important comments on this long process see Harold J. Berman, *The Secularization of American Legal Education in the Nineteenth and Twentieth Centuries*, 27 J. Legal Ed. 382 (1975).

56. See Bernard Dobranski, *New Lawyers for a New Century–Legal Excellence and Moral Clarity: The Founding of Ave Maria School of Law*, 36 U. Tol. L. Rev. 55 (2004) (describing the background and mission of Ave Maria School of Law); Thomas M. Mengler, *What's Faith Got to Do with It? (With Apologies to Tina Turner)*, 35 U. Tol. L. Rev. 145 (2003) (describing the background and mission of the University of St. Thomas School of Law); Sargent, *The Role of the Dean, supra* note 54.

57. See Villanova University School of Law, "Our Catholic Identity," http://www1.villanova.edu/villanova/law/admissions/about/catholicidentity.html (accessed November 19, 2013). Villanova University School of Law, "Patrick McKinley Brennan," http://www1.villanova.edu/villanova/law/academics/faculty/Facultyprofiles/PatrickMcKinleyBrennan.html.

58. See, e.g., Katherine Mangan, "Law Schools Revamp Their Curricula to Teach Practical Skills," *Chron. High. Ed.* 57 (March 4, 2011): 1.

59. See Monte N. Stewart and H. Dennis Tolley, *Investigating Possible Bias: The American Legal Academy's View of Religiously Affiliated Law Schools*, 54 J. Legal Ed. 136 (2004).

60. The experience of Ave Maria School of Law indicates that this would be the case. See, e.g., Robert F. Drinan, "Pizza Bucks Back Hyper-Catholic Law School," *Nat'l. Cath. Rep.* (May 7, 1999) (criticizing the creation of Ave Maria School of Law). See also Monte N. Stewart and H. Dennis Tolley, *Investigating Possible Bias: The American Legal Academy's View of Religiously Affiliated Law Schools*, 54 J. Legal Ed. 136 (2004).

61. Gleason, *Contending with Modernity, supra* note 3 at 322.

62. Catholic social teaching is that body of papal encyclicals, conciliar documents, episcopal statements, and other magisterial texts—beginning with Leo XII's *Rerum Novarum* through Vatican II's *Gaudium et Spes* to Benedict XVI's *Caritas in Veritate*—that address various social problems.

63. See John M. Breen and Lee J. Strang, "The Golden Age That Never Was: Catholic Law Schools from 1930–1960 and the Question of Identity," 7 *J. Catholic Soc. Thought* 489, 515–19 (2010).

64. See John M. Breen, *Justice and Jesuit Legal Education: A Critique*, 36 Loy. U. Chi. L. J. 383 (2005) (arguing that the study of and implementation of justice should be central to Jesuit law schools).

65. *Ex Corde Ecclesiae*, art. 4.4.

Chapter Four

Philosophy of Law

Robert P. George

There is a sense in which modern legal philosophy began on January 8, 1897. Oliver Wendell Holmes, then a justice of the Supreme Judicial Court of Massachusetts, spoke on that day at a ceremony dedicating the new hall of the Boston University School of Law. In his remarks, which would become a famous *Harvard Law Review* essay entitled "The Path of the Law," Holmes purported to debunk the jurisprudence of the past and propose a new course for modern jurists and legal scholars. Holmes's themes—the question of law's objectivity and the relationship between law and morality—have preoccupied legal philosophy ever since.

The opening sentence of his lecture invites his audience—lawyers, law professors, and law students—to consider what it is we study when we study law. We are not, he said, studying a "mystery," but, rather, "a well-known profession."[1] People are willing to pay lawyers to advise and represent them because "in societies like ours the command of public force is intrusted to the judges in certain cases, and the whole power of the state will be put forth, if necessary, to carry out their judgments and decrees."[2] Now, this is a fearsome power. So, "people will want to know under what circumstances and how far they will run the risk of coming against what is so much stronger than themselves, and hence it becomes a business to find out when this danger is to be feared."[3] The object of the study of law, therefore, "is prediction, the prediction of the incidence of the public force through the instrumentality of the courts."[4]

This was the thesis of "The Path of the Law." It was intended, I believe, as a provocation. And, so, Holmes formulated it in provocative ways:

A legal duty so called is nothing but a prediction that if a man does or omits certain things he will be made to suffer in this or that way by judgment of the court.[5]

The prophecies of what the courts will do in fact, and nothing more pretentious, are what I mean by the law.[6]

The duty to keep a contract at common law means a prediction that you must pay damages if you do not keep it,—and nothing else.[7]

Of course, provocation is effective only to the extent that one obscures one's intention to provoke. So Holmes claims merely to be proposing a "business-like understanding of the matter."[8] Such an understanding, he insists, requires us strictly to avoid confusing moral and legal notions. This is difficult, Holmes suggests, because the very language of law—a language of "rights," "duties," "obligations," "malice," "intent," etc.—lays a "trap" for the unwary. "For my own part," he declares in another famously provocative sentence, "I often doubt whether it would not be a gain if every word of moral significance could be banished from the law altogether, and other words adopted which should convey legal ideas uncolored by anything outside the law."[9]

Holmes's implicit denial of law's objectivity is not unconnected to his insistence on the strict separation of moral and legal notions. "One of the many evil effects of the confusion between legal and moral ideas," he states, "is that theory is apt to get the cart before the horse, and to consider the right or the duty as something existing apart from and independent of the consequences of its breach, to which certain sanctions are added afterward."[10] A corrective, according to Holmes, is to adopt the viewpoint of a "bad man" when trying to understand the law as such.

If you want to know the law, and nothing else, you must look at it as a bad man, who cares only for the material consequences which [legal] knowledge enables him to predict, not as a good one, who finds his reasons for conduct, whether inside the law or outside it, in the vaguer sanctions of conscience.[11]

And what exactly is being corrected by adopting the bad man's point of view?

You will find some text writers telling you that [the law] is something different from what is decided by the courts of Massachusetts or England, that it is a system of reason, that it is a deduction from principles of ethics or admitted axioms or what not, which may or may not coincide with the decisions. But if we take the view of our friend the bad man we shall find that he does not care two straws for the axioms or deductions, but that he does want to know what the Massachusetts or English courts are likely to do in fact.[12]

"I am much of this mind. The prophecies of what the courts will do in fact, and nothing more pretentious, are what I mean by the law."[13]

Still for all his skepticism—legal and moral—Holmes denied that his was "the language of cynicism."[14]

> The law is the witness and external deposit of our moral life. Its history is the history of the moral development of the race. The practice of it, in spite of our popular jests, tends to make good citizens and good men. When I emphasize the difference between law and morals I do so with reference to a single end, that of learning and understanding the law.[15]

Going still further, Holmes claimed to "venerate the law, and especially our system of law, as one of the vastest products of the human mind."[16] It was not, he assured his reader, disrespect for the law which prompted him to "criticize it so freely,"[17] but rather a devotion to it which expresses itself in a desire for its improvement.[18]

Holmes's aim is merely, he says, to expose some common fallacies about what constitutes the law. For example, some people—Holmes does not tell us who they are—hold that "the only force at work in the development of the law is logic."[19] This erroneous way of thinking is, Holmes advises his audience, "entirely natural" for lawyers, given their training in logic with its "processes" of analogy, discrimination, and deduction, but it is erroneous nevertheless. Moreover, "the logical method and form flatter that longing for certainty and for repose which is in every human mind."[20] "But," Holmes goes on to say without the slightest hesitation or expression of doubt,

> certainty generally is an illusion, and repose is not the destiny of man. Behind the logical form lies a judgment as to the relative worth and importance of competing legislative grounds, often an articulate and unconscious judgment, it is true, and yet the very root and nerve of the whole proceeding.[21]

The man who would later utter, in another connection, the famous aphorism that "the life of the law has not been logic, it has been experience,"[22] has already told his audience in this lecture that law is a matter of prediction, of prophecies of what courts will do in fact. And he has expressed great skepticism about the role of logic in guiding the decision-making of judges whose rulings, one way or the other, will constitute the law. So, how are those decisions to be rationally guided? What is "the law" from the perspective, not of the "bad man," but of the "good judge," who, facing a disputed question of law, will not be comforted by the assurance that "the law" is a prediction of how he will in fact resolve the case. In fact, what he wishes to do is to resolve the case according to the law. That, he supposes, is his job. He wants to rule on the matter favorably to the litigant whose cause is supported by the superior *legal* argument. But what constitutes *legal* argument? What are the sources of law upon which legal reasoning operates?

Of course, one candidate for inclusion in the list of legal sources is history. According to Holmes, "The rational study of law is still to a large extent the study of history."[23] Is this good or bad? Well, "history must be a part of the study, because without it we cannot know the precise scope of rules which it is our business to know."[24] But then comes the punch line: "It is part of the rational study, because it is the first step toward an enlightened scepticism, that is, toward a deliberate reconsideration of the worth of those rules."[25]

So, history is not a source in the sense that the legal rules uncovered, and whose meaning is clarified, by historical inquiry are authorities that guide the reasoning of the conscientious judge. On the contrary, such study has its value in exposing such rules to "an enlightened skepticism" regarding their value. But, then, by appeal to what standards are such judgments of value to be made? And—most critically—are these standards internal to the law or external? Does the judge discover the proper standards in the legal materials—the statutes, the cases, the learned treatises—or bring them to those materials? If the latter, then what is the discipline from which he derives them?

These are questions that will be central to the theoretical reflections of jurists and legal scholars for a hundred years. They will be answered one way by Jerome Frank and his fellow "legal realists" in the first half of the twentieth century, and precisely the opposite way by Ronald Dworkin and his followers in the second half. H.L.A. Hart, the Oxford scholar who essentially refounded the tradition of English analytical jurisprudence at roughly mid-century, will refer to the realists' answer as the "nightmare" that law does not exist, and to Dworkin's answer, as the "noble dream," that law as such provides a "right answer"—a single uniquely correct resolution—to every dispute which makes its way into the courtroom.

Holmes's own answer was vexingly ambiguous. In "The Path of the Law," he said at one point "I think the judges themselves have failed adequately to recognize their duty of weighing considerations of social advantage."[26] At another point he made this remarkable statement:

> I look forward to a time when the part played by history in the explanation of [legal] dogma shall be very small, and instead of ingenious research we shall spend our energy on a study of the ends sought to be attained and the reasons for desiring them. As a step toward that ideal it seems to me that every lawyer ought to seek an understanding of economics.[27]

Three-quarters of a century later, Richard Posner, Frank Easterbrook, Richard Epstein, Guido Calabresi, and other theorists and practitioners of the "economic analysis of law" would take this last piece of advice quite literally. Their books, law review articles, and—in the cases of Posner, Easterbrook, and Calabresi—judicial opinions would subject legal rules and social policies to cost-benefit tests and other forms of economic analysis to assess their instrumental rationality and, thus, in some cases, their legal validity. What these scholars and jurists do fits pretty well with Holmes's desire for lawyers and judges to "consider the ends which the several rules seek to accomplish, the reasons why those ends are desired, what is given up to gain them, and whether they are worth the price."[28] But, one must ask, would Holmes really approve their doing it?

Although Holmes was, in his politics, "a moderate, liberal reformer,"[29] he was resolutely determined, as a judge, not to "legislate from the bench." Indeed, during a period of unprecedented "judicial activism," he became the symbol of opposition to the judicial usurpation of legislative authority under the guise of interpreting the constitution. As an Associate Justice of the Supreme Court of the United States, he drew as sharp a line as any jurist of his time between "law" and "politics"—even when the politics in question was political economy. In what was perhaps his most celebrated dissent, Holmes castigated the majority in the 1905 case of *Lochner v. New York* invalidating a state law setting maximum working hours for employees in bakeries on the ground that such a regulation violated the "freedom of contract" which was held to be implicit in the due process clause of the Fourteenth Amendment. Holmes argued that this so-called substantive due process doctrine was an invention designed to authorize what was, in fact, the illegitimate judicial imposition of a theory of economic efficiency and the morality of economic relations on the people of the states and the nation. His claim was not that there was anything defective in that theory; on the contrary, its "social darwinist" dimensions held considerable appeal to him. Rather, it was that judges had no business substituting their judgments of efficiency and value for those of the people's elected representatives in Congress and the state legislatures.[30]

Now, it is not that any of this is flatly inconsistent with what Holmes says in "The Path of the Law." Indeed, at one point in that lecture he seems to suggest that training in economics and a due weighing of considerations of social advantage has the salutary effect of encouraging judicial restraint. "I cannot but believe that if the training of lawyers led them habitually to consider more definitely and explicitly the social advantage on which the rule they lay down must be justified, they sometimes would hesitate where now they are confident, and see that really they were taking sides upon debatable and often burning questions."[31] But plainly Holmes, as a judge—and, above all, as a dissenting judge—is supposing that the law is something more than merely a prophecy of what the courts will in fact decide. As a dissenter, he holds that the Courts have decided the case incorrectly. Of course, he does not deny that their rulings—even where incorrect—have the binding force of law, at least until they are reversed by higher courts of appeal. But he does suppose that the judges in the majority "got the law wrong." So, in some significant sense, the courts should be guided by the law; the judges should be faithful to the law. And this presupposes the reality of law, the preexistence of law, as something more than "a prophecy of what courts will do in fact."

So we must press the question: To what standards of legal correctness should the judge look in reasoning to the resolution of a case? Are the standards internal to the legal materials and discoverable, by some method, in them? Or are they external? Do judges "find" the law? Or do they, necessarily, "create" it? Can lawyers predict, or "prophesy" what a good and conscientious judge will do by figuring out what he should do in light of the legal materials which should control his reasoning? If that is all he means by "prediction" and "prophecy," then Holmes's debunking exercise is, for all its provocative language, far less skeptical than it appears.

Drawing their inspiration from Holmes, however, was a group of legal scholars who were prepared, for a while at least, to expose the idea of law to truly radical skepticism. The legal realist movement, which reached the peak of its influence in the 1930s and '40s, advanced the debunking project well beyond the point at which Holmes had left things in "The Path of the Law." Felix Cohen, Karl Llewellyn, Jerome Frank, and others pressed to an extreme the idea of jurisprudence as an essentially "predictive" enterprise. "Law," according to Llewellyn, "was what officials do about disputes." In accounting for their decisions, he insisted, it could only rarely be true to say that they are guided by rules. The trouble is not—or not just—that judges and other officials are willful and thus willing to lay aside the clear command of legal rules in order to do as they please. It is that legal rules are necessarily vague and susceptible of competing reasonable interpretations and applications. Even the problem of selecting which rule to apply to a given set of facts can only rarely be solved by looking to a clear rule of selection. The result is a measure of indeterminacy which makes nonsense of the idea of legal objectivity. The key to understanding the phenomenon of law—accounting for what judges and other officials do, or predicting what they will do, about disputes—is not the analysis of legal rules. It must be something else. True, judges and other officials cite the rules in justifying their decisions. But, if we are to be realistic about what is going on, according to Llewellyn, we must recognize that this is the mere legal rationalization of decisions reached on other grounds.

Frank's realism, was, if anything, still more extreme in its denial of legal objectivity. Going beyond Llewellyn's "rule-skepticism," Frank declared himself to be a "fact-skeptic" as well. Thus he denied law's objectivity even in the rare cases in which a clear rule was clearly applicable. Since rules must be applied to facts in order to generate a legal outcome, everything depends on findings of fact in trial courts and other fact-finding tribunals. And facts are, in most cases, virtually as indeterminate as legal rules. In statements which seem eerily, well . . . realistic, in the aftermath of several high-profile celebrity trials in our own day, Frank argued that our perceptions of facts are deeply influenced by conscious and subconscious beliefs, attitudes, and prejudices which vary among groups and individuals. So the key to understanding law—in legal realist terms—is the understanding of people's beliefs, attitudes, and prejudices, and why they hold them. Since law is a sort of epiphenomenon of human psychology, legal scholarship should be directed to scientific (e.g., psychological) and social scientific studies of human motivation. To be realistic, it should abandon the idea that law preexists and is available to guide legal decisions.

The legal realists' insistence on the indeterminacy of law would, in our own time, be reasserted by advocates of "critical legal studies," though this time in the service of a "new left" political agenda and with nothing like the realists' faith in the objectivity and explanatory power of the natural and social sciences. The realists themselves were, like Holmes, political progressives—moderate liberals—eager to bring instrumental rationality to bear to solve social problems. Many were New Dealers. A few became judges. And those who did were, like Holmes, far less radical in practice than their theoretical views would have led one to predict. Although appeals to the alleged findings of social science became an increasingly common feature of judicial opinions as the twentieth century wore on, realists who became judges rarely cited their own subjective views or prejudices as ground of their decisions. Rather, they cited legal rules as the ultimate reasons for their decisions; and claimed, at least, to lay aside their own preferences in fidelity to the law. (Interestingly, Frank, in the aftermath of the revelation of Nazi atrocities in Europe, declared himself in the preface to the sixth edition of his *Law and the Modern Mind* to be a follower of St. Thomas Aquinas on the basic questions of law and morality. Nothing in his earlier writings, he insisted, was ever meant to suggest otherwise.)

Of course, realism has its appeal precisely because it is, from a certain vantage point, realistic. Trial lawyers take issues of venue and *voir dire* very seriously because they know, and have always known, that who is on the jury can be critical to whether facts are found favorably to their clients. And one of the first questions lawyers at any level of litigation want to know the answer to is who the judge or judges are who will be making determinations of law at the trial or on appeal. Often enough, different jurors or a different judge or judges mean different results. So far forth, the phenomenon of law includes elements of genuine subjectivity.

But the realists overstate their case. They get stuck on the same question we put to Holmes a little while ago. From the point of view of a conscientious judge, the law is not—for it cannot be—a prediction of his own behavior. Often they, like Holmes, are faced with what they themselves perceive to be a duty to follow rules whose application generates outcomes which run contrary to their personal preferences. True, a willful judge can simply give effect to his prejudices under the guise of applying the law, at least until reversed by a higher court of appeal (if there is one). But this is no modern discovery. And it is no more a threat to the possibility of law's objectivity than is the fact that people sometimes behave immorally is a threat to the objectivity of morals. Just as a conscientious man strives to conform his behavior to what he judges to be the standards of moral rectitude, the conscientious judge strives to rule in conformity with the controlling rules of law. And no account of the phenomenon of law which ignores the self-understanding of such a judge—no account which, that is to say, leaves his point of view out of account—can do justice to the facts.

This, I think, was clear to Herbert Hart. He above all other English-speaking juridical thinkers in the wake of legal realism recognized that the shortcomings of legal skepticism and the radical denial of law's objectivity had mainly to do—not with the dangers of its project of debunking to the body politic by its capacity to undermine the public's faith in the rule of law—but rather with realism's inability realistically to account for the phenomenon of law as it functions in human societies. Realist theories failed to fit the facts. And they failed to fit the facts because they approached the phenomenon of law from a purely external viewpoint. The problem, according to Hart, was not that legal realists were bad lawyers; it was that they were bad psychologists and social scientists, even as they looked to psychology and social science to explain the phenomenon of law.

Social phenomena—phenomena created or constituted, at least in part, by human judgment, choice, cooperation, etc.—can never adequately be understood, Hart argues, without adopting what he calls the "internal point of view." This is the point of view of those who do not "merely record and predict behavior conforming to rules," or understand legal requirements as mere "signs of possible punishment," but, rather, "use the rules as standards for the appraisal of their own and others' behavior."[32]

On this score, Hart faults not only the legal realists, but also the leading figures in his own intellectual tradition, the tradition of analytical jurisprudence inspired by Thomas Hobbes and developed by Jeremy Bentham and his disciple John Austin. The problem with their jurisprudential theories, Hart observes, is that they too fail to fit the facts. And they fail to fit the facts because they do not take into account the practical reasoning of people whose choices and actions create and constitute the phenomenon of law—people for whom legal rules function as reasons for decisions and actions.

Hart in no way denies the wide variability of legal rules. Beyond some basic requirements of any legal system—what Hart calls the "minimum content of natural law"—there could be, and, in fact, one finds in the world, a great deal of variation from legal system to legal system. But in all societies which have achieved a legal order—that is, moved from a pre-legal order to a regime of law—law exhibits a certain objectivity and autonomy from other phenomena, including other normative systems. And the law of any system is not truly understood by the theorist proposing to give an intellectually satisfying account of that system until he understands the practical point of the law from the perspective of actors within the system who do not perceive their own deliberations, choices, and actions to be "caused," but rather understand themselves to be making laws for reasons and acting on reasons provided by the laws.

In his masterwork, *The Concept of Law*, Hart invites his readers to treat his analysis as "an exercise in descriptive sociology." But his is a sociology designed to make possible the understanding of legal systems from the inside. So what he proposes, and what the tradition of analytical jurisprudence has now more or less fully accepted as Hart's most enduring contribution, is that even "the descriptive theorist (whose purposes are not practical) must proceed . . . by adopting a practical point of view, [he must] assess importance or significance in similarities and differences within his subject matter by asking what would be considered important or significant in that field by those whose concerns, decisions, and activities create or constitute the subject-matter."[33]

If Hart rejected the externalism of Bentham and Austin—with its understanding of law (in Hobbesian fashion) as constituted by commands of a sovereign ("orders backed by threats") who was habitually obeyed by a populace but who in turn obeyed no one—he retained their commitment to "legal positivism." He described this much misunderstood commitment as the acknowledgment of a "conceptual separation" of law and morals. Although he was yet another moderate liberal in his politics, Hart did not mean by "positivism" the idea that law ought not to embody or enforce moral judgments. True, in his famous debate with Patrick Devlin over the legal enforcement of morals, Hart defended a modified version of J.S. Mill's "harm principle" as the appropriate norm for distinguishing legitimate from illegitimate state enforcement of morality; but he fully recognized that this principle itself was proposed as a norm of political morality to be embodied in, and respected by, the law. Moreover, he understood perfectly well that the content of legal rules reflected nothing so much as the moral judgments prevailing in any society regarding the subject matters regulated by law. So Hart cheerfully acknowledged the many respects in which law and morality were connected, both normatively and descriptively. In what respect, then, did he insist on their "conceptual separation"?

As I read *The Concept of Law*, as well as Hart's later writings, the "conceptual separation" thesis strikes me as rather modest. It has to do above all, I think, with the legitimate aspiration of the descriptive sociologist to keep his descriptions, to the extent possible, free of coloration by his own normative moral views. One can recognize a law, or even a whole legal system, as a law, or legal system, irrespective of whether one believes that that law, or legal system, is just; indeed, even a gravely unjust legal system can be, from a meaningful descriptive viewpoint, a legal system. And what is true of the descriptive sociologist or legal theorist can also be true of the judge, who may conclude in a given case that the law—identified by authoritative criteria or standards of legality—provides a rule of decision in the case at hand which is, from the moral point of view, defective. In repudiating what he takes—wrongly, in my view—to be the defining proposition of the natural law theorist, Hart denies in an unnecessarily wholesale fashion the proposition *lex iniusta non est lex*.

Although his views in fundamental moral theory are frustratingly elusive, nothing in Hart's positivism obviously commits him in any way to the moral skepticism, subjectivism, or relativism characteristic of the positivism of, say, Hans Kelsen or which one detects in the extrajudicial writings of Oliver Wendell Holmes. In fact, the student of Hart's who has remained closest to his views in legal theory, Joseph Raz, combines Hartian legal positivism with a robust moral realism. Hart and Raz have both insisted—rightly, in my view—on the necessity of some conceptual separation of law and morality for the sake of preserving the possibility of moral criticism of law. As John Finnis has observed, the necessary separation "is effortlessly established [by Aquinas] in the *Summa*, [by] taking human positive law as a subject for consideration in its own right (and its own name), a topic readily identifiable and identified *prior* to any question about its relation to morality."[34]

Nevertheless, Hart's positivism generated one of the century's most fruitful jurisprudential debates when it was challenged by Lon L. Fuller in the late 1950s. Fuller—whose careful explication and working out of the diverse elements of the Aristotelian ideal of the Rule of Law constituted a genuine achievement of twentieth century legal philosophy—proposed an argument to show that law and morality were, as a matter of brute fact, more tightly connected than Hart's positivism would allow. He sought to show that law necessarily embodied an "internal morality" that defied Hart's "conceptual separation" thesis. He offered to argue the point, not as a normative matter about moral standards that positive law *ought* to meet, but, rather, on Hart's own terms, as a descriptive proposition about moral standards that law had to embody before even the purely descriptive theorist could recognize it as law.

In his book *The Morality of Law*, Fuller offers an apparently "value-free" definition of law that any legal positivist ought to be able to accept: "Law is the subjecting of human behavior to the governance of norms."[35] Nothing in this definition demands that those who make and enforce the laws be wise, virtuous, benign, or concerned in any way for the common good. Still, some things follow from it. For example, people simply *cannot* conform their behavior to rules which have not been promulgated, or which lack at least some measure of clarity, or apply retrospectively. So promulgation, clarity, and prospectivity are aspects of the Rule of Law. Where they are absent, no legal system exists. And there are other requirements, including some significant measure of reliable conformity of official actions with stated rules. Taken together, Fuller argues, the Rule of Law constitutes a *moral* achievement. While this does not guarantee that a legal system will be perfectly just—in fact, all legal systems contain elements of injustice—it does mean that a certain minimum set of moral standards must be met before a legal system actually exists. And, sure enough, grave injustice is rarely found in systems in which the rulers—whatever their personal vices and bad motives—govern by law. It is in societies in which the Rule of Law is absent that the most serious injustices occur.

Of course, Hart was not buying this for a moment. While he admired, and for the most part accepted, Fuller's brilliant explication of the Rule of Law, he saw no reason to refer to its content as an internal *morality*. Moreover, he argued that there is no warrant for supposing that a system of law could not be gravely unjust, or that the Rule of Law provided any very substantial bulwark against grave injustice. Indeed, Raz argued against Fuller that the Rule of Law was analogous to a sharp knife, valuable for good purposes, to be sure, but equally useful to rulers in the pursuit of evil objectives.

The Hart/Fuller debate (like the Hart/Devlin debate) is an illuminating one. My own judgment is that Fuller scores a point or two in establishing a certain moral value of the Rule of Law, but that Hart rightly resists Fuller's somewhat exaggerated moral claims on its behalf. In any event, I do not think that Fuller undermines the central appeal of the "conceptual separation" thesis": the methodological aspiration to avoid confusing "law as it is" with "law as it ought to be."

Nor do I think that Ronald Dworkin's celebrated critiques of Hart's positivism are telling. Hart's theory has, as I have suggested, certain implications for the question Dworkin is most concerned about, namely, the question of judicial discretion in "hard cases"; but these implications are quite limited. Hart is fundamentally interested in developing methodological tools to enable the descriptive legal theorist to give a refined and accurate account of law in a given society. Thus, for example, he proposes the union of "primary" and "secondary" rules as "the key to the science of jurisprudence"; he distinguishes "duty-imposing" from "power-conferring" rules; and he develops the idea of a rule (or rules) of recognition to which actors in a legal system resort as establishing criteria of legal validity. Hart's jurisprudence is not "court-centered." In this respect, it differs sharply from the jurisprudence of Dworkin and most other American legal philosophers, including, interestingly enough, Holmes and the legal realists.

For Hart, the question of how much law-creating (or "legislative") authority a judge has, if any, or where that authority obtains, is not to be resolved at the level of general jurisprudence. Different legal systems differ—indeed reasonably differ—on the question of how such law-making authority is to be allocated among judges and other actors in the overall political system. To be sure, Hart observes that legal rules are inevitably "open textured," and, thus, in need of authoritative interpretation in their concrete application; and this entails a certain measure of judicial discretion and law-making authority as a matter of fact, even in those systems which exclude it in theory. Does this mean that the wall between legal validity and the moral judgment of judges is porous, even in systems of avowed legislative supremacy? Yes, indeed. Does it vindicate Dworkin's "right answer" thesis? Not at all. Hart's legal positivism is, in fact, completely compatible with the recognition that judges in some legal systems are invited or even bound under the positive law of the constitution to bring moral judgment to bear in deciding cases at law. Hart's is not a theory designed to show judges how they can resolve cases without making moral judgments, though neither is it a theory offering to justify their doing so (as Dworkin's is). The theory simply is not addressed to such questions.

What I think Hart *is* to be faulted for is a certain failure to see and develop the fuller implications of his own refutation of Benthamite and Austinian positivism and of his adoption of the internal point of view. Some of these implications are acknowledged, I think, by Raz in his later work, though he quite resolutely resisted them earlier on, as Hart did. The central or focal case of a legal system, to borrow a principle of Aristotle's method in social study, is one in which legal rules and principles function as practical reasons for citizens as well as judges and other officials because of people's apprehension of their value. Aquinas's famous *practical* definition of law as an ordinance of reason directed to the common good here has its significance in *descriptive* legal theory. As Finnis remarks,

> If we consider the reasons people have for establishing systems of positive law (with power to override immemorial custom), and for maintaining them (against the pull of strong passions and individual self-interest), and for reforming and restoring them when they decay or collapse, we find that only the moral reasons on which many of those people often act suffice to explain why such people's undertaking takes the shape it does, giving legal systems the many features they have—features which a careful descriptive account such as H.L.A. Hart's identifies as characteristic of the central case of positive law and the focal meaning of "law," and which therefore have a place in an adequate concept (understanding and account) of positive law. [36]

Yet Hart himself, in *The Concept of Law* and elsewhere declines to distinguish central from peripheral cases of the internal point of view itself. Thus, he treats cases of obedience to law by virtue of "unreflecting inherited attitudes" and even the "mere wish to do as others do" from morally motivated obedience of fidelity to law. These "considerations and attitudes," like those which boil down to mere self-interest or the avoidance of punishment, are, as Finnis says, "diluted or watered-down instances of the practical viewpoint that brings law into being as a significantly differentiated type of social order and maintains it as such. Indeed, they are parasitic upon that viewpoint."[37] Now, this is in no way to deny any valid sense to the positivist insistence on the "conceptual separation" of law and morality. It is merely to highlight the ambiguity of the assertion of such a separation and the need to distinguish, even more clearly than Hart did, between the respects in which such a separation obtains and those in which it does not. Still less is it to suggest that belief in natural law or other forms of moral realism entail the proposition that law and morality are connected in such a way as to confer upon judges as such a measure of plenary authority to enforce the requirements of natural law or to legally invalidate provisions of positive law they judge to be in conflict with these requirements. Important contemporary work by Finnis and others has clearly identified the misguidedness of such a suggestion. The truth of the proposition *lex iniusta non est lex* is a moral truth, namely, that the moral obligation created by authoritative legal enactment—that is to say, by positive law—is conditional, rather than absolute. The moral obligation to obey the law is *prima facie* and *defeasible*.

What about law's objectivity? Does law exist prior to legal decision? Can judicial reasoning be guided by standards internal to the legal materials? We can certainly improve on Holmes's answers. Yes, the standards to guide judicial reasoning can be internal to the law of a system which seeks to make them so, though never perfectly. Positive law is a human creation—a cultural artifact—though its justifying aims are moral; namely, the establishment and maintenance of justice and the realization of the common good. That is to say, law exists in what Aristotelians would call the order of technique, but it is created in that order precisely for the sake of purposes which obtain in the moral order. So, for moral reasons, we human beings create normative systems of social enforceable rules that enjoy, to a significant extent, a kind of autonomy from morality as such. We deliberately render these rules susceptible to *technical* ("legal") application and analysis (to the extent possible) for purposes of, for example, fairly and finally resolving disputes among citizens, or between citizens and governments, or between governments at different levels. And to facilitate this application and analysis, we create a legal profession, from which we also draw our judges, which is composed of people socialized and trained in programs of study which teach not, or not just, moral philosophy, but the specific tools and techniques of research, interpretation, reasoning, and argument relevant to *legal* analysis.

Now, to stress law's objectivity and relative autonomy from morality is by no means to deny the Thomistic proposition that just positive law is derived from the natural law. For Thomas himself did not suppose that positive law was anything other than a cultural artifact, a human creation, albeit a creation of great moral worth brought into being largely for moral purposes. Nor did he suppose that a single form or regime of law was uniquely correct for all times and places. His stress on *determinationes* by which the human lawmaker translates the requirements of the natural law into positive law for the common good of his community—enjoying, to a considerable extent, the creative freedom Aquinas analogized to that of the craftsman (or architect)—reveals his awareness of the legitimate potentially very wide variability of human laws. Whoever Holmes may have had in mind in criticizing those "text writers" who saw law as a set of deductions from a few axioms of reason, the charge has no applicability to Aquinas. In this, as in so many other respects, the Angelic Doctor was a man of the twentieth century, and—if I may engage in a bit of prediction and prophecy myself—of the twenty-first, and beyond.

NOTES

1. Oliver Wendell Holmes, Jr., *The Path of the Law*, 10 Harv. L. Rev. 457 (1897).
2. Holmes, 10 Harv. L. Rev at 457.
3. Holmes, 10 Harv. L. Rev at 457.
4. Holmes, 10 Harv. L. Rev at 457.
5. Holmes, 10 Harv. L. Rev at 458.
6. Holmes, 10 Harv. L. Rev at 461.
7. Holmes, 10 Harv. L. Rev at 462.
8. Holmes, 10 Harv. L. Rev at 459.
9. Holmes, 10 Harv. L. Rev at 464.
10. Holmes, 10 Harv. L. Rev at 458.
11. Holmes, 10 Harv. L. Rev at 459.
12. Holmes, 10 Harv. L. Rev at 460–61.
13. Holmes, 10 Harv. L. Rev at 461.
14. Holmes, 10 Harv. L. Rev at 459.
15. Holmes, 10 Harv. L. Rev at 459.
16. Holmes, 10 Harv. L. Rev at 473.
17. Holmes, 10 Harv. L. Rev at 473.
18. Holmes, 10 Harv. L. Rev at 474.
19. Holmes, 10 Harv. L. Rev at 465.
20. Holmes, 10 Harv. L. Rev at 466.
21. Holmes, 10 Harv. L. Rev at 466.
22. Oliver Wendell Holmes, *The Common Law: Lecture I* (1881), available at http://www.constitution.org/cmt/owh/commonlaw01.htm (accessed March 5, 2014).
23. Holmes, 10 Harv. L. Rev at 469.
24. Holmes, 10 Harv. L. Rev at 469.
25. Holmes, 10 Harv. L. Rev at 469.
26. Holmes, 10 Harv. L. Rev at 467.
27. Holmes, 10 Harv. L. Rev at 474.
28. Holmes, 10 Harv. L. Rev at 476.
29. J.W. Harris, *Legal Philosophies* (London: Butterworths, 1980), 94.

30. *Lochner v. New York*, 198 U.S. 45, 25 S. Ct. 539 (1905).

31. Holmes, 10 Harv. L. Rev at 468.

32. H.L.A. Hart, *The Concept of Law* (Oxford: Clarendon Press, 1961), 95–96.

33. John Finnis, *Natural Law and Natural Rights* (Oxford: Clarendon Press, 1980), 12.

34. John Finnis, "The Truth in Legal Positivism," in *The Autonomy of Law: Essays on Legal Positivism*, ed., Robert P. George (Oxford: Clarendon Press, 1996).

35. Lon L. Fuller, *The Morality of Law* (New Haven, CT: Yale University Press, 1969).

36. Finnis, "The Truth in Legal Positivism."

37. Finnis, *Natural Law and Natural Rights*, 14.

Chapter Five

Tort Law from a Catholic Perspective

Ronald J. Rychlak

INTRODUCTION

The early Americans' peculiar attachment to the law was one of the first things Tocqueville noticed about this new nation. "The spirit of the law," he wrote, "born within schools and courts . . . infiltrates through society right down to the lowest ranks, till finally the whole people have contracted some of the ways and tastes of a magistrate."[1] In America, the law not only outlines that conduct which is acceptable, it also helps form national views and opinions. All law reflects social and economic interests, but tort law is particularly associated with morality and standards of behavior.

When someone has caused harm to another, it is appropriate that he or she rectify the situation. In many cases, rectification comes without appeal to any other authority. The two parties simply work things out. The offender may offer to repair or replace the damaged item. Perhaps the victim may fully or partially forgive the wrongdoer. In other cases, the parties look to some other mediating institution. They might, for instance, turn to a priest or minister to help resolve things. Children may turn to a teacher or a parent. Members of a club may look to their leader. In any of these cases, at least partial forgiveness is likely to be included in the resolution.

When it is operating properly, the traditional American tort law system serves as "an arbiter between citizens who have a disagreement about who should bear a loss that has already occurred."[2] When the court orders a defendant to pay money damages to a plaintiff, even if the parties disagree strongly about the facts of the case, the decision must be based on reasons that both parties respect—i.e., harm and causation. The parties might disagree about whether harm and causation exist in that particular case, but as long as the standards are respected, a tort claim is a legitimate appeal to the values of free and responsible people. "It communicates to both parties that, even though we live in a world in which losses cannot be avoided, one can, by properly leading one's life, avert tort liability."[3] Such a system reaffirms the free will and self-determination of the parties by carefully evaluating their voluntary actions and decisions.[4]

Free will is, of course, a fundamental precept of Catholic doctrine. The Catholic Church teaches that "man is rational and therefore like God; he is created with free will and is master over his acts."[5] "By free will one shapes one's own life. Human freedom is a force for growth."[6] Following the Protestant Reformation, Sir Thomas More famously challenged Martin Luther's denial of free will.[7]

The Catholic Church also teaches that civil government must provide the rule of law and protect property rights, maintain a stable currency, and ensure efficient public services.[8] Authority has as its purpose the promotion of the common good of society. A viable political framework is, therefore, indispensable because it assures justice. Tort law is an important part of that framework. When individuals or smaller mediating institutions cannot resolve disputes, the government serves the common good by providing a mechanism to resolve them.

Under the Catholic doctrine of subsidiarity, decisions are best handled at the lowest level, and larger entities should only get involved when the smaller entities are unable to resolve issues. To the extent that tort laws encourage a proper resolution of difficult situations, first by encouraging settlement without resorting to the courts and then by providing a mechanism when litigation is necessary, they serve the common good by bringing commutative justice to the society. That is the traditional role of tort law, and that type of system is in line with the Catholic view of justice. It teaches adherence to the Golden Rule, and it encourages people to take account of others' interests even as they advance their own.[9]

THE CATHOLIC UNDERSTANDING OF JUSTICE

Professor Randy Lee, who has written persuasively on the differences between American tort law and the Catholic vision of justice, says: "[a]ny discussion . . . of tort law and Christ's law must begin with the recognition that the two are intended to relate with people in completely different ways. Thus, although they are both labeled as laws, their comparison is more akin to comparing apples and elephants than apples and oranges."[10] He argues that "[w]hile the tort system rejects tenderness, Catholicism hungers for mercy. While the tort system seeks to be blind, Catholicism seeks to see more clearly."[11]

Lee notes that "the framework in which tort law functions is one of duty, breach, injury, and cause," while the Christian viewpoint "meanwhile, mentions none of these requirements. Instead, Christ's instruction functions within a framework of love."[12] These differences, Lee argues, make attempts to compare tort law with a Catholic mentality very frustrating. "[T]ort law differs from Divine Law because tort law favors form over substance and is content with an imitation of truth that is merely a shadow of the real thing. This weakness of tort law is perhaps inescapable given the nature of human law."[13]

Professor Mary Ann Glendon, former U.S. Ambassador to the Vatican, pointed to another important difference between American tort law and the Catholic approach to such matters when she discussed

> the American tort-law doctrine that a person has no legal duty to come to the aid of another person in peril, even if he can do so without harm to himself. The doctrine, as it exists in all but a handful of states, is so profoundly at odds with ordinary moral intuitions that it comes as a shock to most law students. Yet, unless persons have entered into a legally recognized relationship with one another, our tort law treats them as "strangers" having no duty to one another except to avoid the active infliction of harm. The terminology is telling: The drowning man and I are "strangers" rather than fellow citizens or fellow members of the human family. I have no legal obligation to toss him a lifeline. [14]

Professor Glendon is certainly correct in noting that the Catholic Church has generated the body of Canon Law, which requires specific behaviors (including a duty to rescue) at certain times, whereas tort law generally does not demand affirmative actions.[15]

Despite the points made by Professors Lee and Glendon, American tort law stands more in line with Catholic thought than in opposition to it. To a certain extent, the differences noted by Professor Lee are those that would be inherent in any human construct. American tort law, after all, exists in a system in which a plurality of U.S. Supreme Court justices in 1992 announced a theory that endows human personhood with the freedom "to define one's own concept of existence, of the meaning of the universe, and of the mystery of human life." That freedom, they said, "lies at the heart of liberty" because "beliefs in these matters could not define the attributes of personhood were they formed under compulsion of the State."[16] Despite the criticism that this definition of liberty if taken seriously would undermine the basis of all law, the Court reaffirmed that position in 2003.[17]

Existing as it does in this legal system, tort law stands up alongside Catholic values pretty well as compared to other aspects of American law. It advances human responsibility and community in a manner that human constructs are capable of doing. As Professor Lee acknowledges: "Different as the tort system and Catholicism may be, the tort system is still usable as a tool for salvation."[18]

TORT LAW AND THE IMPACT ON SOCIETY

The traditional American tort system encourages acceptance of responsibility—certainly a good thing. Those who have been harmed know that because of the tort law system they will be compensated, and those who have committed the harm know that society ultimately will not let them avoid responsibility. This subtle pressure encourages potential litigants to work things out. The wrongdoer is encouraged to "do the right thing," and the person who has suffered harm is encouraged to be understanding and accept the apology and any associated inconvenience. Acceptance of responsibility by the wrongdoer and reasonable accommodation by the person who has been harmed are forms of charitable conduct in that they affirm the dignity and intrinsic value of the person.

The traditional American tort law system assigns liability in a way that serves to affirm the wrongdoer's basic humanity and advance the common good. As an example, consider the case of A:

> Upon hearing someone call his name [at a party], he inadvertently knocks over the glass [on a nearby table]. Suppose that A could not have been expected to be more careful than he was. Still, it would be perfectly natural for him, as well as expected of him, to feel some embarrassment and to offer to wipe up the spilled wine. . . . By his responsible stance, A reclaims his body from the status of a mere object that he most of the time successfully manipulates and invests it instead with the significance and meaning of an aspect of himself as subject.[19]

Without recognition of such responsibility, A is nothing more than a product of his environment, accountable neither for mistakes nor for great achievement.[20] It is only when the individual chooses to do what he or she does as a matter of free will that responsibility attaches.[21]

The Catholic Church also teaches that people have free will.[22] "The just man is worthy of praise for his honest deeds, since it is in his free choice that he does not transgress the will of God," explained Tatian the Syrian in A.D. 170.[23] Almost two-and-a-half centuries later, Augustine wrote, "God's precepts themselves would be of no use to a man unless he had free choice of will, so that by performing them he might obtain the promised rewards. For they are given that no one might be able to plead the excuse of ignorance, as the Lord says concerning the Jews in the Gospel: 'If I had not come and spoken unto them, they would not have sin; but now they have no excuse for their sin.'"[24]

The traditional American tort system holds a person responsible when he, "as a free agent, has exercised *his* choice in such a way as to make the punishment a necessary consequence."[25] This is where causation becomes a particularly important aspect of the morality of tort law:

> The common law did not aim to compensate every wronged party. Instead, it aimed to ensure that only wronged parties would be compensated, that they would be compensated *only* by wrongdoers, and that the compensation would not be so generous as to encourage fraudulent claims. The common law's many limits on liability and recovery did a reasonably good job of accomplishing that set of modest goals. Though the system plainly did some good, much of what it strived for was to avoid doing harm.[26]

As traditional tort law recognizes, holding wrongdoers responsible (in some cases even punishing them) is "the systematic *moral* response to wrongdoing."[27] This is how society acknowledges the integrity of the person.

If the person is not treated as the author of his or her actions, but a mere instrument, then the person is deprived of the role of creator. The satisfaction of personal achievement is closed to the person.[28] If we are truly to recognize full human potential, we must hold people accountable or release them from liability based upon their blameworthiness.[29] When punishment is given without justification, or when honors are given without merit, basic human will is undermined.

PROBLEMATIC DEVELOPMENTS IN TORT LAW

During the last few decades of the twentieth century, courts and legislatures too often tried to use the tort law system as a social planner. Rather than enforcing agreed and understood values of justice, courts used litigation to shape society.[30] In doing this, however, legal obligations subsumed morality, and the system came into conflict with the common good. Along the way, the system also brought personal responsibility into question, and that presented a challenge to our view of human free will. Needless to say, it significantly pulled away from a Catholic worldview.

Developments in the American tort system began for very reasonable purposes. It was, for instance, often difficult for plaintiffs in environmental exposure actions to prove causation. Courts therefore lessened causation requirements in order to help injured citizens prove their cases. In order to be certain that corporations took corrective action instead of permitting dangerous situations to exist (and dismissing any associated expenses as "costs of doing business"), courts expanded the amount and the availability of "punitive damages." For similar reasons, courts abrogated charitable and governmental immunities, and they eliminated rules like contributory negligence that precluded recovery when the plaintiff was partially at fault.[31] Individually, each of these changes made some sense—at least in specific cases. They corrected minor problems that would occasionally creep up under the traditional tort law system. Their collective and universal application, however, led to great damage.

These changes made lawsuits much easier to bring and made them much more profitable. It did not take long for the entrepreneurial spirit to take hold. Lawyers, who had previously been prohibited from soliciting business, began advertising in order to attract injured plaintiffs.[32] Jury awards became larger, large awards became more frequent, and tort litigation exploded.

With these developments, courts have begun to separate responsibility for the harm from the obligation to make the victim whole. Assigning liability to a party better able to bear the loss, but not actually responsible for the harm, not only violates traditional Christian ideas about responsibility, it also harms the legal system itself. When a court assigns liability without demanding a clear showing of causation, it encourages people to see the court not as a place for justice, but as a place for the transfer of wealth. Rather than responsibility, chance seems to be the operative factor:

> The operation of the tort system is akin to a lottery. Most crucial criteria for payment are largely controlled by chance: (1) whether one is "lucky" enough to be injured by someone whose conduct or product can be proved faulty; (2) whether that party's insurance limits or assets are sufficient to promise an award or settlement commensurate with losses and expenses; (3) whether one's own innocence of faulty conduct can be proved; and (4) whether one has the good fortune to retain a lawyer who can exploit all the variables before an impressionable jury, including graphically portraying whatever pain one has suffered.[33]

This undermines the societal understanding and agreement on which the tort system has been based. People have begun to seek out opportunities to be plaintiffs in tort suits, and that is a movement away from a Catholic view of justice. This has become a problem for the legal system in the second half of twentieth century.[34]

With the changes made to the traditional tort law system and the explosion of litigation, people became reluctant to seek forgiveness. Hesitancy to apologize grew as the fear of being sued expanded. No one wanted to offer an apology only to have it turned into a weapon against him in court. Furthermore, no one wanted to accept an apology and extend forgiveness if it might be used by an opponent before a judge and jury. Too often, those who suffered an injury were urged by television, radio, and print advertisements to call a lawyer who would sue anyone who might be blamed for the problem.

As the tort law system moved away from the concept of personal responsibility, it also moved away from traditional notions of Christian justice. This transformed the legal landscape as well as the message sent forth from the legal system. "Recent developments in Tort can be understood as just such a shift from moral to amoral Tort law; from a body of law assisting private ordering to a court-ordered public policy."[35] These changes put the tort law system into at least partial conflict with the Catholic vision of justice. They adversely impacted both the economy and interpersonal relationships. The net result of these developments was more distrust between members of the society, less human understanding, and damage to the common good.[36]

Any effective government needs to have a tort law system in place, and that is in keeping with the Catholic vision of a good government. Under Catholic thinking, however, litigation should not be the first option. According to the Gospel of Matthew:

> If your brother does something wrong, go and have it out with him alone, between your two selves. If he listens to you, you have won back your brother. If he does not listen, take one or two others along with you: whatever the misdemeanor, the evidence of two or three witnesses is required to sustain the charge. But if he refuses to listen to these, report it to the community; and if he refuses to listen to the community, treat him like a gentile or a tax collector.[37]

Similarly, in his first letter to the Corinthians, St. Paul wrote: "When one of you has a dispute with another believer, how dare you file a lawsuit and ask a secular court to decide the matter instead of taking it to other believers!"[38]

Catholics understand these teachings to relate to disputes within the Church, not as a requirement that all courts must be avoided. St. Paul, after all, taught that God had established legal authorities for the purpose of upholding justice, punishing wrongdoers, and protecting the innocent. For that reason, those people who have not done wrong should not fear the courts: "Magistrates bring fear not to those who do good, but to those who do evil. So if you want to live with no fear of authority, live honestly and you will have its approval."[39] Certainly the modern Church has been involved in a reasonable amount of litigation, but even in older times, St. Paul appealed frequently to the legal system, exercising his right to defend himself under Roman law.[40]

The negative impact that litigation can have on society has been noted by jurists and others. Chief Justice Warren Burger, addressing the 1982 American Bar Association convention asked: "Isn't there a better way?"[41] He noted the failure of litigation to truly resolve human conflict. As he explained, the "result is often drained of much of its value because of the time lapse, the expense, and the emotional stress."[42] Along similar lines, Abraham Lincoln is credited with the statement: "Discourage litigation. Persuade your neighbors to compromise whenever you can. . . . As a peacemaker the lawyer has a superior opportunity of being a good man. There will still be business enough."[43]

With the commercialization of litigation, standards that hold defendants responsible for harm that they did not cause, and potentially huge damages awards, businesses can be ruined and people have to be cautious about potential legal exposure.[44] Lawyers advise potential clients to be silent, not to admit anything. Legal advice wins out over human instinct. This violates subsidiarity and harms the common good.

> Behind the explosion of litigation is a great sense of loss of community, and inordinate focus on rights without a correlative sense of duties, a tendency to try to put financial value on every harm and wrong, the failure of our social institutions to provide support for people who hurt and suffer, and our lack of capacity to observe even minor wrong.[45]

In particular, great harm is done to the crucial value of forgiveness, which traditional tort law rightfully supports.[46]

When the tort law system stops encouraging people to behave correctly; when it causes injured people to seek a financial windfall; when it causes wrongdoers to deny responsibility and to look for excuses; when it causes people to doubt the motivations of others, it does not serve the common good.

Other modern developments in tort law also work against the common good. For instance, about half of the states permit parents to sue doctors for negligently failing to give them information that would have caused them to abort their baby.[47] Some states also permit an individual to sue, arguing that he or she should have been aborted, but the doctors did not advise the mother properly.[48] The impact on individuals involved in such suits (or even those who being similarly situated merely become aware of such suits) is staggering and deeply offensive to the common good.[49]

It is impossible to preserve freedom without an equally strong commitment to personal responsibility. Litigation must be a means of conflict resolution and not a tool for structuring an ideal society with a redistributivist mentality. Fortunately, the tort reform movement that grew into prominence in the 1990s and into the twenty-first century has begun to push back against expansion of the tort system. This is good for society, the economy, and in keeping with Catholic notions of justice.[50]

The goal of tort reform should be toward an evenhanded system based on fault and causation that, insofar as it is possible, places blame for damages on those who caused the damage while not unjustly punishing others (regardless of "deep pockets"). This goal is easier to formulate than to accomplish, if only because the reforms themselves have been heavily influenced by parties who stand to benefit from evading the new law (and may know its ins and outs better than anyone else).

CONCLUSION

The traditional American tort system encourages those who have done harm to be responsible for their actions. It also reassures those who have been harmed that they will be made whole. This recognizes free will, serves the common good, and reflects true Christian justice. It also encourages social harmony and personal responsibility. As such, despite differences in their origin and nature, the American tort law system fits well with Catholic social doctrine. Unfortunately, some of the developments to tort law that have taken place in the twentieth century have pulled the legal system away from its traditions and away from a Catholic vision. Fortunately, many states have noted the problem and are moving to correct them with tort reform legislation. With a return to actual compensation for loss and a more strict view of causation, American tort law is moving toward once again being in accord with a true vision of Catholic justice.[51]

NOTES

1. Alexis de Tocqueville, *Democracy in America*, vol. I, part 1, chapter 8.
2. Michael I. Krauss, "Tort Law, Moral Accountability, and Efficiency: Reflections on the Current Crisis," 2 *Journal of Markets and Morality* (Spring 1999). See also Ronald J. Rychlak, *John Wade: Teacher, Lawyer, Scholar*, 65 Miss. L. J. 1 (1996) (tribute to tort scholar and the author's professor).
3. Krauss, "Tort Law."
4. The American system of justice assumes that people are teleological organisms, which is fully in keeping with the Catholic understanding of human nature. See Ronald J. Rychlak, "Tort Law, Free Will, and Personal Responsibility," 12 *Catholic Social Science Rev.* 51 (2007).
5. *Catechism of the Catholic Church*, ¶1730 [hereinafter *Catechism*].
6. *Catechism*, ¶1731.
7. See Gerard B. Wegemer, *Thomas More: A Portrait of Courage* (Scepter Publishers, 1998) at 64, 97, 123.
8. In the *Summa Theologiae*, Aquinas defined justice as "the habit whereby a man renders to each one his due by a constant and perpetual will." ST II-II q. 58, a. 3. This definition serves as the foundation in Christian social thought upon which the notions of rights (as entitlements), right conduct, and rightness of a situation can be understood. He classified justice as one of four cardinal virtues along with temperance, prudence, and fortitude, and he distinguished the general and the particular senses of justice.
9. William J. Stuntz, "Pride and Pessimism in the Courts," *First Things* (February 1997).
10. Randy Lee, *Reflecting on Negligence Law and the Catholic Experience: Comparing Apples and Elephants*, 20 St. Thomas L. Rev. 3, 4–5 (2007).
11. Lee, *Reflecting on Negligence Law* at 3, 4–5.
12. Lee, *Reflecting on Negligence Law* at 3, 4–5.
13. Lee, *Reflecting on Negligence Law* at 3, 4–5.
14. Mary Ann Glendon, "Looking for 'Persons' in the Law," *First Things* (December 2006). Glendon went on to note:

The Romano-Germanic legal systems, by contrast, impose both civil and criminal penalties for a failure to rescue where the deed could have been accomplished without undue risk to the rescuer. The practical significance of this difference is small, for actual cases of failure to rescue rarely arise. But as a leading French scholar has pointed out, the chief importance of the legal duty to rescue is pedagogical: It is "to serve as a reminder that we are members of society and ought to act responsibly." By the same token, one might speculate that the chief importance of legal silence on this point in the United States is that it represents a lost opportunity to reinforce the sense of being part of a community for which all share a common responsibility.

15. See, e.g., *Codex Iuris Canonici* (1983).

16. *Casey v. Planned Parenthood*, 505 U.S. 833 (1992).

17. *Lawrence v. Texas*, 539 U.S. 558 (2003).

18. Lee, *Reflecting on Negligence, supra* note 10, at 21. See Randy Lee, *A Look at God, Feminism, and Tort Law*, 75 Marq. L. Rev. 369 (1992).

19. Meir Dan-Cohen, *Responsibility and the Boundaries of the Self*, 105 Harv. L. Rev. 959, 978 (1992).

20. "[L]ike a cockroach, you are in no position to make moral choices of your own free will. When you commit some hideous brutality, it is not that you decided to do so. No, on the contrary, external circumstances made you do it. Once that message is fully absorbed by potential criminals as well as by their judges and juries, civility and safety will be doomed." Daniel Lapin, "Darwin Is Dead," *Crisis* (November 1995): 56.

21. See Joseph F. Rychlak and Ronald J. Rychlak, *Mental Health Experts on Trial: Free Will and Determinism in the Courtroom*, 100 W. Va. L. Rev. 193 (1997).

22. When it comes to the legitimacy of moral judgments, the free will issue raises serious questions for both religious and secular institutions. The 1910 *Catholic Encyclopedia* introduces the issue as follows:

> The question of free will . . . ranks amongst the three or four most important philosophical problems of all time. It ramifies into ethics, theology, metaphysics, and psychology. . . . On the one hand, does man possess genuine moral freedom, power of real choice, true ability to determine the course of his thoughts and volitions, to decide which motives shall prevail within his mind, to modify and mold his own character? Or, on the other, are man's thoughts and volitions, his character and external actions, all merely the inevitable outcome of his circumstances?
>
> Augustine said, "Every sin is voluntary." *De Vera Relig.* 14. The corollary, expressed by John Damascene in the eighth century, is that "the involuntary act deserves pardon." *De Fide Orth.* 2:24.

23. Tatain the Syrian, *Address to the Greeks*, 7.

24. St. Augustine, *On Grace and Free Will*, 2:5.

25. Edmund L. Pincoffs, *The Rationale of Legal Punishment* (Humanities Press, 1966), 8.

26. The legal system's vision of itself was not particularly grandiose. Disputes were supposed to be dealt with privately, out of court, if at all possible—hence the difficulty of actually getting a lawsuit into court and before a jury. Not all wrongs were to be righted—at least not in this life. Judicial decision-making was not a virtue but an unfortunate necessity, something we have to have in a world filled with sinful and contentious people, but something we should have as little of as we can get away with. Law was seen not as a way of perfecting the world, but as a means of keeping a lid on the worst sorts of behavior. William J. Stuntz, "Pride and Pessimism in the Courts," *First Things* (February 1997).

27. Robert J. Lipkin, *The Moral Good Theory of Punishment*, 40 U. Fla. L. Rev. 17, 81 (1988).

28. J. Feinberg and H. Gross, eds., *Philosophy of Law*, 2nd ed. (Wadsworth Publishing Company, 1980), 523.

29. As such, it has been argued that there is a fundamental *right* to punishment, which stems from the fundamental right to be treated as a person. Herbert Morris, "Persons and Punishment," 52 *The Monist* 475 (October 1968), *reprinted in Philosophy of Law* at 582. This right to punishment derives from the fundamental right to be treated as a person, and denial of this right implies the denial of all moral rights and duties, hence the denial of the right to be human. Morris; see also Max Scheler, *Formalism in Ethics and Non-Formal Ethics of Values* (Nanfred S. Frings and Roger L. Frank trans., 3rd ed., 1973), 366 (discussing moral right to punishment); Martin R. Gardner, *The Right to Be Punished—A Suggested Constitutional Theory*, 33 Rutgers L. Rev. 838 (1981) (presenting the right to punishment as a constitutional right). *See generally* Ronald J. Rychlak, *Society's Moral Right to Punish: A Further Exploration of the Denunciation Theory of Punishment*, 65 Tulane L. Rev. 299 (1990).

30. See generally Robert A. Levy, *Shakedown: How Corporations, Government, and Trial Lawyers Abuse the Judicial Process* (Cato Institute, 2004) (arguing that the tort system, especially "regulation through litigation," has become an avenue for exploitation rather than justice).

31. Contributory negligence limited the exposure of a defendant when the plaintiff was partially at fault. Similarly, the doctrine of privity of contract often prevented consumers from seeking a tort remedy for injuries caused by defective products. These limitations, like the required causal showing, tended to protect the innocent, reflect and reaffirm societal values, and serve the common good.

32. See *Bates v. State Bar of Arizona*, 433 U.S. 350 (1977) (upholding the right of lawyers to advertise).

33. Jeffrey O'Connell, *The Lawsuit Lottery: Only the Lawyers Win* (Free Press, 1979), 8.

34. When police arrive at the scene of a bus or train accident, one of the first things they have to do is secure the area, lest false "victims pretend to be injured so that they can recover in the lawsuit that is certain to follow." Stephen B. Burbank, professor at the University of Pennsylvania Law School, explained: "There is unquestionably a certain amount of fraud going on in this type of litigation. People who have not been injured and people who have been injured in the most minor ways get swept in with those who are seriously injured." L. Stuart Ditzen, "Mass Diet-Pill Litigation Inflates Settlement Costs to $13.2 Billion," *Philadelphia Inquirer*, April 9, 2002.

35. Krauss, "Tort Law," *supra* note 2.

36. See Ronald J. Rychlak, *Disciples on the Docket: A Christian Response to Tort Reform, Policy Reform* (Acton Institute, 2005).

37. Matthew 18:15–17.

38. 1 Corinthians 6:1–7.

39. Romans 13:3.

40. See Acts 16:37–40; 18:12–17; 22:15–29; 25:10–22.

41. Lynn Buzzard, *With Liberty and Justice: A Look at Civil Law and the Christian* (Victor Books, 1984), 136.

42. Buzzard, *With Liberty and Justice* at 136.

43. Roy P. Basler, ed., *Collected Works of Abraham Lincoln*, vol. 2 (Rutgers University Press, 1953), 82.

44. The effect of massive punitive damage awards has been devastating to many American businesses. The manufacturer of a small product in New York may find himself hauled into court in Arkansas, facing damages that bear no reasonable relationship to the damage actually caused by the product. As a result of this potential exposure, American firms have to be especially cautious. The tort law system forces corporations to create "paper trails" that are unnecessary for any reason other than potential legal exposure. Manufacturers must opt for potentially less effective products and processes, simply because they have been tested in the litigation process. Because the manufacturer does not work toward the newest, most improved product, competitiveness in overseas markets is damaged. See Robert W. Sturgis, *Tort Cost Trends: An International Perspective* 16, (Tillinghast-Towers Perrin, 3rd ed. 1995).

45. Buzzard, *With Liberty and Justice, supra* note 41, at 135.

46. See John Paul II, "No Peace Without Justice, No Justice Without Forgiveness, Message of His Holiness Pope John Paul II for the Celebration of the World Day of Peace," January 1, 2002 (discussing the importance of forgiveness).

47. Amy Lynn Sorrel, "Judging Genetic Risks: Physicians Often Caught Between What Patients Want and What Science Offers," *American Medical News*, posted November 10, 2008, http://www.amednews.com/ ("case law in about 25 states recognizes wrongful birth claims") (accessed February 26, 2014).

48. See, e.g., *Gleitman v. Cosgrove*, 227 A.2d 689 (N.J. 1967); *Becker v. Swartz*, 386 N.E.2d 807 (N.Y. 1978); *Curlender v. BioScience Laboratories*, 106 Cal.App.3d 811 (Cal. Ct. App. 1980); Jay Webber, "Better Off Dead?" *First Things*, May 2002 at 10–12.

49. Two of America's "most outrageous legal absurdities," the horrific claims for "wrongful birth" and "wrongful life" claims are anomalies that can and should be banned by state legislation. See Webber, "Better Off Dead?" *supra* note 48 ("in traditional tort law, in order for one to be liable for the injuries of another, one's actions must actually cause the injuries. But in wrongful birth and life suits, the defendants have not caused any harm to the unborn child. The plaintiffs argue that the child's life itself is an injury, nonexistence being preferable to the child's challenged existence.") See Alan J. Belsky, *Injury as a Matter of Law: Is This the Answer to the Wrongful Life Dilemma?* 22 U. Balt. L. Rev. 185 (1993).

50. See Rychlak, *Disciples on the Docket, supra* note 36.

51. For a more detailed study of these issues, see Ronald J. Rychlak, *Trial by Fury: Restoring the Common Good in Tort Litigation*, monograph 8 in the Christian Social Thought Series (The Acton Institute, 2005).

Chapter Six

American Corporate Law and Catholic Social Thought

John M. Czarnetzky

INTRODUCTION

Catholic legal scholars often emphasize the ethics of business or the effect of businesses and their policies on the community. These are unquestionably important aspects of corporate law that intersect with Catholic social theory ("CST"). Indeed, in the case of the individual ethics of the members of a business, it is vital—no social institution will fulfill its legitimate purpose under CST unless its members pursue and nurture their individual virtue and that of the other members of the firm. Similarly, a corporation that pollutes the environment or whose purpose is illicit does not comport with CST. However, CST provides a deeply nuanced vision of the human person and human institutions. Indeed, it is the purpose of this chapter to apply the insights of CST to American corporate law in order to provide a richer explanation of the law than either materialistic or communitarian critiques have provided to date.

THE THEORETICAL DIVIDE:
SHAREHOLDERS V. STAKEHOLDERS

Legal scholars posit a number of theories to explain or to criticize American corporate law. Two such theories delimit the theoretical debate. The first, derived from the application of neoclassical economics, stresses shareholder primacy—shareholders are the owners of a corporation, and thus the goal of the corporation as an institution is the maximization of shareholder wealth. Scholars working in this tradition stress the perceived problems created by

the separation of ownership from control in the modern corporation. Because
the agent/directors of a corporation, and not the owner/shareholders, largely
control the corporation, agency problems are created by the resultant mis-
alignment of incentives. For such scholars, the primary goal of corporate law
is to ameliorate the agency problem inherent in corporations in order to
achieve the goal of increasing shareholder wealth.

The second major approach is the "stakeholder" model of the corporation.
Proponents of the stakeholder model envision the corporation as an amalgam
of various "stakeholders," each of whom has an interest in the corporation
through their contribution to it. Shareholders contribute capital, managers
contribute their business skills, communities provide a place for the business
to conduct its activities (and sometimes tax breaks and other incentives),
employees contribute their skills and labor, etc. Through these contributions,
stakeholders gain a right to influence the direction of the corporation which
the law ought to recognize. It is thus the community of stakeholders that is
entitled to direct the corporation to one degree or another and to share in its
fruits. [1]

Each of these models of the corporation is founded upon assumptions
about either the human person or social institutions. The shareholder model
assumes that human beings are self-interested, rational, economic maximiz-
ers. The stakeholder model views the corporation as a community to which
all of its members contribute, and thus from which all of its contributors are
entitled to a share. Both models yield important truths about American corporate law, but neither provides a truly humanistic theory of the corporation.
The fault lies in incomplete models of the human person and human institutions.

CST AND ECONOMIC ACTIVITY

CST is grounded in the Church's social anthropology. In developing and
expounding CST, the Church aims to reveal the full truth about humankind,
just as its founder sought to reveal the truth. [2] This effort requires the Church
to "offer a contribution of truth to the question of man's place in nature and
in human society. . . ." [3] Unsurprisingly, corporations, such a large part of
modern economic life, are a topic of concern for modern CST, though some
groundwork must be laid first.

Human Dignity

Human beings are made in *imago Dei*, a perfect unity of material body and
transcendent soul which forms a unique, single nature. That is, the Church
rejects a purely materialist vision of the human person on the one hand, and
spiritualism which rejects the human body on the other hand. Rather, "it is

because of its spiritual soul that the body made of matter becomes a living, human body; spirit and matter, in man are not two natures united, but rather their union forms a single nature."[4]

Each human being is unique and unrepeatable, entitled through his/her unique nature to inherent dignity. Such dignity requires that a person is always a *subject*, not an *object*. Any social doctrine or institution which envisions the human being as something less than human—or treats the human being as a mere object of social doctrine or institutions—is bound to fail. In short, the person is the end of society, never a mere cog forming part of a greater moral whole. CST consists of the development of the implications of the human being as such an end.

Important among those implications is the human capacity for love, which human beings share with their creator. Following Aristotle and Aquinas, the Church recognizes that fully integral development of the human person in all of his or her dimensions is possible only through relationships of love with others. Human beings form families out of conjugal love in which parents are called to radical service of their beloved and their children. Through friendships, another form of love, individuals serve each other, always with a view to the good of the other as required by the golden rule. The family, friendships, and the Church itself serve the common good of society through the development of the human person. Indeed, CST defines the common good of society as "the sum total of social conditions which allow people, either as groups or as individuals to reach their fulfillment more fully and more easily."[5] The Church, like the family, does not exist for its own sake, but rather for the good of its individual members.

Human Work

CST extends this idea beyond the Church and families—which are institutions operating in the order of love—to all social institutions, including those which operate in the purely material world, including human work. Work in its subjective dimension is nothing less than "an essential expression of the person, it is an *'actus personae.'*"[6] This insight has profound import for CST's analysis of economic activity. First, as the essential expression of the human person, work is entitled to the same inherent dignity as the human person. It must not be considered merely a commodity, but rather must always be ordered to the good of the individual. The Church proclaims that *"work is for man and not man for work."*[7] Moreover, CST recognizes that, consistent with human nature, work is inherently a social activity. Cooperation is vital to produce goods and services desired and required by others; more importantly, cooperation is necessary for the individual to realize his potential fully through work. Of course, work must also be ordered to the common good. Thus, society has a role in monitoring work—one's work must serve the common good, and the work itself must be performed according to what constitutes the common good. Finally, work is an obligation of human beings in several respects. It is the means to develop fully as a human being; it is a way to serve other human beings by producing goods and services others desire; it is a moral obligation to provide for one's family and/or fellow human beings; it is an obligation to help develop one's nation and, indeed, the entire human family; finally, work is the way to repay past generations for their work and provide for future generations by easing the burden of work on them.[8]

The subjective dimension of work requires that the individual must be free in economic matters. "Everyone has the right to economic initiative; everyone should make legitimate use of his talents to contribute to the abundance that will benefit all, and to harvest the just fruits of his labor."[9] Experience shows that limiting such initiative limits the development of the individual by destroying the creative subjectivity of that person. "[F]ree and responsible initiative, then, should be given ample leeway," to be limited "only in cases of incompatibility between the pursuit of the common good and the type of economic activity proposed or the way it is undertaken."[10]

The subjective dimension of work also requires the Church to recognize the superiority of work to all other economic factors, including capital.[11] This is not to say that capital and labor are inexorably in conflict, as suggested in some political philosophies. Rather, the urgent need is for "economic systems in which the opposition between capital and labor is overcome."[12]

> In considering the relationship between labor and capital . . . we must maintain that the principal resource and the decisive factor at man's disposal is man himself, and that the integral development of the human person through work does not impede but rather promotes the greater productivity and efficiency of work itself.[13]

Subsidiarity and Solidarity

Two crucial organizing principles flow from CST's social anthropology: subsidiarity and solidarity. Taken together, these CST doctrines help point the way to an answer to the ancient question of how society is to be structured. Subsidiarity defines civil society as "the sum of the relationships between individuals and intermediate social groupings, which are the first relationships to arise and which come about thanks to the creative subjectivity of the citizen."[14] All the components of civil society—from the bowling league to political parties and government itself—are important to the development of the person. Thus, the doctrine of subsidiarity requires that social groups be given leeway to perform their appropriate roles in society without inference, but always with aid where necessary, by other, particularly higher, social institutions.

> Just as it is gravely wrong to take from individuals what they can accomplish by their own initiative and industry and give it to the community, so also it is an injustice and at the same time a grave evil and disturbance of right order to assign to a greater and higher association what lesser and subordinate organizations can do. For every social activity ought of its very nature to furnish help to the members of the body social, and never destroy and absorb them. [15]

Thus, the doctrine of subsidiarity recognizes that there are myriad social institutions that make up civil society, each with its own role in contributing to the common good. Subsidiarity is the doctrine of noninterference in one institution by another, particularly (but not only) a higher institution. Such interference is a "grave evil" because it detracts from the dignity of the lower institution, thus injuring the dignity of the individuals who constitute the lower institution.

The term "solidarity" is potentially a source of misunderstanding given the variety of meanings assigned to it in modern social theory. In CST, solidarity is the principal that "highlights in a particular way the intrinsic, social nature of the human person, the equality of all in dignity and rights and the common path of individuals and peoples towards an ever more committed unity. . . ." [16] The term "highlights the interdependence between individuals and peoples." [17] The Church posits that all social institutions—including the free market itself and its institutions—must replace "structures of sin" with solidarity, which the Church deems *the* "social virtue." [18] Solidarity is not, however, a vague call for compassion; rather, the Church holds that solidarity is the "firm and persevering determination to commit oneself to the common good." [19] It is this concern for all and for each individual that makes solidarity a moral imperative for social institutions.

Subsidiarity and solidarity are therefore intertwined. In social institutions, all must be concerned for the common good of the whole, with the end always being the common good of the individuals who make up the institution. In implementing solidarity, the members of the institution must be prepared to help their fellow members, but always with an eye to the proper role of the individuals.

CST AND AMERICAN CORPORATE LAW

The Purpose of the Corporation

The neoclassical economist views the corporation as a web of contracting parties joined together in an institution whose role is to reduce the bargaining costs among the parties. Shareholders contract with directors who contract with management who contract with labor. The corporate structure is useful only if this web of relationships is achieved more cheaply than could be achieved in the market. The purpose of the corporation is to maximize returns to shareholders.[20]

On the other hand, the stakeholder model views the corporation as an institution which has "stakeholders" beyond its shareholders. The corporation—and therefore American corporate law—must recognize its obligation to persons or institutions outside the corporation who contribute to its success and to those inside the corporation who are not traditionally considered stakeholders. Scholars in this tradition call for the law to provide real influence over the corporation, perhaps through membership on the board of directors, to representatives of local communities in which the corporation operates, and to labor.

CST views the corporation and other business entities as forms of social institutions, which means that they must be oriented to the common good, rather than solely to profits or to the community:

> [n]o expression of social life—from family to intermediate social groups, associations, enterprises of an economic nature, cities, regions, States, up to the community of peoples and nations—can escape the issue of its own common good, in that this is a constitutive element of its significance and the authentic reason for its very existence.[21]

The goal of businesses is twofold. First, a business must serve the common good, through the development of the talents of the individuals who are part of it, by producing goods and services desired by society. In doing so, the successful business produces wealth; however,

> [b]esides this typically economic function, businesses also perform a social function, creating opportunities for meeting, cooperating and the enhancement of the abilities of the people involved. In a business undertaking, therefore, the economic dimension is the condition for attaining not only economic goals, but also social and moral goals, which are all pursued together. A business' objective must be met in economic terms and according to economic criteria, but the authentic values that bring about the concrete development of the person and society must not be neglected. In this personalistic and community vision, "a business cannot be considered only as a 'society of capital goods'; it is also a 'society of persons' in which people participate in different ways and with specific responsibilities, whether they supply the necessary capital for the company's activities or take part in such activities through their labour."[22]

Therefore, the purpose of the corporation is *not* to turn a profit; a profit indicates that the corporation is performing its proper function, but it does not *prove* it.

CST's view of the corporation is closer to that experienced by actual people who work in corporations. Work can be stimulating or drudgery, but there is no question that individuals form bonds in working for a corporation in the same way they do in their bowling leagues or religious institutions. The purposes of the institutions are different, but they are all human institutions.

On the other hand, the corporation is not the property of all of society in which the entire community shares. Rather, it is a social institution in which each member of the institution has a role according to his or her talents, directed to the common good of the institution. The Catholic theory of subsidiarity requires that each group within the corporation leave to other groups their proper roles. The Catholic theory of solidarity requires that each person and each group do all they can to help the other members of the business. If the institution successfully fulfills its role of developing the talents of its members through serving the public good, then the good of all society obviously is enhanced. It is in this way that those who are not members of the corporation benefit. Usurping the fruits of others' labor would be unjust, hurting both the laborer and the usurper.

The Structure of the Corporation

American corporate law places the board of directors at the center of the corporation. They are elected by shareholders, who have very little additional control over corporate affairs. The directors have all residual power in the corporation, which they delegate to managers whom the directors have the power to hire and fire. The managers are the pure agents of the corporation—they implement the business plan through contracts, hire employees, and conduct other business in the market and with governments.

The materialist critique posits that the separation of ownership from control in American corporate law raises the possibility that directors' and officers' interests will diverge from those of the owners. Given the power of the directors, this leads to harm to the owners. The communitarian critique holds that the structure of the corporation in American law does not properly compensate other stakeholders—such as employees or the community—for their contributions to the business.

The Church's understanding of how a corporation serves the common good is humanistic and entrepreneurial.

> Organizing . . . a productive effort, planning its duration in time, making sure that it corresponds in a positive way to the demands which it must satisfy, and taking the necessary risks—all this too is a course of wealth in today's society. In this way, the role of disciplined and creative human work and, as an essential part of that work, initiative and entrepreneurial ability becomes increasingly evident and decisive . . . [M]an's principal resource is man himself. His

intelligence enables him to discover the earth's productive potential and the many different ways in which human needs can be satisfied. [23]

Thus, the corporation must be designed to foster creative, disciplined, entrepreneurial activity in order to mine the greatest of human resources— the person. American law ingeniously, though not flawlessly, does precisely that. The shareholders invest in corporations whose entrepreneurial plans the shareholder judges plausible and potentially profitable. Those plans are made by the directors. Thus, the shareholders' most important role as owners is to pick wise persons as directors who are able to formulate and/or implement entrepreneurial plans. The directors, in fulfilling their roles must hire managers who are able to implement the plans successfully. Managers, in doing so, must hire employees for the myriad tasks that the corporation will face.

If the structure is working properly, aided by the interplay of subsidiarity and solidarity, each group within the corporation is left to develop its talents through its appointed contribution to the business. This is good for the business, but also good for the individual. It is up to each individual and group to encourage the virtues of their peers within the corporation. Because the business is a social institution with a mission of its own, other institutions such as government should not interfere with its inner workings or claim a right to control it. This would violate subsidiarity just as the workers claiming a right to a seat on the board would. A representative of labor could sit on the board, but only if the shareholders, in their role as evaluators of the company's plans, think that such an arrangement will serve the common good of the firm.

Governance of the Corporation

Several critiques of the American law of corporate governance are possible. The materialist view of the corporation might counsel for greater shareholder control in the actual running of the corporation. Shareholder groups often attempt to overturn board decisions despite the difficulty in doing so. As has already been mentioned, communitarians wish the board composition be opened up beyond those chosen by the shareholders. From either perspective, several aspects of the law of corporate governance are difficult to justify through existing models of the corporation.

For example, on the one hand, directors can adopt antitakeover defenses which prevent a hostile takeover even if it might yield a healthy return to shareholders. On the other hand, directors may approve (shareholders would have a vote as well) a merger or sale of substantially all corporate assets without consulting the communities that might be affected. Similarly, the "business judgment rule" holds that directors are not responsible for the consequences of their decisions—even if they are bad ones—as long as the directors act in a reasonable manner in making those decisions. Another example is the fact that boards of directors are often divided into "staggered" boards where only a portion of the board stands for election by shareholders in any given year. This is another measure that seemingly limits the ability of the owners of the corporation to have a significant voice in running their own corporation.

CST provides explanations for these rules. Directors, in virtuously exercising the talents for which they are hired by the shareholders, are uniquely the arbiters of the entrepreneurial direction of the corporation. Shareholders as a group should not do so because they might sacrifice entrepreneurial planning and risk taking for short-term returns. Moreover, in a large, publicly traded company, the shareholders are not equipped as a group to act as entrepreneurs.[24] Specialized employees are hired and receive salaries for the exercise of their talents toward the common good. Human dignity requires that their talents be fostered and their voices be heard by management and the directors, but their role is not to manage or direct the corporation.

It is therefore the directors who must have "maximum leeway" for the development and implementation of the corporation's entrepreneurial plans. Because humans are fallen beings, they have neither perfect knowledge nor judgment. They will make mistakes. If directors are not talented in their role, the shareholders will replace them or the corporation will fail. Until then, they must be given the opportunity to fill their role as platonic guardians of the corporate plans. The law protects the corporation as an institution from hostile, short-term raiders through the poison pill or staggered boards. The plans of the directors are given time to bear fruit. Moreover, if the directors have miscalculated, they should not be punished for honest mistakes. Rather, they should be replaced in due course by the group in the corporation to whom the evaluation of directors is entrusted—the owners of the corporation.

CONCLUSION

Catholic Social Theory's humanistic justification and explanation of human social institutions is a gift that has not yet been fully exploited by scholars in the United States. The goal of this chapter is to stimulate much deeper studies of corporations and American corporate law using CST. Corporations, the individuals who are part of them, and American corporate law will all profit from the exercise.

NOTES

1. These schools of scholarship represent the two dominant models of the corporation which in turn drive critiques of American corporate law. Of course, there are other models which combine the insights of both schools to one degree or another.

2. Pontifical Council for Justice and Peace, *Compendium of the Social Doctrine of the Church* [hereinafter *Compendium*], ¶13.

3. *Compendium*, ¶14.

4. *Compendium*, ¶129, *quoting Catechism of the Catholic Church* [hereinafter *Catechism*], ¶365.

5. *Compendium*, ¶164; *Catechism*, ¶1906.

6. *Compendium*, ¶271.

7. *Compendium*, ¶272 (italics in the original).

8. *Compendium*, ¶274.

9. *Compendium*, ¶336.

10. *Compendium*, ¶336.

11. *Compendium*, ¶276. Note that the Church recognizes the different meanings of the term "capital." They include the financial resources necessary to begin and run the business, the actual physical assets used to produce the business's goods and services, and even "human capital," which refers to the knowledge and creativity which human beings employ to produce labor. *Compendium* ¶, 276. It is in the first two, material senses that this article will use the term "capital."

12. *Compendium*, ¶277.

13. *Compendium*, ¶278.

14. *Compendium*, ¶185; Ronald J. Rychlak and John M. Czarnetzky, *The International Criminal Court and the Question of Subsidiarity*, Third World Legal Studies, Vol. 16, Article 6.

15. *Compendium*, ¶186.

16. *Compendium*, ¶192.

17. *Compendium*, ¶192.

18. *Compendium*, ¶193.

19. *Compendium*, ¶193.

20. This idea is enshrined in the famous case of *Dodge v. Ford Motor Co.*, 170 N.W. 668 (1919) where the Michigan Supreme Court held that Henry Ford's attempts to reward employees of Ford Motor Company or the community as a whole—today we would call them "stakeholders"—at the expense of shareholders was not appropriate.

21. *Compendium*, ¶165.

22. *Compendium*, ¶338 (italics omitted).

23. *Compendium*, ¶337.

24. In a small, closely held company, the person(s) who develop(s) the entrepreneurial plan will also be the primary shareholder(s). Therefore, in such small companies the roles overlap significantly. However, when the shareholder base expands widely, the entrepreneurial expertise formally concentrated in the shareholders is dissipated, and subsidiarity requires the two groups exercise only the power appropriate to their group's role in the business. The Supreme Court took note of the difference between a closely held corporation and one that is not in *Burwell v. Hobby Lobby*, 573 U.S. ___ (2014).

Chapter Seven

The Meaning of Person

A Catholic Legal Perspective

Robert John Araujo, S.J.

The meaning and nature of the human person has long been the subject of debate and discussion. In his 1963 encyclical letter *Pacem in Terris*, Pope John XXIII contended that every human being is a person with rights and duties because he or she is in a developing process where one's intelligence and free will evolve from the moment of conception.[1] At the time of the pope's statement, probably few would have disagreed; however, ten years later in 1973 when *Roe v. Wade* was decided by the United States Supreme Court, the landscape of opinion had changed dramatically. Here it is crucial to consider the transformation of public opinion regarding who the human person is. But in doing so, it is also critical to acknowledge that the Pope's 1963 assertion is not simply theological; it is verifiable by objective scientific, medical evidence. His position is in accord with the elemental science of human embryology that a new human life exists when sperm fertilizes egg.[2] In short, there seems to be no objectively reasoned basis for disagreeing with St. John XXIII. Yet in the present day, there are deep divides about the understanding of who and what a person is. This contribution provides a framework for the Catholic answer to the question: Who and what is a person? But the Catholic answer is not only the Catholic answer; it is, moreover, the answer that should satisfy all who think objectively and critically. In essence, the Church's position is the necessary synthesis of objective human intelligence comprehending the intelligible reality of human nature. In addition, it is a position that should be at the foundation of all lawmaking and judicial opinion regarding the definition of person; however, it is not. Even on issues that are impartially verifiable, the laws of man have not always reflected the truth in the Church's view.

Throughout the history of lawmaking and legal interpretation of many nations and the international community, it has been held that a "person" is one who simultaneously has rights and obligations that exist because of the law. The human person precedes the laws of society and the state which legislates these laws. A person is also a subject of the law who has rights and duties as St. John XXIII noted in 1963. But the understanding of "person" for purposes of the law needs to be considered in light of a variety of disciplines that include scientific understanding about the nature of the human being. After all, sound laws reflect the objective thinking of the intellect comprehending intelligible reality; but flawed laws typically do not follow this crucial pattern because they reflect the will of the lawmaker or judge whose perspective is untethered from objective thinking and comprehension but is fixed on goals that suit the lawmaker or judge's political objectives, the will that directs the lawmaker or judge, and little else.

From the viewpoint of the Catholic understanding about the definition of person, we first remember that each person is a creation of God who bears His divine image. Moreover, every human being has rights and responsibilities as already mentioned. Considering issues of authentic equality, each of us started in the same fashion when the genetic materials of our parents were combined at the moment of conception which defined the beginning of our unique humanity. There are times when the laws of society accord with this straightforward understanding. But there are occasions throughout history when some societies and their laws do not share in this accord.

For example, consider the case of *Dred Scott v. Sanford*, decided by the United States Supreme Court in 1856. A central question of the case was whether Dred Scott and the members of his family were persons. Of course they were—both then in the antebellum period and now. But in 1856 the question was vigorously debated in that some persons thought that other persons were not persons at all because they were slave property. A majority of the Supreme Court, however, was in the camp that thought and concluded that they were not persons because they were African slaves.[3] Nevertheless, two of the justices of the Supreme Court disagreed (Curtis and McLean). From their analysis of the situation, Dred Scott, his wife, and their children were persons because the exercise of right and objective reason—not political or economic considerations or the cultural whimsy of the day—inexorably led to the acceptance of this fact.

The significance of the combination of right or practical reason and the law is relied upon and developed by Thomas Aquinas in his *Treatise on Law*, wherein he states that the first principle of the law is that "good is to be done and pursued, and evil is to be avoided."[4] Right reason is a search for truth that is not only conceptual but also practical. The search for truth is inextricably combined with the application or implementation of the truth. In this way, the rational and the moral merge through the exercise of right reason.[5]

Furthermore, these interrelated searches are capable tasks of the human intellect. In fact, this search has a bearing on the making of law that seeks what is good and eschews that which is not.

The laws of most countries today no longer assert that some people are lesser humans or not persons at all. To disabuse one's self of such a notion, one only needs to consult the Universal Declaration of Human Rights accepted without objection in the early years of the United Nations (1948). No longer do we consider that the fundamental or universal rights of human beings are within the power of any government to grant, modify, or deny. These fundamental rights are natural and are inherent in and inextricably a part of human nature; therefore, they cannot be created by anyone, any government, or any political party or organization. It appears that human law has finally acknowledged in many respects the general understanding that a person is an individual human being—man, woman, or child—and is to be distinguished from a thing or from the lower animals.[6]

Consequently, and in accord with objective intelligence comprehending intelligible reality, *Dred Scott* was effectively reversed and superseded by the Civil War Amendments to the Constitution. The Thirteenth Amendment proscribed slavery in 1865. The complementary Fourteenth Amendment specified that the subjects of the previous amendment were "persons" in fact by using the term. In addition, subsequent legislation such as the Civil Rights Act of 1964 prohibited discrimination in employment situations on the basis of race, color, religion, sex, and national origin. On the international level, the Universal Declaration of Human Rights acknowledged the evils of slavery and involuntary servitude (Article 4) and the fact that everyone is to be recognized as a person before the law (Article 6). What had been denied by the law—i.e., Dred Scott's personhood—is now recognized and protected by the law. But even before the law it was a fact that could not be denied by the objective human intellect comprehending the intelligible reality of the human being and the world.

Notwithstanding these important legal developments in the domestic and international arenas, the definition and understanding of the term "person" still retains ambiguities. These ambiguities are used to question or deny personhood to other human beings even in the present day. This issue has been raised in the context of abortion—is the fetus, is the unborn child a person before the law? From *Roe v. Wade* and its progeny,[7] the legal responses regarding the status of the unborn regarding their personhood have not been promising.

However, if we remove the case of the not-yet-born from the context of the abortion debate, the unborn child has been recognized as a person in the context of having legal rights and therefore status before the law. For example, under some state laws in the United States the unborn child has received a variety of protections or legal recognitions, and therefore rights before the law for wrongful death and homicide.[8] Under particular international legal instruments, the fetus has acknowledged rights that strongly suggest something about his or her status under the law.[9] While this chapter does not address the issue of fetal rights, as it has been traditionally presented in the context of abortion,[10] it does concentrate on the question of personhood and its application to all members of the human family including the unborn.

This investigation necessitates the use of the natural law—as defined by John Courtney Murray—to explain the nature of the human person. Murray argues that the natural law—the use of right and objective reason—is a threefold project. The first element is the realization that the human person is intelligent. This means that those who engage in the political and legal discussions of the day have the innate capacity to think about serious matters not only from their personal perspective but also from the perspective of the fellow sisters and brothers who are members of the human race. The second component then follows: The reality of everything in the universe is intelligible to the human intellect and can be comprehended by the reasoning in which the human mind is capable of doing. Lastly, the intelligible reality of all creation is comprehendible by human intelligence which enables the members of society to identify norms and make laws that further the interest not of specific lobbies but of the common good.[11] It is this threefold realization that is at the root of how the human person as an individual and as a member of society can formulate norms regarding the administration and continuance of a just society in which the "person" is unambiguously identified and protected.

The subject of human intelligence comprehending intelligible reality is critical to the formulation of propositions regarding the nature and essence of the human person. Human intelligence comprehending intelligible reality, moreover, relies on the tools of human intelligence to assist in the formulation of verifiable propositions about human nature. Hence, we can turn to the role of science in helping us understand what the human person is. In this regard, we must turn again to what John XXIII said in *Pacem in Terris*: "What emerges first and foremost from the progress of scientific knowledge and the inventions of technology is the infinite greatness of God Himself, who created both man and the universe."[12] In addition, St. John XIII reminds us that "[r]ecent progress in science and technology has had a profound influence on man's way of life."[13] Thus there is a need to turn to objective science and other means of impartial investigation that are in service to the human person to help understand the nature, the essence of the human person. Human intelligence comprehending intelligible reality would do no less.

The inquiring mind of objective human intelligence would necessarily consider the current developments in medical science which have demonstrated that we humans are a pretty clever lot. Not only can we reproduce ourselves in the manner that we have for thousands of years, but we can also reproduce ourselves through *in vitro* techniques (a procedure fraught with moral implications). We have developed the capability of reproducing human tissue and other components through morally nonoffensive adult stem cell cloning, and this technology is a source of much promise for therapies that could alleviate many ailments that plague humanity through the replication of human tissue of specific types, such as muscle, nerve, and bone. Yet this intelligence also acknowledges that while the replicative science exists, should humans create other humans for the purpose of research that will inevitably lead to the destruction of many of the new human lives generated in a laboratory. At this point one thing becomes imperative to consider: There are certain fundamental principles that need to be considered regarding all new human life and when does it begin, for these matters go to the heart of what is the human person.

We begin with the human embryo, its essence and nature. As Heuster and Street concluded in 1941, "[i]t is to be remembered that at all stages the embryo is a living organism, that is, it is a going concern with adequate mechanisms for its maintenance as of that time."[14] Upon the fertilization of the human egg, which is the *donum* of the mother, by the sperm, which is the *donum* of the father, a new, distinct human life comes into existence.[15] This is fact and not desire or wish. It is an objective certainty comprehendible by objective human intelligence. However, in spite of the fact that every human being—person—has begun in this fashion, we lament as we recall the flawed words of Chief Justice Taney in *Dred Scott*, "[t]he unhappy black race were separated from the white by indelible marks . . . and were never thought of or spoken of except as property."[16] The chief justice may have spoken a political conclusion, but his assertion disregards the truth easily discernable by objective human intelligence that is interested in seeking the universal truth about who and what we are as human beings.

In the context of *Dred Scott*, Taney's view was not the only one that was infused with much politics but little, if any, objective reason. A majority of the Court agreed with his conclusions. So did many legislators if for no other reason than to keep a fragile peace—a peace that would be disrupted by a brutal civil war in less than a decade. This is why it is all the more important to consider what Justice McLean said in his dissent about the difference noted by the chief justice between the white and the black races. McLean argued that the majority view in *Dred Scott* was "more a matter of taste than of law."[17] While history has demonstrated that Justice McLean was right, and Chief Justice Taney was wrong, this examination of the nature of the human person cannot stop here for we must see how investigation in search of the truth—and human intelligence comprehending intelligible reality—can aid us in understanding who is a person not only before the law but who is a person, period.

In the public mind of today, the question of who is person and who or what is not is still passionately contested. But for many, the question remains: Who is person? To begin with, you are, and I am. We think about the members of our families (living and deceased) and our friends. Most assuredly, they are persons too. For those of us who come from the Abrahamic tradition (and, in particular the Catholic faith), we further acknowledge that the divine image is present in our personhood, our humanity.[18] As the investigation about the nature of the human person continues, we think of those who have gone before us, those who presently coinhabit the planet with us, and those who will come after us as persons.

As the investigation expands, we know that personhood or personality is also an important legal concept which is of vital importance to individual persons and to all members of the human family. Under the law of most jurisdictions, one quickly learns about the need to be clear about the distinction between the "natural person" (the live flesh-and-blood type who is a creation of human nature and, for some of us, God's plan) and the "juridical person" (the legal fiction entity such as a corporation which is a creation of the law rather than nature). Here, the concern is on the natural person. While the law can define and redefine the juridical person which is, in essence, a legal fiction, it does not have and should not have the ability to do the same regarding natural persons although this has been attempted in the past in such diverse places as the Germany of National Socialism, the United States of the antebellum era, and the world of *Roe*.[19] When the law is detached from right/ objective reason, it betrays recognition of who is and must be considered a natural person.

There can be ambiguity about the meaning of who the natural person is. For example, we know that the Constitution addresses "persons" in many ways, when, for example, it addresses who can hold office.[20] The Constitution further acknowledges rights, duties, and statuses of persons. We know that persons are to be secure and that their property is protected under the law.[21] In addition, no person can be in jeopardy of the law for the same thing more than once.[22] The Constitution establishes which persons are citizens of the United States; moreover, it asserts that persons who are citizens cannot be denied life, liberty, or property without due process of law.[23] Furthermore, persons are to enjoy equal protection of the law.[24] It is clear that these provisions define who a person is due to some kind of status that not all human beings share. But the distinctions do not stop here. As seen in the *Dred Scott* case, the legal understanding of "person" can be flawed given the context of the natural person who is not a legal fiction but a fact of flesh and blood.

While the various Constitutional contexts mentioned above consider a natural person in specific legal contexts, there is a common denominator underlying each one of these contexts: The subject (the person) is a unique human being whose life was begun in the same fashion and whose existence merits protection from beginning to natural end. It is clear that each reference to person listed in the Constitutional provisions is to the "human" or "natural" person. This point raises the significance associated with understanding the natural person—one who is a subject before the law—and the person's fundamental rights and obligations. When the law is manipulated, as in *Dred Scott*, to deny "personhood" to one who is naturally a part of the human race, violence is done not only to the law but to the natural person as well.

While the American Constitutional structure distinguishes between natural and juridical persons, it is vital to distinguish between the two a little bit more insofar as the fundamental law of a great democracy is concerned. While the state creates or recognizes the juridical person, it has no competence to do the same with the natural person as previously mentioned. It has the competence and capacity to make some distinctions among persons, e.g., who can vote; who can run for office; who can be licensed by the state to conduct some business or profession; but, it does not have the competence to declare that one member of the human family is a person whereas another member is not.

Within the context of common sense that relies on objective human intelligence comprehending intelligible reality, we must acknowledge the inherent truth in the words of the Declaration of Independence that placed the human person and the self-evident truths about him or her in the context of their Creator to again rely on the Declaration's nomenclature. The inherent nature of the human person surfaces in other ways as well. The juridical person is a creation of human law, and while it can have rights and duties as defined by the law, these defining elements of the juridical entity are determined by the state. However, the circumstances of the natural person are remarkably different. The natural person stands in sharp contrast because he or she, first of all, is not a creation of the state. Thus, there are some fundamental rights of the natural person, as noted by the Declaration, that are also not created by the state. If that were the case, whatever the state gives it can retract. This would not bode well for the human person of the natural rights inherent in the natural person's dignity.

In short, there is a dignity which subsists in the human person that is not conferred by the state or any other human agency. The conferral of this dignity is, as Jacques Maritain noted in 1943, in the right of each person to be inviolably respected because "[t]here are things which are owed to man because of the very fact that he is man."[25] In essence, personhood is something which exists in human nature. It exists not in trees, dogs, cats, or any other living being; but in man, the human being regardless of age, regardless of what stage of development, personhood exists where the human being exists. Here we must not take the meaning of the term "man" for granted. For it is this entity, this man, this person who is the holder of rights and corresponding responsibilities that are the rights and duties of no other living entity. It is these rights and their corresponding responsibilities which have a major role in defining the human person and, therefore, personhood. No institution and no other sentient being enjoy or exercise these factors of existence. It is the operation of objective reason[26] that acknowledges the existence of the status of the human person and his or her personhood both of which are endowed by our Creator and God. These values are not generated by political power even though some political powers exaggerate these values or, in the alternative, deny them. Political powers have a duty to acknowledge the person and personhood, but the political authority does not have the capacity to confer or deny personhood. The exclusive source of this activity is the divine.

Here we need to consider the reality of the methods by which particular societies have determined who has and who does not have human rights and therefore the ability to be considered a person. As this investigation gets under way, it is evident that some societies have used subjective means in addressing personhood that depart from the essential element of objective reason. This circumstance and the society that employs these methods are a major limitation in good governance and demonstrate the fundamental defects of positivist legal systems and the language they employ to define and limit fundamental human rights that are constitutive of the human person. The objective meaning of language is therefore critical to the task. As Lewis Carroll reminds us, "'[w]hen I use a word,' Humpty Dumpty said, in a rather scornful tone, 'it means just what I choose it to mean—neither more nor less.'"[27] Such is the problem with subjectivity in the law which is the capricious subjectivity that compromises and corrupts positive lawmaking so that it degenerates into the rank positivism that has proven itself of conferring and denying personhood.

The Catholic method of addressing and resolving the problems posed by positivist subjectivity that eviscerates the meaning of person and personhood is to turn to the objective approach to lawmaking and interpretation that comes from relying on right/objective reason—the foundation of the natural law.[28] If the investigator can objectively identify what is essential about human nature and the rights to be accorded to this nature, he or she can obtain a far better understanding of who the human person is as a subject of the law. As Professor Eibe Riedel has suggested when commenting on the world of international law, "[h]uman rights . . . are rights flowing from human nature. They are transcendental, supernatural or innate rights not necessarily laid down in texts."[29] These rights that are essential to personhood are not restricted to locale, race, sex, age, ethnicity, language, or other similar characteristic because they are universal. As Maritain noted, this universality is crucial to the dignity of the human person—all human persons—because there are things due to the human person because of the very fact that he or she is man.[30] And as Tertulian remarked so long ago, personhood is present at the moment of conception when that unique combination of genetic material given by the father and mother declare the presence of a new person because "he who will one day be man is a man already."[31]

It is through the objective mechanism of right/objective reason that lawmakers, judges, administrators, and citizens come to a better understanding of who are persons before the law (especially when the law is the Constitution) and then who are persons, period. As already noted, law that is based on subjective principles and methodology can be notably flawed. By way of example, the subjective Nationalist Socialist laws of Nuremberg or the laws of the antebellum United States may have made Jews and blacks nonpersons before the law, but these legislations did not take account of the reality of their situations and circumstances and the nature of human beings. These imperfect laws ignored the comprehendible reality of Jews and blacks whose nature and essence are that of any other racial or ethnic group. It is objectivity—the search for what is true as determined by standards that extend beyond the reasoning of the isolated, autonomous self—and the sincere quest for it that makes the law an enduring and just institution. This is the exercise of right/objective reason that is essential to the development of sound legal principles that are universal in both nature and application. Who is a recognized person before the law can be subject to the vagaries of human frailty and limitation when objectivity and right reason are absent. What makes the law firmer in its conviction and persuasion is the degree to which the understanding transcends these frailties. It is the role of right reason to help the lawmaker and the law decider overcome these frailties.

The framers who founded our durable juridical structure and the Constitution they drafted expended the effort to make good law that upheld the dignity and the responsibility of the human person. Good law that serves noble purposes is built on the strong foundation of objective reason, not on the sands of whim or caprice or even well-intentioned subjectivity. So much the better when the reason is right rather than wrong. In the context of assessing the status of the human person, including the ones that each of us were in our human development, many of the sound reasons for protecting them—us—come from the quest for truth that serves humanity and all, not just some, of its members.

NOTES

1. John XXIII, *Pacem in Terris*, ¶9 (April 1963).
2. See Ronan O'Rahilly and Fabiola Müller, *Human Embryology and Teratology*, 2nd ed., (Wiley-Liss, Inc., 1996).
3. *Dred Scott v. Sanford* 60 U.S. 393 (1856). The manner in which the Supreme Court stated the issue was in this fashion: "The question before us is, whether the class of persons described in the plea in abatement compose a portion of this people, and are constituent

members of this sovereignty? We think they are not, and that they are not included, and were not intended to be included, under the word 'citizens' in the Constitution, and can therefore claim none of the rights and privileges which that instrument provides for and secures to citizens of the United States. On the contrary, they were at that time considered as a subordinate and inferior class of beings, who had been subjugated by the dominant race, and, whether emancipated or not, yet remained subject to their authority, and had no rights or privileges but such as those who held the power and the Government might choose to grant them." 60 U.S. at 404–5.

4. Thomas Aquinas, *Summa Theologica*, Part I-II, q. 94, a. 2.

5. For a more contemporary explanation of right reason, see Austin Fagothey, S.J., *Right and Reason: Ethics in Theory and Practice*, 6th ed. (C.V. Mosby Co., 1976), 99–100.

6. *The Oxford English Dictionary*, 2nd ed., s.v. "person" (this is a primary definition of "person" which is applicable to this investigation).

7. *Roe v. Wade*, 410 U.S. 113 (1973).

8. See e.g., *66 Federal Credit Union v. Tucker*, 853 So. 2d 104 (Miss. 2003) (holding that a nineteen-week-old fetus was a "person" for purposes of the state's wrongful death statute and that the mother was entitled to bring a wrongful death action for the death of the nonviable fetus).

9. See e.g., *American Convention on Human Rights*, art. 4(1) (July 18, 1978), 1144 U.N.T.S. 123 (stating "[e]very person has the right to have his life respected. This right shall be protected by law and, in general, from the moment of conception. No one shall be arbitrarily deprived of his life").

10. See Robert John Araujo, S.J., "The Legal Order and the Common Good: Abortion Rights as Contradiction of Constitutional Purposes," http://www.uffl.org/vol11/araujo11.pdf (accessed September 7, 2013).

11. John Courtney Murray, S.J., *We Hold These Truths—Catholic Reflections on the American Proposition* (Sheed and Ward, 1960), 109.

12. *Pacem in Terris*, ¶3.

13. *Pacem in Terris*, ¶130.

14. *Cited in* Ronan O'Rahilly and Fabiola Müller, *supra* note 2.

15. O'Rahilly and Müller, n. 19, at 8 (suggesting that "[a]lthough life is a continuous process, fertilization is a critical landmark because, under ordinary circumstances, a new, genetically distinct human organism is thereby formed. This remains true even though the embryonic genome is not actually activated until 4–8 cells are present, at about 2–3 days").

16. *Dred Scott*, 60 U.S. at 410.

17. *Dred Scott*, 60 U.S. at 533 (McLean, J., dissenting).

18. Genesis 1:27.

19. See, *Byrn v. N.Y.C. Health & Hospital Corp.*, 286 N.E.2d 887, 893 (N.Y. App. Div. 1970) (Burke, J., dissenting) (noting the limitations on the state in determining the reality of who is a natural person and therefore who should be a person before the law). The implication of his dissent was that if the state could do this, the basis for fundamental human rights could be undermined by human whim or caprice.

20. U.S. Const. art. I, § 2, cl. 2; art. I, § 3, cl. 3; amend. XXII.

21. U.S. Const. at amend. IV, V.

22. U.S. Const. at amend. V.

23. U.S. Const. at amend. XIV.

24. U.S. Const. at amend. XIV.

25. Jacques Maritain, *The Rights of Man and Natural Law* (Charles Scribner's Sons, 1951), 65.

26. In the context of Thomas Aquinas's development of the intellect's use of right reason and this reason's connection with universal and transcendental moral principles that are available to each person, see John J. Coughlin, OFM, *Pope John Paul II and the Dignity of the Human Being*, 27 Harv. J. L. Pub. Policy 65 (2003). Pope John Paul II states "[o]nce reason successfully intuits and formulates the first universal principles of being and correctly draws from them conclusions which are coherent both logically and ethically, then it may be called

right reason or, as the ancients called it, *orthós logos, recta ratio.*" John Paul II, *Fides et Ratio,* ¶4 (September 14, 1998).

27. Lewis Carroll, "Through the Looking Glass," in *The Complete Works of Lewis Carroll* (Modern Library, 1936), 133, 214 (*quoted in Tenn. Valley Auth. v. Hill,* 437 U.S. 153, 173, n. 18 (1978).

28. Pope John XXIII offered an insight into this point when he stated, "[b]ut it must not be imagined that authority knows no bounds. Since its starting point is the permission to govern in accordance with right reason, there is no escaping the conclusion that it derives its binding force from the moral order, which in turn has God as its origin and end." *Pacem in Terris,* 47.

29. Eibe Riedel, "Commentary on Article 55(c)," in *The Charter of the United Nations: A Commentary,* 2nd ed., ed. Bruno Simma (Oxford Univesity Press, 2002), vol. 2, 917, 921.

30. See Maritain, *Rights of Man, supra* note 25 and accompanying text.

31. *Quoted in* John Paul II, *Evangelium Vitae,* 61.

Chapter Eight

Church and State

Richard S. Myers

This chapter describes American law relating to church and state and then evaluates the current legal situation from the perspective of Catholic social thought. The principal focus is on the First Amendment's Religion Clauses.[1] The dominant idea in current judicial interpretation of the Religion Clauses is the concept of neutrality. That concept is, in many respects, more desirable than the strict separationist approach that prevailed in the 1960s and 1970s. But, as explained below, this focus on neutrality fails to adequately protect religious liberty in certain important contexts and is in tension with important elements of Catholic teaching on church and state.[2]

With certain narrow exceptions, there was not a great deal of case law on the Religion Clauses until the mid-twentieth century when the Supreme Court applied the Bill of Rights to the states.[3] But beginning in the 1940s, the United States Supreme Court began to play an important role.

From this era, the Court's decisions emphasized the idea of the separation of church and state. In *Everson v. Board of Education*, Justice Black's majority opinion stated: "The 'establishment of religion' clause of the First Amendment means at least this: Neither a state nor the Federal Government can set up a church. Neither can pass laws which aid one religion, aid all religions, or prefer one religion over another. . . . In the words of Jefferson, the clause against establishment of religion by law was intended to erect 'a wall of separation between church and state.'"[4] Although the *Everson* Court upheld the constitutionality of a program that authorized reimbursement to parents for money spent to transport their children to parochial schools on public buses, the emphasis on separation influenced the Court's decisions over the next few decades.

In a series of decisions in the 1960s and 1970s, the Court emphasized the idea that religion had to be privatized.[5] This was particularly true in cases involving government funding of religious schools. The cases were quite hostile to religious schools undertaking any sort of role in a "public" task such as education. Of course, these schools had to be tolerated, but they were confined almost entirely to the realm of private choice. Many of the opinions in this era reflected a negative assessment of the religious schools, as demonstrated by the opinions' frequent references to the schools' purposes of religious indoctrination.[6] To the liberal, secular mindset that figured so prominently in these cases, the "authoritarian" character of these schools was hardly attractive. There was also some straightforward anti-Catholicism. But the Court's view of the religious schools reflected a more general antipathy to the supposedly irrational, freedom-restraining, undemocratic character of traditional religion.[7] The views expressed in one of Justice Brennan's opinions were illustrative:

> [i]t is implicit in the history and character of American public education that the public schools serve a uniquely *public* function: the training of American citizens in an atmosphere free of parochial, divisive, or separatist influences of any sort—an atmosphere in which children may assimilate a heritage common to all American groups and religion. This is a heritage neither theistic nor atheistic, but simply civic and patriotic. . . . The choice which is thus preserved is between a public secular education with its uniquely democratic values, and some form of private or sectarian education, which offers values of its own.[8]

These decisions contributed greatly to the privatization of religion. The title of the 1993 book—*The Culture of Disbelief: How American Law and Politics Trivialize Religious Devotion*[9] —captured this evaluation of the Court's work. In that book, Professor Stephen Carter wrote that American law treats religion as a hobby—like building model airplanes. In this view, religion is "something quiet, something private, something trivial—and not really a fit activity for intelligent, public-spirited adults."[10] Professor Gerard Bradley had earlier noted that "the Court is now clearly committed to articulating and enforcing a normative scheme of 'private' religion."[11]

For the most part, however, that diagnosis is a thing of the past.[12] Establishment Clause law has improved a great deal over the last twenty-five years. The Court no longer seems to place religion under special disabilities. The Court's approach—and this is most clearly seen in *Zelman v. Simmons-Harris*[13] —is that there is no Establishment Clause violation if religion is treated on equal terms with secular alternatives.

In *Zelman*, the Court upheld the constitutionality of the Ohio voucher program. Even though most of the voucher money was used to pay for education at religious schools, the Court held that the program did not violate the Establishment Clause. The Court confirmed prior cases that made it clear that the Court would not be troubled if aid was offered on the basis of neutral, secular criteria that neither favored nor disfavored religion. The choice to use the voucher money at religious schools was made by private actors (parents) and when one considered the government's overall role in education (which included the public school system itself and the state's support for magnet and charter schools), it was clear that the state was not trying to influence the religious choices of poor parents.[14]

According to the Court, however, this neutrality is not required by the Constitution; equal treatment is entirely a matter of legislative grace.[15] This is a serious problem and is an important point where American law diverges from Catholic social teaching.[16] The Court has not really come to grips with the impact of the modern welfare state. The Court does not interpret the Constitution to require that religious schools are afforded an equal share of government support. This results in an injustice. Catholic social thought is far more sensitive to the impact of government funding. The *Compendium of the Social Doctrine of the Church* states:

> Public authorities must see to it that "public subsidies are so allocated that parents are truly free to exercise this right without incurring unjust burdens. Parents should not have to sustain, directly or indirectly, extra charges which would deny or unjustly limit the exercise of this freedom." The refusal to provide public economic support to non-public schools that need assistance and that render a service to civil society is to be considered an injustice.[17]

Federal constitutional law in the United States often results in penalizing parents who exercise their constitutionally protected choice to educate their children outside the government schools. In general, though, the Court no longer expresses the negative views of religion that characterize the earlier cases. The Court seems willing to allow religion an equal role in the political process, and that improvement is worthy of note. We have moved from hostility toward a public role for religion to neutrality.

There are other Establishment Clause issues that deserve discussion. The *Everson* Court's emphasis on official religious neutrality has sometimes been taken to mean that there is a "constitutional command of secular government."[18] This concept has surfaced in a number of areas. One area involves religious displays or religious exercises on public property. The cases in this area are complicated but the Court seems uncomfortable with departures from this idea of secular government.[19] This is reflected in cases that hold as unconstitutional displays or exercises that are too "religious." So, displays of the Ten Commandments or Nativity scenes are permissible only if their religious content is diluted by enough secular items. Similarly, reciting the Pledge of Allegiance in public schools is only permissible if the Pledge is interpreted not to be religious, despite the language "under God."[20] In some of these cases, the Court seems uncomfortable with any public recognition of the importance of religion for maintaining the health of society and rather seems bent on, as Justice Scalia has stated, "a revisionist agenda of secularization."[21] This effort is worlds away from the view of Founders such as George Washington and from the view expressed in *Dignitatis Humanae* that "government . . . ought indeed to take account of the religious life of the citizenry and show it favor, since the function of government is to make provision for the common welfare."[22] These religious symbol cases may not seem that important in practical terms, since there is little risk of coercion of any sort. Yet, to the extent that the cases promote a trend toward secularization, there is a danger.

As Justice Scalia explains in some detail in *McCreary County v. ACLU*,[23] the Framers thought that religion had a unique role to play in maintaining the health of our society. Under this view, there is nothing objectionable about a "governmental affirmation of the society's belief in God. . . ."[24] In fact, such an acknowledgement could be understood as an act of humility. These acknowledgements help to reinforce the society's view that our nation is "under God" and subject to a transcendent order. They help then to "underscore the idea that the health of a political community depends on its acknowledgement that there are 'at least a minimum of objectively established rights not granted by way of social conventions, but antecedent to any political system of law.'"[25] Justice Scalia's concern about the Court being committed "to a revisionist agenda of secularization[,] . . ."[26] resonates well with Pope John Paul II's warning of the risks inherent in the exclusion of God from the cultural life of a nation. In *Evangelium Vitae*, the Pope states:

> When the sense of God is lost, there is also a tendency to lose the sense of man, of his dignity and his life; in turn, the systematic violation of the moral law, especially in the serious matter of respect for human life and its dignity, produces a kind of progressive darkening of the capacity to discern God's living and saving presence. . . . The eclipse of the sense of God and of man inevitably leads to a practical materialism, which breeds individualism, utilitarianism and hedonism. . . . [This loss of a sense of God and of man has the effect of promoting the toleration and fostering of behavior contrary to life, and] encourag[ing] the "culture of death," creating and consolidating actual "structures of sin" which go against life.[27]

So, the stakes in these symbol cases are quite high.

Another area where the command of secular government has surfaced is in the area of public morality. Some argue that the Religion Clauses require that laws be supported by a form of secular rationality. In a few opinions, some Justices have expressed the view that laws are unconstitutional if these laws are based upon religiously informed moral norms.[28] This view is of course inconsistent with Catholic social teaching, which continually has reaffirmed the legitimacy of Catholics seeking to advance their understanding of moral truth in the political realm.[29] Fortunately, a majority of the Court has never clearly accepted the position that laws must only be supported by a form of secular rationality.

> The Court continually reaffirms the idea that a moral position should not be regarded as religious [and therefore illegitimate] simply because it happens to coincide with the tenets of some religious organizations. . . . The Court has consistently refused to restrict the types of moral arguments that are considered a legitimate part of public debate. . . . The Court has not insisted that laws be supported by a certain form of secular reasoning. . . . The Court has adopted a wide understanding that permits the inclusion of a range of comprehensive moral views, even if some might regard one or more of these comprehensive moral views as religious in some sense.[30]

Unfortunately, this situation is highly unstable. Cases such as *Lawrence v. Texas*[31] seem to condemn the state's reliance on religiously informed moral norms, and this notion has played an important role in some of the court cases dealing with same-sex marriage. There is a fair amount of cultural pressure in favor of this position, and so there is still cause for concern.

Another area where the command of secular government has surfaced has been with regard to the divisiveness doctrine. In the 1970s, the Court often expressed concern that political divisiveness that might be engendered by religious involvement in the political process was a warning signal of Establishment Clause problems.[32] Under this divisiveness rubric, the Court expressed concern about religious activism in politics. The solution to potential divisiveness, the Court thought, was privatization. The Court seemed to have buried this doctrine after the mid-1980s. Unfortunately, the doctrine has resurfaced in some recent cases, although its current status is not clear.[33]

The law has also changed in the Free Exercise area. The major debate about the scope of the Free Exercise Clause involves "neutral laws of general applicability" that have the effect of interfering with religiously based conduct. Historically, there has been little support for the idea that the Constitution requires an exemption from laws that burden religious liberty, although an exemption is sometimes provided for in laws or regulations.[34] The Supreme Court's 1879 decision in *Reynolds v. United States* reflects this view.[35]

In *Reynolds*, the Court rejected a religious defense to a bigamy prosecution. The Court stated that as result of the First Amendment "Congress was deprived of all legislative power over mere opinion, but was left free to reach actions which were in violation of social duties or subversive of good order."[36] According to the Court, to allow a religious defense "would be to make the professed doctrines of religious belief superior to the law of the land, and in effect permit every citizen to become a law unto himself."[37]

The law changed in the *Sherbert–Yoder* era in the 1960s and 1970s.[38] In this era, religious claimants were sometimes entitled to constitutionally compelled exemptions from state mandates. The protection provided was in reality quite narrow, and the Supreme Court rejected the doctrine in its 1990 decision in *Employment Division v. Smith*.[39]

In *Smith*, the Court made it clear that the Free Exercise Clause provided very little judicially enforceable protection against laws that mandated conduct that might be viewed as interfering with the religious liberty of an individual or an institution. If the state mandate was a "neutral law of general applicability," then there was no realistic argument that the Constitution provided any basis to resist the mandate. *Smith* involved two individuals who were denied unemployment compensation because of work-related misconduct. The workers were fired from their jobs with a drug rehabilitation organization due to their use of peyote, an illegal drug, even though they used peyote for religious purposes. The Court, in an opinion by Justice Scalia, concluded that Oregon could "include religiously inspired peyote use within the reach of its general criminal prohibitions on use of that drug. . . ."[40] To allow an exemption from laws prohibiting "socially harmful conduct" would allow an individual with a religious objection to such laws "'to become a law unto himself.'"[41]

Under this approach, so long as the state mandate is a neutral law of general applicability, there is no prospect of a court finding that someone with a religious objection to the mandate is entitled to an exemption. One seeking an exemption from such a mandate would be limited to seeking relief from the legislature. Justice Scalia notes that "leaving accommodation to the political process will place at a relative disadvantage those religious practices that are not widely engaged in; [he concludes, though] . . . that unavoidable consequence of democratic government must be preferred to a system in which conscience is a law unto itself or in which judges weigh the social importance of all laws against the centrality of all religious beliefs."[42]

It is important to note that *Smith* has not had as dramatic an impact as some suggest. The *Sherbert–Yoder* doctrine is actually quite narrow,[43] and so the Court's rejection of that doctrine has not brought significant change.[44] There are, in addition, a variety of exceptions to *Smith*. There are exceptions in federal constitutional law,[45] in federal statues,[46] and in various state laws.

There would seem to be considerable tension between the Court's current view of the Free Exercise Clause (as reflected in *Smith*) and Catholic teaching.[47] The Catholic bishops in the United States have in recent years been outspoken in their advocacy for a right to conscientious objection, particularly in the context of the Department of Health and Human Services ("HHS") mandate.[48] In so doing, the bishops have relied on *Dignitatis Humanae*, the Vatican II Declaration on Religious Liberty. *Dignitatis* contains a ringing endorsement of religious liberty:

The Vatican Council declares that the human person has a right to religious freedom. This freedom means that all men are to be immune from coercion on the part of individuals or of social groups and of any human power, in such wise that no one is to be forced to act in a manner contrary to his own beliefs, whether privately or publicly, whether alone or in association with others, within due limits. The Council further declares that the right to religious freedom has its foundation in the very dignity of the human person as this dignity is known through the revealed word of God and by reason itself. This right of the human person to religious freedom is to be recognized in the constitutional law whereby society is governed and thus is to become a civil right. [49]

Yet, *Dignitatis* does not establish an unlimited idea of religious liberty or conscience. *Dignitatis Humanae* defends an idea of civil immunity from coercion and notes that the right protected must be understood "within due limits."[50] The Declaration notes that these limits include

the need for the effective safeguard of the rights of all citizens and for the peaceful settlement of conflicts of rights, also out of the need for an adequate care of genuine public peace, which comes about when men live together in good order and in true justice, and finally out of the need for a proper guardianship of public morality."[51]

The Declaration does not change the traditional view that "error has no rights." The Catechism explicitly states: "The right to religious liberty is neither a moral license to adhere to error, nor a supposed right to error, but rather a natural right of the human person to civil liberty, i.e., immunity, within just limits, from external constraint in religious matters by political authorities."[52]

Some of the parallels between the constitutional law in the United States and Church teaching are striking.

It is intriguing that, at a formal level, the constitutional doctrine and Church teaching on religious liberty have much in common. Both are quite skeptical of the idea that someone should have a presumptive right to an exemption from a law. Both critique the idea that an individual ought to be treated as a law unto himself. Both share the concern that such a broad view of freedom would degenerate into subjectivism and ultimately to the tyranny of a majority. [53]

Church teaching does, however, depart from the constitutional law in significant respects. The doctrine set forth in *Smith*—no constitutionally compelled exemptions—is completely independent of both the content of the religious choice and of the state interest reflected in the law. The Court's understanding operates at a formal level (with a focus on whether the law is neutral) and does not focus on the impact of laws on religious liberty. Church teaching, in contrast, is more concerned with whether a law has an effect on religious liberty. In addition, the Catholic understanding of religious liberty is profoundly influenced by both the nature of the choice in question and by the state interest being asserted. The Church repeatedly states, in the words of Pope Pius XII, "that which does not correspond to truth or to the norm of morality objectively has no right to exist."[54] Moreover, Church teaching does not simply accept the state interests being claimed. As Pius XII states, "No human authority, no state, no community of states, whatever be their religious character, can give a positive command or positive authorization to teach or to do that which would be contrary to religious truth or moral good."[55] Furthermore, the Church also maintains that it is the Church that is the authoritative interpreter of the natural law.[56]

In a society with a sound understanding of the demands of the natural law, there would be a limited role for a right to conscience. So, for example, in a society that banned abortion or assisted suicide, there would be no need for a Catholic doctor to assert a right to conscience since his beliefs would conform to the laws of the society. And, those who asserted a right to conscience (e.g., that their religion required them to perform an abortion or assist in a suicide), would not be successful in receiving an exemption since the right to religious liberty is limited by the requirements of objective morality.

The principal strategy for defending Catholics and others with traditional views on moral issues ought to be to rebuild a proper understanding of the demands of the natural law. A society with sound laws on abortion, for example, would not have a need for strong protection for conscience.

To the extent a society departs from a sound understanding of the natural law, there is a need for stronger protection for a right to conscience. One can see this increasingly in the United States. As state laws increasingly depart from the moral norms taught by the Church, the potential for legitimate claims of conscience, according to the Church's understanding, increases. When moral evils (e.g., abortion or contraception or same-sex marriage) are elevated to the status of fundamental rights and compelling government interests, then the need for an exemption increases. In such a situation, the Church—which advocates a limited idea of religious liberty—increasingly supports a right to conscience, although there are some significant risks attached to pursuing an exemption strategy.[57]

CONCLUSION

My overall assessment of constitutional law dealing with church and state is a very qualified endorsement. The Establishment Clause cases through about 1985 dealing with public funding issues had serious flaws. The cases, which were influenced by a strict separationist orientation, were supportive of the idea of the privatization of religion, and religious entities were sometimes treated with hostility. But it is important to recognize that this has largely changed. The current approach emphasizing neutrality affords religious institutions an equal opportunity to participate, although unfortunately this is a matter of legislative grace. This leaves religious individuals and institutions at the mercy of the political process, and in the area of education it has led to serious injustice for parents who choose to educate their children outside the government schools. This is an area where there is serious tension between federal constitutional law and Church teaching, which is far more supportive of the rights of parents to choose a religious education for their children.

In certain other areas, Establishment Clause doctrine is not clearly settled. As explained above, there is some support in the cases for a more aggressive enforcement of the idea that there is a constitutional command of secular government. If this is pursued more aggressively, there would be some significant risks and tension with Catholic teaching.

The principal reservation about the Court's Establishment Clause jurisprudence is that the Court's approach makes it difficult to acknowledge a special role for religion. This contributes to a "revisionist agenda of secularization" and that approach is ultimately threatening to religious liberty and to human rights more generally.

With respect to the Free Exercise doctrine, the Court's current approach is not as bad as some suggest. There are, in truth, some important similarities between current constitutional doctrine and Church teaching. Yet, it is important to note some key problem areas. The Court's approach fails to reflect a proper understanding of the demands of the moral law. This is particularly troublesome as laws in the United States increasingly diverge from Catholic moral teaching, as the increasing acceptance of same-sex marriage illustrates. Fortunately, current law affords Catholics an opportunity to advance their views on moral issues, and we see some progress in certain areas (e.g., abortion).[58]

NOTES

1. The First Amendment provides, in relevant part: "Congress shall make no law respecting an establishment of religion, or prohibiting the free exercise thereof." U.S. Const. amend. I.

2. For background and citations to other literature on the topic, see Richard S. Myers, "Current Legal Issues Regarding Rights of Conscience in Health Care," 16 *Josephinum J. Theology* 394 (2009) [hereinafter Myers, "Conscience"]; Richard S. Myers, *A Critique of John Noonan's Approach to Development of Doctrine*, 1 U. St. Thomas L. J. 285 (2003). Because this chapter focuses on federal constitutional law, it does not address in any detail the idea of the "freedom of the Church," which is a key to a broader understanding of Church thought on these questions.

3. *Cantwell v. Connecticut*, 310 U.S. 296 (1940) (incorporating the Free Exercise Clause); *Everson v. Board of Education*, 330 U.S. 1 (1947) (incorporating the Establishment Clause).

4. *Everson*, 330 U.S. at 15–16. For a critique of the wall of separation metaphor, see generally Philip Hamburger, *Separation of Church and State* (Harvard University Press, 2004).

5. For a discussion of this theme, see Richard S. Myers, *The Supreme Court and the Privatization of Religion*, 41 Cath. U. L. Rev. 19 (1991).

6. See Myers, *Supreme Court and Privatization, supra* note 5, at 29.

7. See Myers, *Supreme Court and Privatization, supra* note 5, at 29.

8. *Abington Township v. Schempp*, 374 U.S. 203, 241–42 (1963) (Brennan, J., concurring).

9. Stephen L. Carter, *The Culture of Disbelief: How American Law and Politics Trivialize Religious Devotion* (Basic Books, 1993).

10. Carter, *Culture of Disbelief* at 22.

11. Gerard V. Bradley, *Dogmatomachy—A "Privatization" Theory of the Religion Clause Cases*, 30 St. Louis U. L. J. 275, 276–77 (1986).

12. See Richard S. Myers, *The Privatization of Religion and Catholic Justices*, 47 J. Cath. Legal Stud. 157 (2008).

13. *Zelman v. Simmons-Harris*, 536 U.S. 639 (2002).

14. For discussion of the school choice issue, see Richard S. Myers, "School Choice: The Constitutional Issues," 8 *Cath. Soc. Sci. Rev.* 167 (2003).

15. See *Locke v. Davey*, 540 U.S. 712 (2004) (upholding the constitutionality of a state program that excluded a student from a student scholarship because the student majored in theology from a "devotional perspective").

16. See Richard S. Myers, *Same-Sex Marriage, Education, and Parental Rights*, 2011 BYU Educ. & L. J. 303 at 318–320.

17. *Compendium of the Social Doctrine of the Church*, ¶241 (2004) (*quoting* The Charter of the Rights of the Family, art. 5(b) [1983]).

18. This phrase is from Justice Blackmun's opinion in *County of Allegheny v. ACLU*, 492 U.S. 490, 611 (1989).

19. For discussion of these cases, see Richard S. Myers, "The Ten Commandments Cases and the Future of the Religion Clauses of the First Amendment," 11 *Cath. Soc. Sci. Rev.* 245 (2006).

20. Myers, "Ten Commandments," *supra* note 19, at 246–47 (discussing the Pledge of Allegiance cases and other cases involving the national motto ("In God We Trust") and various state mottoes. *Town of Greece v. Galloway* is currently pending before the United States Supreme Court 681 F. 3d (2d Cir. 2012), *cert. granted*, 133 S. Ct. 2388 (2013). The case involves the constitutionality of prayers before town board meetings. A major issue in the case is whether the prayers are sectarian or nonsectarian, which is similar to the "religious intensity" issue noted in the text.

21. *McCreary County v. ACLU*, 545 U.S. 844, 910 (2005) (Scalia, J., dissenting).

22. Vatican Council II, *Dignitatis Humanae*, ¶3 (December 7, 1965). For a discussion of George Washington's views, see Richard S. Myers, "The United States Supreme Court and the Privatization of Religion," 6 *Cath. Soc. Sci. Rev.* 223 (2001).

23. *McCreary County*, 545 U.S. 844, 885–94 (2005) (Scalia, J., dissenting).

24. *McCreary County*, 545 U.S. at 889 (Scalia, J., dissenting).

25. Richard S. Myers, *A Comment on the Death of Lemon*, 43 Case W. Res. L. Rev. 903, 909 (1993).

26. *McCreary County*, 545 U.S. at 910 (Scalia, J., dissenting).

27. Pope John Paul II, *Evangelium Vitae* (1995), ¶¶21, 23, 24.

28. See Myers, *Privatization of Religion, supra* note 12, at 164–65.

29. Congregation for the Doctrine of the Faith, *Doctrinal Note on Some Questions Regarding the Participation of Catholics in Political Life* (November 24, 2002).

30. Richard S. Myers, *Same-Sex "Marriage" and the Public Policy Doctrine*, 32 Creighton L. Rev. 45, 63–64 (1998).

31. *Lawrence v. Texas*, 539 U.S. 558 (2003). For a critique of *Lawrence*, see Richard S. Myers, *Pope John Paul II, Freedom, and Constitutional Law*, 6 Ave Maria L. Rev. 61 (2007).

32. For a discussion of this point, see Myers, *Supreme Court and Privatization, supra* note 5, at 37–38.

33. Myers, "The Ten Commandments," *supra* note 19, at 251. This doctrine is in considerable tension with Catholic thought, which strongly defends the right and obligation of Catholics to participate in political life. See *Doctrinal Note, supra* note 29.

34. Richard S. Myers, *Right to Conscience and the First Amendment*, 9 Ave Maria L. Rev. 123 (2010) at 124.

35. *Reynolds v. United States*, 98 U.S. 145 (1879).

36. *Reynolds*, 98 U.S. at 164.

37. *Reynolds*, 98 U.S. at 167.

38. The references are to *Sherbert v. Verner*, 374 U.S. 398 (1963) and *Wisconsin v. Yoder*, 406 U.S. 205 (1972). See Myers, *Right to Conscience, supra* note 34, at 126–28.

39. *Employment Division v. Smith*, 494 U.S. 872 (1990).

40. *Smith*, 494 U.S. at 874.

41. *Smith* (quoting *Reynolds v. United States*, 98 U.S. 145, 167 [1879]).

42. *Smith*, 494 U.S. at 890.

43. See Myers, *Right to Conscience, supra* note 34, at 128–29. One issue that explained the narrow protection prior to *Smith* was that courts often gave less protection to religiously based conduct as opposed to freedom of belief and worship. See Richard S. Myers, "United States Law and Conscientious Objection in Healthcare," in *Cooperation, Complicity, and Conscience: Moral Problems in Healthcare, Science, Law, and Public Policy*, ed. Helen Watt (Linacre Center, 2006), 296, 307–9 (discussing this point). The Obama Administration has created much controversy by persisting in describing religious freedom as freedom of worship. Catholics do not, of course, draw a sharp separation between religious and secular activities. The United States Conference of Catholic Bishops has emphasized that religious freedom ought to be protected when religious institutions and individuals are "out in the world" running hospitals or schools, for example. Some argue that for-profit corporations are not entitled to protections afforded religious freedom. For a critique of this view, see Mark Rienzi, *God and the Profits: Is There Religious Liberty for Money-Makers?* 21 Geo. Mason L. Rev. 59 (2013).

44. See Myers, *Right to Conscience, supra* note 34, at 128–29.

45. In *Hosanna-Tabor Evangelical Lutheran Church & Sch. v. EEOC*, 132 S. Ct. 694 (2012), the Court held that the Religion Clauses bar the government from applying employment discrimination laws to the decision of a religious group to fire one of its ministers.

46. Congress passed the Religious Freedom Restoration Act, 42 U.S.C. § 2000bb, in 1993. The Act was held unconstitutional as applied to state and local laws, see *City of Boerne v. Flores*, 521 U.S. 507 (1997), but the Act still provides a basis to argue for an exemption to federal mandates.

47. One area where this is most apparent is with regard to the rights of parents to control the education of their children. In addition to the funding issue noted above, conflicts have arisen when parents have objected that the curriculum in public schools interferes with their religious liberty. These cases are typically decided in favor of the public schools. See Myers, *Same-Sex Marriage, Education and Parental Rights, supra* note 16 at 308–13(discussing cases).

48. See, e.g., United States Conference of Catholic Bishops Ad Hoc Committee for Religious Liberty, *Our First, Most Cherished Liberty: A Statement on Religious Liberty* (2012). See *Sebelius v. Hobby Lobby Stores, Inc.*, 723 F. 3d 1114 (10th Cir. 2013), *cert. granted*, 2013 U.S. LEXIS 8418 (November 26, 2013); *Conestoga Wood Specialties Corp. v. Sebelius*, 724 F. 3d 377 (3d Cir. 2013), *cert. granted*, 2013 U.S. LEXIS 8418 (November 26, 2013).

49. *Dignitatis Humanae*, at ¶2.

50. *Dignitatis Humanae*, at ¶2.

51. *Dignitatis Humanae*, at ¶7.

52. *Catechism of the Catholic Church*, ¶2108 (footnotes omitted).

53. See Myers, "Conscience," *supra* note 2, at 404.

54. Pope Pius XII, *Ci Riesce*, Discourse to the National Convention of Italian Catholic Jurists, §V (December 6, 1953).

55. *Ci Riesce*, § V.

56. See *Doctrinal Note, supra* note 29, at no. 3 (footnote omitted). ("It is, however, the Church's right and duty to provide a moral judgment on temporal matters when this is required by faith or the moral law.")

57. See Myers, "Conscience," *supra* note 2, at 407–10. The major risk is that describing a claim for an exemption as based on "religion" creates a risk of delegitimizing the moral views that ought to be advanced (e.g., the immorality of abortion or contraception). That is because

some influential segments of our society (including the courts on occasion) view "religious" views as "irrational superstitious nonsense," see Suzanna Sherry, *Outlaw Blues*, 87 Mich. L. Rev. 1418, 1427 (1989), and, therefore, not a fit subject for public action. Characterizing a view as "religious" may suggest to some that it is idiosyncratic and not publicly accessible, and this line of thinking may well promote a subjectivism and relativism that ultimately threatens the protection of human rights.

58. After *Roe v. Wade*, 410 U.S. 113 (1973), many thought that the Court had settled the abortion issue by endorsing a view that seemed to reflect the inevitable direction of public opinion. But that is not what happened. Those with pro-life views have continued to advance their views and significant progress has been made. Strong and effective advocacy for pro-life views has also made an exemption, when that is necessary, more acceptable. See Myers, "Conscience," *supra* note 2, at 407.

Chapter Nine

First Amendment Freedoms and the Right of Privacy

The Necessary Connection Between Rights and Human Dignity That the U.S. Supreme Court Often Fails to Make

Stephen M. Krason

We can recall the famous "mystery passage" in the U.S. Supreme Court's 1992 *Planned Parenthood v. Casey* opinion, in which it reaffirmed its 1973 abortion decisions: "At the heart of liberty is the right to define one's own concept of existence, of meaning, of the universe, and of the mystery of human life."[1] In an article about the mystery passage, Catholic legal scholar Michael Scaperlanda commends the Court for understanding that liberty is essential to human dignity but faults it for failing to see that such liberty—to sustain itself—must be acknowledged as grounded in "the objective reality of the person," in "objective truth."[2] This makes one think about Pope John Paul II's profound statement in *Centesimus Annus*: "A democracy without values easily turns into open or thinly disguised totalitarianism."[3] The First Amendment freedoms of speech, assembly, press, petitioning for a redress of grievance, and association, and also the notion of human privacy—which the Supreme Court is purporting to protect in its abortion decisions—embody the fundamental connection between rights and human dignity that the Church stresses. As in its abortion decisions, the Court has often not seen the correct connection and has embraced a perspective about liberty that, in the final analysis, undermines human dignity. This chapter examines key constitutional cases, makes an assessment about the extent to which the Court conforms to the Church's teaching and, alternatively, deviates from it.

CHURCH TEACHING

A number of teachings of the Church are pertinent to the rights found in the First Amendment. Pope John XXIII's encyclical *Pacem in Terris* presents a catalogue of the natural rights of man. First are rights categorized as "rights pertaining to moral and cultural values," which include the rights to one's "good reputation . . . to freedom in searching for truth and in expressing and communicating his opinions . . . and . . . the right to be informed truthfully about public events."[4] *Inter Mirifica* (*Decree on the Means of Social Communication*) from the Second Vatican Council calls on the state to "defend and safeguard . . . a true and just freedom of information . . . guarantee[ing] to those who use the media the free exercise of their lawful rights."[5] This all, of course, parallels the First Amendment rights to free speech and press. Another category of rights concerns "assembly and association." As part of this, the encyclical says men have the right to form societies (or organizations) in order to achieve goals.[6] In the apostolic exhortation *Familiaris Consortio*, John Paul II makes clear that this is not just a right of individuals. Families have the right "to form associations with other families and institutions" in order to better fulfill their role.[7] Here is a parallel to the First Amendment's explicit right to assembly and implied right of association. Another category concerns rights in the political order, including "the right to take an active part in public affairs and to contribute one's part to the common good."[8] To be able to do this obviously involves freedom of speech, assembly, petition, and association. John Paul's *Sollicitudo Rei Socialis* calls for "democratic and participatory" forms of government to replace authoritarian ones.[9] All of these rights are part of the former.

The Church makes many expressions of the importance of privacy, rightly considered. The seal of confession is an obvious expression of protecting a right of the individual to privacy.[10] In discussing the Eighth Commandment, the *Catechism of the Catholic Church* exhorts everyone to "observe an appropriate reserve concerning persons' private lives," and admonishes the media not to infringe upon "the private lives of persons" in the public arena.[11] Also relating to privacy is the sin of detraction, which the *Catechism* defines as disclosing a person's faults and failings to another without a good reason.[12] One of the rights of the family listed in *Familiaris Consortio* is the right to the intimacy of conjugal and family life.[13] Pope Leo XIII emphasized family privacy way back at the time of *Rerum Novarum* (1891) when he condemned those in his time who claimed that the state "should at its option intrude into and exercise intimate control over the family." State intervention is justified only if the family is in "exceeding distress" or if within it "there occur grave disturbance of mutual rights."[14]

Clearly, these rights of the individual and the family are not absolute. The latter quote states, in effect, a limitation on family privacy. What is said about the media having to respect the privacy of "public people" shows a limitation on its rights. Indeed, *Pacem in Terris* makes clear that the rights it lists have "just as many respective duties."[15] As noted above, one's rights or liberty cannot be disconnected from the truth, from the natural moral law. One cannot in the name of his rights violate the rights of another or undermine the common good, which involves respect for the human person and the promotion of society's well-being.[16] So, additionally, *Inter Mirifica* insists that the rights of the media impose on it a corresponding obligation to see to it that "the content of the communication be true and . . . complete," and also "be communicated honestly and properly."[17] While there is a right of association, *Rerum Novarum* says that public authorities can prohibit associations "which are evidently bad, unlawful, or dangerous to the State."[18]

Freedom of the press is not open-ended in other respects. Nor is the freedom of speech. Pope Leo XIII emphasizes in *Libertas Praestantissimum* that these freedoms do not imply that there is a right to promulgate falsehood and vice. The latter "should be diligently repressed by public authority." Leo insists that true liberty is more secure when license is restrained.[19] As for the media, the Church is concerned that they not offend decency or human dignity, have a corrupting effect on youth, or convey distorted conceptions of groups of people that can stir up prejudice.[20] The Church has frequently addressed the problem of "unwholesome entertainment," such as movies. For example, she has called not just for discretion and restraint among users of media and ecclesiastical ratings, but also for "enforcement of . . . provident laws."[21] The same is true of pornography, generally. The *Catechism of the Catholic Church* insists that "civil authorities should prevent the production and distribution of pornographic materials."[22] It is an offense against chastity and injures the dignity of all who participate in it, especially women.[23] Besides not violating privacy, the media also may not act in such a way as to damage reputations or defame people.[24]

The Church obviously rejects the reasoning that would use the right of privacy as grounds to permit the taking of innocent human life, as not just in abortion but also euthanasia and assisted suicide. She also makes clear that the law must prohibit such destruction of the innocent.[25] The Church further rejects the claim that the "emancipation of women" justifies abortion. As the *Declaration on Procured Abortion* says, "No one can exempt women, any more than men, from what nature demands of them. Furthermore, all publicly recognized freedom is always limited by the certain rights of others."[26] In other words, no one is exempted from the demands of the natural moral law and in the name of his rights one cannot violate the rights of another (in this case of the unborn child). Indeed, in *Sollicitudo Rei Socialis*, John Paul mentions as an "especially" important right "the right to life at every stage of its existence."[27]

The Church clearly does not view a right of privacy as grounds for protecting homosexual acts—which the Church teaches "are intrinsically disordered and can in no case be approved of—or of sexual acts between people of the opposite sex outside of marriage.[28]

AN EVALUATION OF SUPREME COURT DECISIONS ON THE FIRST AMENDMENT IN LIGHT OF CATHOLIC TEACHING AND THE CATHOLIC UNDERSTANDING OF HUMAN DIGNITY

Let us now turn to the leading decisions of the Supreme Court in the areas of the First Amendment under consideration and compare them and the perspective they embrace to the Church's understanding about human dignity. We first consider freedom of speech. From the end of World War I to the beginning of the current century, the Court decided several major cases and set down significant constitutional doctrines on free speech that provide a good basis for evaluation.

The Court's First Amendment free speech jurisprudence took shape with a string of decisions that concerned the speech and activities of political radicals: *Schenck v. U.S.* (1919),[29] which upheld a prosecution for passing out anticonscription leaflets during World War I in violation of the Espionage Act of 1917; *Abrams v. U.S.* (1919),[30] which upheld the Sedition Act of 1918 that punished a range of utterances against the American form of government, Constitution, armed forces, or flag or that in any way expressed support for Germany in World War I; and *Gitlow v. New York* (1925) and *Whitney v. California* (1927),[31] which upheld criminal syndicalism statutes used, respectively, to punish pamphleteering to urge a worker revolution and participation in the Communist party. In the decades right after World War II, the Court addressed similar cases, but with more mixed results: *Dennis v. U.S.* (1951),[32] which upheld application of the Smith Act (that criminalized the advocacy of the violent overthrow of the U.S. Government and organizing of a group to do this) to several American Communist Party leaders; *Yates v. U.S.* (1957),[33] where the Court made a distinction between theoretical advocacy of such overthrow and advocacy aimed at imminent action; *Scales v. U.S.* (1961),[34] which permitted a prosecution under the Smith Act for mere Communist Party membership (although it involved some very limited active steps toward violent action); and *Brandenburg v. Ohio* (1969),[35] which overturned the conviction of a Ku Klux Klansman under a statute forbidding "violence or unlawful methods" of accomplishing "industrial or political reform" for a speech at a Klan rally calling for revenge against governmental repression (the Court saying that advocacy may not be proscribed except when likely to incite imminent lawless action). In these different decisions, the Court applied different constitutional tests or doctrines that it had fashioned. The clear-and-present-danger test was the standard of *Schenck* and *Abrams* (since the Court ostensibly reasoned that the war effort could be harmed) and later of *Yates* (since the Court seemingly reasoned that the possibilities of a Communist revolution in the U.S. were remote). In the *Gitlow*, *Whitney*, and *Dennis* decisions, the Court used what has been called the bad tendency test (where the Court defers overwhelmingly to legislative judgment about when political speech can be curtailed, regardless of any imminent danger). *Scales* was sort of in between these two tests. *Brandenburg* represented another test, the incitement test (which is a shade more permissive than the clear-and-present-danger test, as it requires the likelihood of *immediate* lawless action). In 1968, the Court's *U.S. v. O'Brien* decision[36] went essentially in the same direction as *Schenck*, as it sustained a young man's prosecution for burning his draft card in protest of the Vietnam War. *Schenck* had protested and urged noncompliance with the World War I draft. *Texas v. Johnson* (1989) and *U.S. v. Eichman* (1990)[37] went in the opposite direction of *Abrams* and struck down statutes that criminalized burning the American flag.[38]

Political speech cases such as the above are difficult to evaluate in light of Church teaching because the Church tends to avoid immersing herself in debates about public lawmaking unless there is a clear moral question involved and because she is aware of the large realm of prudential judgment that must be left to legislators. Still, a few points can be made. First, there is no question that the state can act to stop action that can threaten it or harm the community. As *Rerum Novarum* states, "The safety of the commonwealth . . . is government's whole reason for existence."[39] Obviously, the Church's stress on rights and participation and her practical preference for democracy (i.e., representative government or what might best be called a democratic republic)[40] means that a state could not use this rationale for suppressing legitimate political speech, although it is not at all clear that this is what was happening in these cases.

The cases involving Communist Party activists cross into freedom of association, and Pope Leo makes clear that bad and dangerous associations can be suppressed. Further, the Church has consistently condemned communism and, more broadly, totalitarianism, which intrinsically are threats to the very dignity of the individual and are destructive of good political life.[41] The Church also might be accepting of the suppression of speech in a case like *Brandenburg*, since it perhaps represents a distortion of the truth about certain groups and the promotion of prejudice (as above) and thereby is an attack on human dignity. To be sure, however, the Church would probably recognize the role of prudential judgment that judges and other governmental officials could rightfully exercise in cases such as this: They might be reluctant to proscribe such speech because of the "slippery slope" argument.

In light of the connection the Church makes between decency and human dignity, it is likely that she would hold that even if speech is political in character that does not mean that the law may not regulate it according to time, place, and manner considerations. Even though this is also the Court's prevailing doctrine on speech and assembly,[42] it has not always given attention to these considerations even where they seem pertinent. In its 1971 *Cohen v. California* decision,[43] it overturned a young man's disturbing-the-peace conviction for wearing a jacket in a county courthouse with the words "F--- the draft" emblazoned on it. With her stress on the need for decency and its relationship to human dignity, the Church would not likely agree with the Court's decision. Moreover, she would hardly endorse the relativism of Justice John Marshall Harlan II's opinion where he claims, "One man's vulgarity is another's lyric." The Church's reaction here would be along the same lines as what it says about pornography. Similarly, although she would be sympathetic to the cause of the small group of Negro men who staged a silent sit-in in March 1964 at a Louisiana public library to protest racial segregation of the library system, she would not necessarily agree with the Court's decision in *Brown v. Louisiana* (1966)[44] that freedom of speech and assembly protect such behavior.[45] The Church stresses the necessity of order and obedience to civil authority.[46] Further, the moral analysis to be employed to justify such civil disobedience is probably similar to that for armed resistance to the state or just war, and two of the criteria are whether all other means for redress have been attempted and no better solution is available.[47] That clearly was not the case here, when the civil rights revolution was at its peak, passage of the Civil Rights Act of 1964 only months away, and the opportunity for ready legal redress available.

Also on the question of manner, the Church would almost certainly have no reservation about the Court's "fighting words" doctrine, which permits the suppression of abusive language that is likely to provoke retaliation, cause disturbance of the peace, and harm public morality.[48] Again, the Church stresses the need for order that, among other things, is needed to foster respect for human dignity. Furthermore, such abusive utterances can easily offend human dignity.

It is clear that the Court's line of decisions dealing with obscenity/pornography from at least the late 1950s until the early 1970s—essentially paralleling the period of the Warren Court—was on a collision course with the Church's teaching. The Court's "libertarian era" on this subject began with the 1957 *Roth v. U.S.* decision,[49] which held that obscenity was not constitutionally protected speech but nevertheless set out a standard that made prosecutions for it very difficult. It said that something could not be determined to be obscene/pornographic unless to "the average person, applying contemporary community standards, the dominant theme of the material taken as a whole appeals to prurient interest.[50] Actually, *Roth* was not a sudden shift of direction. For almost three decades before that decision, American law had begun to adopt a relativistic standard about obscenity. It moved away from the traditional *Hicklin* rule, which sought to protect the most vulnerable in the population from moral corruption, to a standard of what was acceptable to "contemporary standards" and whether a work's literary or scientific merit outweighed its prurient appeal. (Very often, of course, the level of acceptability was fashioned by secular opinion and the thinking of current cultural trendsetters.[51])

Less than a decade after *Roth*, the Court became even more permissive in the *Fanny Hill* case when it held that for material to be considered as pornographic it had to be "patently offensive" and "utterly without redeeming social value."[52] The Court went yet one step further when it ruled in *Stanley v. Georgia* (1969)[53] that private possession of pornography was protected by the First Amendment. After the Warren era, the Court somewhat pulled back on national standards for obscenity. In *Miller v. California* (1973),[54] it left the criteria more up to state and local judgment, so long as material lacked "serious value." Since that time, however, there has been limited prosecution of obscenity around the country, except for child pornography.[55] Perhaps the permissive legal regime that for so long was nationally mandated by the Warren Court helped fashion a widespread attitude of acceptance.[56]

The Court's permissiveness and its embracing of relativistic, shifting standards about what is obscene and pornographic—which reflected, implicitly, an acceptance or at least toleration of an amoral perspective about the depiction of sex and the use of these materials (seen very well by the quote from Harlan, above)—readily illustrates its severing of freedom from truth. These opinions betray a view of freedom as autonomy—the individual rightfully being his own moral arbiter—and show little awareness that it can undermine an objective notion of human dignity. There is no concern about the effects, of any sort, of pornography on the people who produce or act in pornography, the users, people connected to the users (e.g., their families), or the moral tone of the broader culture. The Church would not be oblivious to the fact that decision-making about censorship can be difficult. Fr. John Courtney Murray, S.J., said that it "is no job for the amateur,"[57] but unlike Justice Harlan the Church would say that the line can clearly be drawn. That is, it is possible to determine what is obscene or pornographic and what certainly may be proscribed.[58]

Another free speech subject concerns blasphemy, which today is hardly even thought about in the Western world. In the United States, blasphemous utterance was prosecuted into the twentieth century without any sense that it violated the First Amendment. In fact, as late as 1952 (as hard as it might be to believe today) New York State suppressed films for that reason. That year the Court, reviewing one of New York's decisions, held in *Burstyn v. Wilson*[59] that the First Amendment precluded such an action. By taking an

amoral stance about blasphemy—forcing the political order to tolerate anyone's outrageous public assaults against the Almighty—the Court not only
showed itself impervious to how the dignity of the person can be harmed by
allowing him to do this and the bad example he gives to others (perhaps
leading them into conduct that can undermine *their* dignity), but also to the
duties owed by the political society to God. This is something that Leo XIII
specifically mentions in *Libertas Praestantissimum*.[60] Suppressing blasphemy is a minimal part of such duties and the least that should be expected of
the state.

The proscribing of virtually any kind of officially sanctioned religious
expression in the public schools since the *Engel v. Vitale* and *Abington
School District v. Schempp* decisions of the early 1960s[61] —and often even
when it is not officially sanctioned[62] —represents a similar disregard of the
duties that the political society owes to God. In this case, its duty is simply to
acknowledge Him, and encourage the young to acknowledge Him, in at least
the minimal way of starting a school day with prayer. In both these areas of
blasphemy and religious expression, the Court shows no understanding of the
central belief of the Church that there can be no true human dignity without
God who is the source of morality and all truth.[63] To be sure, the Church
would not be oblivious to the problems of religious pluralism in the United
States, but likely would favor an accommodationist approach for governmental institutions like public schools instead of the strict separationist position
the Court has taken since shortly after World War II. Accommodationism
holds that government should encourage religious expression and be tolerant
of a great variety of it (so long as the type of expression does not harm the
public good) because it is good for the state and its people. As with the
Court's handling of pornography and blasphemy, its separationist jurisprudence is contrary to earlier American legal and constitutional practice.[64]

The Court has been very solicitous about protecting freedom of the press,
as we usually think of the term. This was illustrated by such major twentieth-
century decisions as *Near v. Minnesota* (1931), *Grosjean v. American Press
Company* (1936), and *New York Times Company v. U.S.* (1971).[65] *Near* held
that the First Amendment freedom of the press provision applied to the states
by virtue of the Fourteenth Amendment, as it invalidated a Minnesota statute
that gave the state the power to shut down any malicious, scandalous, or
defamatory publication (the statute permitted truth as a defense). *Grosjean*
nullified a Huey Long–initiated tax on Louisiana's daily newspapers, almost
all of which opposed him. The *Times* decision (the "Pentagon Papers" case)
made clear that government bore a very heavy burden to meet for prior
restraint of publication to be upheld, even when national security is invoked.
Even on libel, the Court drew a line far in the direction of protecting the
interests of the press. The standing rules were set down in *New York Times v.
Sullivan* (1964) and *Curtis Publishing Company v. Butts* (1967), which held,

respectively, that public officials and prominent persons who were not public officials could sue for libel only if they could meet the highly improbable standard of proving "actual malice." *Hustler Magazine v. Falwell* (1988) held that even plainly false, off-color parodies were constitutionally protected.[66]

The Church in an absolute sense might view these decisions as giving too much leeway to media interests in light of what is said above about her concerns that they not damage people's reputations. Still, aware of the dangers of allowing legitimate free speech to be suppressed, she would almost certainly give public decision-makers—judges and legislators—much room for prudential judgment on this. While scurrilous reporting on people violates human dignity, so does using libel as a rationale for suppressing the truth by, say, restraining investigative reporting which unearths corruption by public officials. This is an area that demands line-drawing, and Catholic teaching would not fault the Court for where it has drawn the line.

Another area of libel concerns group libel, as seen in the Court's *Beauharnais v. Illinois* decision (1952).[67] In that case, the Court narrowly upheld a statute that criminally punished the portrayal of members of any racial or religious group as depraved or criminal. In principle, as the above indicates, the Church would support such a law. Again, there would have to be a large area for prudential judgment because public officials and interest groups could try to use the law to suppress legitimate public debate about policy issues (e.g., affirmative action, racial quota systems, and the causes of sociopolitical problems within minority communities).[68] Also, some groups could try to use the law to stop criticism of immoral activity, as seen with the homosexualist movement.[69]

The Court's protection of freedom of association mostly conforms to the Church's teaching above. The first decision that formally recognized the right "as a derivative of the speech and assembly clauses" was *NAACP v. Alabama* (1957).[70] It held that a private organization has the right to withhold its membership list to avoid harassment that could threaten its and its members' constitutionally protected liberties. The Court has also refused to permit state antidiscrimination laws to thwart what it calls "expressive association," which concerns an organization's right to keep intact the content of its message. If it is forced to permit into its ranks individuals who would oppose its message—that is, forcing it to associate with people who would reject what it is seeking to convey or whose presence would suggest an alteration of its message—this violates its First Amendment rights. The two leading decisions concern a moral issue—the acceptance of homosexuality— that would make the Church particularly intent about seeing free association upheld.[71] To dilute free association in such cases would essentially compromise moral truth—the homosexualist movement makes no practical distinction between a condition of same-sex attraction, which is not immoral, and homosexual practice, which is—which by definition signals the undermining of human dignity. While the above makes clear that the right of association is not unlimited in either the Church's or the Court's thinking, it is not so clear that the Church—which has long had a history of separate men's and women's organizations, to say nothing of religious orders—would agree with the Court that it should be limited when it comes to nonreligiously affiliated fraternal clubs excluding women members. In the 1980s, the Court held that state antidiscrimination statutes trumped freedom of association on this.[72] The most recent major freedom of association decision again concerns the acceptance of homosexuality and is troublesome from a Catholic standpoint; it also raises religious liberty concerns. In *Christian Legal Society v. Martinez* (2010),[73] the Court held that a state university law school could refuse to recognize a Christian student group if it excluded homosexuals as full members.

AN EVALUATION OF SUPREME COURT DECISIONS ON PRIVACY IN LIGHT OF CATHOLIC TEACHING AND THE CATHOLIC UNDERSTANDING OF HUMAN DIGNITY

Most of the Court's decisions on the right of privacy—which primarily have come in the last fifty years—have put it at odds with the Church. *Griswold v. Connecticut* (1965)[74] is generally viewed as the godfather of this line of cases, but its legalization of contraception for married couples is only partly troublesome in a legal sense. While contraception, of course, is morally illicit in all cases, the constitutional right of marital privacy—which is the supposed basis for the decision—is something the Church would readily support as part of the broader notion of family privacy above. The right of entities to sell or distribute contraceptives or disseminate contraceptive information— which, in fact, is what really was involved in the case since the only persons prosecuted were the head of Planned Parenthood of New Haven, Connecticut, and a collaborating physician—is a different matter. The case essentially involves the promotion of immorality and a practice that undercuts the dignity of individuals, married couples, and families (and very often harms physical health).[75] As we have said, the Church insists that there is no right to promote falsehood and vice.[76]

Two years after *Griswold*, the other noteworthy exception to the general thrust of the Court's modern privacy doctrine came in *Loving v. Virginia*.[77] This decision struck down Virginia's legal prohibition against interracial marriage, a decision in line with the Church since she teaches the fundamental equality of all human persons.

Within seven years of *Griswold*, the Court transformed the right of marital privacy respecting reproductive matters into strictly a right of individual privacy. *Eisenstadt v. Baird* (1972)[78] held that unmarried persons had the same right to have contraceptives, and even distribution to them could not be proscribed. Then, of course, in the following year came the Court's infamous decisions in *Roe v. Wade* and *Doe v. Bolton*,[79] holding that the right of privacy encompassed the abortion decision. Those decisions legalized abortion (for all practical purposes) up until birth. The Court betrayed an utterly myopic view about freedom, embracing an almost abstract notion of an autonomous decision-maker (as it did with pornography). It virtually absolutized freedom when it came to reproductive decisions. The pregnant woman's "right" was exalted and anyone else's rights—the father's, it shortly turned out the parents' in the case of a minor, and even the unborn child's who could now be destroyed—melted into irrelevance. It even paid no attention to how this new freedom might hurt the woman herself.[80] The Court rode the wave of the abstract feminist way of thinking that had taken hold of informed opinion in the Western world. It was an aspect of the notion of freedom disconnected from truth—after all, informed opinion was unwilling to acknowledge that there was such a thing as moral truth on many things—so it fixated on a right to abortion for the sake of women's liberation. As stated above, however, the Church—whatever the merits of improving the condition of women in general—could never accept this for the very reason that the abortion decision was a use of freedom inimical to moral truth. This goes right back to the mystery passage, where the individual shapes a personal destiny without any apparent awareness of how freedom can turn on itself and impair the human dignity that it makes possible. Quite the contrary, as the Church said in the *Declaration on Procured Abortion*, "One cannot invoke freedom of thought to destroy . . . [unborn] life." She also insisted that for the state to withhold punishment for the taking of life in abortion would be viewed by many as a sign of its acceptability.[81]

To be sure, the Court did not take the next logical step and say that the freedom to master one's own destiny means even the right to choose to destroy oneself. In the companion cases of *Washington v. Glucksberg* and *Vacco v. Quill*,[82] it held that there was no constitutional right, under privacy doctrine, to suicide or to assisted suicide. This would have been the ultimate subversion of human dignity in the name of choice.[83]

This, however, did not signal a reversal of privacy jurisprudence oblivious to moral truth and considerations of human dignity. In *Lawrence v. Texas* (2003),[84] the Court declared statutes criminalizing same-sex sodomy unconstitutional (seventeen years previously, it had not been willing to take this step).[85] The Church's concern about a behavior being declared legal—to say nothing of its being protected by a nation's fundamental law—indicating to people its moral acceptability and the effects individual behavior, at least when carried out by numerous people, may have on the social fabric is something that (again) escaped the Court. Whether the Church would necessarily insist on criminal punishment for sodomy, she certainly could not agree with its being viewed as a right. Further, one wonders how human dignity would not be undermined by a behavior that ignores the rightful end of human faculties, embodies the notion of sex as devoid of a procreative dimension, completely collides with the reality of male–female complementarity, and tends to have profound and abundant physical and psychological consequences for its practitioners. [86]

CONCLUSION

The Supreme Court's constitutional jurisprudence has been inconsistent from a Catholic standpoint. Sometimes it has been in harmony with the Church's teaching, sometimes not. It has been particularly problematical on questions relating to sex, procreation, and human life. This is probably for three reasons: First, the Court has bought into a secular worldview—an ideological atmosphere—that has made the rejection of traditional, Judeo-Christian teaching about sex its hallmark. Second, the Court has fallen prey (at least in some sense) to an individualistic outlook. [87] Third, perhaps because of this individualism—it is fair to say that many of the justices have lacked a deep, solid philosophical formation—the Court has often not been able to understand the full social character of man, and so cannot sufficiently fathom the fact that his individual actions and even at times utterances (even if involving only a small, visible minority) can have a profound effect on the social fabric. They fail to grasp the notion of the common good, which involves the good of society and of each individual person in it, and understand that the two can never be radically disconnected. Part of the reason they cannot grasp the notion of common good is the very problem of the separation of freedom from moral truth that has been discussed. As the mystery passage illustrates, the justices—or at least many of them—do not fathom that man does not truly create his own destiny, that his end is ingrained in his very being. It is that end that is the basis for the notion of the common good. It is that end which the common good helps move man toward, which is the true basis for human dignity. True freedom does not consist in man acting as if he is a god, trying to fashion his own end, but in his cooperating with the inclination toward his rightful end that God has written into his nature. In other words, true freedom is acting responsibly—even if it is at times difficult—to subject oneself to the moral order whose basis is in the very nature of his Creator. Rights are not dictated by desires, but are prerogatives to do things that help one achieve his end or retain the dignity that is tied up with that end. Finally, the Court's failures reflect—in a very pronounced way—a fundamental weakness of the American political order. [88] It does not look to the Church as the authoritative interpreter of the natural law. In the absence of the true magisterium, substitute magisteria appear. The Court, in some sense, is perhaps America's, although it is itself shaped by prevailing cultural trends, ideologies, legal philosophies, etc. This is something that American constitutional law could largely "get away with" for much of our history because of a common law and constitutional tradition forged in the cauldron of medieval Catholic England. As that "moral capital" has waned, however, we increasingly see the damaging cultural and human consequences, and the need to look to the Church for moral direction becomes ever more apparent.

NOTES

1. 505 U.S. 833, 851 (1992).
2. Michael Scaperlanda, *Rehabilitating the "Mystery Passage": An Examination of the Supreme Court's Anthropology Using the Personalistic Norm in the Philosophy of Karol Wojtyla*, 45 J. Cath. Legal Stud. 638 (2006).
3. Pope John Paul II, *Centesimus Annus (The Hundredth Year)* (1991), ¶46 [hereinafter *CA*].
4. Pope John XXIII, *Pacem in Terris (Peace on Earth)* (1963), ¶12 [hereinafter *PT*].
5. Vatican II, *Inter Mirifica (Decree on the Means of Social Communication)* (1963), ¶12 [hereinafter *IM*].
6. *PT*, ¶23.
7. Pope John Paul II, *Familiaris Consortio (Apostolic Exhortation on the Family)* (1982), III, 3 [hereinafter *FC*].
8. *PT*, ¶26.
9. Pope John Paul II, *Sollicitudo Rei Socialis (The Social Concern of the Church)* (1987), ¶44 [hereinafter *SRS*].
10. *Catechism of the Catholic Church*, ¶2490 [hereinafter *Catechism*].
11. *Catechism*, ¶2492.
12. *Catechism*, ¶2477.
13. *FC*, III, 3.
14. Pope Leo XIII, *Rerum Novarum (The Condition of Labor)* (1891), ¶14 [hereinafter cited as *RN*].
15. *PT*, ¶28.
16. *Catechism*, ¶¶1907, 1908.
17. *IM*, ¶5.
18. *RN*, ¶52.
19. Pope Leo XIII, *Libertas Praestantissimum (Human Liberty)* (1888), ¶23 [hereinafter *LP*]. John Paul commended this encyclical in *CA*, ¶4.
20. See, e.g., Pope Pius XI, *Divini Illius Magistri (Christian Education of Youth)* (1929), in William J. Gibbons, S.J., *Seven Great Encyclicals* (Paulist Press, 1963), 64; Pope Pius XI, *Vigilanti Cura (On Motion Pictures)* (1936), (St. Paul Edns.), 12.
21. See Catechism, ¶2496; Pope Pius XII, "Address to Representatives of the Italian Movie Industry (June 21, 1955), in *The Pope Speaks, The Teachings of Pope Pius XII*, Michael Chinigo, ed. (Pantheon, 1957), 192; Pope Pius XII, "Address to Catholic Women" (February 20, 1942), in Chinigo, 104. "Address to Catholic Women" in Chinigo, 103. The quotes are from the latter statement, 103, 104.
22. *Catechism*, ¶2354.
23. *Catechism*, ¶2354; *FC*, III, 1.
24. *Catechism*, ¶¶2497–2498.
25. See Sacred Congregation for the Doctrine of the Faith, *Declaration on Procured Abortion* (1974), ¶20 [hereinafter *DPA*]; Sacred Congregation for the Doctrine of the Faith, *Declaration on Euthanasia* (1980), III.

26. *DPA*, ¶15.

27. *SRS*, ¶33.

28. Sacred Congregation for the Doctrine of the Faith, *Declaration on Certain Questions Concerning Sexual Ethics* (1975), VIII, VII.

29. 249 U.S. 47.

30. 250 U.S. 616.

31. 268 U.S. 652 and 274 U.S. 357, respectively.

32. 341 U.S. 494.

33. 354 U.S. 298.

34. 367 U.S. 203.

35. 395 U.S. 444.

36. 391 U.S. 367.

37. 491 U.S. 397 and 496 U.S. 310, respectively.

38. The source for this discussion of these cases and the constitutional tests is Alpheus Thomas Mason and Donald Grier Stephenson, Jr., *American Constitutional Law: Introductory Essays and Selected Cases*, (9th ed. Prentice-Hall, 1990 and 16th ed. Longman, 2012), 373–77 and 453–58, respectively.

39. *RN*, ¶35.

40. See, e.g., *CA*, ¶46.

41. See Pope Pius XI, *Divini Redemptoris (On Atheistic Communism)* (1937), ¶¶4, 9–13; *CA*, ¶¶19, 23–24.

42. Donald A. Downs, "Time, Place, and Manner Rule," in *The Oxford Companion to the Supreme Court of the United States*, ed. Kermit L. Hall (Oxford University Press, 1992), 874–975.

43. 403 U.S. 15.

44. 383 U.S. 131.

45. See Mason and Stephenson (9th ed.), *supra* note 38 at 376–77.

46. See Pontifical Council for Justice and Peace, *Compendium of the Social Doctrine of the Church*, ¶¶384, 394, 398, 400 [hereinafter *Compendium*].

47. See *Compendium*, ¶401.

48. See *Chaplinsky v. New Hampshire*, 315 U.S. 568 (1942).

49. 354 U.S. 476.

50. 354 U.S. at 476, 488.

51. Stephen M. Krason, *The Public Order and the Sacred Order: Contemporary Issues, Catholic Social Thought, and the Western and American Traditions*, vol. 1 (Scarecrow Press, 2009), 363.

52. *Memoirs of a Woman of Pleasure v. Massachusetts*, 383 U.S. 413 (1966).

53. 394 U.S. 557.

54. 413 U.S. 15.

55. Stephen M. Krason, *The Transformation of the American Democratic Republic* (Transaction, 2012), 417, 434–435.

56. See Mason and Stephenson (9th ed.), *supra* note 38 at 383–84.

57. John Courtney Murray, S.J., *We Hold These Truths: Catholic Reflections on the American Proposition* (Sheed and Ward, 1960), 171.

58. Elsewhere, I propose criteria for a reasonable regimen of censorship that conforms to a sound philosophical understanding, Church teaching, and traditional American practice. (See Krason, *The Public Order and the Sacred Order*, *supra* note 51 at 355–75).

59. 343 U.S. 495.

60. *LP*, ¶21.

61. 370 U.S. 421 and 374 U.S. 203, respectively.

62. The Court has even declared student-initiated prayer at public school athletic events to be unconstitutional (*Santa Fe Independent School District v. Doe*, 530 U.S. 290 [2000]). Federal courts have generally rejected student-initiated and conducted prayers at graduations. See Brook R. Whitted and Malcolm C. Rich, "Religion in Our Schools: Balancing First Amendment Rights," http://www.wct-law.com/resource-links/publications/180.html (accessed June 28, 2013).

63. See, e.g., *Compendium*, ¶¶396–98.

64. For a discussion of the changing character historically of the Court's church-state juris-prudence and about how it could be reshaped along the lines of the earlier accommodationist perspective, see Krason, *The Public Order and the Sacred Order*, *supra* note 51, 201–28.

65. 283 U.S. 697, 297 U.S. 233, and 403 U.S. 713, respectively.

66. The citations for these cases are, respectively, 376 U.S. 254, 388 U.S. 130, and 485 U.S. 46. See Mason and Stephenson (16th ed.), *supra* note 38, 463–64.

67. 343 U.S. 250. See Mason and Stephenson (16th ed.), *supra* note 38, 468.

68. The Church also makes clear that minority groups may not "exalt beyond due measure anything proper to their own people" (*PT*, ¶97).

69. Homosexuals and their advocacy organizations have used civil rights law to force busi-nesses to offer services for same-sex "weddings" in this country and clergy have been brought before "human rights" tribunals in Canadian provinces for publicly opposing homosexual activity.

70. 357 U.S. 449.

71. The leading decisions here are *Hurley v. Irish-American Gay, Lesbian and Bisexual Group*, 515 U.S. 557 (1995) and *Boy Scouts of America and Monmouth Council v. Dale*, 530 U.S. 640 (2000).

72. The decisions are *Roberts v. U.S. Jaycees*, 468 U.S. 609 (1984), *Rotary International v. Rotary Club of Duarte*, 481 U.S. 537 (1987), and *New York State Club Association v. New York City*, 487 U.S. 1 (1988). See Mason and Stephenson (16th ed.), *supra* note 38, 462.

73. 561 U.S ___.

74. 381 U.S. 479.

75. For a brief overview of the health risks and consequences of contraceptive use, see John F. Kippley and Sheila K. Kippley, *The Art of Natural Family Planning* (Couple to Couple League International, 2003), 6–18. Professor Janet E. Smith has written about the full range of bad effects of contraceptive use, for marriages, for women, for children, and for the culture (see, e.g., "Birth Control—the Pill—Why Use Contraception?" available at www.janetsmith.excerptsofinri.com [accessed June 28, 2013]).

76. Some might think that "vice" to too strong a word to apply to contraceptive use, but that is how it was viewed in earlier American history (until the twentieth century). A well-known history of the issue is James Reed, *From Private Vice to Public Virtue: The Birth Control Movement and American Society Since 1830* (Basic Books, 1978).

77. 388 U.S. 1.

78. 405 U.S. 434.

79. 410 U.S. 113 and 410 U.S. 179, respectively.

80. See, e.g., Elizabeth Ring-Cassidy and Ian Gentiles, *Women's Health after Abortion: The Medical and Psychological Evidence* (DeVeber Institute for Bioethics and Social Research, 2002).

81. *DPA*, ¶20.

82. 521 U.S. 702 and 521 U.S. 793, respectively.

83. This does not mean, however, that the Court would have stood in the way of any state legislating to permit these. In other words, it probably would not have stood in the way of allowing such a subversion of human dignity by legislative enactment.

84. 539 U.S. 558. See Mason and Stephenson (16th ed.), *supra* note 38, 557–58, 561–63.

85. The previous case was *Bowers v. Hardwick*, 478 U.S. 186 (1986).

86. On the adverse physical and psychological effects of same-sex sexual activity, see Peter Sprigg and Timothy Dailey, eds., *Getting It Straight: What the Research Shows about Homo-sexuality* (Family Research Council, 2004), chap. 4; James E. Phelan, Neil Whitehead, and Philip M. Sutton, "What Research Shows: NARTH's Response to the APA's Claims on Homo-sexuality," *Journal of Human Sexuality*, vol. 1 (2009): 41–87.

87. See Krason, *The Transformation of the American Democratic Republic, passim*. This individualistic outlook progressively took hold in certain areas over the course of our history and arguably had its roots in the Enlightenment influence on our Founding itself.

88. See generally, Krason, *The Transformation of the American Democratic Republic*, *supra* note 55.

Chapter Ten

Equal Protection, Free Speech, and Religious Worship

Timothy J. Tracey

The argument that religious worship is "similarly situated" to ordinary, everyday speech devalues and degrades worship. It equates the celebration of the Mass with cheering for a football team on a Monday night. Nonetheless, the argument has gained currency because some public libraries and public schools have barred Christian churches from renting space for Sunday morning worship services.[1] Though most of these churches are Protestant, Catholic groups are facing similar opposition.[2]

Historically, the U.S. Supreme Court has held that the government must grant religious groups "equal access" to government-run facilities.[3] So if the school board allows the Boy Scouts to hold meetings on a Tuesday evening to teach boys about character and patriotism, then the First Amendment mandates that the board also allow religious groups access to do the same from a religious perspective. But in these equal access cases, the Supreme Court only requires schools to give religious groups use of public facilities to talk about an already permitted subject matter. Schools allowing community groups to discuss childrearing must allow religious groups to show films discussing the same subject matter from a religious perspective.[4] And schools allowing students to meet for an after-school book club must allow religious groups to host Bible studies—essentially a book study from a religious perspective.[5]

Undergirding these religious "equal access" decisions is the Court's reliance on a principle of equal protection—that the speech proposed by the religious group is "similarly situated" to the nonreligious speech already permitted by the government.[6] The religious group's speech furthers the government's purpose (e.g., promoting the welfare of the community or fostering a robust, academic debate on a college campus) to the same extent as the nonreligious groups' speech already permitted by the government.

The Court has never said that the government must open its facilities to religious worship. In fact, it seems to imply the opposite. "[Q]uintessentially religious activities"—like Sunday morning worship services—the Court suggests, may be excluded because there is no secular analog to worship.[7] Worship is not just a religious perspective on character or childrearing. It is wholly different—"similarly situated" to no secular activities. The Church calls the Celebration of the Mass on Sunday mornings the "fount and apex of the whole Christian life."[8] When believers gather together for the Mass, they "unite [themselves] with the heavenly liturgy and anticipate eternal life, when God will be all in all."[9]

Heaven is the place where the whole community of God's people will dwell with Him forever, praising His name and delighting in His glory.[10] When believers gather for corporate worship, it is a snapshot of that experience—one that believers can enjoy in this life.

There is a temptation to equate the Mass with secular, speech-related activities to squeeze it into the mold of the Court's equal access cases. But the ramifications of casting worship as simply a religious version of a tailgate party are significant. It cheapens worship. It strips it of its spiritual meaning. It may be a convenient way for churches to seek access to government facilities, and perhaps even a successful one, but it should be offensive to Catholic believers.

Catholics dare not jettison the spiritual significance of worship for mere pragmatic purposes. Yes, an equation of the Mass to a meeting may allow the thousands of churches meeting in public buildings, like schools, to continue to do so. But the cost is too great.

THE GENERAL PRINCIPLES OF EQUAL PROTECTION

The Equal Protection Clause of the Fourteenth Amendment commands that no state shall "deny to any person within its jurisdiction the equal protection of the laws."[11] Though nothing in the Constitution's text imposes a similar restriction on the federal government, the U.S. Supreme Court has construed the Fifth Amendment Due Process Clause as "contain[ing] an equal protection component prohibiting the United States from invidiously discriminating between individuals or groups."[12] Under most circumstances, the Amendments afford the same protections.

But the Equal Protection Clause does not prohibit government from discriminating in all circumstances. Indeed, all laws classify people at some level. They impose burdens or confer benefits on a selective basis, singling out some people or activities for treatment different from that accorded to other people. A police officer who enforces a speed limit pulls over fast drivers and allows other drivers to pass by unchecked. A law regulating child labor treats employers who hire ten-year-olds differently from those who hire twenty-five-year-olds. The government discriminates in both instances; yet no court would hold that the government has run afoul of the Equal Protection Clause.

The Equal Protection Clause, thus, aims only at prohibiting arbitrary or invidious discrimination—that is, from employing classifications that cannot be justified on the basis of a legitimate government interest or that are adopted merely for the sake of harming a particular group of persons. [13] The government, for instance, violates equal protection when it offers public education to whites but not to blacks [14] or permits women to drink at age eighteen, but forces men to wait until age twenty-one. [15] Someone's race is irrelevant to whether he should be provided a public education, and someone's gender has no bearing on the risk she presents when driving drunk. But when government excludes persons with no athletic ability from playing for the state university's football team, the government no doubt discriminates but it can hardly be called arbitrary or invidious. Someone's athletic prowess has everything to do with his ability to meaningfully contribute on the football field.

The prerequisite to any equal protection claim is proof that the individuals or groups alleged to have been treated differently are "similarly situated with respect to the purpose of the law." [16] In other words, the individuals or groups must present the same evil the government seeks to prevent or present the same good that the government seeks to promote. And yet the government nonetheless treats these individuals or groups differently. [17]

Look back at the drinking-age example above. Presumably, the legislature's purpose in passing the law is to promote highway safety. The legislature chooses to accomplish that purpose by raising the drinking age for men but not women. The legislature's decision to discriminate against men in favor of women violates equal protection. It does so not simply because the law distinguishes between men and women, but, rather, because the law treats men and women differently even though they are "similarly situated with respect to the purpose of law." Both men and women present the same evil the legislature is trying to prevent—hazardous driving while drunk—and yet the legislature treats them differently by penalizing men but not women. [18]

But assume that the legislature has credible evidence that men are more likely to drink and drive than women are. In that case, men and women would no longer be "similarly situated with regard to the purpose of the law." Men would present the evil of drunk driving to a greater degree than women. The legislature may then distinguish between men and women without transgressing the Equal Protection Clause.

To treat people differently who are "similarly situated" offends fundamental standards of fairness. It runs contrary to the American, democratic
principle that all persons stand equal before the law. But, more significantly,
it contradicts the teaching of the Church concerning human dignity. The
Church teaches that "[t]he divine image is present in every man."[19] And
because all persons are "created in the image of the one God and equally
endowed with rational souls" and "have the same nature and the same origin," they enjoy an "equal dignity."[20] Any "form of social or cultural discrimination in fundamental personal rights," the Church says, is "incompat-
ible with God's design."[21] Our "equal dignity as persons demands that we
strive for fairer and more humane conditions."[22] In short, the equal dignity of
human persons requires equal treatment under the law.

Just like the Court's equal protection jurisprudence has recognized that
not all discrimination is bad, the Church's teaching does too. The Church
teaches:

> On coming into the world, man is not equipped with everything he needs for
> developing his bodily and spiritual life. He needs others. Differences appear
> tied to age, physical abilities, intellectual or moral aptitudes, the benefits de-
> rived from social commerce, and the distribution of wealth. The "talents" are
> not distributed equally.
>
> These differences belong to God's plan, who wills that each receive what
> he needs from others, and that those endowed with particular "talents" share
> the benefits with those who need them. These differences encourage and often
> oblige persons to practice generosity, kindness, and sharing of goods; they
> foster the mutual enrichment of cultures.[23]

This diversity within the body of Christ ought to be acknowledged and celebrated even if that means in some circumstances treating people differently
because of their varying talents and abilities.

THE CONNECTION BETWEEN EQUAL
PROTECTION AND FREE SPEECH

This equality principle carries over to the realm of free speech. "In adjudicat-
ing First Amendment issues of freedom of speech and expression," Michael
Paulsen points out, "the Supreme Court has borrowed freely from the conceptual apparatus of its equal protection doctrine."[24] According to the Court,
free speech "intersects with" and "closely intertwine[s] with" the "guarantee
of equal protection."[25] Equal protection, said the Court, is "fused [into] the
First Amendment."[26] It guarantees that the government will treat the expression of viewpoints and ideas evenhandedly.

Necessarily, then, under the Equal Protection Clause, not to mention the First Amendment itself, government may not grant the use of a forum to people whose views it finds acceptable, but deny use to those wishing to express less favored or more controversial views. And it may not select which issues are worth discussing or debating in public facilities. There is an "equality of status in the field of ideas," and government must afford all points of view an equal opportunity to be heard.[27]

Thus, as Paulsen observes, "This First Amendment equality principle is clearly the core element in cases of a purported 'public forum.'"[28]

For instance, the Supreme Court struck down a City of Chicago ordinance that prohibited picketing outside of Chicago public schools except for "peaceful picketing of any school involved in a labor dispute." Earl Mosley, a city resident, sought to walk "the public sidewalk adjoining [Jones Commercial High School], carrying a sign that read: 'Jones High School practices black discrimination. Jones High School has a black quota.'" The City's picketing ordinance barred Mosley from protesting racial discrimination outside of the high school, but allowed teachers' unions to protest low wages outside the very same high school. The government's uneven treatment of these protests—First Amendment free speech—the Court said, "denied [Mosley] equal protection of the law in violation of the First and Fourteenth Amendments."[29]

The Court's reasoning hinged on Mosley's desired speech being "similarly situated" to the speech the City of Chicago already permitted. Mosley wanted to picket just like the teachers' unions could picket. The city claimed it passed the ordinance to combat the evil of "school disruption." Mosley and the teachers' unions were "similarly situated" with regard to this evil. Protests by both created the same risk of interfering with school activities. Yet the City of Chicago permitted labor protests by teachers' unions but not a civil rights protest by Mosely. "Such unequal treatment," said the Court, "is exactly what was condemned" by the principle of equal protection.[30]

Now if Mosley had wanted to hold a rock concert outside of the school, that would have been a different case. A rock concert is not "similarly situated" to a peaceful labor protest. It creates a much greater risk of school disruption than a peaceful protest. Because Mosley's rock concert would not be "similarly situated" to the speech already permitted by the City of Chicago—the peaceful, labor picketing—the city could prohibit the rock concert while allowing the protest without any concern for running afoul of the Equal Protection Clause. The *Mosley* court put it this way: The City of Chicago could prohibit Mosley's speech if it was "clearly more disruptive than the picketing Chicago already permits."[31] But that was not the case.

THE APPLICATION OF EQUAL
PROTECTION TO RELIGIOUS SPEECH

The Court has made frequent recourse to its equal protection doctrine, in particular, when addressing government regulation of religious speech. In *Niemotko v. Maryland*,[32] for example, a city denied a group of Jehovah's Witnesses a permit to use a city park for Bible talks, though other groups were permitted to use the park for picnics and Flag Day ceremonies. The Court concluded that the city's uneven treatment of the Jehovah's Witnesses violated "[t]he right to equal protection of the laws, in the exercise of those freedoms of speech and religion protected by the First and Fourteenth Amendments."[33] The Court followed *Niemotko* in *Fowler v. Rhode Island*,[34] where again the Jehovah's Witnesses were refused permission to conduct religious services in a city park. "Catholics could hold mass in Slater Park and Protestants could conduct their church services there without violating the ordinance."[35] The Court determined that the ordinance "as so construed and applied violated the First and the Fourteenth Amendments of the Constitution." For the park to allow "all religious groups" except for Jehovah's Witnesses, said the Court, was "discrimination" barred by the Free Speech and Equal Protection Clauses.[36]

Equal protection, in fact, became the dominant method by which the Supreme Court analyzed religious speech claims starting with *Widmar v. Vincent* in 1981.[37] In *Widmar*, the Court relied on equal protection cases like *Mosley* and *Fowler*, to hold that "if a university permits students and others to use its property for secular purposes, it must also furnish facilities to religious groups for the purposes of worship and the practice of their religion." The university said, "The overall goal [of its student activities program] was to develop social and cultural awareness as well as intellectual curiosity." The provision of university facilities to a religious student group, Cornerstone, according to the Court, furthered this goal just as much as giving access to secular student groups like the Students for a Democratic Society and the Young Socialist Alliance. They were, thus, "similarly situated" with regard to this goal. So by opening school facilities to secular student groups, but denying those same facilities to religious student groups, the university violated "equal protection and freedom of speech under the First and Fourteenth Amendments to the Constitution of the United States." The equal protection doctrine embedded in the Court's free speech jurisprudence mandated that the university provide religious speakers use of school facilities "on equal terms with others."[38] This basic principle became known as "equal access."

The Court repeatedly reaffirmed the principle of equal access over the next thirty years. The Court discussed these cases in terms of free speech—referring to speech forums, permissible subject matters, and viewpoint discrimination. But its rationale remained rooted in equal protection. "The necessities of confining a [speech] forum to the limited and legitimate purposes for which it was created," said the Court, "may justify the State in reserving it for certain groups or for the discussion of certain topics."[39] Or, to put it in terms of equal protection, the government need only open its forum to speakers "similarly situated" to the speakers already permitted in the forum. The Constitution, said the Court, does not require government to ignore the purpose for which it allowed speech in the first instance.

Thus, underlying the Court's equal access decisions is the determination that the proposed religious speech is "similarly situated" to the nonreligious speech already permitted by the government. The proposed speech raises the same evils and promotes the same goods as the already allowable speech.

For instance, in *Lamb's Chapel v. Center Moriches Union Free School District*,[40] the Court held that the First Amendment required a New York school district to provide meeting space for a church to show Christian films about childrearing. The district opened its facilities to community groups for the purpose of "social, civic and recreational meetings and entertainments, and other uses pertaining to the welfare of the community." The Court's reasoning turned on the fact that the church's proposed speech—showing the films—and the speech already permitted by the district were "similarly situated" with respect to the purpose of the forum. Both promoted the same good—"the welfare of the community." The only difference being that the church's films did so from a religious perspective.[41]

In *Rosenberger v. Rectors and Visitors of the University of Virginia*,[42] the Court again applied its equal protection doctrine to vindicate the free speech rights of a religious group. The Court held that the First Amendment required the University of Virginia to fund a religious student newspaper, called *Wide Awake*, out of the Student Activity Fund ("SAF"). "The purpose of the SAF," said the Court, "is to support a broad range of extracurricular student activities that are related to the educational purpose of the University." The university funded a wide gamut of student groups out of the SAF, including "student news, information, opinion, entertainment, or academic communications media groups." Just as in *Lamb's Chapel*, the Court's decision rested on the parity between *Wide Awake*'s proposed religious speech and the secular speech already permitted by the university. *Wide Awake*'s speech was "similarly situated" with respect to "the educational purpose" of the SAF. The "subjects discussed [by *Wide Awake*]," said the Court, "were otherwise within the approved category of publications." *Wide Awake* simply sought to address the subjects from a religious perspective.[43]

The Court once more relied on its equal protection doctrines in *Good News Club v. Milford Central School District* to analyze a religious speech claim.[44] The Court held that the First Amendment required a New York school district to give classroom space to a Good News Club for its after-school meetings. The school district opened classrooms to community groups for the purpose of promoting the "welfare of the community." The district allowed groups, like the Boy Scouts and the 4H Club, to meet to "teach morals and character development to children," but denied meeting space to the Good News Club to teach the same subjects from a religious perspective. The Court once again rooted its decision in the similarity between the Good News Club's proposed speech and the speech of the Boys Scouts and the 4H Club already permitted by the district. "What matters for purposes of the Free Speech Clause," said the Court, "is that we can see no logical difference in kind between the invocation of Christianity by the Club and the invocation of teamwork, loyalty, or patriotism by other associations to provide a foundation for their lessons." The Club's speech was "similarly situated" to the already allowed speech—both furthered the district's objective of promoting the "welfare of the community."[45]

Yet the Court has not always found that religious speech is "similarly situated" to nonreligious speech. Most recently, the Court held in *Christian Legal Society v. Martinez* that Hastings College of the Law could deny classroom space, bulletin boards, and money to a religious student group, a chapter of the Christian Legal Society ("CLS"), without transgressing the Constitution.[46] CLS required that voting members and leaders—the students who control the group—affirm their commitment to the group's core beliefs by signing a Statement of Faith. That was a problem for Hastings. Hastings insisted that all student groups seeking recognition and its accompanying benefits must maintain an all-comers policy with regard to membership and leadership. "[I]n order to be a registered organization," the school said, "you have to allow all of our students to be members and full participants if they want to."[47]

The purpose of the all-comers policy, according to Hastings, was to "ensure that the leadership, educational, and social opportunities afforded by [registered student groups] are available to all students." The nonreligious student groups already recognized by Hastings complied with the policy. They had agreed to "allow any student to participate, become a member, or seek leadership positions in the organization, regardless of [the student's] status or beliefs." CLS had not. It "exclude[d] students who [held] religious convictions different from those in the Statement of Faith." It could not claim to be "similarly situated" to the already-recognized groups "with respect to the purpose of the law."[48]

Equal protection principles undergirded each of the Court's "equal access" decisions. The central question—although cast in free speech terms— was whether the proposed religious speech was "similarly situated" to the speech already permitted by the government.

EQUAL PROTECTION AND RELIGIOUS WORSHIP

But state and local governments are testing the limits of the Court's application of its equal protection doctrines to free speech claims. Local governmental entities, such as school districts, libraries, and public colleges, are now regularly denying churches access to school facilities to hold Sunday morning worship services, and the trend is significant. A study from the North American Mission Board reports that 12 percent of churches meet in public school buildings. Another 8 percent meet in community halls such as public libraries.[49] Though most of the churches seeking access to government-run facilities are not Catholic, Catholic student groups, such as the Newman Center, increasingly face problems at public colleges and universities.

The most high profile case occurred in New York City. The dispute involved the Bronx Household of Faith—an evangelical Christian church seeking to use public school facilities for its Sunday worship services. The city denied the church use of the facilities for its services based on a school board policy that prohibited the use of school property for "religious worship services, or otherwise using a school as a house of worship."[50]

In 2011, the Second Circuit upheld the city's denial. The court distinguished the Supreme Court's decisions in *Lamb's Chapel*, *Good News Club*, and *Rosenberger* as resting on the fact that the proposed religious speech was "similar situated" to the speech already allowed by the schools.[51]

But religious worship is different. Bronx Household's worship service is not just a religious perspective on childrearing or character or the latest news. "[T]here is no real secular analogue to religious 'services,'" the court said. To argue that the church's worship services were "similarly situated" to a supposed category of "non-religious worship services," the court said, was a "canard."[52]

> There is no difference in usage between a "worship service" and a "religious worship service"; both refer to a service of religious worship. We think, with confidence, that if 100 randomly selected people were polled as to whether they attend "worship services," all of them would understand the questioner to be inquiring whether they attended services of religious worship. While it is true that the word "worship" is occasionally used in nonreligious contexts, such as to describe a miser, who is said to "worship" money, or a fan who "worships" a movie star, the term "worship services" has no similar use; meetings of a celebrity's fan club are not described as "worship services." Worship services are religious; the rule describes the entire category of activity excluded. The meaning of the rule's exclusion of "religious worship services" would be no different if it identified the excluded activity as "worship services."[53]

A worship service is, thus, *sui generis*. "[It] is," as Judge Calabresi put it, "something entirely different."[54] New York City's exclusion of worship services, said the court, "is no restraint on the free expression of any point of view." [55] Unlike *Lamb's Chapel*, *Good News Club*, and *Rosenberger*, the exclusion applies only to the conduct of a certain type of activity—the conduct of religious worship services—and not to the free expression of religious views on an otherwise secular subject. A worship service by its very nature is not "similarly situated" to any other speech allowed by the city.[56]

Court rulings, like those of the Second Circuit, no doubt pose a setback for churches seeking to rent public buildings for Sunday morning worship. But the response should not be to gut worship of its distinct, spiritual character in a desperate grab for meeting space. Indeed, attempts to squeeze worship into the mold of *Lamb's Chapel*, *Good News Club*, and *Rosenberger* are misguided. Each of those cases depends on the proposed religious speech—whether showing a video series from a religious perspective, teaching character from religious perspective, or publishing a newspaper from a religious perspective—being "similarly situated" to the secular speech already permitted by the government. The government already allows speakers to use classroom space to speak on childrearing, character, and current events. And endeavors to speak on those subjects from religious groups are "similarly situated" in every sense except for their religious perspectives.

The religious groups' speech in these cases furthers the government's purpose—promoting the welfare of the community, fostering academic debate on campus, etc. It brings a religious perspective on a subject the government has already chosen for discussion. But the purpose of a religious worship service is not to promote community welfare or foster academic debate. Rather, when the Church gathers for worship, it "blesses the Father by her worship, praise, and thanksgiving and begs him for the gift of his Son and the Holy Spirit."[57] The aim of worship is nothing less than to glorify God.

The character of true, Christian worship is such that it can never be deemed "similarly situated" to any form of secular speech. As the Second Circuit notes, worship has no "secular analogue." The Apostle Paul writes that the gospel is "folly to those who are perishing."[58] "The natural person," says Paul, "does not accept the things of the Spirit of God, for they are folly to him, and he is not able to understand them because they are spiritually discerned."[59] Christian worship then is foreign and perhaps even odd to the watching world.

It is true that in some sense the school booster club "worships" the basketball team, or the marching band "worships" at the school pep rally; however, the sacredness of the worship of God, the Creator of the Universe, cannot with any sincerity and right reverence, be equated to cheering for the school football team.

When the local church body comes together for the Mass, it "is joined to the action of Christ, the high point both of the action by which God sanctifies the world in Christ and of the worship that the human race offers to the Father, adoring him through Christ, the Son of God, in the Holy Spirit."[60]

> [W]hen the church assembles for worship she is not at all like the world. She invokes the name of Christ. She prays and sings to a God who cannot be seen. She hears words said by a man commissioned by Christ that become, by the work of the Holy Spirit, the power of God unto salvation. She eats a holy meal whose portions are tiny, but which, by the blessing of Christ, nourishes God's people for eternal life. In these ways the church at worship is different from the world. All elements of worship look weak and foolish to those outside the house of God. But to God's people they are manna that sustains for eternal life.[61]

Stripping worship of its spiritual character may be pragmatic; it may even help thousands of churches gain access to public school buildings. But at what cost? Without the spiritual trappings perhaps churches may more easily equate worship with ordinary, everyday nonreligious speech already allowed in government-run facilities. But what's left can hardly be called worship. Ultimately, is worship really worship at all if it lacks any sense of coming into the presence of the transcendent God of the Universe?

In the past, the Church roundly criticized such attempts to "secularize" Christianity as a mere tool to get from point A to point B. In the mid-1800s, for instance, Horace Mann, Alexander Campbell, and William Ruffner pushed the teaching of a stripped-down concept of Christianity in public schools as a means to creating a virtuous citizenry for "easy" governing. The Church protested the government "turn[ing] the Jesus of the faith into a model citizen, a figure several steps removed from the revered second person of the trinity."[62]

In particular, when Boston public schools called for students to recite the Ten Commandments as part of their daily religious instruction, the local Roman Catholic Bishop objected that Catholic students could not "present [themselves] before the Divine presence in what would be for [Catholics] a merely simulated union of prayer and adoration." In other words, "what for Boston's public school officials and teachers was simply a generic, unobjectionable reading from an age-old source of Christian morality, to Roman Catholics was an act of religious devotion that needed to be performed in a setting properly reserved for worship."[63] The Church would not stand for separating Christian morality from Christian spirituality in the hope of teaching Americans "the morality necessary for a republican form of government."[64]

The temptation even now to divorce the Christian faith from Christian spirituality in the name of expediency remains the same. It would certainly be easier to rent space for Sunday morning worship in government-run buildings by just downplaying the unique, spiritual elements of Christianity. But the Church rejected such a utilitarian approach to religion in the past; it should do so again. Catholics cannot call religious worship "similarly situated" to everyday, ordinary speech without quelling what makes it distinct and sacred. And that frankly would not be worship at all.

NOTES

1. See, e.g, *Bronx Household of Faith v. Board of Educ.*, 650 F.3d 30 (2d Cir. 2011), *cert. denied*, __ U.S. __,132 S. Ct. 816 (2011) (school district denying church meeting space for Sunday morning worship service); *Faith Ctr. Church Evangelistic Ministries v. Glover*, 480 F.3d 891 (9th Cir. 2007), *cert. denied*, 552 U.S. 822 (2007) (public library denying church meeting space for Sunday morning worship service); *Badger Catholic, Inc. v. Walsh*, 620 F.3d 775 (7th 2010), *cert. denied sub nom, Walsh v. Badger Catholic, Inc.*, __ U.S. __, 131 S. Ct. 1604 (2011) (university denying Catholic student group funding for worship services).

2. See, e.g., *Badger Catholic*, 620 F.3d at 776–77 (university refused to fund Catholic student group at the University of Wisconsin because its activities included "worship, proselytizing, or religious instruction"); Bob Smietana, *Anti-Bias Policies Drive Some Religious Groups off Campuses*, USA Today, April 2, 2012 (explaining how Catholic student groups are being kicked off university campuses). Catholic groups have, historically, faced opposition to celebrating the Mass in public parks. See, e.g., *Doe v. Village of Crestwood*, 917 F.2d 1476 (7th Cir. 1990) (holding that city park could bar the celebration of the Mass as part of a "Touch of Italy" festival); *O'Hair v. Andrus*, 613 F.2d 931 (D.C. Cir. 1979) (reviewing National Park Service's refusal to allow the celebration of the Mass by Pope John Paul II on the National Mall).

3. See, e.g., *Widmar v. Vincent*, 454 U.S. 283 (1981) (university must provide religious student group equal access to school facilities); *Lamb's Chapel v. Center Moriches Union Free School District*, 508 U.S. 384 (1993) (school district must provide church equal access to show religious film series in school classrooms); *Rosenberger v. Rectors & Visitors of Univ. of Va.*, 515 U.S. 819 (1995) (university must provide religious news publication equal access to student activity fee funding); *Good News Club v. Milford Central School*, 533 U.S. 98 (2001) (school must provide Christian after-school club equal access to school facilities).

4. See *Lamb's Chapel*, 508 U.S. at 394. ("The film series involved here no doubt dealt with a subject otherwise permissible . . . and its exhibition was denied solely because the series dealt with the subject from a religious standpoint.")

5. See *Good News Club*, 533 U.S. at 108.

6. The Supreme Court in *Police Dept. of the City of Chicago v. Mosley*, 408 U.S. 92 (1972), analyzed the effect of a Chicago ordinance that barred all forms of picketing except for laboring picketing. The Court explained:

> Because Chicago treats some picketing differently from others, we analyze this ordinance in terms of the Equal Protection Clause of the Fourteenth Amendment. Of course, the equal protection claim in this case is closely intertwined with First Amendment interests; the Chicago ordinance affects picketing, which is expressive conduct; moreover, it does so by classifications formulated in terms of the subject of the picketing.

Mosley, 408 U.S. at 94–95.

See also *Carey v. Brown*, 447 U.S. 455, 463 (1980) (analyzing almost identical picketing statute and stating, "Necessarily, then, under the Equal Protection Clause, not to mention the First Amendment itself, government may not grant the use of a forum to people whose views it finds acceptable, but deny use to those wishing to express less favored or more controversial views").

7. See *Good News Club*, 533 U.S. at 112 n. 4 ("[W]e conclude that the Club's activities do not constitute mere religious worship, divorced from any teaching of moral values"); *Rosenberger*, 515 U.S. at 840 (distinguishing between a news publication taking a religious editorial viewpoint, which the First Amendment requires a university to fund, and "religious organizations . . . whose purpose is to practice a devotion to an acknowledged ultimate reality or deity," which the First Amendment perhaps *allows* a university to fund but does not *require* it).

8. Pope Paul VI, *Lumen Gentium*, ¶11 (1964).

9. *Catechism of the Catholic Church*, 2nd ed., ¶1326 [hereinafter *Catechism*].

10. See *Catechism* at ¶1023–29. ("Heaven is the blessed community of all who are perfectly incorporated into Christ.")

11. U.S. Constitution, amend. XIV.

12. *Washington v. Davis*, 426 U.S. 229, 239 (1976).

13. See *Loving v. Virginia*, 388 U.S. 1, 10 (1967). ("[T]he Equal Protection Clause requires the consideration of whether the classifications drawn by any statute constitute an arbitrary and invidious discrimination.")

14. See *Brown v. Board of Education*, 347 U.S. 483 (1954).

15. See *Craig v. Boren*, 429 U.S. 190 (1976).

16. Joseph Tussman and Jacobus tenBroek, *The Equal Protection of the Laws*, 37 Cal. L. Rev. 341, 346 (1949).

17. See Tussman and tenBroek. ("The purpose of a law may be either the elimination of a public 'mischief' or the achievement of some positive public good.")

18. See *Craig*, 429 U.S. at 199–204.

19. *Catechism*, ¶1702.

20. *Catechism*, ¶1934.

21. Pope Paul VI, *Gaudium et Spes*, ¶29, § 2 (1965).

22. *Gaudium et Spes*, ¶29, § 3.

23. *Catechism*, ¶¶1936–37.

24. Michael A. Paulsen, *Religion, Equality, and the Constitution: An Equal Protection Approach to Establishment Clause Adjudication*, 61 Notre Dame L. Rev. 311, 327 (1986).

25. *Mosley*, 408 U.S. at 95; *Carey*, 447 U.S. at 462–63.

26. *R.A.V. v. City of St. Paul*, 505 U.S. 377, 384 n. 4 (1992).

27. *Mosley*, 408 U.S. at 96; see also *Carey*, 447 U.S. at 462–63.

28. Paulsen, *Religion, Equality, supra* note 24, at 328.

29. *Mosley*, 408 U.S. at 94–98.

30. *Mosley*, 408 U.S. at 100–101.

31. *Mosley*, 408 U.S. at 100.

32. *Niemotko v. Maryland*, 340 U.S. 268 (1951).

33. *Niemotko*, 340 U.S. at 272.

34. *Fowler v. Rhode Island*, 345 U.S. 67 (1953).

35. *Fowler*, 345 U.S. at 69.

36. *Fowler*, 345 U.S. at 68–69.

37. *Widmar*, 454 U.S. 263 (1981).

38. *Widmar*, 454 U.S. at 269–70.

39. *Rosenberger*, 515 U.S. at 829.

40. *Lamb's Chapel*, 508 U.S. 385.

41. *Lamb's Chapel*, 508 U.S. at 394–95.

42. *Rosenberger*, 515 U.S. 819.

43. *Rosenberger*, 515 U.S. at 832–35.

44. *Good News Club*, 533 U.S. 98.

45. *Good News Club*, 533 U.S. at 108–10.

46. *Christian Legal Society v. Martinez*, 561 U.S. __, 130 S. Ct. 2971 (2010).

47. Brief for Petitioner at 14, *Martinez*, 130 S. Ct. 2971 (No. 08–1371), 2010 WL 711183 at *14 (emphasis omitted).
48. *Martinez*, 130 S. Ct. at 2993.
49. See Ed Stetzer and Phillip Connor, *Church Plant Survivability and Health Study*, Research Report, Center for Missional Research, North American Mission Board, 7 (2007), available at http://pcamna.org/churchplanting/documents/CPMainReport.pdf. Other studies suggest that it is rare for a Roman Catholic Church to meet at a public school building. See National Congregations Study, Panel Data Set, Association of Religion Data Archives (1998 and 2006–2007), available at http://www.thearda.com/Archive/Files/Analysis/NCSPANEL/NCSPANEL_Var511_1.asp (reporting that 0 percent of Catholic Churches responded that they meet in a school).
50. See *Bronx Household of Faith*, 650 F.3d at 33–34.
51. See *Bronx Household of Faith*, 659 F.3d at 36–39.
52. *Bronx Household of Faith*, 659 F.3d at 38–39.
53. *Bronx Household of Faith*, 659 F.3d at 38–39.
54. *Bronx Household of Faith*, 659 F.3d at 51 (Calabresi, J., concurring).
55. *Bronx Household of Faith*, 659 F.3d at 39.
56. The Court in *Widmar, supra*, questioned whether government could constitutionally draw a distinction between ordinary, religious speech and religious worship. It said:

> [E]ven if the distinction drew an arguably principled line, it is highly doubtful that it would lie within the judicial competence to administer. Merely to draw the distinction would require the university—and ultimately the courts—to inquire into the significance of words and practices to different religious faiths, and in varying circumstances by the same faith. Such inquiries would tend inevitably to entangle the State with religion in a manner forbidden by our cases.

Widmar, 454 U.S. at 269–70 n. 6.

The recent religious worship cases, like *Faith Center*, *Badger Catholic*, and *Bronx Household of Faith*, do not raise these same entanglement concerns because the churches themselves identify their speech as religious worship. The churches are coming to local school districts and libraries and asking to rent facilities for the express purpose of holding Sunday morning worship services. The government, thus, has no need to troll through a church's religious speech to determine whether it qualifies as mere, religious speech as opposed to religious worship.
57. *Compendium of the Catechism of the Catholic Church*, ¶67, Q. 221 (2009).
58. 1 Corinthians 1:18 (English Standard Version).
59. 1 Corinthians 2:14 (English Standard Version).
60. United States Conference of Catholic Bishops, *General Instructions of the Roman Missal*, no. 16 (March 17, 2003).
61. D.G. Hart and John R. Muether, *With Reverence and Awe* (P & R Publishing, 2002), 34.
62. D.G. Hart, *A Secular Faith* (Ivan R. Dee, 2006), 77–83.
63. Hart, *Secular Faith* at 83–84.
64. Hart, *Secular Faith* at 78.

Chapter Eleven

United States Immigration Law and Policy Through a Catholic Lens

Michael A. Scaperlanda

The people of the United States have long had a love–hate relationship with immigrants and immigration. "Give me your tired, your poor, your huddled masses yearning to breathe free"[1] stands in stark tension with, for example, California's attempt to get Congress to exclude "Chinese laborers" because they have had "a baneful effect upon the material interests of the State, and upon public morals; that their immigration was in numbers approaching the character of an Oriental invasion, and was a menace to our civilization."[2] We are a nation of immigrants. In 1910, an estimated 14.7 percent of our population was foreign born, a century later it was 12.9 percent.[3] Yet, some immigrants are met with a less than enthusiastic welcome as evidenced by the Dillingham Commission's conclusion a century ago that Mexicans lacked "ambition and thrift."[4]

Tension abounds in the early twenty-first century as some argue for comprehensive immigration reform, including some form of amnesty for those who reside in the United States illegally. Others want piecemeal legislation beginning with border security. With respect to legal immigration, some would like to see the United States give preference to highly skilled immigrants while others emphasize family reunification.

How should Catholics frame their thinking about immigration law and policy?[5] The Catholic Church does not bind the consciences of American Catholics to adopt particular immigration policies at particular times in response to particular situations or crises. Instead, she calls us to exercise prudential judgment guided by a Catholic understanding of the human person and the role of community in forming and sustaining human persons. This

137

chapter provides the framework; I leave to the reader the task of applying it in the context of current and future immigration debates.

LIMITING THE PUSH FACTORS

"[E]migration is in some aspects evil."[6] These startling words by John Paul II strike at the heart of a Catholic anthropology. Each human person possesses an inviolable dignity, rooted in the *imago dei* and nurtured in community. In other words, people and place matter. Rather than untethered beings, human persons are born into, grow, and are in some sense bound by a particular family within a particular culture with that family's and that culture's unique history, language, and traditions. If "wines embody, and are shaped by, the places they come from—their distinctive combination of geography and climate,"[7] how much more true is that for human persons?

At the very least, emigration unsettles the ties between person and community. Gustavo Pérez Firmat's autobiographical account, *Next Year in Cuba: A Cubano's Coming of Age in America*, describes refugees as

> amputees. Someone who goes into exile abandons not just possessions but a part of himself. . . . Just as people who lose limbs sometimes continue to ache or tingle in the missing calf or hand, the exile suffers the absence of the self he left behind. I feel the loss of that Cuban boy inside me. He's my phantom limb, at times dogging me like a guilty thought, at other times accompanying me like a guardian angel.[8]

John Paul II describes the loss to the community left behind: "[T]he departure of a person who is also a member of a great community united by history, tradition and culture. . . . [I]t is the loss of a subject of work, whose efforts of mind and body could contribute to the common good of his own country, but these efforts, this contribution, are instead offered to another society which in a sense has less right to them than the person's country of origin."[9]

Given the connectedness of person to place, the first pillar of sound immigration policy lies outside of what is traditionally viewed as immigration law and policy: limiting the factors pushing people to emigrate. Inability to flourish due to lack of economic or educational opportunity, political instability, persecution or oppression, famine, and violence or civil war cause individuals and families to uproot and seek a better life elsewhere. As the Bishops of Mexico and the United States said: "[P]ersons should have the opportunity to remain in their homeland to support and to find full lives for themselves and their families. This is the ideal situation for which the world and both countries must strive."[10]

It is too much to expect that push factors will be eliminated. Desperate individuals and families will flee their homes in search of a better life. [11] How should we respond?

OPENNESS TO THE IMMIGRANT

"All social life is an expression of its unmistakable protagonist: the human person." [12] Part of this drama is human migration both voluntary and forced. In 2012, over forty-five million people "were forcibly displaced worldwide a result of persecution, conflict, generalized violence, and/or human rights violations." [13] Add to this, economic refugees who cannot adequately support themselves or their families and the magnitude of the issue takes shape. Many of these displaced persons can and do return to their homes once the cause of the displacement passes. How should the United States respond to those who end up at our doorstep seeking a new life in the United States?

Each human person has an inherent dignity, which all are bound to recognize and accept across cultures and national boundaries. As the Catechism states, "[b]eing made in the image of God the human individual possesses the dignity of a person, who is not just a something, but someone." [14] Because of our common origin in God, "the human race forms a unity," [15] and in solidarity we must pursue the common good recognizing that "we are *all* really responsible *for all*." [16] One way that we pursue the good in common is to recognize the universal destination of goods; that is, to recognize that all goods, even goods that belong to me or the people of the United States, must be used for the benefit of all. [17]

With this general understanding, we can begin to sketch an answer. Part of contributing to the common good is for each person, family, entity, and nation to take care of its own obligations. Toward this end, the state has an obligation to serve the common good by putting in place institutions, structures, and laws that create rightly ordered liberty, supplying the conditions for "integral human growth." [18] Therefore, sovereign states have a *qualified* right to limit immigration, especially where immigration would threaten the goods held in common by the civil society of the nation. [19] But, where civil society would not be threatened by immigration, the sovereign has a *duty* to admit those who seek entry if they cannot flourish in their countries of origin. "When there are just reasons in favor of it, he must be permitted to emigrate to other countries and take up residence there." [20] In short, state sovereignty "cannot be exaggerated to the point that access to this land is, for inadequate or unjustified reasons, denied to needy and decent people from other nations, provided of course, that the public wealth, considered very carefully, does not forbid this." [21]

Not surprisingly, Catholic social teaching corresponds with the older notions of international law with its natural law underpinnings. Quoting Leviticus and referencing Popes Pius XII and Paul VI, James Nafziger points out: "Before the late 19th century, there was little, in principle, to support the absolute exclusion of aliens. . . . Biblical injunctions, which influenced the articulation of international law by 17th- and 18th-century publicists, favored free transboundary movement."[22] With a thicker understanding of the common good and the universal destination of goods than is generally accepted today, seventeenth and eighteenth century scholars, including Hugo Grotius, Francisco de Vitoria, Christian Wolff, Samuel Pufendorf, and Emer de Vattel, all recognized a duty to admit foreigners who "had lawful reasons, including economic ones, for seeking admission," unless the entry of said aliens would cause grave danger to the commonwealth.[23]

Faithful Catholics in the United States will come to different prudential judgments about when the admission of aliens creates grave danger to civil society and the goods we hold in common as a country. As the earth's number one economy, we must, however, heed the words of the bishops of the United States and Mexico: "More powerful economic nations, which have the ability to protect and feed their residents, have a stronger obligation to accommodate migration flows."[24] Therefore, the burden is on those who argue for restrictive immigration laws to provide adequate reasons for their position.[25] But, what about the undocumented who have entered the United States without permission or who have overstayed their visas?

WHAT ABOUT THE UNDOCUMENTED?

The Department of Homeland Security estimates that 11.5 million unauthorized immigrants lived in the United States in January of 2011.[26] This is not a good thing.[27] As Father Hesburgh, then president of the University of Notre Dame, said nearly thirty years ago, illegal immigration should be brought under control.[28] Without proper papers, the illegal migrant lives in the shadows, fearful of deportation and subject to exploitation by employers and others. Without labor market tests, some of the undocumented might be taking jobs from the neediest among us or depressing wages for vulnerable workers authorized to work in the United States. National security and rule of law concerns, both real and imagined, shape a national narrative of suspicion toward aliens generally. Closing the "back door" of illegal immigration, if possible, creates optimal conditions to allow the "front door" of legal migration to remain healthy and open.[29]

We do not live in utopia, and the fact remains that millions of people live and will continue to live in the United States without authorization. Should the law tolerate aid and comfort to those who are here without permission from the United States government? And, should we consider some form of amnesty for these unauthorized immigrants?

The first question is easy to answer; absolutely, the law ought to tolerate individuals and faith communities in ministering to the undocumented. With Congress' inability to reform our nation's immigration laws and stem the tide of illegal migration, states began to take matters into their own hands, with some states making it illegal to transport, conceal, harbor, or shelter the undocumented.[30] The United States Conference of Catholic Bishops has listed these laws as one of many threats to religious liberty in the United States.[31] In response to an Oklahoma law, then Archbishop Beltran and several members of the clergy responded with a letter to the governor: "Our faith tradition instructs us to do good to all peoples. There is no exemption clause for those persons who do not have documentation or their citizenship status. We will not show partiality to those who are in need of humanitarian assistance."[32]

Now to the second question: Should we consider some form of amnesty for those who reside here without the state's permission? When I speak about the possibility of amnesty for undocumented aliens, particularly to certain Christian audiences, I encounter two responses: "Illegal" aliens are line jumpers and lawbreakers.

Many of the interlocutors argue that "illegal" entrants are line jumpers, cutting in front of those who have waited patiently to enter the United States legally.[33] They argue that fairness dictates making the "illegal" immigrant leave the United States and go to the back of the line. In reality, no line exists. Aliens can immigrate to the United States based on certain family ties or employment prospects. Within employment immigration, the United States only allows 10,000 unskilled workers to immigrate to the United States annually. If the United States created a line just for the 11.5 million illegal aliens residing in the United States in January 2011 and allowed 10,000 to immigrate a year, the one millionth would be eligible to receive a visa in the year 2111 and the ten millionth in the year 3011.[34]

The second objection rests on the illegality of the alien's presence in the United States. Prooftexting scripture, Arizona Christian University's president, Len Munsil, argues that "[t]hose who violate our immigration laws by jumping the fence are, in essence, stealing rights of citizenship (to live and work in America) and, in essence, coveting and stealing their neighbors' property."[35] These arguments lack the sophistication and nuance that St. Thomas Aquinas brings to the issue.

Aquinas recognizes that a person's "superabundance is due, by natural law, to the purpose of succoring the poor." Since "[i]n the cases of need all things are common property," if a person's "need be so manifest and urgent . . . then it is lawful for a man to succor his own need by means of another's property by taking it either openly or secretly: nor is this properly speaking theft or robbery."[36] Five hundred years later, Vattel reiterated Aquinas's conclusion: "The earth was designed to feed its inhabitants; and he who is in want of everything is not obliged to starve, because all property is vested in others. . . . Extreme necessity revives the primitive communion, the abolition of which ought to deprive no person of the necessaries of life. . . . The same right belongs to individuals, when a foreign nations [*sic*] refuses them a just assistance."[37]

Many unauthorized immigrants are lawbreakers only in the sense of evading a broken immigration system by risking their lives and fortunes to seek a better life for themselves and their families in the United States. "[T]hey are lawless in the way that Jean Valjean is lawless in 'Les Misérables,' stealing bread to feed his family."[38]

How the law ought to respond, and whether the response ought to include a form of amnesty for some or all of those residing in the United States without permission, requires the exercise of prudential judgment. In formulating our judgments, the Catholic perspective calls us to make a vital distinction between positive law and natural law in assessing the wrongness or illegality on the part of the unauthorized immigrant. Additionally, a Catholic analysis ought to begin with the attitude of the bishop responding in mercy and love to Valjean rather than that of Inspector Javert who spent his energy and resources—indeed his very life—chasing a bread thief in the pursuit of a cold and rigid justice.

CONCLUSION: SHAPING IMMIGRATION LAW AND POLICY

For a Catholic, indeed for any Christian, the starting point for developing immigration law and policy must be the human face—the suffering face of the human person yearning to build a life for himself and his family. Seeing the face of Christ in the person of the immigrant and refugee is not the end point but must be the starting point. As Pope Pius XII taught:

> The émigré Holy Family of Nazareth, fleeing into Egypt, is the archetype of every refugee family. Jesus, Mary and Joseph, living in exile in Egypt to escape the fury of an evil king, are, for all times and places, the models and protectors of every migrant, alien and refugee of whatever kind who, whether compelled by fear of persecution or by want, is forced to leave his native land, his beloved parents and relatives, his close friends, and to seek a foreign soil.[39]

In the immigration context and with the Holy Family in mind, Pope Francis calls us to a "culture of encounter" and away "from attitudes of defensiveness and fear, indifference and marginalization—all typical of a throwaway culture."[40]

With this starting point, I conclude this chapter with a brief sketch of my own judgments on some of the most pressing immigration issues of our day and leave to the reader a determination of whether these judgments show prudence.

With respect to legal immigration, current United States immigration law places a higher priority on family unity than the needs or desires of the labor market. As a result, 670,000 people became permanent residents of the United States in 2012 based upon family connections while only 144,000 immigrated based upon employment skills.[41] By prioritizing the unity of the family, United States immigration law and policy is in accord with a Catholic understanding of the human person and her relationship with the world. Family unity is important for the person because "[i]t is in the family that children learn their first and most important lessons of practical wisdom, to which the virtues are connected."[42] Family unity is also important for society: "A society built on a family scale is the best guarantee against drifting off course into individualism or collectivism, because within the family the person is always at the centre of attention as an end and never as a means."[43]

Pressure has been building to diminish or reverse this ratio, placing greater emphasis on attracting workers to build the United States economy.[44] This movement, which reduces persons to human capital, giving priority to *homo economicus*, should be resisted in favor of a policy rooted in anthropological foundations that understand the person as body, mind, soul, and spirit living in community and contributing to that community in ways that go beyond economic potential. And, although "initial differences in earnings between family-based and employment-based immigrants" exist, these differences "tend to narrow dramatically over time."[45]

For the most part, illegal migration presents a messier problem. But first, two issues with easy answers. The law ought to respect the right and the duty of the Church and its members to minister to all persons regardless of immigration status or religious affiliation. It would be unjust of the state to threaten to punish Christians for following the dictates of Matthew 25 in feeding the hungry, welcoming the stranger, clothing the naked, etc. Congress also ought to enact what has become known as the DREAM Act, granting amnesty to the undocumented immigrants who were brought to the United States as children.[46]

The United States must devise a way to successfully stem the tide of unauthorized migration. Two measures, beyond border security, can aid in this effort. Since most undocumented migrants come to the United States for work, sanctioning employers who hire unauthorized workers should decrease unauthorized immigration. To be effective, the sanctions must be heavy enough that businesses do not consider them merely a cost of doing business; the system must be structured in such a way that the employer cannot plausibly claim that it did not know that its employees lacked authorization, and the government must devote the resources necessary to ensure compliance. Given the government's poor track record with enforcing existing employer sanctions, I am skeptical that the United States has the political will to address this problem.

In addition to employer sanctions, the United States should expand the availability of nonimmigrant "guest-worker" visas in a way that ebbs and flows with the economy. When the supply of available workers who are authorized to seek employment in the United States equals the demand, the employment of unauthorized workers should decrease, especially as the probability of real sanctions increases. Two features of a guest-worker program are essential. First, the law ought to allow the worker employment mobility. Without mobility, an abused employee faces two choices, continued suffering under the abusive employer or quitting and being forced to leave the country. Second, the guest worker ought to be allowed only a short stay in the United States or a path to eventual citizenship. I am ambivalent between these options, but the option that should be avoided is long term guest-workers who only develop shallow roots in the community.

Even if we stem the tide of future undocumented immigration, the question remains what to do about the eleven million plus people currently residing in the United States without authorization. A path to legalization should be made available to many if not most of them. As amnesty critic, Andrew McCarthy, said during the immigration debates late in the second term of President George W. Bush:

> To be clear, no one should say the status of illegal immigrants should be off the table. There is an unavoidable human aspect to this. The equities are such that compelling some illegal aliens to leave at this point would be unduly harsh—many have been here for a decade or more, have strong community ties, and no longer have any meaningful connection to their native lands. There is no good reason to target such people at this point. [47]

This does not require strict amnesty and could involve the payment of a fine, a longer path to citizenship, or other similar measures.

In sum, many complex factors enter into the immigration law and policy equation. A Catholic perspective provides a few concrete answers but leaves most of the field to the exercise of prudential judgment within a framework that sees the value and dignity of each person and the importance of family and community to human flourishing.

NOTES

1. Emma Lazarus, *The New Colossus*, Statue of Liberty National Monument, available at http://www.libertystatepark.com/emma.htm.
2. See *Chae Chan Ping v. U.S.*, 130 U.S. 581, 595 (1889).

3. United States Census Bureau, "How Do We Know? America's Foreign Born in the Last 50 Years," available at http://www.census.gov/how/infographics /foreign_born.html (accessed March 14, 2014).

4. See United States Congress Joint Immigration Commission [Dillingham Commission], *Reports of the Immigration Commission*, Vol. 1 (1911), 683.

5. For a different emphasis on the same question, see Michael Scaperlanda, "Immigration Justice: A Catholic Christian" in *Recovering Self-Evident Truths: Catholic Perspectives on American Law*, ed., Michael Scaperlanda and Teresa S. Collett (CUA Press, 2007). See also Michael Scaperlanda, *Aliens, Pilgrims, and Solidarity: Reflections in the Mirror*, 9 Regent J. Int'l. L. 1 (2012); Michael Scaperlanda, *Religious Freedom in the Face of Harsh State and Local Immigration Laws*, 5 Tulsa J. Comp. & Int'l. L. 165 (2008); William Chip and Michael Scaperlanda, "The Ethics of Immigration: An Exchange," *First Things* (May 2008); Michael Scaperlanda, *Reflections on Immigration Reform, the Workplace and the Family*, 4 U. St. Thomas L. J. 508 (2007); Michael Scaperlanda, *Immigration and Evil: The Religious Challenge*, 83 U. Det. Mercy L. Rev. 835 (2006); and Michael Scaperlanda, *Who Is My Neighbor? An Essay on Immigrants, Welfare Reform and the Constitution*, 29 Conn. L. Rev. 1587 (1997).

6. Pope John Paul II, *Laborem Excercens*, ¶23 (1981). For a more complete treatment of this, see Scaperlanda, *Immigration and Evil, supra* note 5.

7. Wine Spectator Maps of Wine Regions, available at http://www.wine spectator.com/webfeature/show/id/42427.

8. Gustavo Pérez Firmat, *Next Year in Cuba: A Cubano's Coming of Age in America* (New York: Doubleday, 1995), 22. Although Firmat distinguishes between the "immigrant" and the person in "exile," I suspect that the loss, even if not as pronounced, is felt by the immigrant as well.

9. *Laborem Excercens*, ¶23.1.

10. United States Conference of Catholic Bishops [USCCB], *Strangers No Longer: Together on the Journey of Hope, A Pastoral Letter Concerning Migration from the Catholic Bishops of Mexico and the United States*, ¶59 (2003). See also Pope Francis, "Message for the World Day of Migrants and Refugees," August 5, 2013, available at http://www.vatican.va/holy_father/francesco/messages/migration/documents/papa-fran cesco_20130805_world-migrants-day_en.html (accessed March 14, 2014). ("[C]ooperation [among nations] begins with the efforts of each country to create better economic and social conditions at home, so that emigration will not be the only option left for those who seek peace, justice, security and full respect of their human dignity.")

11. See e.g., *Dying to Live: A Migrant's Journey*. Film synopsis available at http://dyingtolive.nd.edu/.

12. Pontifical Council for Justice and Peace, *Compendium of the Social Doctrine of the Church*, ¶106 (2004) [hereinafter *Compendium*].

13. United Nations High Commissioner for Refugees [UNHCR], *2012 Statistical Yearbook*, available at http://www.unhcr.org/52a722559.html (including 28.8 million internally displaced people).

14. *Catechism of the Catholic Church*, ¶357 [hereinafter *Catechism*].

15. *Catechism* at ¶360.

16. *Compendium*, ¶193 (emphasis in original).

17. *Catechism* at ¶¶171–84.

18. *Catechism* at ¶394.

19. See *Strangers No Longer*, ¶36, *supra* note 10.

20. Pope John XXIII, *Pacem in Terris*, ¶25 (1963).

21. Pope Pius XII, *Exsul Familia Nazarethana* (Apostolic Constitution) (1952) *quoting* letter to American bishops (December 24, 1948), available at http://www.papal encyclicals.net /Pius12/p12exsul.htm (accessed March 14, 2014).

22. James Nafziger, *The General Admission of Aliens Under International Law*, 77 Am. J. Int'l. Law 804, 809 (1983).

23. See Nafziger, *General Admission of Aliens* at 810–14.

24. See *Strangers No Longer*, ¶38, *supra* note 10.

25. *Cf. Exsul Familia Nazarethana, supra* note 21.

26. Department of Homeland Security, Office of Immigration Statistics, *Estimates of the Unauthorized Immigrant Population Residing in the United States: January 2011*, Michael Hoefer, et al. (March 2012), available at https://www.dhs.gov/sites/default/files/publications/ois_ill_pe_2011.pdf (accessed March 14, 2014).

27. See Scaperlanda, *Reflections on Immigration Reform, supra* note 5, at 523–25 and Beth Lyon, *When More "Security" Equals Less Workplace Safety: Reconsidering U.S. Laws That Disadvantage Unauthorized Workers*, 6 U. Pa. J. Lab. & Emp. L. 571, 595–96 (2004).

28. Immigration Reform and Control Act of 1985: Hearings before the Senate Subcomm. on Immigration and Refugee Policy of the Senate Comm. on the Judiciary, 99th Cong. (1985) (statement of Rev. Theodore Hesburgh, Chairman of the Select Commission on Immigration and Refugee Policy predicating the Commission's recommendation for amnesty "on one condition: that somehow the sieve that we call a border could be tightened up, that somehow we would bring our illegal immigration under control").

29. *Cf.* H.R. Rep. No. 99-682(I), at 46 (1986), *reprinted in* 1986 U.S.C.C.A.N. 5649–50.

30. See e.g., Scaperlanda, *Religious Freedom, supra* note 5.

31. USCCB, *Our First, Most Cherished Liberty: A Statement on Religious Liberty* (2012), available at http://www.usccb.org/issues-and-action/religious-liberty/upload/Our-First-Most-Cherished-Liberty-Apr12-6-12-12.pdf (accessed March 14, 2014).

32. Letter from Council of Priests, Archdiocese of Oklahoma City to Governor of Oklahoma Brad Henry, *Pledge of Resistance*, available at http://sites.saintmarys.edu/~incandel/resistance-pledge.pdf. ("Because this law is overly punitive and makes a felony of the act of providing humanitarian assistance to an undocumented person in need; we the undersigned clergy, religious leaders, and lay people of conscience will not and can not obey this law. We will continue to aid and assist all people regardless of their legal citizenship status, with charitable care and spiritual counsel.") See also Michael Scaperlanda, "Immigration and the Bishops," *First Things* (February 2008), available at http://www.firstthings.com/article/2008/01/003-immigration-and-the-bishops-9 (accessed March 14, 2014).

33. e.g., Len Munsil, *Justice and Compassion: Applying Biblical Truth to the Problem of Illegal Immigration*, 9 Reg. J. Int'l. L. 11, 17–18 (2012).

34. Scaperlanda, *Aliens, Pilgrims, and Solidarity, supra* note 5, at 7.

35. Munsil, *Justice and Compassion, supra* note 33, at 17. "Everyone is to obey the governing authorities. For there is no authority that is not from God, and the existing authorities have been placed where they are by God. Therefore, whoever resists the authorities is resisting what God has instituted. . . . But if you do what is wrong, be afraid! Because it is not for nothing that he holds the power of the sword; for he is God's servant, there as an avenger to punish wrongdoers." Munsil at 15 (quoting Romans 13:1–4).

36. Thomas Aquinas, *Summa Theologica* II-II, Question 66, Article 7 (Fathers of the English Dominican Province trans., Christian Classics, 1981). See also Scaperlanda, *Aliens, Pilgrims, and Solidarity, supra* note 5, at 8.

37. Emer de Vattel, *The Law of Nations*, ed. J. Chitty (1839), § 120 at 178, *quoted in* Nafziger, *General Admission of Aliens, supra* note 22 at 814.

38. Scaperlanda, *Aliens, Pilgrims, and Solidarity, supra* note 5, at 7.

39. *Exsul Familia Nazarethana.*

40. Pope Francis, "Message for the World Day of Migrants," *supra* note 10.

41. See Department of Homeland Security, Office of Immigration Statistics, *Yearbook of Immigration Statistics 2012*, available at https://www.dhs.gov/yearbook-immigration-statistics-2012-legal-permanent-residents (accessed March 14, 2014).

42. *Compendium* at ¶210.

43. *Compendium* at ¶213.

44. See generally Associated Press, "Immigration Reform in the Senate looks at family-based vs. employment-based immigrants," *Patriot-News*, February 19, 2013.

45. Immigration Policy Center, "The Advantages of Family-Based Immigration," March 14, 2013, available at http://www.immigrationpolicy.org/just-facts/advantages-family-based-immigration (accessed March 14, 2014).

46. See Michael Scaperlanda, "DREAM Act Would Align Immigration Policy with U.S. Legal Culture," *Our Sunday Visitor*, December 8, 2010.

47. Andrew McCarthy, "Close the Immigration Vault with Employer Enforcement," National Review Online, March 5, 2007, available at http://www.nationalreview.com/articles/220172/close-immigration-vault-employer-enforcement/andrew-c-mccarthy (accessed March 14, 2014).

Chapter Twelve

Human Dignity and the Death Penalty

Comparing Catholic Social Teaching and Eighth Amendment Jurisprudence

Dorie Klein

INTRODUCTION

At the heart of Catholic social teaching is the belief that every person possesses an inherent human dignity. A belief in inherent human dignity also underlies the Eighth Amendment to the U.S. Constitution, which bans "cruel and unusual punishments." In modern times, especially since the 1995 encyclical *Evangelium Vitae* of Pope John Paul II, the Catholic Church has stood strongly against the imposition of death as a criminal punishment, even for those convicted of the most heinous crimes. The Eighth Amendment also has, in recent years, served as the basis for U.S. Supreme Court decisions ruling that the death penalty is an excessive, and therefore unconstitutional, punishment, at least as applied to certain offenders and for certain offenses.

This chapter explores the commonalities between Catholic social teaching and Eighth Amendment jurisprudence regarding the death penalty in general and, more specifically, regarding respect for human dignity as a ground for opposing the death penalty. The first part presents a brief discussion of the Catholic Church's opposition to the death penalty as presented in the Catechism, the *Evangelium Vitae* of Pope John Paul II, and statements of the U.S. Conference of Catholic Bishops. The belief expressed in these sources that all human life is created by God in the image of God and as such possesses inherent dignity establishes the foundation for the Church's opposition to the death penalty.

The second part focuses on recent decisions of the U.S. Supreme Court ruling that the death penalty is a "cruel and unusual punishment" and therefore prohibited by the Eighth Amendment. Historically, many Eighth Amendment decisions include rhetorical references to human dignity but do not translate that rhetoric into decisions that actually limit the application of the death penalty. In recent years, though, the Supreme Court has in a handful of cases ruled that the death penalty is unconstitutional for certain offenders and for certain offenses. While these cases do not adopt the position advocated by the Church—the position that the death penalty is a violation of human dignity—these cases do offer hope that the Supreme Court is perhaps moving toward an understanding of the Eighth Amendment which recognizes that the death penalty is inconsistent with respect for human dignity.

CATHOLIC SOCIAL TEACHING AND THE DEATH PENALTY

In the past several decades, the Catholic Church has become a strong and influential voice in opposition to the death penalty. The Church's involvement in the death penalty debate is motivated by the belief that every human person possesses an inherent human dignity. This dignity results from having been created by God, in God's image. Because every person exists in a relationship with God, it is a violation of the moral order for the state to kill any person for the purpose of punishing that person. The Church concedes, at least for the purpose of argument, that killing a (guilty) person would be permitted if it were the only way to save the lives of other people. Yet this concession does not detract from the absolute position that killing a person for the sole purpose of punishing that person is not permitted.

The Church's opposition to the death penalty is presented in numerous sources, including the 1995 encyclical *Evangelium Vitae* (*The Gospel of Life*) of Pope John Paul II, the Catechism, and several statements of the U.S. Conference of Catholic Bishops.[1] In his encyclical, Pope John Paul II presents an extended argument in favor of the "culture of life" and against the "culture of death." The starting point for this argument is the belief in "the incomparable worth of the human person."[2] This "incomparable worth" exists because of each person's relationship to God: "Man is called to a fullness of life which far exceeds the dimensions of his earthly existence, because it consists in sharing the very life of God."[3] Accepting that all people possess an inherent worth because of their relationship with God is the foundation of the "culture of life."

> Why is life a good? This question is found everywhere in the Bible, and from the very first pages it receives a powerful and amazing answer. The life which God gives man is quite different from the life of all other living creatures, inasmuch as man, although formed from the dust of the earth, is a manifesta-

tion of God in the world, a sign of his presence, a trace of his glory. This is what Saint Irenaeus of Lyons wanted to emphasize in his celebrated definition: "Man, living man, is the glory of God." Man has been given a sublime dignity, based on the intimate bond which unites him to his Creator: in man there shines forth a reflection of God himself.[4]

The death penalty is part of what the Pope terms a "culture of death." Respect for the inherent dignity of all people allows the state to take a (guilty) human life only when no other means exists to protect the lives of other people. Thus, criminal punishment "ought not go to the extreme of executing the offender except in cases of absolute necessity: in other words, when it would not be possible otherwise to defend society."[5] In support of this conclusion, the Pope quotes the 1995 Catechism: "If bloodless means are sufficient to defend human lives against an aggressor and to protect public order and the safety of persons, public authority must limit itself to such means, because they better correspond to the concrete conditions of the common good and are more in conformity to the dignity of the human person."[6]

Because of the effectiveness of modern prisons, the cases in which the bloodless means of incarceration cannot protect society are rare, if they exist at all. The Catechism, revised in 1997 to reflect Pope John Paul II's teachings in *Evanglium Vitae*, explains that because "of the possibilities which the state has for effectively preventing crime, by rendering one who has committed an offense incapable of doing harm—without definitely taking away from him the possibility of redeeming himself—the cases in which the execution of the offender is an absolute necessity 'are very rare, if not practically nonexistent.'"[7]

The U.S. Conference of Catholic Bishops has issued several extensive statements explaining its opposition to the death penalty. For example, the 2005 document, *A Culture of Life and the Penalty of Death*, argues,

> Each of us is called to respect the life and dignity of every human being. Even when people deny the dignity of others, we must still recognize that their dignity is a gift from God and is not something that is earned or lost through their behavior. Respect for life applies to all, even the perpetrators of terrible acts. Punishment should be consistent with the demands of justice and with respect for human life and dignity.[8]

This belief that the dignity of all people is a grounds for opposing the death penalty is consistent with the bishops' 1980 *Statement on Capital Punishment*, which argues, "It is the recognition of the dignity of all human beings that has impelled the Church to minister to the needs of the outcast and the rejected and that should make us unwilling to treat the lives of even those who have taken human life as expendable or as a means to some further end."[9]

Dorie Klein

[handwritten: When the court determines Death Pen is cruel and unusual]

The Church thus stands firmly against the death penalty, believing that imposing death as a punishment for criminal acts denies the human dignity that is inherent in every person. The U.S. Supreme Court, meanwhile, has issued decisions in recent death penalty cases that offer hope that in assessing the constitutionality of the death penalty the Court might in the not-so-distant future come to agree that imposing death as a criminal punishment is inconsistent with respect for human dignity.[10]

[handwritten: ① means ② SCOPE ③ Inad. Trial Procedure]

THE EIGHTH AMENDMENT AND THE DEATH PENALTY

The Eighth Amendment of the U.S. Constitution prohibits "cruel and unusual punishments." Part of what this prohibition means is that states must respect the human dignity of those it punishes. According to the U.S. Supreme Court, "The basic concept underlying the Eighth Amendment is nothing less than the dignity of man."[11] The dignity that underlies the Eighth Amendment is dignity that the state must respect in all of its subjects. As Justice Brennan explains in his concurring opinion in *Furman v. Georgia*, the 1972 case that invalidated all then-existing death penalty statutes, "The Cruel and Unusual Punishments Clause prohibits the infliction of uncivilized and inhuman punishments. The State, even as it punishes, must treat its members with respect for their intrinsic worth as human beings. A punishment is 'cruel and unusual,' therefore, if it does not comport with human dignity."[12]

For the Church, the conclusion that the death penalty is a violation of the moral order follows closely from the belief that all people, even those who have committed horrendous crimes, possess an inherent human dignity. For the Supreme Court, what the Eighth Amendment's embrace of inherent human dignity means for the death penalty is not nearly so straightforward. The Court as a whole has never concluded that the death penalty is always "cruel and unusual"; in cases where the Court has ruled that the death penalty is unconstitutional, the decisions have all been limited in scope, to prohibiting or requiring certain ways of implementing the death penalty, or to excluding certain offenders or certain offenses from eligibility for the death penalty. Even those individual Supreme Court justices who have concluded that the death penalty should in all cases be ruled unconstitutional have based their conclusions on a mix of moral as well as practical considerations. For example, Justice Blackmun's famous 1994 assertion "I no longer shall tinker with the machinery of death" was based primarily on his determination that no set of procedures for administering the death penalty could "eliminate arbitrariness while preserving fairness."[13]

For many years, death penalty commentators complained that the Supreme Court's death penalty jurisprudence was overburdened with procedural requirements yet lacking in substantive limitations.[14] For example, the

[handwritten: 4. REHAB 5. SELF DEFENSES]

Court had decided cases concerning the selection of jurors in death penalty cases,[15] the presentation of mitigating evidence at the sentencing phase,[16] and the specification of aggravating factors that could warrant imposing the death penalty,[17] yet the Court had largely avoided addressing the substantive appropriateness of death as a punishment.

In 2002, however, the Court took a sharp turn toward substantive regulation of the death penalty in *Atkins v. Virginia,* ruling that death was a "disproportionate" and therefore "cruel and unusual" punishment for the crime of murder when the offender was mentally retarded. The Court had previously held, in the 1976 case *Gregg v. Georgia,* that the death penalty must be reserved for the "worst of the worst" offenders.[18] The Court in *Atkins* reasoned that because of their cognitive deficits, people with mental retardation were less culpable for their criminal acts and thus could not be among those "worst of the worst" offenders who were eligible for the death penalty.[19]

Atkins certainly does not declare that the death penalty is an excessive punishment for all offenders. Yet in assessing the potential of the Eighth Amendment to perhaps one day be a source of such a declaration, *Atkins* is a giant step forward. In particular, the Court's willingness to apply its own independent judgment, rather than afford uncritical deference to state legislative judgments as is its general practice regarding the proportionality of criminal punishments,[20] provides a basis for hoping that a continued examination of the death penalty might lead the Court to decide that the death penalty is in all cases "cruel and unusual."[21]

Cases subsequent to *Atkins* further fuel such a hope. In the 2005 case *Roper v. Simmons,* the Court again relies on its "independent assessment" to decide that the death penalty is a "cruel and unusual" punishment for people who commit their crimes when they are juveniles.[22] The Court reasons that like people with mental retardation, juveniles lack certain psychological abilities and are therefore less culpable for their crimes. Additionally, juveniles' personalities are still developing, making reformation more likely.

Although the Court's opinion is limited to juvenile offenders, the Court's rejection of the death penalty in part on the grounds that it forecloses the possibility of reformation could logically apply to adult offenders as well. Even if it is true that "a greater possibility exists that a minor's character deficiencies will be reformed,"[23] certainly some possibility exists that adults' character deficiencies will be reformed.[24] Moreover, the Court writes, "When a juvenile offender commits a heinous crime, the State can exact forfeiture of some of the most basic liberties, but the State cannot extinguish his life and his potential to attain a mature understanding of his own humanity."[25] But the harm that comes from denying an offender the opportunity to "attain a mature understanding of his own humanity"—what the Church might view as the opportunity for repentance and reconciliation[26] —is of course a harm that is potentially experienced by all whom the state executes.

The Court further explores the moral consequences of the death penalty in the 2007 case *Panetti v. Quarterman,* which concerns the standard for mental competency to be executed.[27] In this case, the Court rules that it is "cruel and unusual" to execute a person who lacks a "rational understanding" of the reasons for his execution. Among the reasons that the Court offers for its ruling are "the natural abhorrence civilized societies feel at killing one who has no capacity to come to grips with his own conscience or deity" and the observation that "it is uncharitable to dispatch an offender into another world, when he is not of a capacity to fit himself for it."[28] The Court expressly limits its decision to those offenders whose understanding is compromised by a psychotic disorder. Still, the Court's detailed recognition of specific moral consequences of an execution—consequences that are not logically limited to those who are psychotic—is perhaps a reason to hope that the Court will someday conclude that all executions are "abhorrent" and "uncharitable" denials of offenders' inherent humanity.

In its most recent substantive death penalty case—*Kennedy v. Louisiana,* decided in 2008—the Supreme Court rules that the death penalty is an excessive punishment for an offense that does not cause, and was not intended to cause, the death of the victim. The Court again explores the moral implications of the decision whether to allow the death penalty, observing that "[t]he standard of extreme cruelty is not merely descriptive, but necessarily embodies a moral judgment"[29] and that "[e]volving standards of decency must embrace and express respect for the dignity of the person, and the punishment of criminals must conform to that rule."[30] The Court also again discusses the harm of foreclosing the possibility of reformation, reasoning that "[i]n most cases justice is not better served by terminating the life of the perpetrator rather than confining him and preserving the possibility that he and the system will find ways to allow him to understand the enormity of his offense."[31]

As in *Simmons* and *Panetti,* the Court has recognized an appropriate reason for ruling that the death penalty is unconstitutional—the desirability of preserving the possibility that the offender will come to "understand the enormity of his offense"—but has unnecessarily and perhaps even illogically limited the application of this reason. An offender who has committed murder likely has, as the *Kennedy* Court concludes, caused a more grievous harm than an offender who has committed any other crime, but the possibility of his reformation does not matter any less, and might in fact matter more, because of the enormity of his crime.

CONCLUSION

Human dignity informs both Catholic social teaching and Eighth Amendment jurisprudence regarding the death penalty. According to the Church, all people possess an inherent dignity, because they are created by God in God's image and exist always in a relationship with God. Respect for this inherent human dignity means that the death penalty can be justified only when no other way exists to protect the lives of other people. Human dignity also underlies the Eighth Amendment's ban on "cruel and unusual punishments." In the view of the U.S. Supreme Court, states must not impose punishments that deny the human dignity of their subjects. This view of human dignity has not (yet?) caused the Court to rule that the death penalty is in all cases unconstitutional. In some of its recent death penalty cases, however, the Court has drawn upon not only the broad principle of respect for human dignity but also more specific moral concepts, particularly the desirability of allowing for the possibility of reformation, to rule that the death penalty is unconstitutional as applied to certain offenses and certain offenders. Although the Court's position is still a long way from the Church's, these recent cases offer hope that the Court is moving in the right direction.

NOTES

1. This chapter accepts that the Church's current teachings regarding the death penalty are consistent with tradition. The precise contours of the relationship of the current teachings to tradition are controversial. For an in-depth discussion of the death penalty within the Christian tradition, see James J. Megivern, *The Death Penalty: An Historical and Theological Survey* (Mahwah, NJ: Paulist Press, 1997).

2. Pope John Paul II, *Evangelium Vitae: Encyclical Letter on the Value and Inviolability of Human Life*, ¶2 (March 25, 1995).

3. *Evangelium Vitae*, ¶2.

4. *Evangelium Vitae*, ¶34.

5. *Evangelium Vitae*, ¶56.

6. *Evangelium Vitae*, ¶56 (*quoting Catechism of the Catholic Church*, ¶2267 [1995]) [hereinafter *Catechism*].

7. *Catechism*, ¶2266 (1997) (*quoting* Pope John Paul II, *Evangelium Vitae*, ¶56 [1995]).

8. U.S. Conference of Catholic Bishops [hereinafter USCCB]. *A Culture of Life and the Penalty of Death: A Statement of the United States Conference of Catholic Bishops Calling for an End to the Death Penalty* (2005), 11, available at http://www.usccb.org/issues-and-action/human-life-and-dignity/death-penalty-capital-punishment/upload/penaltyofdeath.pdf.

9. USCCB, *Statement on Capital Punishment* (1980), available at http://www.usccb.org/issues-and-action/human-life-and-dignity/death-penalty-capital-punishment/statement-on-capital-punishment.cfm.

10. This is not to argue that any direct causal connection exists between the Church's position and the Supreme Court's decisions. Such a connection is possible, of course; however, the goals of this chapter are simply to explore how far apart the Church and the Court are and to suggest that perhaps the distance between the two is diminishing.

11. *Trop v. Dulles*, 356 U.S. 86, 100 (1958).

12. *Furman v. Georgia*, 408 U.S. 238, 270 (1972) (Brennan, J., concurring).

13. *Callins v. Collins*, 510 U.S. 1141, 1145 (1994) (Blackmun, J., dissenting).

14. See, e.g., Carol S. Steiker and Jordan M. Steiker, *Atkins v. Virginia: Lessons from Substance and Procedure in the Constitutional Regulation of Capital Punishment*, 57 DePaul L. Rev. 721 (2008). ("In its first two decades regulating capital punishment in the modern era, the U.S. Supreme Court focused primarily on procedure rather than substance.")

15. See *Witherspoon v. Illinois*, 391 U.S. 510 (1968).

16. See *Woodson v. North Carolina*, 428 U.S. 280 (1976).

17. See *Proffitt v. Florida*, 428 U.S. 242 (1976).

18. *Gregg v. Georgia*, 428 U.S. 153 (1976). The Court has reaffirmed this narrowing requirement in recent cases; for example, in *Kennedy v. Louisiana*, 554 U.S. 407 (2008), the Court wrote, "[W]e have explained that capital punishment must be limited to those offenders who commit a narrow category of the most serious crimes and whose extreme culpability makes them the most deserving of execution." *Kennedy*, 554 U.S. at 420 (internal quotation marks omitted) (*quoting Roper v. Simmons*, 543 U.S. 551, 568 [2004] (*quoting Atkins v. Virginia*, 536 U.S. 304, 319 [2002]) (citing *Gregg v. Georgia*, 428 U.S. 153 [1976]).

19. *Atkins*, 536 U.S. at 319–20 (noting that the "deficiencies" of people with mental retardation "do not warrant an exemption from criminal sanctions, but they do diminish their personal culpability" and that "[i]f the culpability of the average murderer is insufficient to justify the most extreme sanction available to the State, the lesser culpability of the mentally retarded offender surely does not merit that form of retribution").

20. See, e.g., *Medina v. California*, 505 U.S. 437, 446 (1992) (noting the need to show "substantial deference" toward legislative judgments).

21. Not everyone views the Court's exercise of its independent judgment as preferable to affording uncritical deference to state legislative judgments. An in-depth discussion of this issue is beyond the scope of this chapter.

22. *Roper v. Simmons*, 543 U.S. 551, 590 (2005). ("It is for us ultimately to judge whether the Eighth Amendment permits imposition of the death penalty.") (*quoting Enmund v. Florida*, 458 U.S. 782, 797 [1982]). As in *Atkins*, the Court also considered whether a national consensus exists against the death penalty for juveniles. *Simmons* at 564. That issue is beyond the scope of this chapter.

23. *Simmons*, 543 U.S. at 570. ("From a moral standpoint it would be misguided to equate the failings of a minor with those of an adult, for a greater possibility exists that a minor's character deficiencies will be reformed.")

24. Examples of adult offenders who, according to anecdotal evidence, reformed after committing crimes that warranted death sentences include Paul Crump and Karla Faye Tucker. See B. Douglas Robbins, *Resurrection from a Death Sentence: Why Capital Sentences Should Be Commuted upon the Occasion of an Authentic Ethical Transformation*, 149 U. Pa. L. Rev. 1115, 1160, 1163 (2001).

25. *Simmons*, 543 U.S. at 573–74.

26. Saint Augustine, for example, argued on these grounds against the execution of the offender who had murdered a Catholic priest:

> We do not object to wicked men being deprived of their freedom to do wrong, but we wish it to go just that far, so that, without losing their life or being maimed in any part of their body, they may be restrained by the law from their mad frenzy, guided into the way of peace and sanity, and assigned to some useful work to replace their criminal activities. It is true, this is called a penalty, but who can fail to see that it should be called a benefit rather than a chastisement when violence and cruelty are held in check, but the remedy of repentance is not withheld?

Saint Augustine, Letters, in 3 The Fathers of the Church 6–7 (1953).

27. *Panetti v. Quarterman*, 551 U.S. 930 (2007).

28. *Panetti*, 551 U.S. at 958 (*quoting Ford v. Wainwright*, 477 U.S. 399, 407 [1986]).

29. *Kennedy v. Louisiana*, 554 U.S. 407, 420 (2008) (*quoting Furman v. Georgia*, 408 U.S. 238, 382 (1972) (Burger, C. J., dissenting).

30. *Kennedy*, 554 U.S. at 407, 420.

31. *Kennedy*, 554 U.S. at 407, 448.

Chapter Thirteen

Fidelity and Fairness in Marital Commitments, Covenants, and Contractual Relationships

Mulieris Dignitatem's Wisdom

Kevin H. Govern

[A] man shall leave his father and mother and be joined to his wife, and the two shall become one flesh, so they are no longer two, but one flesh [there remains in force the law which comes from God himself:] [t]herefore, what God has joined together, [let no man put asunder].[1]

In secular terms, a contract is a "promise, or set of promises, for breach of which the law gives a remedy, or the performance of which the law in some way recognizes as a duty."[2] In a spiritual context, the contract of marriage is both a covenant and a sacrament between a man and a woman, with inherent obligations of fidelity—the commitment to promise keeping—and to fairness—the commitment to giving from one spouse to the other their due and to equitably allocate the marital resources. With other covenants and contractual relationships guided by faith and reason, there too exists a similar commitment to fidelity and fairness.

This chapter illuminates the clarity, wisdom, and beauty expressed in the Roman Catholic Church's Magisterium relating to marital commitments, covenants, and contractual relationships, so inspirationally expressed by His Holiness Pope John Paul II some twenty years ago in his Apostolic Letter—*Mulieris Dignitatem (On the Dignity and Vocation of Women)*. In so doing, the Supreme Pontiff acted in his capacity as *magister*, or teacher, fulfilling a duty toward the people of God to enlighten them so they might serve each other and serve the Word itself, especially in relations between men and women, in light of (and even in contrast to) American legal traditions regarding such commitments, covenants, and contractual relationships.

BEYOND "NUDE PACTS" TO A NATURAL LAW OF AGREEMENTS BETWEEN MEN AND WOMEN

In Roman law a mere agreement between two parties to give, do, or refrain from doing something was a "nude pact" (*nudum pactum*) which gave rise to no civil obligation, and no action lay to enforce it; for instance a valid contract to conclude a sale required a *justa causa*, namely, a good legal reason.[3] Much later in the development of secular law, the English law of simple contracts required a valuable consideration. In like manner as by Roman law, there was needed a *justa causa*. At common law, as practiced in England and America, a contract was further defined as:

> [T]he union of several persons in a coincident expression of will by which their legal relations are determined. This "co-incident expression" consists of an agreement and promise enforceable in law, and "on the face of the matter capable of having legal effects," "an act in the law" "whereby two or more persons capable of contracting," "of doing acts in the law," "declare their consent as to any act or thing to be done or forborne by some or one of those persons for the use of the others or other of them."[4]

At English and American law, so-called moral consideration was said to be "nothing in law," [and] moral obligation of a contract is of "an imperfect kind," and "addressed to the conscience of the parties under the solemn admonitions of accountability to the Supreme Being,"[5] but "not to an earthly court of justice."[6]

If there is a nonterritorial, eternal law, how might these principles be equally applied to men and women alike regarding agreements between and with each other? Might moral considerations, if not the legal term of "moral consideration," count significantly in equal and fair relations between the genders? According to St. Thomas Aquinas, the natural law is "nothing else than the rational creature's participation in the eternal law."[7] Gender equality means an equal visibility, empowerment, and participation of both sexes in all spheres of public and private life. "Gender equality is the opposite of gender inequality, not of gender difference."[8] It is completely consistent with how God chose his people to keep his Revelation, and how he trained the Chosen People to fulfill their mission: "God created man in his image; in the divine image he created him; male and female he created them."[9]

Christ pledged to protect the teachings of the Church to men and women alike when he said: "Whoever listens to you listens to me. Whoever rejects you, rejects me. And whoever rejects me rejects the one who sent me."[10]

This must be remembered in conjunction with the fact that Sacred Scripture begins with the creation and union of man and woman and ends with the wedding feast of the Lamb.[11] In its reflection on this, the U.S. Conference of Catholic Bishops ("USCCB") has observed that "[s]cripture often refers to marriage, its origin and purpose, the meaning God gave to it, and its renewal in the covenant made by Jesus with his Church,"[12] and that the Catechism of the Catholic Church ("CCC") teaches that "[t]he Church attaches great importance to Jesus' presence at the wedding at Cana. She sees in it the confirmation of the goodness of marriage and the proclamation that thenceforth marriage will be an efficacious sign of Christ's presence."[13]

THE MAJESTY OF THE MAGISTERIUM ON THE DIGNITY OF WOMEN—AND MEN

The full breadth of the Roman Catholic Church's Magisterium, or teaching authority regarding marital commitments, covenants, and contractual relationships, would be worthy of a doctoral dissertation. Yet adherents and observers of the Roman Catholic Faith can find much inspiration in *Mulieris Dignitatem*'s beauty and the truth inherent in its passages relating to how men and women are to serve each other, and serve the Word itself, in advancing fundamental fidelity and fairness between men and women,[14] and further, how Catholics committed to their faith and their families can and do abide by U.S. law in so doing.

Saint Pope John Paul II wrote:

> [T]he dignity and vocation of women—a subject of constant human and Christian reflection—have gained exceptional prominence in recent years. This can be seen, for example, in the statements of the Church's Magisterium present in various documents of the Second Vatican Council, which declares in its Closing Message: "The hour is coming, in fact has come, when the vocation of women is being acknowledged in its fullness, the hour in which women acquire in the world an influence, an effect and a power never hitherto achieved."[15]

Inherent to the cardinal virtues of faith, hope, and love is a promise of commitment to do good for others and with others—a promise that transcends one's own physical and spiritual self to require a pure and unalloyed commitment to God and the community which he created. Regarding this purity of purpose, Saint Pope John Paul II wrote further that:

> The Church herself is a virgin, who keeps whole and pure the fidelity she has pledged to her Spouse. This is most perfectly fulfilled in Mary. The Church, therefore, "imitating the Mother of her Lord, and by the power of the Holy

Spirit . . . preserves with virginal purity an integral faith, a firm hope, and a sincere charity.[16]

Attorney-author Eugene Harper has written how Aquinas synthesized Aristotle's philosophy with the teachings of Christ to change *Eudaimonia* to beatitude, the first principle of practical reason being "good is to be done and pursued, and evil . . . avoided," and the cardinal virtues finding perfection through the Christian virtues of faith, hope, and love.[17]

Scholar Susan Brinkmann found that *Mulieris Dignitatem* created a "renaissance" for Catholic women in their commitments toward each other and with men; it fostered the notion that "[m]en and women were not created to compete with each other, but to complete one another."[18] Contrary to the "man-eating feminism" of the 1980s, Brinkmann found His Holiness Pope John Paul's writing of a "[F]emininity [which] informs everything she does: the way she loves, works and thinks, whether at home or in the public square. Far from being a weakness, John Paul II said, this is woman's 'genius.'"[19]

Citing author Dawn Eden, Brinkmann further said that "[b]elonging to a husband, a father, a brother," were mistakenly believed to be about "submitting to another's power." To the contrary, Eden said, "The pope is all about celebrating our dependence upon others as being a representation of our dependence upon God. It's in showing the world how we receive the love of God that we become truly feminine."[20]

Archbishop William E. Lori has written that as women and men form a communion of love, the couple "[c]ooperates with God in the procreation of new human life. This truth, etched into the design of creation, is at the heart of the Church's teaching against contraception expressed in Pope Paul VI's 1968 encyclical *Humanae Vitae* (*Of Human Life*)."[21]

Archbishop Lori goes on to explain how human love imitating divine love must move away from being "calculated, measured or exchanged as a commodity." In a full, faithful, and fair manner of dealing with each other, women and men should strive to make their love "holy, moving toward the eternal."[22]

Unlike the legal measuring sticks used to evaluate conventional, secular contracts and the objects subject to them, the Sacrament of Marriage is a covenant, which is more than a contract, involving lives and souls, a relationship between natural persons. The USCCB states that the marriage covenant refers to the "[R]elationship between the husband and wife, a permanent union of persons capable of knowing and loving each other and God [and t]he celebration of marriage is also a liturgical act, appropriately held in a public liturgy at church. Catholics are urged to celebrate their marriage within the Eucharistic Liturgy."[23]

IN THIS WORLD IF NOT OF THIS WORLD: COMPARING AND CONTRASTING U.S. LAW AND *MULIERIS DIGNITATEM*

What should the *magisters*, the teachers, and the leaders, elected and otherwise, do with respect to advancing a pure, faithful, inspired genius of femininity coexisting in a world of/with male or "masculine" presence? The paradox of living in an ordered, lawful society, yet freeing oneself from worldly affairs, is nothing new. Of note to Catholicism and the system of common law rooted in English heritage, King Alfred the Great of England (871–899) said in his preface to the *Cura Pastoralis*:

> Thanks be to God almighty that we now have any supply of teachers. Therefore I command you to do as I believe you are willing to do, that you free yourself from worldly affairs as often as you can, so that wherever you can establish that wisdom that God gave you, you establish it. Consider what punishments befell us in this world when we neither loved wisdom at all ourselves, nor transmitted it to other men; we had the name alone that we were Christians, and very few had the practices. [24]

From the time of the Saxons to the time of American Colonies, a certain male-dominated attitude pervaded law and society. At its very inception, the nascent nation's state of the law and the dignity and rights of women were captured in these words from Abigail Adams to her husband on March 31, 1776: "In the new Code of Laws which I suppose it will be necessary for you to make I desire you would Remember the Ladies, and be more generous and favorable to them than your ancestors."[25] In response, the future president of the United States, John Adams wrote, "I cannot but laugh. Depend upon it, we know better than to repeal our masculine systems."[26]

The new Constitution's promised rights were fully enjoyed only by certain white males. Women were treated according to social tradition and English common law and were denied most legal rights. In general they could not vote, own property, keep their own wages, or even have custody of their children. In 1923, Alice Paul put forward the first "Equal Rights Amendment," or "ERA," proposing that "men and women shall have equal rights throughout the United States and every place subject to its jurisdiction" and that "Congress shall have power to enforce this article by appropriate legislation."[27]

It would not be until August 18, 1920, that the Nineteenth Amendment to the U.S. Constitution would correct that alluded-to inequality of participation in governance. The Nineteenth Amendment prohibits each of the states and the federal government from denying any citizen the right to vote because of a citizen's sex.[28] By 1972 the proposed but not ratified ERA evolved into language stating that "Equality of Rights under the law shall not be denied or abridged by the United States or any state on account of sex."[29]

There has been a significant expansion, development, or a (d)evolution (depending upon one's perspective) of American women's legal rights within the family, in the workplace, and in society as a whole during the twentieth and early twenty-first centuries. In particular, since the 1980s, domestic violence including rape, incest, and battering; child custody; child support; and marriage and divorce law generally have all been redefined in the United States as women's experiences. [30]

Mulieris Dignitatem speaks of "God's *instituting marriage* as an indispensable condition for the transmission of life to new generations, the transmission of life to which marriage and conjugal love are by their nature ordered." [31] The Church's teaching "maintains *that beneath all changes there are many realities which do not change and which have their ultimate foundation in Christ*, who is the same yesterday and today, yes and forever." [32]

While the Constitution's First Amendment provides "Congress shall make no law respecting an establishment of religion," U.S. jurisprudence has long recognized the importance of marriage as a social institution which is favored in law and society. As early as 1888, marriage was described as an American institution, which is the foundation of society "without which there would be neither civilization nor progress." [33]

One eloquent decision from twentieth-century American jurisprudence set forth the inexplicable tie between the bounds of marriage, religion, and the state:

> While we may speak of marriage as a civil contract, yet that is a narrow view of it. The consensus of opinion in civilized nations is that marriage is something more than a dry contract. It is a contract different from all others. . . . It marks the line between the moral of the barnyard and the morals of civilized men, between reasoning affection and animal lust. In time, it rises to the dignity of a status in which society, morals, religion, reason and the state itself have a live and large interest. [34]

Mulieris Dignitatem notes regarding the sovereignty of God and the society of mankind, that

> *in calling only men as his Apostles*, Christ acted *in a completely free and sovereign manner*. In doing so, he exercised the same freedom with which, in all his behaviour, he emphasized the dignity and the vocation of women, without conforming to the prevailing customs and to the traditions sanctioned by the legislation of the time. [35]

Recognizing a different sort of sovereign authority with regard to marriage, the U.S. Supreme Court found that state laws are subject to certain constitutional limitations; namely, those laws which violate the right to marry also violate a fundamental liberty protected by the Due Process Clause of the Fourteenth Amendment.[36]

Mulieris Dignitatem does not *per se* recognize a right of privacy within relations between women and men, observing instead that man was alone among surrounding creatures before woman:

> In the description found in Gen[esis] 2:1 8–25, the woman is created by God "from the rib" of the man and is placed at his side as another "I", as the companion of the man, who is alone in the surrounding world of living creatures and who finds in none of them a "helper" suitable for himself.[37]

The U.S. Supreme Court by way of contrast (and, to some, with vexatious expansiveness) has observed a "penumbra of constitutional privacy rights" between women and men. Such "penumbra," or body of rights held to be guaranteed by implication, include not only the right to marry, but also a right to privacy within marriage.[38]

Mulieris Dignitatem exhorts people of faith to consider that:

> [T]he child's upbringing, taken as a whole, should include the contribution of both parents: the maternal and paternal contribution. In any event, the mother's contribution is decisive in laying the foundation for a new human personality.[39]

In the United States, marital support rests equally upon husband and wife and should be shared equally in proportion to their individual abilities.[40] In fact, with regard to *Mulieris Dignitatem*'s "prevailing customs and . . . traditions sanctioned by the legislation of the time,"[41] equality of woman and man includes in many states a constitutional prohibition of any denial or abridgment of rights on account of sex. U.S. courts have held it is a "form of sexual discrimination to impose the duty of support solely on husbands."[42] All states have adopted the "best interests of the child" standard in deciding custody matters between two biological parents.[43] Courts typically consider a number of factors in determining what is in the child's best interests. According to the U.S. Supreme Court:

> It is cardinal with us that the custody, care and nurture of the child reside first in the parents, whose primary function and freedom include preparation for obligations the state can neither supply nor hinder. . . . And it is in recognition of this that these decisions have respected the private realm of family life which the state cannot enter.[44]

Mulieris Dignitatem speaks of women—and men sharing in "a common responsibility for the destiny of humanity":

> Therefore the Church gives thanks for each and every woman: for mothers, for sisters, for wives; for women consecrated to God in virginity; for women dedicated to the many human beings who await the gratuitous love of another person; for women who watch over the human persons in the family, which is the fundamental sign of the human community; for women who work professionally, and who at times are burdened by a great social responsibility; for "perfect" women and for "weak" women—for all women as they have come forth from the heart of God in all the beauty and richness of their femininity; as they have been embraced by his eternal love; as, together with men, they are pilgrims on this earth, which is the temporal "homeland" of all people and is transformed sometimes into a "valley of tears"; as they assume, together with men, a common responsibility for the destiny of humanity according to daily necessities and according to that definitive destiny which the human family has in God himself, in the bosom of the ineffable Trinity.[45]

In a less eloquent—but nonetheless potent manner—U.S. law of the twentieth century has at least in two notable instances promoted women and men sharing in a common responsibility toward each other and their shared families. Title I of the Employee Retirement Income Security Act ("ERISA"), helps to ensure the equality of rights for spouses through payment of joint and survivor pension annuities (unless the spouses consent to another form of payment or absent other planned protections).[46] Promoting a "healthier balance between work and family responsibilities, ensuring that family development and cohesiveness are encouraged by this nation's public policy," the U.S. Congress enacted the Family and Medical Leave Act of 1993 ("FMLA").[47]

Mulieris Dignitatem noted the changes in man's understanding of the bonds of marriage, moving away from the Mosaic "certificate of divorce," as considered at Matthew 19:7, where

> Jesus answers: "For your hardness of heart Moses allowed you to divorce your wives, but from the beginning it was not so." Jesus appeals to the "beginning," to the creation of man as male and female and their ordering by God himself, which is based upon the fact that both were created "in his image and likeness." Therefore, when "a man shall leave his father and mother and is joined to his wife, so that the two become one flesh," there remains in force the law which comes from God himself: "What therefore God has joined together, let no man put asunder."[48]

Reflective of a secular society, U.S. jurisprudence has traditionally allowed divorce upon a showing of one of several fault-based grounds such as adultery, desertion, or cruelty. Today, every state grants "no-fault" divorces, with most states providing for both a no-fault basis and a fault basis for dissolving marriages.[49] The seventy-five million Catholics in the United

States, however, should be inspired and guided by the Church's teachings on the insolubility of marriage.[50]

EXTRAORDINARY TIMES CALL FOR EXTRAORDINARY MEASURES—FUTURE PRACTICES, POLICIES AND LAWS AFFECTING MEN, WOMEN, AND FAMILIES AS SHAPED BY PRAYER AND ACTIVE PARTICIPATION

To address the many challenges to the covenant of marriage and the ties that bind together families, His Holiness Pope Francis called an extraordinary general assembly of the Synod of Bishops in October 2014.[51] In his letter to families ahead of the Synod, the Pontiff wrote of this "important meeting (that) will involve all the People of God—bishops, priests, consecrated men and women, and lay faithful of the particular Churches of the entire world—all of whom are actively participating in preparations for the meeting through practical suggestions and the crucial support of prayer."[52] He continued:

> Such support on your part, dear families, is especially significant and more necessary than ever. This Synodal Assembly is dedicated in a special way to you, to your vocation and mission in the Church and in society; to the challenges of marriage, of family life, of the education of children; and the role of the family in the life of the Church.[53]

The assembly will "examine the popular reception of Church teachings on marriage and the family, assess the problems of putting them into practice, identify which teachings are most criticized and ignored, and consider how best to communicate them."[54] In turn, "the findings of this extraordinary assembly will set the stage for another general assembly of the Synod of Bishops . . . in 2015 . . . on pastoral strategies and guidelines for dealing with marriage and family issues."[55]

CONCLUSION

After the extraordinary assembly in September 2015 the Church in Philadelphia will host the Eighth World Meeting of Families. Whatever happens, the World Meeting of Families will be a major high point in the life of married couples, those who intend to be joined in holy matrimony, and those whose lives are touched by those bound by the covenant of marriage. May that grace described in *Mulieris Dignitatem*, an indispensable gift from God for development, improvement, and character expansion, guide individuals, couples, organizations, and societies towards harmonious, if not shared, conceptualizations of fidelity and fairness in spiritual and secular commitments, covenants, and contractual relationships.

NOTES

1. Matthew 19:6 (New American Bible).

2. *Williston on Contracts*, § 1.1 (Richard A. Lord, ed., 1990); *Restatement (Second) of Contracts* 1, n. 1 (1981), *cited in* Joseph Calamari and John Perillo, *Calamari and Perillo on Contracts* (St. Paul, MN: West, 2003) at 1.

3. *The Catholic Encyclopedia*, Vol. 4 (New York: Robert Appleton Company, 1908), s.v. "Contract."

4. Frederick Pollock, *Principles of Contract*, 3rd Amer. ed. (New York, 1906), 58, 1, 2, 3.

5. Joseph Story, *Commentaries on the Constitution of the United States*, 5th ed. (Boston, 1891), § 1380, *cited with authority in* Pollock, *Principles of Contract.*

6. Story, *Commentaries*, § 1380.

7. St. Thomas Aquinas, *Summa Theologica*, I-II.94 (2nd and rev. ed., 1920).

8. Fact sheet on Equality Between Women and Men, Council of Europe homepage, September 2008, available at http://www.coe.int/t/e/human_rights/equality/01._overview/2._background_documents/001_Factsheet.asp.

9. Genesis 1:27.

10. Luke 10:16.

11. Revelation 19:7, 19:9.

12. "Matrimony," U.S. Conference of Catholic Bishops Website, 2014, http://www.usccb.org/prayer-and-worship/sacraments/matrimony/.

13. *Catechism of the Catholic Church* (*CCC*), ¶1613.

14. *Mulieris Dignitatem*, *supra* note 2.

15. *Mulieris Dignitatem*, ¶1.

16. *Mulieris Dignitatem*, ¶22.

17. Eugene Harper, *The Conception of the Human Person*, St. John's L. Rev., Vol. 75, Issue 2 (2001), 297.

18. Susan Brinkmann, "A Renaissance for Catholic Women," *Columbia Magazine*, August 1, 2008.

19. Brinkman, "Renaissance" at 300.

20. Brinkman, "Renaissance."

21. William E. Lori, "Male and Female He Created Them," *Columbia Magazine*, August 1, 2008 (*citing* Pope Paul VI, *Humanae Vitae*, July 25, 1968).

22. Lori, "Male and Female."

23. "Matrimony," *supra* note 13.

24. King Alfred the Great, *Preface to Cura Pastoralis*, available at http://www.departments.bucknell.edu/english/courses/engl440/pastoral/translation.shtml.

25. Abigail Adams, "'Remember the Ladies' Abigail and John Adams Exchange Views, 1776" in *The Way We Lived* (Boston: Houghton Mifflin, 2004), 130, *cited in* Rachael Pifer, "Abigail Adams and the Doomed Rhetoric of Revolutionary Era Women," *Drake Undergrad. Soc. Sciences Journal* 2 (2005).

26. Letter from John Adams (March 31, 1776) *in* Alice S. Rossi, *The Feminist Papers: From Adams to de Beauvoir* (New York: Columbia University Press, 1973).

27. See, e.g., *Equal Rights Amendment*, available at http://equalrightsamendment.org/.

28. U.S. Const. amend XIX.

29. *Equal Rights Amendment*, *supra* note 28. The Equal Rights Amendment passed the U.S. Senate and then the House of Representatives, and on March 22, 1972, the proposed 27th Amendment to the Constitution was sent to the states for ratification. The ERA was reintroduced in Congress on July 14, 1982, and has been before every session of Congress since that time without obtaining passage by a two-thirds vote in each house of Congress or ratification by 38 states.

30. U.S. Report Under the International Covenant on Civil and Political Rights: Art. 23—Protection of the Family, § VIII (July 1994) [hereinafter U.S. Report]. U.S. Department of State Electronic Research Collection, available at http://dosfan.lib.uic.edu/ERC/law/Covenant94/Specific_Articles/23.html.

31. *Mulieris Dignitatem*, ¶6.

32. *Mulieris Dignitatem*, ¶28.

33. *Maynard v. Hill*, 125 U.S. 190, 211 (1888).

34. *Bishop v. Brittain Inv. Co.*, 129 S.W. 668, 676 (Mo. 1910).

35. *Mulieris Dignitatem*, ¶26.

36. See *Loving v. Virginia*, 388 U.S. 1 (1967). In that case, the U.S. Supreme Court struck down a Virginia law that prohibited interracial marriages. The Court held that the Virginia statute limiting the right to marry, "similar to those in effect in 15 other states at the time, discriminated on the basis of race in violation of the Equal Protection Clause of the Fourteenth Amendment."

37. *Mulieris Dignitatem*, ¶6.

38. *Griswold v. Connecticut*, 381 U.S. 479, 485 (1965) (overturning Connecticut statutes forbidding the use or sale of contraceptives to married persons).

39. *Mulieris Dignitatem*, ¶18.

40. See, e.g., Cal. Civ. Code § 5100 (1983); Conn. Gen. Stat. Ann. § 46b-37 (1986). In 1978, the Supreme Court invalidated a state law that authorized alimony payments only for wives as a violation of the Equal Protection Clause of the Fourteenth Amendment. *Orr v. Orr*, 440 U.S. 268 (1979), *cited in* U.S. Report, § III, *supra* note 31.

41. *Mulieris Dignitatem*, ¶26.

42. See, e.g., *Rand v. Rand*, 374 A.2d 900 (1977); *Henderson v. Henderson*, 327 A.2d 60 (1974).

43. See, e.g., *In re Marriage of Ellerbroek*, 377 N.W.2d 257 (Iowa App. 1985); *Pikula v Pikula*, 374 N.W.2d 705 (Minn. 1985) *cited in* U.S. Report, *supra* note 31.

44. *Prince v. Massachusetts*, 321 U.S. 158, 166 (1944).

45. *Mulieris Dignitatem*, ¶31.

46. Employee Retirement Income Security Act (ERISA), 29 U.S.C. § 1001 *et seq.* (1974).

47. Family and Medical Leave Act (FMLA), 29 U.S.C. § 2601 *et seq.* (1993).

48. Matthew 19:6–8.

49. U.S. Report, § VI, *supra* note 31.

50. "The Global Catholic Population," Pew Research Religion and Public Life Project, February 13, 2013, available at http://www.pewforum.org/2013/02/13/the-global-catholic-population/. That same study noted that Catholics still comprise about half (50 percent) of Christians worldwide and 16 percent of the total global population.

51. Archbishop Charles J. Chaput, "Marriage, Family and Some Help for Pope Francis," Zenit.org, November 25, 2013.

52. "Pope Francis Issues Letter to Families Ahead of Extraordinary Synod," *Catholic Herald.co.uk*, February 25, 2014, available at http://www.catholicherald.co.uk/news/2014/02/25/pope-francis-issues-letter-to-families-ahead-of-extraordinary-synod/.

53. Pope Francis' letter, *supra* note 53.

54. Chaput, "Help for Pope Francis."

55. Chaput, "Help for Pope Francis."

Chapter Fourteen

Catholic Perspectives on Family Law

Bill Piatt

Unlike some areas of the law, family issues affect virtually all Catholics. Both the legal system and the Church recognize the importance of marriage. Both establish requirements for entering into, and for withdrawal from, that status. While the requirements and concerns overlap in many regards, there are some critical differences between the approaches to the institution of marriage by the Church and by the secular legal system. This chapter explores these issues beginning with an understanding of how each institution views the nature of the marital relationship. Then it examines the requirements each institution imposes for entering into and dissolving a marriage. It concludes by examining the dilemma and the solutions for Catholics facing the breakdown of a marriage. More detailed information on these, and other topics involving the views of the legal system and the Church on a number of areas, can be found in the book *Catholic Legal Perspectives.* [1]

HOW DOES THE CHURCH VIEW MARRIAGE?

Marriage is of the utmost importance to the Catholic Church. It is recognized by the Church as one of the seven sacraments. According to Canon Law:

> The matrimonial covenant, by which a man and a woman establish between themselves a partnership of the whole of life, is by its nature ordained toward the good of the spouses and the procreation and education of offspring; this covenant between baptized persons has been raised by Christ the Lord to the dignity of a sacrament. [2]

The importance of marriage was underscored by Pope Benedict XVI on February 4, 2007, and on February 22, 2007:

> The family . . . is the "cradle" of life and of every vocation. We are well aware that the family founded on marriage is the natural environment in which to bear and raise children and thereby guarantee the future of all of humanity. However, we also know that marriage is going through a deep crisis and today must face numerous challenges. It is consequently necessary to defend, help, safeguard, and value it in its unrepeatable uniqueness. If this commitment is in the first place the duty of spouses, it is also a priority duty of the Church and of every public institution to support the family by means of pastoral and political initiatives that take into account the real needs of married couples, of the elderly and of the new generations. [3]

"Marriage and the family are institutions that must be promoted and defended from every possible misrepresentation of their true nature, since whatever is injurious to them is injurious to society itself." [4]

The United States Conference of Catholic Bishops ("USCCB") followed in 2009 with a pastoral letter entitled *Marriage: Love and Life in the Divine Plan.*

> Marriage is a natural institution established by God the Creator. It is a permanent, faithful, fruitful partnership between one man and one woman, established by their free mutual consent. It has two purposes: the good of the spouses, called the unitive purpose, and the procreation and education of children.
>
> Marriage is not merely a private institution. It is the foundation of the family, where children learn values and virtues that make them good Christians as well as good citizens. Marriage is important for the upbringing of the next generation, and therefore it is important for society. . . . No other relationship symbolizes life and love as marriage does. [5]

HOW DOES THE LEGAL SYSTEM VIEW MARRIAGE?

The legal system, of course, does not identify relationships in sacramental terms. Nonetheless, marriage is afforded a great deal of importance by the legal system because of its impact on, and role in, the formation of societal relationships. While the agreement to marry and live as husband and wife is recognized as involving elements of a contract between the spouses, it has always been viewed as more than just a contract between two people. [6] The State has a direct interest in the creation, maintenance, and dissolution of the marriage relationship because of the concerns associated with children, property, and general good order in society. Thus the State identifies who is eligible to marry, under what circumstances the marriage can be dissolved, and how child custody, visitation, and property allocation and distribution is to occur if the marriage breaks down. [7] One summary of the nature of marriage provides: "Marriage is a unique institution by which those who are married enter into a legally recognized personal relationship." [8]

The United States Supreme Court has long recognized the importance of the institution of marriage. In 1888, it characterized marriage as "the most important relation in life,"[9] and as "the foundation of the family and of society, without which there would be neither civilization nor progress."[10]

The right to marry is considered a fundamental right under the Due Process Clause of the Constitution of the United States.[11] While states generally have the right to identify the qualifications necessary to enter into a marriage, they cannot enact restrictions, such as racial restrictions, which would violate this Constitutional principle, and that of the Equal Protection Clause of the Fourteenth Amendment to the Constitution.[12] Because of the constitutional importance of this right to marry, even incarcerated inmates have a constitutional right to marry; however, they do not have the right to consummate the marriage.[13]

WHO IS ELIGIBLE TO MARRY?

The Church

Just as with the civil authorities, the Church also identifies certain requirements for marriage. Marriages which do not meet these requirements are considered non-sacramental and invalid. A succinct summary of these requirements appears in Scott P. Richert's note *Can I Get Married in the Catholic Church?*[14]

Richert identifies five basic requirements. First, a Catholic can only marry a baptized Christian. A Catholic seeking to marry a non-Catholic Christian must obtain permission from the Catholic's bishop. Second, the parties must not be too closely related. In some cases, though, the Church will allow a dispensation for first cousins to marry. Third, Richert notes, the partners must be free to marry. If either party has been previously married, he or she can only remarry in the Catholic Church if the Church declares the previous marriage "null." Fourth, the parties must be one man and one woman. The Church does not recognize same-sex marriage. Finally, the Catholic partner must be in good standing with the Church.

The Catholic Church does not recognize common-law marriages or other informal marriage or marriage-like arrangements. This position was made clear by the Vatican's Pontifical Council for the Family in its statement on *Family, Marriage and "De Facto" Unions* set out in 2000.[15] The document runs thirty pages and includes extensive analyses of the Church's opposition to recognizing "de facto" unions. As might be expected, the Catholic Church takes a negative view regarding the creation of a state-sanctioned homosexual marriage. The June 24, 2011, Statement of the Bishops of New York State is illustrative:

The passage by the Legislature of a bill to alter radically and forever humanity's historic understanding of marriage leaves us deeply disappointed and troubled. We strongly uphold the Catholic Church's clear teaching that we always treat our homosexual brothers and sisters with respect, dignity, and love. But we just as strongly affirm that marriage is the joining of one man and one woman in a lifelong, loving union that is open to children, ordered for the good of those children and the spouses themselves. This definition cannot change, though we realize that our beliefs about the nature of marriage will continue to be ridiculed, and that some will even now attempt to enact government sanctions against churches and religious organizations that preach these timeless truths.

We worry that both marriage and the family will be undermined by this tragic presumption of government in passing this legislation that attempts to redefine these cornerstones of civilization.

Our society must regain what it appears to have lost—a true understanding of the meaning and the place of marriage, as revealed by God, grounded in nature, and respected by America's foundational principles.[16]

The Legal System

The legal system, like the Church, imposes qualifications on who can marry. These restrictions are generally left to the states. Typically, states impose minimum-age restrictions for marriage. Also, prohibitions against marriage between people related by blood, adoption, or between those who are, or who have been, in a step-child or step-sibling relationship are common. Typically, states require some formalities in creating the marriage relationship. That is, usually the parties are required to obtain a marriage license, have the marriage ceremony performed by an authorized officiant, and then the license must be recorded noting the date and location of the marriage ceremony. These records are usually maintained in the county where the marriage license is issued.

Note that the requirements within the legal system for entering into marriage actually have some basis in the Old Testament. For example, in Leviticus 18, there is a series of prohibitions against sexual relations and therefore marriage, between a man and his mother (v.8), his father's wife (v.8), his sister by either his father or mother (v.9), his son's daughter or his daughter's daughter (v.10), daughter of his father's wife (v.10), his father's sister (v.12), his mother's sister (v.13), his father's brother's wife (v.14), his daughter-in-law (v.15), his brother's wife (v.16), both a woman and her daughter, her son's daughter or her daughter's daughter (v.17), and a wife's sister while the wife is living (v.18).[17]

However, some states allow people to enter into "common law" marriages, without the need for a formal license or ceremony. In these states, the parties essentially declare themselves to be husband and wife, hold themselves out to be spouses, and live in a husband–wife relationship. A common-law marriage is just as valid as a ceremonial marriage. That means that generally all the laws governing married couples apply, including the laws that require the entry of a formal divorce decree to dissolve marriages.

GROWING DISAGREEMENT OVER SAME-SEX MARRIAGE

There is now growing disagreement between the Church and the legal system regarding same-sex marriages. Marriage has only been recognized, traditionally, by both the legal system and the Catholic Church as those unions between one man and one woman. Currently, twenty-nine states include the "one man, one woman" requirement in their statutes or constitutions, prohibiting same-sex marriages in those states; however, in the last few years several states and the District of Columbia have recognized "same-sex marriages," either by judicial decree or by legislative enactment. This process has been controversial and, obviously, political. One of the most controversial involves the state of California, where voters enacted a constitutional amendment outlawing same-sex marriages. The constitutionality of that act was challenged in the courts. The state's governor and attorney general refused to defend the act in court. The Supreme Court of the United States concluded that the people who appeared to defend the act did not have the legal "standing" to do so. As a result, a lower-court decision declaring the act to be unconstitutional was left in place.[18]

There has been controversy on the federal level as well. In 1996, the Congress of the United States passed, and the President signed into law, the Defense of Marriage Act ("DOMA").[19] That Act reads as follows:

> *§1738C. Certain acts, records, and proceedings and the effect thereof:* No State, territory, or possession of the United States, or Indian tribe, shall be required to give effect to any public act, record, or judicial proceedings of any other State, territory, possession, or tribe respecting a relationship between persons of the same sex that is treated as a marriage under the laws of such other State, territory, possession, or tribe, or a right or claim arising from such relationship.

The impetus for the enactment of DOMA was the concern that if some states began to recognize same-sex marriage, other states, even those with constitutional prohibitions against same-sex marriage, would nonetheless be required to recognize the marriage under the Full Faith and Credit Clause of the Constitution of the United States.

On February 23, 2011, President Obama ordered the United States Department of Justice to stop defending DOMA. The Archbishop of New York, Timothy M. Dolan, as president of the United States Conference of Catholic Bishops issued the following statement on March 3, 2011:

The announcement on February 23 that the President has instructed the Department of Justice to stop defending the Defense of Marriage Act (DOMA) is an alarming and grave injustice. Marriage, the union of one man and one woman as husband and wife, is a singular and irreplaceable institution. Only a man and a woman are capable of the "two-in-one-flesh" union of husband and wife. Only a man and a woman have the ability to bring children into the world. Along with that ability comes responsibility which society historically reinforces with laws that bind mothers and fathers to each other and their children. This family unit represents the most basic and vital cell of any society, protecting the right of children to know and be known by, to love and be loved by, their mother and father. Thus, marriage represents the bedrock of the common good of society, its very foundation and future. [20]

In 2013, the United States Supreme Court, in a 5–4 decision, determined that DOMA was unconstitutional. [21] However, while the federal government will now recognize the validity of same-sex marriages if they are valid under the state law which created them, no state is required to enact statutes allowing those marriages.

UNDER WHAT CIRCUMSTANCES MAY A MARRIAGE BE DISSOLVED?

As might be expected, while the Church and the legal system each view the institution of marriage as very important, the Church holds a much more permanent view.

The Legal System

Just as states provide the basis and the qualifications for marriage, so too do the states provide the legal requirements for a divorce. Historically, the party seeking the divorce was required to prove that there was fault on the part of the other person in order to obtain a divorce. The most commonly cited ground was that of adultery.

Because the basis of obtaining a divorce required the proving of fault of the other parties, the person against whom the divorce was filed could raise defenses to the divorce. If one party had behaved in an inappropriate fashion, and was served with a divorce petition, that party could defend by showing that his or her marital partner had engaged in behavior, usually cruelty or adultery, of the same character. This defense was known as "recrimination." This produced the very curious results that a couple with intense disagreements, even rising to the level of mutual cruelty or adultery, would nonetheless be denied a divorce and forced to remain in a marriage. If one of the parties had engaged in misconduct and the other had forgiven the misconduct, usually by resuming the marital relationship, the forgiving party might be precluded from obtaining a divorce due to the defense of "condonation."

By the late 1960s and early 1970s, states began to create and implement "no fault" provisions in their divorce laws. The ground of "insupportability," or "incompatibility," or similar grounds in other jurisdictions, now provided the basis for the awarding of most divorces in the United States. Parties no longer had to plead and prove fault. Theoretically, this allowed for a less acrimonious dissolution of the marriage. Reducing the hostilities should be of particular benefit when there are minor children of the parties.

Even though states have moved toward a no-fault divorce in most instances, alternative fault-based grounds for obtaining a divorce still exist. These grounds are invoked in order to persuade a court to enter an unequal division of property on behalf of the aggrieved spouse. Fault-based divorce petitions are also used in order to gain an advantage in child custody matters.

In a divorce action, the person seeking the dissolution of the marriage is asking that a court declare an otherwise valid marriage to be dissolved. There may, however, be reasons, including religious reasons, why one party might choose, instead of dissolving the marriage, to have it declared annulled. If an annulment is granted, a court determines that the marriage was voidable when entered into and one of the parties is allowed to have the court declare that the marriage does not exist. Annulment statutes typically provide that the enumerated ground for obtaining the annulment makes the marriage voidable. That is, unless someone affirmatively brings an annulment action, the marriage remains valid and in effect.

There is however a category of "void" marriages which means that the marriage never took place in the first place. In most jurisdictions, marriages that are entered into where the parties are too closely related are void marriages. Another basis for obtaining a declaration that the marriage is void is if there is a prior marriage still in effect at the time of the contracting of the offending marriage.

In many jurisdictions, short of a divorce or an annulment, parties to a marriage are able to obtain a legal separation. The legal separation maintains the legal existence of the marriage but provides for a division of property, might contain orders related to children and child support, and identifies the property rights of the spouses. Why would a married couple enter into a separation agreement? It might be that for religious reasons the couple feels that a divorce is morally wrong. It might be that the parties are attempting to determine whether the more dramatic step of divorce is necessary or whether, during a time of separation, the parties might be able to reconcile any differences and resume the marital relationship.

Just because the couple is divorced, separated, or the marriage annulled, state statutes provide for ongoing supervision of relationships particularly in the area of child support and sometimes in the area of spousal support. While the divorce, annulment, or separation proceeding might terminate or reduce the legal relationship between husband and wife, the parties are required to interact peaceably in order to provide as much stability as the court can enforce regarding children.

The Church

Because the Church views marriage as a sacrament and of great importance not only to the individuals but to the Church itself, it should come as no surprise that that Catholic Church takes a very restrictive approach to the dissolution of marriage. Canon Law explicitly states: "[a] marriage that is *ratum et consummatum* can be dissolved by no human power and by no cause, except death."[22]

The Catholic doctrine on divorce may be summed up in the following propositions:

- In Christian marriage, which implies the restoration, by Christ Himself, of marriage to its original indissolubility, there can never be an absolute divorce, at least after the marriage has been consummated;
- Non-Christian marriage can be dissolved by absolute divorce under certain circumstances in favor of the Faith;
- Christian marriage before consummation can be dissolved by solemn profession in a religious order, or by an act of papal authority;
- Separation from bed and board (*divortium imperfectum*) is allowed for various causes, especially in the case of adultery or lapse into infidelity or heresy on the part of husband or wife.[23]

Thus the Church would recognize an absolute divorce only in the rarest of circumstances.

Separation is permitted by the Church. It is permissible for the offended spouse to turn out the adulterer. "Canon Law makes it clear that if one party is guilty of adultery, the other has the right to effect a permanent separation, and this indeed without any intervention of ecclesiastical authority. The marriage bond itself remains, however, and precludes remarriage."[24]

In the case of a Catholic-to-Catholic marriage, divorcees are not free to remarry unless an annulment is granted by the Church. The process of annulment is described by the USCCB as follows:

> The tribunal process seeks to determine if something essential was missing from the couple's relationship from the moment of consent, that is, the time of the wedding. If so, then the Church can declare that a valid marriage was never actually brought about on the wedding day.
>   . . . Several steps are involved. The person who is asking for the declaration of nullity—the petitioner—submits written testimony about the marriage

and a list of persons who are familiar with the marriage. These people must be willing to answer questions about the spouses and the marriage. The tribunal will contact the ex-spouse—the respondent—who has a right to be involved. The respondent's cooperation is welcome but not essential. In some cases the respondent does not wish to become involved; the case can still move forward.

Both the petitioner and the respondent can read the testimony submitted, except that protected by civil law (for example, counseling records). Each party may appoint a Church advocate who could represent the person before the tribunal. A representative for the Church, called the defender of the bond, argues for the validity of the marriage. After the tribunal has reached a decision, it is reviewed by a second tribunal. Both parties can participate in this second review as well.[25]

The process can take more than a year to complete.

Just as in a civil annulment, the aggrieved party seeking to obtain an annulment must have entered into the marriage without knowledge that the grounds for annulment existed. Moreover, it appears that historically the Church would allow an annulment proceeding to be brought by someone other than a party to the marriage. That could result in the married couple defending their marriage in a proceeding.

THE DILEMMA AND THE SOLUTIONS FOR CATHOLICS WHO FACE THE BREAKDOWN OF A MARRIAGE

The sad and unfortunate reality is that some marriages, even Catholic marriages, will break down, as the result of many possible factors. Consider the situation where this has occurred and there is no feasible way, except for recourse to the judicial system, for a Catholic to protect property rights, arrange for custody of minor children and their support, or other similar circumstances. Does the Church preclude divorce in such a circumstance? The answer is, no, it does not. Section 2383 of the Catechism provides, in part, "If civil divorce remains the only possible way of ensuring certain legal rights, the care of the children, or the protection of inheritance, it can be tolerated and does not constitute a moral offense."[26] It is also not a sin for the Catholic who has been divorced by his/her spouse under the circumstances set out in Section 2386: "It can happen that one of the spouses is the innocent victim of a divorce decreed by civil law; this spouse therefore has not contravened the moral law. There is a considerable difference between a spouse who has sincerely tried to be faithful to the sacrament of marriage and is unjustly abandoned, and one who through his own grave fault destroys a canonically valid marriage."

Under either of the scenarios above, the Catholic has not committed sin and is free to continue to receive the sacraments. Even where the Catholic has brought or caused a divorce, under circumstances outside of these situations, he/she can confess the sin through the sacrament of Reconciliation, and continue to receive the sacraments. The difficulty arises, however, if the divorced Catholic, even one who would be covered under the provisions of Section 2383 or Section 2386, remarries. The Church has made clear that unless the first marriage has been annulled by the Church, the parties are not free to remarry, and are thus not free to take the sacraments. See the words of then-Cardinal Ratzinger in a letter to the world's bishops on October 14, 1994, "Concerning the Reception of Holy Communion by Divorced-and-Remarried Members of the Faithful":

> The mistaken conviction of a divorced-and-remarried person that he may re-ceive Holy Communion normally presupposes that personal conscience is con-sidered in the final analysis to be able, on the basis of one's own convictions, to come to a decision about the existence or absence of a previous marriage and the value of the new union. However, such a position is inadmissible. Marriage, in fact, both because it is the image of the spousal relationship between Christ and his church as well as the fundamental core and an impor-tant factor in the life of civil society, is essentially a public reality. [27]

There is one narrow circumstance under which a divorced and remarried Catholic could receive the sacraments. That is the situation where the Catho-lic and his/her new spouse repent of their sin and live together as brother and sister. "This means, in practice, that when for serious reasons, for example, for the children's upbringing, a man and a woman cannot satisfy the obliga-tion to separate, they take on themselves the duty to live in complete conti-nence, that is, by abstinence from the acts proper to married couples. In such a case they may receive Holy Communion as long as they respect the obliga-tion to avoid giving scandal." [28]

Obviously, most Catholics would not view this as a realistic option. And, they view with concern the position of the Church that would treat their attempt to enter into a new and loving marriage, with all the protection afforded to that relationship by the legal system, as the equivalent of unre-pentant adultery. In his book *On Heaven and Earth* Pope Francis states: "Catholic doctrine reminds its divorced members who have remarried that they are not excommunicated—even though they live in a situation on the margin of what indissolubility of marriage and the sacrament of marriage require of them—and they are asked to integrate into the parish life." [29]

Francis continued this theme with a statement to journalists on September 16, 2013. Reuters reported that the Pope: ". . . called for 'another way' of treating divorcees who remarry—a thorny issue since Catholics who wed a second time are currently not allowed to receive Holy Communion at mass. Catholic faithful should 'feel at home' in parishes and those who have remar-ried should be treated with 'justice' the pope is quoted as saying by *Roma-*

sette, the local newspaper for the diocese of Rome. 'Our duty is to find another way in justice,' he said."[30]

Perhaps the Church will find its way to bring back to the sacraments the many who long for that inclusion. Divorced and divorcing Catholics should also consider resources such as the "Catholic's Divorce Survival Guide," or similar offerings, which provide some advice and assistance.[31] Finally, then-Cardinal Ratzinger assigned an *imprimatur* to the following statement regarding the role of conscience:

> Conscience, as "moral judgment" and as "moral imperative," constitutes the final evaluation of an act as good or evil before God. In effect, only God knows the moral value of each human act, even if the Church, like Jesus, can and must classify, judge, and sometimes condemn some kinds of action.[32]

NOTES

1. Bill Piatt, *Catholic Legal Perspectives*, 2nd ed. (Carolina Academic Press, 2014).

2. *Code of Canon Law*, c. 1055 (1983); *see also New Catholic Encyclopedia* (Gale Publishing, 2003), s.v. "Sacrament of Matrimony."

3. Pope Benedict XVI, "Message at Weekly *Angelus*" (February 4, 2007), available at http://www.vatican.va/holy_father/benedict_xvi/angelus/2007/documents/hf_ben-xvi_ang_20070204_en.html (accessed March 4, 2014).

4. Pope Benedict XVI, "Post Synodal Apostolic Exhortation *Sacramentum Caritatis*" 98 (February 22, 2007).

5. United States Conference of Catholic Bishops [hereinafter USCCB], "Marriage: Love and Life in the Divine Plan, A Pastoral Letter by the Catholic Bishops of the United States," (November 2009).

6. See generally 52 Am. Jur. 2d *Marriage* § 7 (2013).

7. See generally 24 Am. Jur. 2d *Divorce and Separation* § 16 (2013).

8. See generally 52 Am. Jur. 2d *Marriage* § 1 (2013).

9. *Maynard v. Hill*, 125 U.S. 190, 205 (1888).

10. *Maynard*, 125 U.S. at 211.

11. *Zablocki v. Redhail*, 434 U.S. 374, 384 (1978).

12. *Loving v. Virginia*, 388 U.S. 1, 12 (1967).

13. *Turner v. Safley*, 482 U.S. 78, 94, 96 (1987).

14. Scott P. Richert, "Can I Get Married in the Catholic Church?" http://catholicism.about.com/od/catholicliving/f/FAQ_Marriage.htm (accessed October 1, 2011).

15. Vatican's Pontifical Council for the Family, "Statement on Family, Marriage and 'De Facto' Unions" (July 26, 2000).

16. N.Y. State Catholic Conference, "Statement of the Bishops of N.Y. State on Same-Sex 'Marriage' Vote" (June 24, 2011), http://www.nyscatholic.org/2011/06/statement-of-the-bishops-of-new-york-state-on-same-sex-marriage-vote/ (defining marriage as a union between a man and a woman) (accessed March 4, 2014).

17. Leviticus 18: 8–10, 12–18 (New Catholic Version).

18. *Hollingsworth v. Perry*, 133 S. Ct. 2652 (2013).

19. 28 U.S.C. § 1738C (2000).

20. USCCB Office of Media Relations, "Archbishop Dolan Calls Refusal to Defend Defense of Marriage Act an 'Alarming and Grave Injustice'" (March 3, 2011), http://www.usccb.org/news/2011/11-043.cfm (accessed March 4, 2014).

21. *U.S. v. Windsor*, 133 S. Ct. 2675 (2013).

22. *Code of Canon Law*, c. 1141 (1983).

23. *The Catholic Encyclopedia* (Kevin Knight, ed., 1993), s.v. "Divorce (in Moral Theology)," available at http://www.newadvent.org/cathen/05054c.htm (last visited October 9, 2011). (Although this text was written from 1908 to 1912, these premises are still current.)

24. *New Catholic Encyclopedia* (Gale Publishing, 2003), s.v. "Adultery."

25. For Your Marriage, "Annulments" (October 1, 2013), http://www.foryourmarriage.org/catholic-marriage/church-teachings/annulments (accessed March 4, 2014).

26. *Catechism of the Catholic Church*, "Article 6: The Sixth Commandment," ¶2383 (1993).

27. Joseph Cardinal Ratzinger, "Letter to Bishops of the Catholic Church Concerning the Reception of Holy Communion by Divorced and Remarried Members of the Faithful," ¶7. The Congregation for the Doctrine of the Faith (October 14, 1994).

28. Ratzinger, "Letter to Bishops," ¶4.

29. Carl Bunderson, "Pope Francis Desires to Draw Remarried People to Christ," *National Catholic Register*, May 5, 2013.

30. "Pope Calls for 'Another Way' for Catholic Divorcees" (September 17, 2013), http://www.straitstimes.com/breaking-news/world/story/pope-calls-another-way-catholic-divorcees-20130917.

31. *The Catholic's Divorce Survival Guide*, http://www.catholicsdivorce.com/.

32. International Theological Commission, "Memory and Reconciliation: The Church and the Faults of the Past" (December 1999), available at http://www.vatican.va/roman_curia/congregations/cfaith/cti_documents/rc_con_cfaith_doc_20000307_memory-reconc-itc_en.html.

Chapter Fifteen

The Odd Couple

Comparing U.S. Military Law and Roman Catholic Ideology

Richard V. Meyer

At first glance, military service appears incongruent with Catholic values. It subjects individuals to horrendous conditions, separates families, denies access to religious service,[1] punishes disobedience even when it is based upon honest moral objection,[2] requires sometimes conflicting loyalties, and trains individuals to be experts at killing other humans. This first glance would be deceiving, however. Military service in the United States may actually be much closer to the ideal Catholic community than most others.

The Pastoral Constitution, *Gaudium et Spes*, describes multiple aspects of the proper community: it has clear authority tasked with the common good that citizens must obey; it promotes solidarity and sacrifice and transcends individual morality; it supports the family; provides proper work conditions and opportunities for leisure; respects the individual; cultivates patriotism; works to preserve peace; and fosters respect for enemies.[3] As Avery Cardinal Dulles further espouses, a community must have shared virtue so that laws can be framed with a view toward the common good rather than self-interest and that inner freedom comes from self-control that is the product of training and discipline.[4] The United States military community, in accordance with its unique system of law and regulation, possesses every one of these attributes. That said, however, there are still areas of improvement, particularly in the regulation of armed conflict.

The purpose of this chapter is to evaluate U.S. military law through a Roman Catholic lens, identifying strengths and areas of improvement. The first part is a brief introduction to the field of military law followed by an analysis of each of the three subfields of military law.

THE FIELD OF MILITARY LAW

Colonel William Winthrop, a man who has been referred to as the "Blackstone of Military Law,"[5] separated this legal field into three parts: the military law proper, the law of war, and civil functions and relations of the military.[6]

Winthrop defines military law proper as the "branch of the public law which is enacted or ordained for the government exclusively of the military state, and is operative equally in peace and in war."[7] It contains both written and unwritten elements, and its primary purpose is "to provide a prompt, ready at hand means of compelling obedience and order"[8] within "a specialized society separate from civilian society"[9] to enable it "to prepare for and perform its vital role" of defending the nation.[10]

The current "bible" of American military law is the 2012 edition of the Manual for Courts-Martial. It is a single volume that includes a unique criminal code, the Uniform Code of Military Justice [U.C.M.J.]; an equally unique criminal process, the Rules for Courts-Martial [R.C.M.]; and a comparatively standard evidentiary system in the Military Rules of Evidence [M.R.E.]. The U.C.M.J. was first enacted by Congress in 1950 and represented a tectonic shift in the field of military law. Prior to 1950, the Army (and Air Force) fell under the Articles of War originally passed by the Second Continental Congress and the Navy and Marine Corps fell under the Articles for the Government of the Navy. The U.C.M.J. not only unified military justice, but it finally incorporated many of the due process protections that had evolved in American criminal law over the previous century and a half. The core substantive articles, Articles 77–134, remained largely unaltered, both then and now, from those concepts that the fledgling United States elected to adopt from the British Empire nearly two-and-a-half centuries ago. It is these articles that are to blame for the tremendous breadth of modern military law.

Article 92, for example, criminalizes violations of the myriad of general orders, directives, and punitive regulations issued by the military services and commanders. As long as these orders or regulations "relate to military duty" and do not violate the Constitution or federal law, they are considered lawful orders subjecting those who disobey to the possibility of years of confinement. Military duty includes activities reasonably necessary to accomplish a military mission, protect or promote the morale, discipline, and usefulness of service members of the command and those connected to the maintenance of good order and discipline.[11] Add in Article 134, arguably the broadest criminal statute in the United States, which criminalizes any and all conduct deemed detrimental to good order and discipline or conduct that would bring "discredit" to the armed forces, and one can start to see the incredible reach of "military law proper."[12]

Winthrop defines the second branch of military law, the law of war, as a branch of international law that "prescribes the rights and obligations of belligerents."[13] Now more commonly referred to as international humanitarian law, the law of war has expanded since Winthrop's day. It still regulates all actions related to the conduct of armed conflict, or *jus in bello*; however, since the Nuremberg tribunal cited the Kellogg-Briand Pact of 1929 as the legal basis for the crime of aggression, the law of war now includes the regulation of the initial decision to go to war/engage in armed conflict, or *jus ad bellum*.[14] Thus the Catholic Church's long-held "just war theory" has mutated from moral belief to the law of the world.

Though the law of war may have expanded to include *jus ad bellum*, the field of military law has not, since *jus ad bellum* concerns the decisions of the state and not the military *per se*. The United States Conference of Catholic Bishops ("USCCB") has issued multiple opinions concerning *jus ad bellum* decisions to the point that the topic merits its own article, but it is too divergent to be included in this piece. That said, the decision of the individual soldier or conscripted citizen to refuse to serve in what he/she deems to be an unjust war remains well within the field of military law.

The third branch of military law identified by Winthrop concerns the relationship of soldiers to the civilian government and legal system. This section includes a brief discussion of the concepts of military conscription and the Department of Defense ("DoD") practice of "stop-loss."

CATHOLICISM AND THE UNITED STATES MILITARY LAW PROPER

Soldiers live and operate in a separate society under the authority of commanders. Commanders are burdened with the ultimate responsibility to accomplish the mission and empowered with a broad range of authority to do so. Far more than just an employer or supervisor, the military commander is legislator,[15] mayor,[16] and police chief[17]; accuser, judge and executioner[18]; and teacher, mentor, and arguably even parent.[19] The commander is tasked with the responsibility of developing a disciplined and cohesive community capable of performing its mission to defend the United States.

The military community is organized around shared values. Selfless service is a core value of the United States Air Force and one of the seven Army Values.[20] It is more than merely an aspirational value, but a foundational principle for the military community where self-interest, even when appropriate, is generally derided. Honor and integrity are also shared military values, but both are backed by the prescription of law. A soldier that makes a false statement in the course of his/her duties could be punished by up to five years in prison.[21]

"Family values" is a frequent catchphrase of American politics, but it is a way of life in the military. Morality-based crimes that have faded from civil codes, such as adultery, indecent language, and private acts of sexual indecency are still punishable under military law in certain circumstances.[22] Compared to other employers, the military excels in the variety of support it provides military families. Soldiers with families are eligible for family housing or additional pay,[23] additional pay when families are forced to be separated due to deployment[24]; free or nearly free health care, on-post child care and education, youth services, legal assistance, tax assistance, financial counseling, relocation assistance, and access to hundreds of recreational facilities around the globe.[25] The military goes beyond merely providing support as an organization, it grants the commander the authority to order soldiers to provide financial support to their families even without a court order.[26] Commanders can also ensure that single parents have an adequate plan in place for the care of children in the event of a deployment.[27]

The military also stands out when it comes to supporting the religious faiths and activities of its members. The Chaplain Corps is composed of clergy from a variety of faiths, including a large number of Catholic priests. These chaplains as well as religious facilities and services are funded by the military,[28] and the seal of confession is fully protected in courts-martial by Military Rule of Evidence 503. Further, the military has a mandatory policy of religious accommodation as long as it does not adversely affect military readiness.

In addition to complying with the federal requirements of equal opportunity,[29] the U.S. military makes respect for others a priority for all soldiers. It is one of the core Army values,[30] and it is enforced both by law and regulation.[31] Soldiers are also prohibited from participating in any organization that advocates hate.[32]

Military service is respected by the Church and it is congruous with basic Catholic values.[33] That potentially explains why Catholics are slightly overrepresented within the population of the military.[34] No system is perfect, however, and there are areas where military law can improve.

One issue of prominence was the use of military authority to prevent Catholic chaplains from complying with the instructions of their religious supervisor. On January 26, 2012, the Archbishop of the U.S. Military Diocese, Timothy Broglio, instructed all Catholic chaplains to read his pastoral letter at Sunday Mass. The letter criticized the U.S. government's policy of forcing Catholic employers to fund artificial birth control for their employees even if that act violated Catholic doctrine, and called on Catholics to resist implementation of this policy. The military stepped in and issued an order preventing the reading of the letter during Mass, but allowed the letter to be distributed at the back of each church after Mass.[35] The military felt that Archbishop Broglio's call for noncompliance with the law was subversive toward the law and the administration. Secretary of the Army McHugh felt that this could be misunderstood as a call for civil disobedience.[36] The use of command authority to prevent the dissemination of a pastoral letter should probably be reserved for more extreme circumstances.

The divergence between United States military law and Catholic ideology is more pronounced in the laws regulating armed conflict.

CATHOLICISM AND COMBAT

In large part, the United States' approach to the rules/laws governing armed conflict is very similar to that of the Holy See. For the most part, they have ratified the same international conventions governing *jus in bello*, and both mandate compliance with these treaties. *Gaudium et Spes* requires that "conventions . . . aimed at rendering military action and its consequences less inhuman . . . must be honored."[37] It further requires that all public authorities and law of war specialists "do all in their power to improve these conventions and thus bring about a better and more effective curbing of the savagery of war.[38] Mirroring both the intent and letter of *Gaudium et Spes*, DoD Directive 2311.01E requires all DoD components to comply with the law of war in all conflicts and military operations.[39] This requirement applies no matter how the conflict is politically characterized.[40] The Directive also requires that every soldier receive regular training on the law of war and that experts work to update and improve these rules.[41] There are also mandatory instructions concerning the reporting and investigation of all potential violations of the conventions.[42] Further, in resolving the conflict between the legal requirement to obey orders and the moral and legal requirement to obey the laws of war, U.S. soldiers have not only the legal right, but the responsibility to refuse to obey any order to commit a violation of the conventions.[43] Thus, United States military law concerning *jus in bello* largely complies with the Catholic approach mandated by *Gaudium et Spes*; however, there are some significant divergences, particularly in targeting enemy combatants, privileged belligerency, and conscientious objection.[44]

Under the United States interpretation, enemy combatants are lawful targets and their destruction is a military advantage in and of itself and not subject to direct limitation by the four principles of the law of war. These principles, rooted in natural law as well as the conventions, are: military necessity, proportionality, distinction, and unnecessary suffering.

Military necessity justifies "those measures not forbidden by international law which are indispensable for securing the complete submission of the enemy as soon as possible."[45] It is notionally linked to both the principle of unnecessary suffering, which prohibits combatants from employing methods and armaments that cause superfluous pain, and the principle of proportionality, which requires the collateral damage to civilians and civilian property by an attack be exceeded by the military advantage gained.[46] For an unnecessary suffering example, consider the employment of a glass-filled grenade against enemy combatants. The military advantage is the grenade will scatter glass fragments, wounding or killing enemy combatants, removing them from combat; however, unlike metal fragments, glass fragments do not show on x-rays and thus surgically removing them is much more difficult. This additional military advantage, preventing the effective treatment of a wounded enemy combatant, is vastly exceeded by the unnecessary suffering caused to this individual and thus the use of glass-filled munitions is prohibited. Regarding proportionality, if there is an innocent civilian riding in a car with three enemy combatants, an attack to destroy the car would probably be lawful despite the civilian's incidental death. In that scenario, the military advantage of killing three enemy combatants would exceed the collateral damage. Conversely, blowing up a bus full of innocent civilians in order to kill a single enemy combatant also present would probably be a violation.

Distinction requires combatants to distinguish both themselves and their attacks from the civilian populace. Thus, lawful combatants are required to wear uniforms and carry arms openly to assist the enemy in identifying them as lawful targets. They must also endeavor to keep themselves separate from the civilian populace since the combatants' mere presence places innocent people and property at risk of being collateral damage of a lawful attack. Distinction also mandates that enemy soldiers who surrender, are wounded to the point that they can no longer fight, eject from a downed aircraft, or are captured are no longer combatants and cannot be the intended target of attacks.

Returning to the idea of targeting enemy combatants, however, none of these principles appear to place a limitation on their intentional killing. Consider this scenario. A United States commander is aware of a much smaller enemy force that is poorly armed and tightly grouped on a hill in the direction of his unit's advance. The commander must choose between a surprise artillery attack that would kill every member of the tightly grouped force or providing the enemy an opportunity to surrender. Though the commander believes that this group will probably surrender, he would lose the advantage of a surprise attack, allowing the enemy to disperse and prepare their defenses, thus increasing the probability of American causalities.

From the American military law perspective, military necessity justifies eliminating the military assets of the enemy; the attack will be with lethal force, so unnecessary suffering is not implicated; there are no civilians or civilian property present, so proportionality does not apply; and his forces are in uniform and attacking the enemy military, so distinction is also not a relevant limitation. Under American military law, an attack without providing these enemy soldiers the opportunity to surrender is legal. Further, most American commanders would probably order the attack if they felt that providing the opportunity to surrender would place the lives of their own men and women at greater risk. Taking care of one's troops is an American mandate overcome only by the needs of the mission and the requirements of law. An American commander would much rather (lawfully) kill one hundred enemy soldiers than lose one of his own.

The Catholic approach to the law of war principles in this scenario would be significantly different, particularly in the area of proportionality. Both the Catechism ("The use of arms must not produce evils and disorders graver than the evil to be eliminated")[47] and the United States Conference of Catholic Bishops ("The overall destruction expected from the use of force must be outweighed by the good to be achieved")[48] combine all damage, against enemy military and against civilians, when evaluating the evil consequences of an attack that must be exceeded by the good achieved. Thus it appears that the Catholic view would require the commander to forgo the surprise attack and offer surrender. This is an overly simplistic scenario, but it identifies the disconnect between the Catholic approach and that of the American military. Lawful damage to enemy soldiers, regardless of how significant and/or potentially avoidable, carries little weight when balanced against any increase of threat to a commander's own troops.

A second area of conflict deals with engaging in combat without acquiring privileged belligerency.[49] As shown by its persistent objection to the Additional Protocol I to the Geneva Conventions, the United States has been more hesitant than most in the granting of lawful combatant/privileged belligerent status.[50] Denying lawful combatant status/privileged belligerency means that the individual, if captured, is subject to prosecution for acts of combat as violations of the domestic law (murder) even if those acts otherwise comply with the laws of war. Subject to the limited exceptions (detailed in The Hague and Geneva Conventions) the United States believes that only uniformed military should be considered lawful combatants; a position originally opposed by the Soviet Union and currently opposed by the Taliban and Al Qaeda. Limiting lawful combatant status to uniformed military strongly supports the Catholic belief that states and certain legitimate revolutions are permitted to engage in war.[51]

In addition to violating the law of war principle of distinction, granting lawful combatant status to members of certain groups could be used to add legitimacy to acts that the United States would otherwise label terrorism. In this stance the United States' position does not necessarily diverge from the Holy See. Inconsistently, however, it appears the United States is willing to direct individuals to engage in armed conflict without being lawful combatants.[52] CIA personnel are not members of the uniformed military; when they engage in combat by attacking the enemy with drone strikes, they do not possess immunity from domestic prosecution for murder in the country where the strike occurs.

The United States is hiding behind a technology gap in the law of war. The concept of privileged belligerency did not contemplate that one could engage in combat from thousands of miles away without being at risk of capture by the enemy or local authorities. Thus these CIA operatives are operating with *de facto* immunity even though they have not earned *de jure* immunity. By refusing to acknowledge who or even if operatives are piloting attack drones, the CIA protects these individuals from extradition and prosecution for crimes they did, in fact, commit. This positivist approach violates the natural law foundations of privileged belligerency.

As *Gaudium et Spes* dictates, *jus in bello* is the product of natural law. As such, *jus in bello* carved out an exception to the Fifth Amendment prohibition against murder for lawful combatants.[53] This exception does not apply to CIA operatives. The administration may find the use of CIA operatives more convenient and flexible than using the uniformed military for drone strikes, but that does not provide moral or legal justification, *de facto* immunity aside, for the immoral act of murder.

The third area of conflict between morality and legal pragmatism in this area is the concept of selective conscientious objection, or the ability of an individual to morally refuse to participate in a given war, rather than a refusal to participate in all wars. *Gaudium et Spes* calls for each state to allow a humane provision for conscientious objectors, allowing them to serve their country in some means other than as a combatant.[54] In the wake of the Vietnam War, the USCCB has gone one step further, requesting that the United States allow individuals who feel that a specific conflict is unjust or not approved by competent authority to refuse to serve as combatants.[55] While the United States does recognize and respect the concept of conscientious objection, it continues to refuse selective conscientious objection.[56] In this conflict, however, pragmatism may take precedence over moral aspiration.

The entire just war concept is an acquiescence to the practicality of the current world. Even though war is fundamentally evil, as long as there are states that will attack, other states must be prepared to defend. The denial of selective conscientious objection is a parallel acquiescence to pragmatism. The military invests a significant amount of money and resources in the recruitment, pay, and initial training of each and every member of the all-volunteer military.[57] The Church recognizes that these individuals are "custodians of the security and freedom of their fellow countrymen."[58] Despite this, the U.S. military is still willing to respect and reassign an honest conscientious objector, even if that individual was not a conscientious objector at the time he/she entered military service; however, it requires that the soldier's objection be to war in any form, be linked to religious training or belief, and be "firm, fixed, sincere and deeply held."[59] The strict criterion exists to prevent the use of conscientious objection as a subterfuge for malingering.

The vast majority of soldiers do not want to go to war, and some are willing to go to great lengths to avoid it. Young men and women who enlist to gain valuable training and college benefits may have a sudden change of heart when faced with the realities of deployment.[60] The Church places the responsibility for the *jus ad bellum* decision with "those who have the responsibility for the common good,"[61] rather than the individual citizen. Selective conscientious objection effectively reverses this stance, forcing the state to respect the disagreement of each and every citizen. Further, in declaring criteria for a just war that are largely subjective, the Church provides ample ammunition for those wishing to avoid conflict purely out of self-interest.[62] The USCCB has subsequently conceded that the concept of selective conscientious objection poses complex substantive and procedural problems.[63] Consequently, like the goal of abolishing war, practicality requires selective conscientious objection to remain aspirational at this time.

THE CATHOLIC VIEW OF CIVIL-MILITARY RELATIONS

Vatican II recognizes the right and the responsibility of governments to fight defensive wars,[64] and the USCCB has further recognized the right of a government to require military service of its citizens when necessary[65]; however, the USCCB is very cautious in its discussion of draft registration and conscription.

> Registration: We acknowledge the right of the state to register citizens, for the purpose of military conscription, both in peacetime and in times of national emergency. Therefore, we find no objection in principle to this action by the government. However, we believe it necessary to present convincing reasons for this at any particular time.

> Military Conscription: We are opposed to any reinstitution of military conscription except in the case of a national defense emergency. We support the present standby draft system which requires the chief executive to obtain a new authorization to induct a specific number of men into the armed forces if clear purposes of adequate defense demand conscription.[66]

While the registration system is largely unchanged since 1980 and the draft has not been reinstituted, the DoD practice of "stop-loss" may implicate and conflict with the spirit of this statement.

Stop-loss is the practice of refusing to allow soldiers to leave service following the expiration of their enlistment contract. Federal law allows the president to "suspend any provision of law relating to . . . separation applicable to any member of the armed forces."[67] The U.S. courts have upheld the practice because each enlistment contract includes the provision that allows the term of service to be involuntarily extended in the event of war.[68]

The standard for the president to institute stop-loss is merely if he determines the continued service of the individual is "essential" to national security.[69] In providing the president with extensive flexibility, this creates a more accessible standard than the "national defense emergency" the Conference requires for conscription. The stop-loss standard does not even require the existence of or threat of an armed conflict, but rather a "circumstance" that the president feels justifies the action.[70] At a minimum this negates the moral contractual obligation in the event of a "war." Procedurally, stop-loss only requires the determination of one person as compared to Congressional approval required for the draft. While national conscription is far more significant to the citizenry than extending one individual's term of service, to that individual the effect is the same: involuntary service to his government. Worse, this individual has already provided more service to that government than the vast majority of the populace. Although the Conference has not issued an opinion specifically on the subject, the moral foundations of the 1980 statement on conscription would appear to apply equally to stop-loss and require an equivalent determination of national emergency.

THE LESSON LEARNED

Despite appearances to the contrary, U.S. military law is generally aligned with Catholic ideology. Of the three subfields of military law, the one most in compliance, military law proper, is also the one least susceptible to the whims of political winds. At its core, military law proper is extremely traditional and resistant to change. Those with primary control over it share and operate within a value system congruous with the Roman Catholic faith. The law of war, however, is more susceptible to varied interpretation by those with conflicting values or national self-interests, separating it from its natural law foundation; from the Catholic perspective, it aspires to be much more than it has achieved so far. Finally, civil military relations implicate fewer moral issues though they appear inextricably linked to political expediency.

Just like Felix Unger and Oscar Madison, U.S. military law and Roman Catholic ideology are an odd couple with differences that are largely superficial and cores that are remarkably similar.

NOTES

Professor Meyer is the Director of the Foreign LL.M. Program at Mississippi College School of Law [MC Law]. This work was supported in part by a grant from MC Law. I would like to thank my lovely wife Melissa for her assistance in editing this piece. Any errors, however, are purely my own.

1. The military works to ensure that soldiers have the opportunity to attend religious services, but the mission sometimes makes this impossible.

2. Disobedience is only justified if the order is unlawful, not merely immoral. See Article 90, Uniform Code of Military Justice [hereinafter U.C.M.J.].

3. See Pope Paul VI, *Gaudium et Spes* or *The Pastoral Constitution* [hereinafter *GS*] §§ 25, 27, 28, 30, 52, 67, 75, 78.

4. Avery Cardinal Dulles, "Truth as the Ground of Freedom: A Theme of John Paul II," in *Recovering Self-Evident Truths: Catholic Perspectives on American Law*, ed. Michael Scaperlanda and Teresa Stanton Collett (Catholic University of America Press, 2007) at 71, 82. The Army of One recruitment campaign is founded on the same solidarity ideology promoted by Vatican II and Cardinal Dulles.

5. Joshua E. Kastenberg, *The Blackstone of Military Law* (Scarecrow Press, 2009).

6. William Winthrop, *Military Law and Precedents* (Government Printing Office, 1920) at 15.

7. Winthrop, *Military Law* at 17.

8. *United States ex rel. Toth v. Quarles*, 350 U.S. 11 (1955).

9. *Parker v. Levy*, 417 U.S. 733 (1973) at 743.

10. *Schlesinger v. Councilman*, 420 U.S. 738 (1975) at 757; for a more detailed discussion, see Gregory E. Maggs and Lisa M. Schenck, *Modern Military Justice* (Thomas Reuters, 2012), 2–3.

11. Article 92, U.C.M.J.

12. Article 134, U.C.M.J. See alsoArticle 133 which broadly criminalizes conduct unbecoming an officer.

13. Winthrop, *supra* note 6.

14. This was reinforced by the prohibition of all but defensive or officially sanctioned war in the United Nations Charter.

15. Officers and noncommissioned officers have the ability to create new law merely by issuing an order. Articles 90–92, U.C.M.J.

16. Commanders are responsible for the organization, upkeep, policing, and protection of all buildings, housing areas, and installations under their command. Army Regulation 600-20, *Army Command Policy* (Washington, D.C., March 18, 2008) [hereinafter AR 600-20] at 2–5. (While many citations are to Army sources, the concepts are consistent across the military services.)

17. AR 600-20. The military police work for the installation commander and commanders have investigative authority under R.C.M. 303.

18. The nonjudicial punishment process under Article 15 of the U.C.M.J. has the commander file the "charges," sit in judgment of guilt, and decide on the punishment. Manual for Courts-Martial (MCM) 2012 Edition, Part V., Non-judicial Punishment.

19. The commander is responsible for the training, counseling, and personal development of all the soldiers in the command. AR 600-20, *supra* note 16.

20. "Put the welfare of the nation, the Army and your subordinates before your own. Selfless service is larger than just one person. In serving your country, you are doing your duty loyally without thought of recognition or gain." http://www.army.mil/values/. See also, Army Regulation [hereinafter AR] 600-100, figure 1-1.

21. Article 107, U.C.M.J.

22. Article 134, U.C.M.J. ¶¶62 & 89; Article 120, U.C.M.J.

23. Department of Defense [DoD] Financial Management Regulation, 7000-14.R, June 2011, Chapter 7A.

24. DoD 7000-14.R.

25. See generally, The Army Family, Morale and Recreation Program at http://www.armymwr.com/.

26. AR 608-99, Family Support, Child Custody and Paternity, October 29, 2003, at 2–6.

27. AR 600-20 at 5-5.

28. AR 600-20, § 5-6.

29. AR 600-20 at 6-1.

30. AR 600-100, figure 1-1

31. Article 93, U.C.M.J.; AR 600-20 at 4-20 and 7-1.

32. AR 600-20 at 4-12.

33. United States Conference of Catholic Bishops, Pastoral Letter, "The Challenge of Peace: God's Promise and Our Response" (May 3, 1981) at 309 [hereinafter "Challenge of Peace"].

34. See generally, Military Leadership Diversity Commission Issue Paper #22, "Religious Diversity in the Military," June 2010. Anecdotally, I believe that the numbers of Catholics in the military to be much higher, especially among the officer corps.

35. "Military Chaplains Instructed Not to Read Letter Against HHS Mandate," *National Catholic Register*, February 7, 2012.

36. *National Catholic Register, supra* note 35.

37. *GS*, § 79.

38. *GS*, §79.

39. DoD Directive 2311.01E, incorporating Change 1, November 15, 2010, § 4.1.

40. DoD Directive 2311.01E, incorporating Change 1, § 4.1.

41. DoD Directive 2311.01E at 5.72; 5.1.

42. DoD Directive 2311.01E at 6.3; 5.8.3. Although violations of the law of war are often charged as common-law crimes such as murder under Article 118 of the U.C.M.J., this does not mean that the United States fails to properly punish these offenses. The United States military has a long tradition of charging law of war violations under the existing code rather than creating separate enumerated offenses. In fact the world's first modern codification of the laws of war, the Lieber Code, was actually a General Order issued to the Union troops during the Civil War rather than an amendment to the Articles of War. General Order 100 was developed by a committee chaired by Francis Lieber at the direction of Union Commander General Henry W. Halleck in 1863. This code is credited as providing the foundation of the modern law of war. See Gary Solis, *The Law of Armed Conflict* (Cambridge University Press, 2010) at 39–40.

43. Article 90, U.C.M.J. c. (2) and United States Department of the Army, *Field Manual FM27-10, The Law of Land Warfare* (Government Printing Office, 1956) ¶509a. *The Catechism of the Catholic Church* [hereinafter *Catechism*] has similar language at ¶2313.

44. The brevity of this piece prevents a discussion of the also important conflicts dealing with the possession and use of nuclear weapons and rules of engagement that require soldiers to observe and not prevent certain travesties.

45. *Law of Land Warfare, supra* note 43 at 4.

46. Think of the three principles as residing on a scale, where on one side is the military advantage gained and on the other is the physical suffering of enemy combatants and collateral damage to civilians. In simplistic terms, if the military advantage to the attacker exceeds the sum of the unnecessary suffering plus incidental damage to civilians, the attack is lawful. Solis, *supra* note 42, 250–85.

47. *Catechism*, ¶2309.

48. Excerpts from the Church's Teaching on War and Peace, *found at* http://old.usccb.org/sdwp/peace/hojexcer.pdf. See also, "The Challenge of Peace," *supra* note 33 at 105.

49. "Privileged belligerency" is the law of war concept that lawful combatants cannot be prosecuted for their lawful acts of conflict, even if they are a violation of domestic laws.

50. This chapter uses the terms of lawful combatant and privileged belligerent interchangeably.

51. *Catholic Encyclopedia* (online edition), s.v. "War," http://www.catholic.org/encyclopedia/view.php?id=12206 (accessed January 1, 2014). "The right of war is the right of a sovereign state." See also, *GS*, § 79: "governments cannot be denied the right of lawful self-

defense" and "The Challenge of Peace," 89–96, discussing legitimate revolutions and the requirement of a competent authority. A just war must also have a legitimate chance of success.

52. Gary Solis, "CIA Drone Attacks Produce America's Own Unlawful Combatants," *The Washington Post*, March 12, 2010.

53. *Jus in bello* envisions two different uniformed militaries taking all reasonable steps to segregate themselves from the civilian populace, both geographically and cosmetically. The wearing of uniforms creates a legal and moral reciprocity: I can shoot you because you can shoot me. It is dissimilar to the use of force in a civilian context, where you must be an imminent threat to me and my response must be proportional to that threat. In combat, I can lawfully kill you while you are sleeping and unarmed.

54. *GS*, § 79.

55. "Challenge of Peace," 232, 233.

56. DoD Directive 1300.06, Conscientious Objectors, May 5, 2007. See also, *Gillette v. United States*, 401 U.S. 437 (1971).

57. AR 635-200, Enlisted Separations, June 6, 2005, ¶¶1–15.

58. *GS*, § 79.

59. Note 39 at ¶4.1.1; 5.1.

60. Rosita Johnson, "Soldier Refuses Army's Order to Go to Iraq," *People's World*, April 9, 2005 available at http://peoplesworld.org/soldier-refuses-army-s-order-to-go-to-iraq/ (accessed March 9, 2014).

61. *Catechism*, ¶2309.

62. "The strict conditions for legitimate defense by military force require rigorous consideration. The gravity of such a decision makes it subject to rigorous conditions of moral legitimacy. At one and the same time: the damage inflicted by the aggressor on the nation or community of nations must be lasting, grave, and certain; all other means of putting an end to it must have been shown to be impractical or ineffective; there must be serious prospects of success; and the use of arms must not produce evils and disorders graver than the evil to be eliminated." *Catechism*, ¶2309.

63. United States Conference of Catholic Bishops, Pastoral Letter, "The Harvest of Justice Is Sown in Peace," November 17, 1993.

64. *GS*, §79.

65. United States Conference of Catholic Bishops, "Statement on the Registration and Conscription for Military Service," February 14, 1980, and "Challenge of Peace," 232.

66. "Statement on the Registration and Conscription for Military Service," and "Challenge of Peace," 232.

67. 10 U.S.C. § 12305.

68. DoD Form 4/1, § 10 (b). See *Qualls v. Rumsfeld*, 412 F. Supp. 2d 40 (D.D.C. 2006); *Doe v. Rumsfeld*, 435 F. 3d 980 (9th Cir. 2006).

69. 10 U.S.C. § 12305(a) "the President may suspend any provision of law relating to promotion, retirement, or separation applicable to any member of the armed forces who the President determines is essential to the national security of the United States."

70. 10 U.S.C. § 12305(b)(2).

Chapter Sixteen

Property Law

D. Brian Scarnecchia

INTRODUCTION

In antiquity property was held in common by a patriarchal chief in trust for his clan and kin. Over time, social structures more respectful of individual human dignity and private property evolved.[1] Today property law has come full circle. Political pressure and legal action are being brought across the United States and around the world to collectivize natural resources in order to ensure sustainable development, avert ecological crisis, and protect the rights of nature.

A sound Catholic perspective on property law, however, must balance the universal destination of goods with the right to private property, not sacrificing one for the other.[2] This dynamic tension rests upon a proper understanding of human nature, one that is common to all human beings with innate laws of human flourishing, a "human ecology."[3] The right to property, and all other human rights, does not depend upon one's talents. Might does not make right. Rather, inalienable human rights are founded upon the essential *relationship* of the human person with God: The origin of each person is from God; each person is called to eternal union with God; and each person is made in the image of God.[4] Pope Benedict XVI reminded the United Nations that God, not might, not human consensus, makes human rights: It is evident that the rights recognized and expounded in the *Universal Declaration of Human Rights* apply to everyone by virtue of the common origin of the person, who remains the high point of God's creative design for the world and for history.[5]

In this chapter those principles and applications of property law that are compatible with authentic human flourishing will be examined from the perspective of Catholic social thought.

"LOOSE-FISH, FAST-FISH": THE RULE OF CAPTURE

In *Moby Dick*, Herman Melville tersely explained the whaling law of his day: "A Fast-Fish belongs to the party fast to it. . . . A Loose-Fish is fair game for anybody who can soonest catch it."[6] This principle, known as the "rule of capture," stands for the proposition that the first person to take possession of a wild animal, *ferae naturae*, is its rightful owner. Adages such as "first in time is first in right" and "possession is nine-tenths of the law" express this legal norm that legitimizes the acquisition of personal property.[7]

Timing, control, and intent are crucial to the rule of capture. For instance, it is not the first person to mark a tree with the intent to take possession of a wild beehive who acquires the right to the beehive. Rather, it is the first person who "hives" the wild bees, by placing them into a hive with the intent to keep the bees, who possesses and legally owns the bees.[8] In *Pierson v. Post* the court ruled against a mounted hunter who, with a pack of hounds baying, first gave chase to a fox in favor of a lone hunter on foot who first shot and killed that fox.[9] The colloquial expression, "dead to rights," sums up the common-law rule of capture. Killing a wild animal, "stopping it dead in its tracks," not merely wounding it, gives one "rights" to it.[10] The capture of an animal in a trap or training a wild animal in the habit of returning to its pen (*animus revertendi*) also entitles one to possess the creature as private property.[11] Once an animal is killed, one may tag or waif it, leave temporarily, and return a short time later better equipped to haul it away.[12] The common-law doctrine of *ratione soli* entitles the owner of the soil to take possession of all the plants and animals thereon.[13] Also, one who owns a parcel of land owns everything from the heavens above to the center of the earth below the ground under the *ad coelum* doctrine.[14]

Haslem v. Lockwood illustrates the extension of the rule of capture to inanimate objects, for example, horse manure abandoned on a public road. It was the person who arrived on the scene first and effectively captured the loose manure, raking it into neat piles, and not he who deftly shoveled those piles of manure into a wheelbarrow and hauled it off to his garden, who had the right to own it:

> [I]f a party finds property comparatively worthless, as the plaintiff found the property . . . owing to its scattered condition upon the highway, and greatly increases its value by his labor and expense, does he lose his right if he leaves it a reasonable time to procure the means to take it away, when such means are necessary for its removal?[15]

American case law soon extended the rule of capture to other things that bear resemblance to mobile wild animals that must be caught in some fashion, from home-run baseballs flying into the bleachers to underground deposits of oil and gas. [16]

THE RIGHT TO PRIVATE PROPERTY — BY THE SWEAT OF YOUR BROW

John Locke, in his *Second Treatise of Government* (1689) justified the acquisition of private property based on the human labor. Originally, he said, all the goods of the earth were bestowed on humanity in common, however, through human labor a person mixes something of himself with what nature provides and converts what is common to all into her own property. "Whatsoever then he removes out of the state that nature hath provided, and left it in, he hath mixed his labour with, and joined to it something that is his own, and thereby makes it his property." [17]

In the era of the founding of the United States, the Supreme Court recognized the natural law origin of private property and that persons enter into political society in order to better secure the enjoyment of private property:

> [T]he right of acquiring and possessing property, and having it protected, is one of the natural, inherent, and unalienable rights of man. Men have a sense of property: Property is necessary to their subsistence, and correspondent to their natural wants and desires; its security was one of the objects that induced them to unite in society. No man would become a member of a community, in which he could not enjoy the fruits of his honest labours and industry. [18]

Catholic social teaching recognizes that private property is necessary for all people to fulfill their duty to sustain their life. [19] Therefore, everyone has a right to own the property they have toiled over with the sweat of their brow:

> By means of work and making use of the gift of intelligence, people are able to exercise dominion over the earth and make it a fitting home: "In this way, he makes part of the earth his own, precisely the part which he has acquired through work; this is the origin of individual property." [20]

Moreover, equal access to the means of acquiring private property is necessary for a just social and economic order and for personal and political freedom. [21]

The Church, however, insists that the right to private property is "not absolute," but qualified. It must serve the original "universal destination of goods." Therefore, in cases of dire necessity, surplus private property reverts to its common usage in order to relieve human want:

> Christian tradition has never recognized the right to private property as absolute and untouchable: "On the contrary, it has always understood this right

within the broader context of the right common to all to use the goods of the whole of creation: the right to private property is subordinated to the right to common use, to the fact that goods are meant for everyone."[22]

The universal destination of goods is the "first principle of the whole ethical and social order." It is a "natural right" that is "innate in individual persons" and it has "priority" to any legal system concerning goods and is a "serious and urgent social obligation." The right to free trade must facilitate the application of the universal destination of all goods.[23]

TAKING PROPERTY—BY "THEFT," ADVERSE POSSESSION, AND LAND REFORM

Lethal force is permitted to save one's life or that of another, if no other means of self-defense or defense of a third party is available.[24] Likewise, one is permitted to take the surplus personal property of another to preserve one's life as St. Thomas Aquinas explains:

> [W]hatever certain people have in superabundance is due, by natural law, to the purpose of succoring the poor. For this reason Ambrose says: "It is the hungry man's bread that you withhold. . . ." [I]f the need be so manifest and urgent, that it is evident that the present need must be remedied by whatever means be at hand . . . then it is lawful for a man to succor his own need by means of another's property, by taking it either openly or secretly: nor is this properly speaking theft or robbery.[25]

Although it may be morally licit to take without permission the surplus food of another to save one's life, it is legally a crime to do so. During the Great Depression, starving workers made an orderly demand for more food to the Red Cross commissar. Being told no more food would be given them, they took food anyway. Even though no acts of vandalism occurred, the court convicted all who took part in the raid: "In larceny cases, economic necessity is frequently invoked in mitigation of punishment, but has never been recognized as a defense."[26]

On the other hand, the law of adverse possession recognizes that the taking of real property against the will of its owner is not always unlawful. A person, not the legal owner of a parcel of land, but who, nonetheless, occupies that parcel continuously, openly, notoriously, and adversely to the exclusion of others, may become the rightful owner of that land.[27]

In the Philippines, claims for adverse possession against absentee owners had been defeated by long-term lease agreements, creating a large rural population of subsistence sharecrop farmers. The Catholic Bishops of the Philippines supported the right of these farmers in their struggle with a small but powerful landed oligopoly stretching back to a period of colonial rule.[28]

Catholic social teaching recognized that land reform and the redistribution of real property interests may be "indispensable in some cases."[29]

The universal destination of good also informs the Church's stance on international assistance to the Least Developed Countries. The Holy See urged the United Nations to formulate "incisive measures for the cancellation of the debt of poorer countries," an "increase of development aid," and "wider access to markets."[30] Pope Paul VI said, "The superfluous goods of wealthier nations ought to be placed at the disposal of poorer nations."[31]

TAKING PROPERTY: THE RULE OF CONQUEST AND THE FIFTH AMENDMENT

Was America in 1492 a loose-fish? Just as a whaler in his small skiff first harpoons and kills a whale, then waifs (tags) the dead whale by planting the ship's flag in the behemoth as a sign of possession, so too, explorers and conquistadors planted the flags of their sovereigns in the soil of newly discovered or conquered territories, as Melville explains: "What was America in 1492 but a Loose-Fish in which Columbus struck the Spanish standard by way of waifing it for his royal master and mistress?"[32]

Europeans generally felt justified taking the land of Native Americans because, as Supreme Court Chief Justice, John Marshall, said in 1823, "the character and religion of its inhabitants afforded an apology for considering them as a people over whom the superior genius of Europe might claim ascendency."[33] Native Americans were granted limited sovereignty under federal law; that is, they are the true owners of their land but they may not transfer their land to private parties or foreign nations without the federal government's approval.[34]

On the contrary, when the Age of Discovery had just begun, Francisco de Vitoria, O.P. (d. 1546), raised his voice in defense of the rights of newly discovered indigenous people in the Americas. He argued that even though they were not baptized or civilized by European standards they were truly rational and the true owners of the land in which they dwelt. Europeans, therefore, had no right to attack and conquer indigenous people in order to take their land and property.[35]

The outright taking by despotic power of the property of one person in order to transfer it to another violates both Judeo-Christian morality and American constitutional law. Supreme Court Chief Justice Paterson noted that no person ought to suffer the loss of the whole value of his property without compensation—"such an act would be a monster in legislation, and shock all mankind."[36] The Fifth Amendment to the United States Constitution specifically provides: "Nor shall private property be taken for public use, without just compensation."

The Supreme Court has ruled that the state may take private property for a public purpose, provided just compensation is paid, in cases of complete physical takings, no matter how small[37]; in cases of regulatory takings, when all economic value is eliminated from one's reasonable "investment backed expectations"[38]; and, possibly, in instances of judicial takings that effectively wipe out all economic value.[39] On the other hand, in cases of nuisance,[40] or government price-fixing in times of war,[41] or in cases of partial physical invasions,[42] or when zoning regulations merely reduce but do not eliminate all economic value in private property,[43] the Supreme Court has held that no taking has occurred and therefore no compensation is due.

In *Susette Kelo v. City of New London, Connecticut* the city council instituted an eminent domain proceeding against several holdouts in order to transfer their private property to another private entity so as to stimulate economic growth, provide a greater tax base, and hopefully, increase employment in the city of New London.[44] Justice O'Connor in her dissenting opinion complained: "Under the banner of economic development, all private property is now vulnerable to being taken and transferred to another private owner, so long as it might be upgraded. . . ." She also warned: "The specter of condemnation hangs over all property. Nothing is to prevent the State from replacing any Motel 6 with a Ritz-Carlton, any home with a shopping mall, or any farm with a factory."[45]

Kelo, however, left open the possibility that states, under their own constitutions and laws, may place further restrictions on eminent domain takings beyond "the federal baseline."[46] The popular backlash to *Kelo* drove through the doors of state legislatures more new legislation than any previous Supreme Court decision in an attempt to ward off the extended reach of the federal government's power to take private property for a public purpose.[47]

Kelo's analysis of public takings relied heavily on "private takings" authorized under the constitutions and statues of several Western states concerning natural resource development.[48] It was widely believed that in order for the newly constituted states of the interior West to develop, large natural resource development corporations (timber, coal, oil, and gas companies, etc.) needed a free hand to condemn and take what property they thought necessary to further their private enterprise, which would boost the economic prosperity of the entire state: "The present prosperity of the state is entirely due to the mining development already made, and the entire people of the state are directly interested in having the future developments unobstructed by the obstinate action of any individual or individuals."[49]

Is the power to take and redistribute property for the economic benefit of large corporations a valid application of the principle of the universal destination of goods? Some suggest it is merely "a tool used by private industry to promote private interests at the expense of other private parties."[50] In the Philippines, the native landed oligopoly gave international corporations exclusive contracts for timber, land use, and mining extraction. The Catholic bishops of the Philippines opposed these special interests.[51] The principle of the universal destination of goods requires "a preferential option for the poor," not the rich.[52]

TAKING PROPERTY: THE PUBLIC TRUST DOCTRINE

Was the moon in 1969 a loose-fish? By virtue of the Outer Space Treaty the moon may never be made a fast-fish. Exploration of the moon is a "common interest of all mankind" and all outer space exploration should be carried on for the benefit of all people. When astronaut Neil Armstrong stuck a United States of America flag in the moon, he did so as an envoy of mankind.[53] Outer space "is not subject to national appropriation by claim of sovereignty, by means of use or occupation, or by any other means."[54]

Today many academics and activists believe that not only the moon but the earth's atmosphere must be considered a common interest of humanity and placed in trust to be managed by national and international trustees. They argue that the common-law "public trust doctrine" ought to be expanded beyond its original scope and moorings in lands subjected to tidal waters to include the atmosphere in order to avert global warming.[55]

Originally the public trust doctrine of England and America guaranteed the right of the public in coastal waters subject to the influence of the tides. The state holds these lands in trust for the public's benefit:

> At common law, the title and dominion in lands flowed by the tide water were in the King for the benefit of the nation. . . . Upon the American Revolution, these rights, charged with a like trust, were vested in the original States within their respective borders, subject to the rights surrendered by the Constitution of the United States.[56]

The state cannot convey land subject to public trust in fee simple to a private party. If such lands have been conveyed, they may be reclaimed by the state without just compensation.[57]

In *American Electric Power v. Connecticut* (2011) the Supreme Court held that all federal common-law claims for atmospheric pollution were displaced by the Clean Air Act. However, a state common-law nuisance claim might still be possible.[58] One year later, Texas district court judge, Gisela D. Triana, invalidated a Texas Commission on Environmental Quality finding that the public trust doctrine applied only to water. She distinguished the case before her from *American Electric Power*. The Clean Air Act, she said, is a "floor, not a ceiling, for the protection of air quality."[59] She opined that "the [public trust] doctrine includes all natural resources of the State including the air and atmosphere."[60]

The tide of political pressure to collectivize all natural resources is rising. Already many developing nations have amended or interpreted their national constitutions to include all natural resources as trust property.[61] Moreover, the public trust doctrine may provide an effective legal strategy for attaining the United Nation's Sustainable Development Goals:

> [T]he Public Trust Doctrine (PTD) provides a legal foundation and implementation framework for achieving sustainable resource use. Two key topics at Rio + 20 in particular could be clarified by applying the PTD: 1) protecting the rights of future generations to functioning ecosystems and 2) governing resources beyond national jurisdictions.[62]

The Church points out that global warming should be neither "exaggerated nor minimized."[63] Certainly the universal destination of goods includes the atmosphere. However, although the universal destination of goods conditions the right to private property, it does not abrogate it. In fact, Leo XIII criticized those who wanted to collectivize all natural resources for the alleged benefit of the people:

> [I]t seems amazing that some should now be setting up anew certain obsolete opinions. . . . They assert that it is right for persons to have the use of soil and its various fruits, but that it is unjust for anyone to possess outright either the land on which he has built or the estate which he has brought under cultivation. But those who deny these rights do not perceive that they are defrauding man of what his own labor has produced.[64]

In light of Leo XIII's warning, perhaps the evolving concept of a "judicial taking" ought to apply to any expansion of the scope of the public trust doctrine. A judicial taking occurs when "a *court* declares that what was once an established right of private property no longer exists, it has taken that property, no less than if the State had physically appropriated it or destroyed its value by regulation."[65] The problem with the public trust doctrine is that it lacks "a readily defensible stopping point. The public trust doctrine has the potential to reach—and to lead to restrictions on the behavior of—all parties that contribute collectively to an ecological problem, even if the casual link of any individual party is attenuated."[66] Some suggest that behind an environmental cloak of green lies a collectivist red agenda.[67]

MARITAL PROPERTY: A LOOSE-FISH?

Is a marriage a loose-fish? Melville tells us about a man who divorced his wife and "abandoned her upon the seas of life; but in the course of the years, repenting of that step, he instituted an action to recover possession of her" or at least regain the marital property he had bestowed upon her. After their divorce, however, "she became a loose-fish; and therefore when a subsequent gentleman re-harpooned her, the lady then became that subsequent gentleman's property, along with whatever harpoon might have been found sticking in her."[68]

Melville's Cupid with harpoon in hand capturing property in the bonds of matrimony is a good metaphor for the redistribution of marital property occurring today. Marriage has become a loose-fish. One may harpoon any "marital object." The law increasingly regards a spouse simply as an indifferent object that one hooks in order to obtain profitable property interests.

After the Supreme Court neutered natural marriage, breaking the link between marriage, procreation, and childrearing by legalizing contraception and abortion,[69] it was only a matter of time until the allocation of marital property exclusively to natural marriage between a man and a woman would seem unreasonable. If, when a man and a woman marry, they choose to render their sex acts artificially infertile through legal contraceptives and abortion, why can't persons with homosexual desires legally marry since their sex acts are naturally infertile? The Supreme Court of Vermont recognized this irony and extended the legal benefits of marriage to homosexual couples:

> [M]any opposite-sex couples marry for reasons unrelated to procreation, that some of these couples never intend to have children, and that others are incapable of having children. Therefore, if the purpose of the statutory exclusion of same-sex couples is to "further the link between procreation and child rearing," it is significantly under-inclusive. The law extends the benefits and protections of marriage to many persons with no logical connection to the stated governmental goal.[70]

Baker v. Vermont held that the benefits formerly apportioned exclusively to natural marriage, based on what they regarded as the missing-link between sexual activity and childbearing ought to be redistributed because "access to a civil marriage license and the multitude of legal benefits, protection, and obligations that flow from it significantly enhance the quality of life in our society." The court listed fifteen valuable marital property interests that were unreasonably withheld from homosexual couples who wish to marry.[71]

However, the judicial taking of marital property in the case of same-sex marriage violates the innate laws of human flourishing: "If, from the legal standpoint, marriage between a man and woman were to be considered just one possible form of marriage, the concept of marriage would undergo a radical transformation, with grave detriment to the common good."[72] Moreover, the rationale used to legitimize same-sex marriage may "be asserted with equal validity for polyamorous partnerships, polygamous households, [and] even . . . incestuous relationships."[73]

HUMAN DNA, ORGANS, AND EMBRYOS: LOOSE-FISH, TOO?

What about us? Are we, too, just loose-fish? Are our thoughts, our sincerely held religious convictions, and our very genetic identity all up for grabs as Melville suggests?

> What are the Rights of man and the Liberties of the World but Loose-Fish? What all men's minds and opinions but Loose-Fish? What is the principle for religious belief in them but a Loose-Fish: What to the ostentatious smuggling verbalists are the thoughts of thinkers but Loose-Fish. . . . And what are you, reader, but a Loose-Fish and a Fast-Fish, too?[74]

Recently, the Supreme Court ruled unanimously that "[a] naturally occurring [human] DNA segment is a product of nature and not patent eligible merely because it has been isolated."[75] This author signed an *Amici Curiae* brief with the Supreme Court in *Association for Molecular Pathology v. Myriad Genetics, Inc.*[76] That brief argued that "the patenting of DNA sequences treats as private property what is a part of the common and innate nature of the human person. Patents on DNA sequences will open the door to further commodification of the gene pool reflecting a eugenic mentality as, for instance, in germ line cell therapy."[77]

Human beings do not *own* themselves—"God alone is sovereign."[78] Our individual existence and our human nature is God's unalienable gift to us:

> Permitting a corporation or person to own this fundamental component of a person corrupts the relationships between human beings and the Creator, and between human beings. The person should not be treated as a commodity for sale to the highest bidder, and property must be recognized in a way that respects all the members of society.[79]

John Paul II warned that human DNA must not be patented "because it is a gift written into nature itself."[80] Man can no more be separated from his DNA than from his spirit and any attempt "to divvy up the person to the highest bidder for commercial purposes runs the 'serious risk of suppressing the person's very nature' and reducing him to a mere object."[81]

There are chilling similarities between slavery and the granting of human genetic patents: "Marketing human life is a form of genetic slavery. Instead of whole persons being marched in shackles to the market block, human gene sequences are labeled, patented, and sold to the highest bidders."[82] Now that the Supreme Court has held that human gene sequences may not be sold to the highest bidder, why should American law continue to allow whole frozen human embryos to be auctioned off? In *Davis v. Davis* the Supreme Court of Tennessee held that frozen human embryos are neither persons nor property and can be destroyed.[83] It disregards the findings of fact made by the trial court (based on evidence presented by the world-renowned geneticist, Dr. Jerome Lejeune) that frozen embryos are "tiny persons" locked in a "concentration can," so, allowing them to be born would be in their best interests. [84]

The morality of the prenatal adoption of frozen embryos is still under consideration by the Magisterium of the Catholic Church. [85] However, Catholic social teaching clearly condemns in vitro fertilization, cryopreservation, and embryo destructive research. [86] Moreover, human organs must not be sold because organ donation is a noble and lifesaving gift of self. [87] However, death must not be hastened so as to procure organs for transplant. [88]

CONCLUSION

Ancient law knew nothing of the individual. The patriarchal chief held in his hand the lives of the members of his clan and all their property which he held in trust for the clan. [89] Today, the denial of free will and despair in human altruism serves to justify collectivizing all natural resources so as to protect us all from ruinous human activity. This approach will only compound the problem. The centralized planned economies of the former Communist countries "were not only terribly inept at producing and distributing goods to their own people, they were also among the worst polluters and most reckless environmental regimes in history." [90]

The ancient world saw time as cyclic. Christians, on the other hand, see time as linear and tending toward perfection. [91] Post-modernity has lost hope in human progress. Its prophets and experts propose "sustainable development" as the best we can expect of the future. [92] Such deterministic and pessimistic models have been used to justify coercive population control. Pope Paul VI warned the United Nations that international programs should not eliminate the "guests" but, rather, should increase the bounty at "the banquet of life." [93]

Finally, the ancient world believed nature was divine. Today, more and more, nature is viewed as a living being, a goddess, "Gaia." [94] Pope Emeritus, Benedict XVI, explained that there are two errors we must avoid—that of "total technical domination over nature" seen as "a heap of scattered refuse" versus "considering nature an untouchable taboo," a "position that leads to attitudes of neo-paganism or a new pantheism." [95] Yes, environmental degradation threatens world peace. However, people must not resort to "an inhuman ecology," which sees humanity "as an irredeemable threat to the earth, whose population and activity need to be controlled by various drastic means." [96]

The answer to the abuse of private property during the Industrial Revolution was not found in Proudhon's socialist denunciation—"Property is theft!" [97] Rather, it was Leo XIII who struck the proper balance between private property and the universal destination of goods. Today the Vicar of Christ reminds us that America was "grounded in a worldview shaped not only by faith but a commitment to certain ethical principles deriving from nature and nature's God."[98] Catholic social teaching provides perspective on property—declaring which fish are fast and which are loose—so we can rebuild a cultural consensus concerning true human ecology, a regard for authentic human flourishing that America once understood and must relearn.

NOTES

1. Henry Sumner Maine, *Ancient Law*, "The Early History of Property" (New York: Cosimo Classics, 2005), 153; see also Pontifical Council for Justice and Peace, *Compendium of the Social Doctrine of the Church* (Libreria Editrice Vaticana, English translation, 2004), ¶180 [hereinafter *Compendium*].

2. *Compendium,* ¶¶176–77.

3. See John Paul II, *Centesimus Annus*, ¶38 (1991); *Evangelium Vitae*, ¶42 (1995); Benedict XVI, *Message for the 2007 World Day of Peace*, ¶7; Benedict XVI, *Caritas in Veritate*, ¶51 (2009); Benedict XVI, "Address to the Members of the Diplomatic Corps," January 11, 2010, http://www.vatican.va/holy_father/benedict_XVI/speeches/2010/january/documents/hf_be; *Cf. Compendium*, ¶463.

4. *Catechism of the Catholic Church* (Libreria Editrice Vaticana, English translation, 1994), ¶1937, ¶1934.

5. Benedict XVI, "Address to the General Assembly of the United Nations," April 18, 2008, *accessible at* http://www.vatican.va/.../benedict_xvi/speeches/2088/april/documents/hf_ben-xvi_spe_20080418_un-visit_en.html-24k-2011-10-10.

6. Herman Melville, *Moby Dick*, Chapter 89, "Fast-Fish and Loose-Fish" (1851).

7. I am indebted to Professor Howard Bromberg who allowed me to use as a textbook his unpublished manuscript, *Course Pack, Property I* and *Course Pack, Property II*. These legal maxims are taken from *Bromberg Course Pack*, *Property I*, 9.

8. *Gillet v. Mason*, 7 Johns. 16 (N.Y., 1859).

9. *Pierson v. Post*, 3 Cai. R. 175, 179, 1805 N.Y. LEXIS 311 (1805).

10. *Buster v. Newkirk*, 20 Johns. 75, 1822 N.Y. LEXIS 63, 1822 WL 1651 (1822).

11. See *Reese v. Hughes*, 144 Miss. 304, 109 So. 731, 1926 Miss. LEXIS 357 (1926); see also *State v. Mallory*, 73 Ark. 236, 244 (Ark. 1904).

12. *Taber v. Jenny*, 1856 U.S. Dist. LEXIS 45, 23 F. Cas. 605, 1 Sprague 315, 19 Law Rep. 27 (1856).

13. Literally, "by reason of the soil." See *Gillet*, 7 Johns. 16, 17.

14. Literally, "to the sky." See *United States v. Causby*, 328 U.S. 256, 260–61 (1946).

15. *Haslem v. Lockwood*, 37 Conn. 500 (1871).

16. *Popov v. Hayaski*, WL 31833731 Ca. Sup. Ct. (2002) (Barry Bonds's record-setting homerun baseball set off a dispute between two parties each of whom claimed to have gained possession of the ball); *Kelly v. Ohio Oil Co.*, 49 N.E. 399 (Ohio, 1897); *Coastal Oil & Gas Corp. v. Garza Energy Trust*, 268 S.W.3d 1 (Tex., 2008) (in 1889, "the doctrine of law of capture was applied to oil. Private property rights in oil were assigned only upon extraction"); *Cf.* David Feeny, et al. "The Tragedy of the Commons: Twenty-Two Years Later," *Human Ecology*, Vol. 18, No. 1, 1990: 6.

17. John Locke, *The Second Treatise of Government*, Chapter 5, ¶27 (1689) (New York: Mentor Books, 1960), 328–29.

18. *Vanhorne's Lessee v. Dorrance*, 2 Dall. 304, 310 (Paterson, Justice) (1795), http://laws.lp.findlaw.com/getcase/us/vol/getcase/US/2/304.html.

19. Leo XIII, *Rerum Novarum* (1891), ¶9.

20. *Compendium*, ¶176, *citing* John Paul II, *Centesimus Annus* (1991), ¶31. *See also Rerum Novarum* (1891), ¶9: "Now, when a man turns the activity of his mind and the strength of his

body towards procuring the fruits of nature, by such act he makes his own that portion of nature's field which he cultivates—that portion on which he leaves, as it were, the impress of his personality; and it cannot be but just that he should possess that portion as his very own, and have a right to hold it without anyone be justified in violating that right."

21. *Compendium,* ¶176, *citing, Centesimus Annus,* ¶6 and *Gaudium et Spes,* ¶71.

22. *Compendium,* ¶177, *citing* John Paul II, *Laborem Exercens* (1981), ¶14.

23. *Compendium,* ¶172, *citing* Paul VI, *Populorum Progresso* (1967), ¶22. See also *Laborem Excercens,* ¶19.

24. *Evangelium Vitae,* ¶55; *cf.,* American Law Institute, Model Penal Code (1981), §3.02 (limits the necessity defense to circumstances when the evil sought to be avoided is greater than the activity sought to be prevented by the law).

25. Thomas Aquinas, *Summa Theologica,* I-II, q. 66, a. 7.

26. *Washington v. Moe,* 174 Wash. 303, 307–8, 24 P.2d 638, 640.

27. See *Naab v. Nolan,* 174 W.Va. 390, 327 S.E.2d 151, 1985 W.Va. LEXIS 476 (1985).

28. The land reform act of the Philippines, *Comprehensive Agrarian Reform Law* (CARP), Republic Act No. 6657, June 10, 1988, broke up the large concentrations of land held in the hands of a few absentee owners worked by sharecrop farmers. CARP was endorsed by the Catholic Bishops Conference of the Philippines. "Pastoral Statement of the Philippine Hierarchy on the Year of Social Action," May 1968, http://cbcponline.net/v2?p=8013; *see also* "Statement of Appeal to the Government of the Philippines," July 2009, http://cbcponline.net/v/?p=572 ("We, the Catholic Bishops of the Philippines . . . appeal to the Government on behalf of our small farmers") (accessed October 13, 2013).

29. *Compendium,* ¶300; see also Pope Paul VI, *Populorum Progressio* (1967), ¶24: "If certain landed estates impede the general prosperity because they bring hardship to peoples or are detrimental to the interest of the country, the common good sometimes demands their expropriation."

30. Cardinal Angelo Sodano, Secretary of State for the Holy See, "Statement at the Millennium Summit," September 8, 2000, http://www.vatican.va/romancuria/secretariatstate/documents/rcseg-stdoc 20000908 (accessed October 2, 2013).

31. *Populorum Progressio,* ¶49.

32. Melville, *Moby Dick,* Chapter 89.

33. *Johnson v. McIntosh,* 21 U.S. (8 Wheat) 543, 573 (1823).

34. *Johnson,* 21 U.S at 574.

35. See Robert Araujo and John Lucal, *Papal Diplomacy and the Quest for Peace* (Naples, FL: Sapientia Press, 2004), 29–32.

36. *Vanhorne's Lessee v. Dorrance,* 2 Dall. 304, 310 (Paterson, Justice) (1795); see also *New American Bible,* 1 Kg 21:1–16 (King Ahab's theft of Naboth's vineyard).

37. See *Loretto v. Teleprompter Manhattan CAVT Corp.,* 458 U.S. 419 (1982).

38. See *Penn Central Transportation Co. v. New York City,* 438 U.S. 104, 124 (1978).

39. See *Stop the Beach Renourishment, Inc. v. Florida Department of Environmental Protection,* 560 U.S. ___, 130 S. Ct. 2592, 2602 (2012).

40. See *Spur Industries, Inc. v. Del E. Webb Development Co.,* 108 Ariz. 178, 494 P.2d 700 (1972).

41. See *United States v. Commodities Trading Corp.,* 339 U.S. 121 (1950).

42. See *Hadacheck v. Sebastian,* 239 U.S. 394 (1915).

43. *Village of Euclid v. Amber Realty Co.,* 272 U.S. 365 (1926).

44. *Susette Kelo, et al. v. City of New London, Connecticut,* et al., 545 U.S. 469, 473–77 (2005).

45. *Kelo,* 545 U.S. at 494, 503–4 (O'Connor, J., dissenting).

46. *Kelo,* 545 U.S. at 488.

47. Ilya Somin, *The Limits of Backlash: Assessing the Political Response to Kelo,* Minn. L. Rev. Vol. 93, No. 6 (June 2009): 2100, 2102.

48. *Kelo,* 545 U.S. at 477–78, 481, 483, 485. See also Alexandra B. Klass, *The Frontier of Eminent Domain,* 79 U. Colo. L. Rev. 651, 671 (2008).

49. Klass, *The Frontier of Eminent Domain citing Dayton Gold & Silver Mining Co. v. Seawell,* 11 Nev. 394, 409–10 (1876).

50. Klass, *The Frontier of Eminent Domain* at 676.

51. Catholic Bishops' Conference of the Philippines, *A Statement on Mining Issues and Concerns "Do not defile the land where you live and where I dwell" (Num. 35:34)*, http:// www.cbcponline.net/documents/2000s/html/2006-AStatementonminingissuesandcon-cerns.html (accessed October 25, 2013). See also note 32, *supra*.

52. *Compendium*, ¶182.

53. United States State Department, *Treaty on Principles Governing the Activities of States in the Exploration and Use of Outer Space, Including the Moon and Other Celestial Bodies (Outer Space Treaty)* (1967), Preamble and Article V., http://www.state.gov/www/global/arms/ treaties/space1.html (accessed November 2, 2013).

54. *Outer Space Treaty*, Article II.

55. *Arnold v. Mundy*, 6 N.J.L. 1 (N.J., 1821); *Martin v. Waddell*, 41 U.S. 367 (1842) (subjecting lands beneath tidal waters to public trust); see www.ourchildrenstrust.org (all natural resources should be subject to public trust doctrine).

56. *Shively v. Bowlby*, 152 U.S. 1, 14–15 (1894).

57. See *Illinois Central Railroad Co. v. State of Illinois*, 146 U.S. 387, 453 (1892).

58. *American Electric Power v. Connecticut*, 564 U.S.___ (2011), 131 S. Ct. 2527, 2537, 2540 (2011).

59. *Inside EPA.Com*, "Judge Rules Atmosphere Public Trust," http://insideepa.com/ 201207132404508/epa-blog/the-inside-story/judge-rules-atmosphere-public-trust (last accessed July 13, 2012).

60. Philip Bump, "Gristmill, a Beacon in the Smog," http://grist.org/news/texas-judge-rules-the-atmosphere-is-protected-under-the-public-trust-doctrine, *citing* Judge Gisela Triana's opinion, *Angela Bonser-Lain, et al. v. Texas Commission on Environmental Quality*, Case No. D-1-GN-11-002194 (July 9, 2012) (accessed December 24, 2013).

61. Developing countries that include all natural resources as held in public trust include India, Pakistan, Philippines, Uganda, Kenya, Nigeria, South Africa, Brazil, and Ecuador. See Blumm and Guthrie, *Internationalizing the Public Trust Doctrine*; 45 U. C. Davis L. R. 741, 760–800.

62. See Turnipseed, et al., *The Public Trust and Rio+20*, February 2012 Syllabus available at http://wildmigration.org/pdf_bin/Brief_201202_PublicTrustDoctrine-Rio20_brief.pdf (accessed October 26, 2013).

63. *Change entitled "The Future Is in Our Hands: Addressing the Leadership Challenge of Climate Change"*, United Nations, New York, September 24, 2007, http://www.vatican.va/ roman_curia/secretariat_state/2007/documents/rc_seg-st_20070924_ipcc_en.html (last accessed February 24, 2014). See also John Paul II, "Message of His Holiness Pope John Paul II for the Celebration of the World Day of Peace, 'Peace with God the Creator, Peace with all of Creation,'" January 1, 1990, http://www.vatican.va/holy_father/john_paul_ii/messages/peace/ documents/hf_jp-ii_mes_19891208_xxiii-world-day-for-peace_en.html (last accessed February 24, 2014); Benedict XVI, "Message of His Holiness Pope Benedict XVI for the Celebration of the World Day of Peace, 'If You Want to Cultivate Peace, Protect Creation,'" January 1, 2010, http://www.vatican.va/holy_father/benedict_xvi/messages/peace/documents/hf_ben-xvi_mes_20091208_xliii-world-day-peace_en.html (last accessed February 24, 2014); Wolfgang Sachs, *Climate Change and Human Rights: Interactions between Global Change and Human Health*, Pontifical Academy of Sciences, 106 Scripta Varia 349, Vatican City, 2006, accessible at http://www.uibk.ac.at/peacestudies/downloads/peacelibrary/climatechange.pdf (last accessed February 24, 2014).

64. *Rerum Novarum*, ¶10.

65. *Stop the Beach Renourishment*, 560 U.S. ___, 130 S. Ct. 2592, 2602 (2012). (Justice Scalia writing for the plurality, emphasis in the original.)

66. Albert C. Lin, *Public Trust and Public Nuisance: Common Law Peas in a Pod?* 45 U. C. Davis L. Rev. 1075, 1089 (2012).

67. Elaine Dewar, *Cloak of Green: The Links Between Environmental Groups, Government and Big Business* (Toronto: James Lorimer & Co., 1995).

68. Melville, *Moby Dick*, Chapter 89.

69. *Planned Parenthood of Southeast Pennsylvania v. Casey*, 505 U.S. 833, 856, 112 S. Ct. 2791, 2809 (1992). (Note the link between contraception and abortion as a cultural norm and economic driver: "[F]or two decades of economic and social developments, people have organized intimate relationships and made choices that define their views of themselves and their places in society, in reliance on the availability of abortion in the event the contraception should fail. The ability of women to participate equally in the economic and social life of the Nation has been facilitated by their ability to control their reproductive lives.")

70. See *Baker v. Vermont*, 744 A.2d 864, 881 (1999).

71. *Baker*, 744 A.2d at 883–84: "The benefits and protections incident to a marriage license under Vermont law . . . include, for example, the right to receive a portion of the estate of a spouse who dies intestate and protection against disinheritance through elective share provisions . . ., preference in being appointed as the personal representative of a spouse who dies intestate . . ., the right to bring a lawsuit for the wrongful death of a spouse . . ., the right to bring an action for loss of consortium . . ., the right to workers' compensation survivor benefits . . ., the right to spousal benefits statutorily guaranteed to public employees, including health, life, disability, and accident insurance . . ., the opportunity to be covered as a spouse under group life insurance policies issued to an employee . . . the opportunity to be covered as the insured's spouse under an individual health insurance policy . . . the right to claim an evidentiary privilege for marital communications . . . homestead rights and protections . . . the presumption of joint ownership of property and the concomitant right of survivorship . . . hospital visitation and other rights incident to the medical treatment of a family member . . . and the right to receive, and the obligation to provide, spousal support, maintenance, and property division in the event of separation or divorce."

72. Congregation for the Doctrine of the Faith, *Consideration Regarding Proposal to Give Legal Recognition to Unions Between Homosexual Persons* (2003), ¶ 8. Cf. Congregation for the Doctrine of the Faith, *Some Considerations Concerning the Response to Legislative Proposals on the Non-discrimination of Homosexual Persons*, ¶15 (critical of health care benefits for homosexual partners).

73. Robert George, Timothy George, and Chuck Colson, *The Manhattan Declaration* (2009), http://www.manhattandeclaration.org (accessed December 16, 2013).

74. Melville, *Moby Dick*, Chapter 89.

75. *Association for Molecular Pathology, et al. v. Myriad Genetics, Inc., et al.*, 569 U.S. ___ (2013).

76. "Brief for Amici Curiae of the Ethics & Religious Liberty Commission of the Southern Baptist Convention and Prof. D. Brian Scarnecchia in Support of Petitioners," *Association for Molecular Pathology, et al. v. Myriad Genetics, Inc., et al.*, On Writ of Certiorari to the United States Court of Appeals for the Federal Circuit, January 31, 2013, http://www.americanbar.org/content/dam/aba/publications/supreme_court_preview/briefs-v2/12-398_pet_amcu_southernbaptist.authcheckdam.pdf (accessed November 27, 2013).

77. "Brief for Amici Curiae of the Ethics & Religious Liberty Commission" at 2.

78. Jacques Maritain, *Man and the State* (Chicago: The University of Chicago Press, 1951), 24.

79. "Brief for Amici Curiae of the Ethics & Religious Liberty Commission" at 13.

80. "Brief for Amici Curiae of the Ethics & Religious Liberty Commission" at 5, *citing* John Paul II, "Message of the Holy Father for Lent 2002," October 4, 2001, ¶2, http://www.vatican.va/holy_father/john_paul_ii/messages/lent/documents/hf_jp-ii_mes_ 20020205_lent-2002_en.html (accessed November 27, 2013).

81. "Brief for Amici Curiae of the Ethics & Religious Liberty Commission" at 8, 10, *citing* John Paul II, "Address to the Pontifical Academy of Sciences" (October 28, 1994), available at http://www.its.caltech.edu/~nmcenter/sci-cp/sci94111.html.

82. Ethics & Religious Liberty Commission, Southern Baptist Convention, BRCA, "Statement of Support from the Ethics & Religious Liberty Commission," May 12, 2009, 16, http://www.aclu.org/free-speech/brca-statement-support-ethics-religious-liberty-commission-southern-baptist-convention (accessed November 27, 2013).

83. *Davis v. Davis*, 842 S.W.2d 588, 597 (1992). ("We conclude that pre-embryos are not, strictly speaking, either "persons" or "property," but occupy an interim category. . . .")

84. *Davis*, 842 S.W.2d at 593.

85. See Congregation for the Doctrine of the Faith, *Dignitas Personae*, ¶19. See also, Brian Scarnecchia, *Bioethics, Law, and Human Life Issues: A Catholic Perspective on Marriage, Family, Contraception, Abortion, Reproductive Technology, and Death and Dying* (Lanham, MD: Scarecrow Press, 2010), 172–86, n. 157; Brian Scarnecchia, *Public Policy Recommendations Concerning Prenatal Adoption of Frozen Embryos in Light of Fetal Microchimerism*, vol. 11.2 Ave Maria L. Rev . 263, 276–88 (2013).

86. See Congregation for the Doctrine of the Faith, *Donum Vitae*, Part I, 6; Part II, a; and Part III.

87. John Paul II, "Address to the 18th International Congress of the Transplantation Society," August 29, 2000, ¶3.

88. United States Conference of Catholic Bishops, *Ethical and Religious Directives for Catholic Health Care Services*, 4th ed. (2001), ¶30: 60.

89. Maine, *Ancient Law*, 152, 86.

90. Acton Institute, *The Catholic Church and Stewardship of Creation, Part VI: A Better Sense of Perspective*, http://www.acton.org/public-policy/environmental-stewardship/theology-e/catholic-church-and-stewardship-creation (accessed October 12, 2013).

91. Maine, *Ancient Law*, 43–44: "The tendency to look not to the past but to the future for types of perfection was brought into the world by Christianity. Ancient literature gives few or no hints of a belief that the progress of society is necessarily from worse to better."

92. See H.E. Mr. Vuk Jeremic and Dr. Jeffrey Sachs, "The United Nations in the Age of Sustainable Development," Executive Summary, Office of the President of the General Assembly, the High-Level Advisory Panel (an example of post-modern despair at humanity meeting the challenges of today other than by limiting human population and activity), http://www.un.org/en/ga/president/67/statements/statements/September13/hlap_sus_dev09092013.shtml (accessed December 1, 2013).

93. Paul VI, "Address to the General Assembly of the United Nations," October 4, 1965, http://unyearbook.un.org/1965YUN/1965_P1_SEC1_CH16.pdf (accessed December 1, 2013).

94. Pontifical Council for Culture and the Pontifical Council for Interreligious Dialogue, *Jesus Christ Bearer of Water: A Christian Reflection on the "New Age"* (2003), ¶2.3.1., http://www.vatican.va/roman_curia/pontifical_councils/interelg/documents/rc_pc_interelg_doc_20030203_new-age_en.html (accessed January 7, 2014).

95. Benedict XVI, *Caritas et Veritate*, ¶48.

96. Pietro Parolin, *The Future Is in Our Hands: Addressing the Leadership Challenge of Climate Change* (September 24, 2007), http://www.vatican.va/roman_curia/secretariat_state/2007/documents/rc_seg-st_20070924_ipcc_en.html (accessed October 22, 2013).

97. Pierre-Joseph Proudhon, *What Is Property? An Inquiry into the Principle of the Right and of Government*, Chapter 1 (1840), http://www.marxists.org/reference/subject/economics/proudhon/property/ch01.htm (accessed December 1, 2013).

98. Benedict XVI, "Address to the Bishops of the United States of America on Their Ad Limina Visit," January 19, 2012, http://www.vatican.va/holy_father/benedict_xvi/speeches/2012/january/documents/hf_ben-xvi_spe_20120119_bishops-usa_en.html (accessed October 12, 2013).

Chapter Seventeen

The Call to Stewardship

A Catholic Perspective on Environmental Responsibility

Lucia A. Silecchia

In recent years, the state of the natural environment—on the local, national, and international levels—has received great attention. This attention has been both contentious and pessimistic as discussion of the nature and scope of humanity's responsibility to care for creation is fraught with bitter scientific, legal, economic, and moral debate. In response, various religious congregations have begun to interject their voices into these discussions. Catholic leaders have brought the traditional principles of Catholic social thought to the conversation, proposing that these principles, with ancient biblical origins, offer guidance to those navigating the modern challenges of responsible environmental stewardship.

DEVELOPMENT OF ENVIRONMENTAL LAW IN THE UNITED STATES

For much of American history, a delicate balance has existed between environmental protection and preservation of other interests.[1] For many years, environmental questions received little attention in American public policy. While many theories exist as to why this was the case, three seem to be of primary importance.

First, the notion of limited resources that now shapes the debates was not a central part of the national consciousness centuries ago. The vastness of the nation, its rapid expansion, and the seemingly limitless possibilities for exploration and settlement created great optimism about the sustainability of great growth.[2] Thus, the emphasis was on encouraging the development and settlement of untamed land rather than on careful attention to conservation, for which the perceived need was not as great.

Second, health and safety questions were traditionally perceived to be prerogatives of state and local governments. While some early attempts at environmental regulation were introduced on the federal level,[3] for many years this was not a widespread development in American law. Environmental matters were seen primarily as health and safety questions—and, thus, matters of local concern.

Third, the early eras of American history were periods of great expansion in economic and industrial capability, both in and beyond the urban centers of the northeast. During this time, the focus of government and economic activity was on developing these opportunities and responding to the immediate challenges that they raised. Little attention was paid to the long-term urban or rural environmental consequences of these activities.

Much began to change in the early twentieth century. Rapid urbanization gave rise to a number of well-publicized urban environmental health threats.[4] These threats prompted state and local officials to begin some small scale initiatives to protect the public. However, it was in the 1930s, when the New Deal legislation and related public works projects expanded the scope of the federal government and generated projects with significant environmental impacts, that the early stirrings of a national environmental regulatory structure began.

It would be well over thirty years before those early stirrings led to the federal framework that characterizes today's environmental law. However, in the early 1970s, four important events took place that shaped the current state of environmental law, both domestically and internationally.

First, on January 1, 1970, President Richard M. Nixon signed into law the National Environmental Policy Act of 1969 ("NEPA").[5] NEPA articulated, for the first time, a broad set of principles and goals to guide U.S. environmental policy-making.

Second, the Environmental Protection Agency ("EPA") was created by President Nixon on December 2, 1970.[6] For the first time, a specialized agency was charged with administering the environmental regulatory program of the United States. Although the EPA's structure would evolve over time, the basic framework and division of tasks by sector were established in these early years.[7]

Third, the decade between 1970 and 1980 saw the passage of major environmental statutes. In addition to NEPA, these statutes included the Clean Air Act ("CAA"),[8] Clean Water Act ("CWA"),[9] Resource Conservation and Recovery Act ("RCRA"),[10] Endangered Species Act ("ESA"),[11] Toxic Substances Control Act ("TSCA"),[12] Safe Drinking Water Act ("SDWA"),[13] Occupational Safety and Health Act ("OSHA"),[14] and the Comprehensive Environmental Response, Compensation, and Liability Act

("CERCLA," better known as "Superfund"),[15] along with untold pages of regulations implementing them and thousands of judicial opinions fleshing out their precise meanings in concrete, often unanticipated, circumstances. This panoply of statutes adopted a wide range of structures, philosophies, and enforcement mechanisms, including technology-based and harm-based controls, outright bans, warning and labeling requirements, storage requirements, compensation obligations for past harms, emergency planning requirements, financial accountability mandates, criminal and civil penalties, citizen suit mechanisms, and financial incentives for both responsibility and creativity.

Finally, on the international level, 1972 was a year of pivotal importance as well. The United Nations Environment Programme ("UNEP") was established.[16] In addition, the landmark United Nations' Conference on the Human Environment ("Stockholm Conference") was held, with an unprecedented 113 nations represented. At this meeting, the Declaration of the United Nations Conference on the Human Environment ("Stockholm Declaration") was adopted with much consensus among nations with diverse traditions, economies, and environmental circumstances.[17] In a manner reminiscent of NEPA, the Stockholm Declaration set forth a global set of goals and priorities to guide decision-making and planning. Although it did not create strict legal obligations, the Stockholm Declaration laid the groundwork for the future development of international environmental law. Most notably, it paved the way for the 1992 United Nations Conference on Environment and Development (commonly called the "Rio Conference" or "Earth Summit") which generated "hard" law.[18]

CATHOLIC SOCIAL THOUGHT ON ECOLOGICAL MATTERS

Coinciding with the coming of age of American and international environmental law was the articulation of a Catholic vision of environmental responsibility. While ecological concerns had previously been raised, one of the most explicit warnings came in 1971, precisely at the dawn of modern American environmental law. In *Octogesima Adveniens*, Pope Paul VI lamented:

> [B]y an ill-considered exploitation of nature [man] risks destroying it and becoming in his turn the victim of this degradation. . . . [N]ot only is the material environment becoming a permanent menace—pollution and refuse, new illness and absolute destructive capacity—but the human framework is no longer under man's control, thus creating an environment for tomorrow which may well be intolerable. This is a wide-ranging social problem which concerns the entire human family. [19]

In one sense, it is a misnomer to say that the Catholic perspective is new. In many respects, the Catholic approach to environmental questions is simply to take traditional principles and apply them to new circumstances raised by modern environmental concerns. That is, the Catholic perspective does not create new ecological theories or doctrine. Instead, it draws on a long tradition—dating back to the Old Testament—and applies principles from that tradition to current questions.

On the other hand, what is new is the way in which these connections have been made explicit and the prominence that ecological questions have enjoyed in recent decades.[20] In 1990, Pope John Paul II's message, *Peace with God the Creator, Peace with All Creation*, became the first major papal document devoted solely to ecology.[21] Twenty years later, Pope Benedict XVI's message, *If You Want to Cultivate Peace, Protect Creation*, repeated many of these themes, developed them more fully, and gave them a new urgency.[22] While there are a number of ways in which the basic principles may be stated, there are six basic themes around which to organize the teachings of the Catholic Church on ecological questions.[23] It is through these six lenses that the environmental regulatory regime of the United States—or any nation—may be considered.

First and foremost, Catholic social thought begins by putting human life and human dignity at the center of consideration of all public policy questions. That is, the Church's consideration of environmental issues begins with the vision of the human person created in the image and likeness of God with "abilities and gifts which distinguish the human being from all other creatures."[24] The centrality of human dignity lies at the heart of the Church's teaching on all social questions, and ecology is no exception. Thus, it rejects any approach to environmental questions that vilifies humanity or fails to consider the impact of environmental action and inaction on the human person.[25]

Some aspects of American environmental law incorporate this concern for human dignity in important ways. For example, the harm-based approach found in a number of American statutes prioritizes human health and directs limited resources toward curbing those threats that most directly impact human health. When environmental statutes are enforced, it is generally true that those violations that harm human health are pursued with harsher consequences—recognizing the importance of the human person. Greater attention has been paid, of late, to questions of environmental justice—asking whether environmentally beneficial activities are concentrated in wealthy, politically active communities while less desirable uses or lax enforcement are disproportionately concentrated in poorer or minority communities where advocacy for public health may be less robust.[26] This advances the notion central to Catholic social teaching that the inherent and equal dignity of all is of priceless, nonnegotiable value. In addition, and ironically, there has also been greater attention paid to the ways in which environmental dangers may pose a threat to unborn children.[27] Sadly, in areas of environmental policy-making that emphasize population reduction, the safety of unborn children is not protected in the same way. Yet, this recognition acknowledges, at least in theory if not in practice, the Catholic Church's teachings on the inviolability of equal dignity.

Concern for human dignity also fosters two additional values central to Catholic thought—that of solidarity, or unity, with all others even if separated by distance, time, and circumstance,[28] and the preferential option for the poor,[29] which prioritizes concern for those most vulnerable whenever decisions are being made.

Unfortunately, there are also areas in which the current structure of American environmental law is inconsistent with these aspects of human dignity in some critically important ways. First, there is much in common ecological rhetoric that demeans the human person, casting doubt on the unique role of the human person in creation.[30] In a particular way, this takes place in debates concerning foreign development aid that condition aid on human population control. In addition, environmental laws often do not factor in the costs of heavy regulation on those who are poor and may depend on or need the industrial jobs often created by polluters. Designing a structure that helps create and retain economic well-being while simultaneously caring for environmental concerns has not been a great strength of American environmental regulation which often posits an irreconcilable conflict between them.

A second basic principle of Catholic thought on ecology is that stewardship is the appropriate model for environmental responsibility. This has biblical roots in the notion that "God entrusted the whole of creation to the man and woman."[31] Pope John Paul II elaborated on this, explicating stewardship in the context of its Old Testament roots:

> *[T]he riches of Creation were . . . a common good of the whole of humanity.* Those who possessed these goods as personal property were really only stewards, ministers charged with working in the name of God who remains the sole owner in the full sense, since it is God's will that created goods should serve everyone in a just way.[32]

Pope Benedict XVI more fully explicated this act of entrusting creation to humanity, saying:

> [T]he true meaning of God's original command . . . was not a simple conferral of authority, but rather a summons to responsibility. . . . Everything that exists belongs to God who has entrusted it to man, albeit not for his arbitrary use. . . . Man thus has a duty to exercise responsible stewardship over creation, to care for it and to cultivate it.[33]

Pope Francis, in his inaugural homily expressed a similar sentiment. He used the word "protector" rather than "steward," but still emphasized the importance of this responsibility.[34]

In important ways, American environmental law reflects this principle. NEPA certainly proposes the ideal of humanity as creation's guardian in its aspirational guidelines. The ESA powerfully incorporates this when it aims to protect all species—not simply those appearing to have immediate value or popularity. Additionally, in a convoluted way, the history of environmental law in the United States reflects a notion of stewardship. Many have observed that American environmental law is highly reactive.[35] That is, potential threats often receive little attention until a high-profile problem occurs. Then, a political and legal response quickly follows. The Love Canal tragedy stirred public support for CERCLA. Graphic photographs of the "burning" Cayuga River spurred progress on the CWA. The oil spill in Prince William's Sound (Exxon-Valdez incident) was the impetus for the Oil Pollution Control Act of 1990. The Three Mile Island incident generated renewed interest in insuring the safety of America's nuclear energy sources. From a legal perspective, this is a poor way to create law; however, it does reflect sensitivity to the obligations of stewardship and the notion that newly appreciated harms require decisive action.

In addition, for a remarkably long period of time, the United States has had an extensive network of national parks and other areas held for conservation. This began in 1872, when Yellowstone National Park was established as the first national park in the United States. These protected lands have potentially high commercial value. Yet, decisions made through the generations to set this expanse aside for preservation, conservation, and simple appreciation is a powerful testament to the importance of stewardship as a national priority. Ever since 1916, the National Park Service has served as steward of these priceless treasures, balancing a complex array of often competing interests.[36]

Obviously, though, there are both theoretical and practical difficulties in fostering responsible stewardship. The theoretical difficulty is that to propose stewardship as the model presupposes that the human person is unique in the created world. Stewardship is certainly not an obligation borne by other parts of creation; however, it is harder to propose and act on this model given the rhetoric that often critiques the notion that the human person is special and thus has a unique array of obligations.

More practically, the stewardship model is difficult to apply because often there are both long- and short-term interests that demand protection. Unfortunately, at times these interests conflict. For example, a long-term interest in cleaning a body of water may be stewardship's clear demand. In the short term, however, this may require radical changes in the way local people use that water—changes that may result in short-term harm to them in economic and other ways. Thus, while it is simple to say that one should act as a steward, discerning what that actually means and demands of individual populations and economies is difficult.

This conundrum is closely related to the next principle that Catholic social teaching brings to bear on ecological questions, which is that future generations must be considered in environmental decision-making. That is, lawmakers and policy advocates must be guided by demands of intergenerational responsibility and solidarity. Often, what is helpful in the short term is politically more popular and easily accomplished than something that will be beneficial in the long term but not have immediate benefits. Yet, the Catholic approach has strongly supported the notion of solidarity across time, recognizing that the human family of tomorrow deserves respect in the decision-making of today.[37]

The link between RCRA and CERCLA offers an interesting study in intergenerational responsibility. CERCLA was a response to the wrongs of past generations. It recognized that carelessness, ignorance, or worse, in handling hazardous wastes created serious problems as those wastes leaked into the ground, wreaking havoc when released. CERCLA tried—in some ways wise, in other ways draconian—to correct this problem by imposing cleanup liability on responsible parties wherever possible. However, this alone was insufficient. RCRA, best viewed as a companion to CERCLA, attempts to avert future harms. RCRA aims to require that today's hazardous waste handlers behave in such a way that their actions do not harm future generations. Thus, for example, they must handle hazardous substances with caution, have a plan for closing facilities, report any spills and emergencies to authorities, and create a plan of fiscal responsibility that continues far into the future. Addressing this link between present conduct and future effects is a responsible way to protect future generations.

One of the most helpful theories in which American law fosters intergenerational responsibility is through the "precautionary principle." This principle posits that when the likelihood of a future harm exists, the lack of definitive scientific proof of that harm should not discourage reasonable steps to avert the danger.[38] This protects future generations from harm inflicted today, even when the full scope of that danger is not yet apparent. The precautionary principle is applied in cases where, for example, standards of safety incorporate a meaningful margin of error to account for unknown harms or when research is directed toward identifying new problems in their early stages.[39]

In other circumstances, however, the precautionary principle is not applied, or the interests of future generations are not weighed as heavily as they should be. This is most often true when the costs of a regulation or policy are obvious now, but the benefits will come only in the future. Here, it is often difficult to see intergenerational responsibility in play because the needs of current parties are far easier to discern and far harder to ignore.

A fourth principle of Catholic teaching applied to environmental concerns is respect for subsidiarity and wise allocation of environmental responsibility among various entities and levels of society.[40] Subsidiarity has been defined multiple times, but perhaps the best known is that found in *Quadragesimo Anno*, in which Pope Pius XI explained:

> Just as it is gravely wrong to take from individuals what they can accomplish by their own initiative and industry, and give it to the community, so also is it an injustice and at the same time a grave evil and disturbance of right order to assign to a greater and higher association what lesser and subordinate organizations can do. For every social activity ought of its very nature to furnish help to the members of the body social, and never destroy and disturb them.[41]

Here, American law faces interesting challenges resulting, in part, from the federal structure of government. Originally, environmental law was the province of the states. This was consistent with the Constitutional system of enumerated powers, which largely limited Congressional influence by explicitly reserving to states all powers not specifically listed as federal prerogatives.[42] This was also consistent with the view that, in a largely agrarian society, most environmental harms were localized and unlikely to travel beyond state borders. Thus, if the state and local levels were the appropriate sphere at which harms could be addressed, this was consistent with subsidiarity. It also had practical benefits. It helped ensure that those with accurate knowledge of local conditions were making decisions. It also gave different states the opportunity to experiment with various approaches that could later be copied by others—or, if ineffective, more easily abandoned because of their smaller scale.

In the past century, however, this model has been challenged. Constitutionally, a more expansive interpretation of the Commerce Clause extended the reach of the federal government into environmental matters.[43] Perhaps more importantly, as the scope of environmental harms grew and more became known about ecology, it became clearer that certain issues could not be properly or effectively addressed by state or local authorities. As industrialization progressed, environmental problems—particularly those involving air and water—could not be locally contained. Thus, on some matters, the federal government became the appropriate and most effective place at which to address environmental matters. This also had practical benefits. By setting uniform federal standards, economies of scale with respect to research could be achieved. In addition, uniform federal standards created a more level playing field, curbing the noxious "race to the bottom" which gave states political and economic incentives for lax regulation. Consistent with the Catholic view of subsidiarity, where the higher authority of a national government is needed to regulate in an effective way, it is commendable to do so.

Taking this notion a step further, there are also circumstances in which ecological problems do not respect national borders, are on such a large scale that expensive solutions are needed, or involve poorer nations unable to assist themselves. In these cases, subsidiarity requires the international community to create an effective solution.[44]

A challenge for American law—and, indeed, for all regimes trying to respect subsidiarity—is to determine in which situations which level is appropriate. Given the political and economic interests that often drive decisions, it is difficult to determine whether this is done wisely and well. In addition, subsidiarity does not address itself only to the proper roles of government. It also proposes appropriate, robust roles for so-called intermediary institutions such as families, neighborhoods, schools, workplaces, associations, and religious organizations, as well as individuals.[45] There is little in American environmental law that encourages activity by these institutions. Perhaps there is little that law *can* do to accomplish this; however, in assessing whether subsidiarity is fully respected, the roles of these groups must be considered. It is worth asking whether American law gives appropriate incentives for nongovernmental communities to play their proper role in environmental protection.

The next principle of Catholic social teaching that must be brought to bear on ecological matters is a dual one. It is the proposition that the right to private property and the mandate to use property for the common good must both be respected.[46] In environmental laws and policies, it is necessary to ensure that the tradition of privately owned property is respected while fostering the awareness that such property comes with a "social mortgage"—an obligation to use it in ways consistent with the common good and the teaching that "the earth is ultimately a common heritage, the fruits of which are for the benefit of all."[47] This is particularly true with respect to those who may be harmed by another's use of private property.

Striking the balance between these goals has not been an easy task for American law. In one sense, all "command and control" regulations are a way of ensuring that the use of private property does not diminish the common good. The uses of property that pollute the air, contaminate a stream, allow industrial waste to destroy the land, or decimate the habitat of an endangered species are not allowed to go unfettered if contrary to the common good. Thus, as the owners of private property—both real property and other forms of property—contemplate activities that will be environmentally harmful, American law poses some burdens for the common good.

Less clear, of course, is where the proper boundaries of those burdens lie. The development of takings law illustrates this conundrum quite clearly, particularly in the context of the Clean Water Act and the Endangered Species Act. With respect to the former, development on privately owned land can be curtailed if to do so would fill a wetland in violation of the Clean Water Act. With respect to the latter, development can be curtailed if doing so would destroy the critical habitat of a protected species. Obviously, these results burden private landowners. As the law in this area ebbs and flows, American law has yet to develop a consistent approach to defining those circumstances in which the public at large should bear the burden of compensating a landowner for the costs these regulations impose and when this is simply an obligation of private owners. Catholic social teaching does not posit that this balance is easy, and the American legal experience suggests this is not the case.

The final principle of Catholic social teaching in this field is one that is profoundly important, and one that American law does not fully address—because in many respects it lies beyond the law. This is the proposition that environmental concerns are moral concerns that demand rethinking of a consumer culture.[48] Indeed, Pope John Paul II taught that "we must go to the source of the problem and face in its entirety that profound moral crisis of which the destruction of the environment is only one troubling aspect."[49] In the view of Catholic social teaching, there is a personal imperative to rethink a lifestyle that values things over people. Extravagance over simplicity. Gathering rather than sharing. Discarding rather than conserving. Having over being. Accumulating rather than preserving.

Catholic teaching encourages sober examination of whether and how the pursuit of a wealthy, modern life marked with possessions has an environmental cost borne by our sisters and brothers today and tomorrow—the reality that "[i]f an appreciation of the value of the human person and of human life is lacking, we will also lose interest in others and in the earth itself."[50] This, of course, is extraordinarily difficult for any law to dictate. It is a call for a change in attitude and heart that cannot be found in statute or regulation:

> *The attitude that must characterize the way man acts in relation to creation is essentially one of gratitude and appreciation; the world . . . reveals the mystery of God who created and sustains it. . . .* This realm opens the path of man to God, Creator of heaven and earth. *The world presents itself before man's eyes as evidence of God, the place where his creative, providential and redemptive power unfolds.*[51]

In the end, this may be the most important challenge the Catholic perspective brings to the call to stewardship.

NOTES

1. This discussion is not intended to be a full history of environmental law and policy in the United States. For background reading on this topic, see generally Richard N.L. Andrews, *Managing the Environment, Managing Ourselves: A History of American Environmental Policy* (Yale University Press, 1999); Richard J. Lazarus, *The Making of Environmental Law* (University of Chicago Press, 2004); and Karl Boyd Brooks, *Before Earth Day: The Origins of American Environmental Law 1945–1970* (University Press of Kansas, 2011). A wealth of additional information may be found at the websites of the American Society for Environmental History, available at http://aseh.net and the Environmental History Timeline, available at http://www.environmentalhistory.org (accessed January 16, 2014).

2. Indeed, this same optimism about unlimited resources characterized some earlier writings in Catholic teaching as well. See, e.g., Pope Leo XIII, *Rerum Novarum*, ¶7 (1891): "Man's needs do not die out, but forever recur; satisfied today, they demand fresh supplies for tomorrow. Nature, accordingly must have given to man a source that is stable and remaining always with him, from which he might look to draw continual supplies. And this stable condition of things he finds solely in the earth and its fruits"; see also, *Rerum Novarum*, ¶9: "[T]hat which is required for the preservation of life and for life's well-being is produced in great abundance from the soil, but not until man has brought it into cultivation"; see also, Pope John XXIII, *Mater et Magistra*, ¶189 (1961): "[T]he resources which God in his goodness and wisdom has implanted in Nature are well nigh inexhaustible, and he has the same time given man the intelligence to discover ways and means of exploiting these resources for his own advantage and his own livelihood."

3. See, e.g., Rivers and Harbors Appropriation Act of 1899, 33 U.S.C. §403 (1899).

4. Many of these issues involved the urban health issues that emerged from overcrowding in unsafe residences, the increased output of pollution from burgeoning industry, and problems caused by poor sewage facilities as exemplified in the landmark water pollution dispute in *Missouri v. Illinois*, 180 U.S. 208 (1901).

5. National Environmental Policy Act, 42 U.S.C. §4321 *et seq.* (1969).

6. For historical documents related to the creation of the EPA, see generally http://www2.epa.gov/aboutepa/epa-history (accessed January 16, 2014).

7. Initial Organization of the Environmental Protection Agency, EPA Order 1110.2 (December 4, 1970), available at http://www2.epa.gov/abovtepa/epa-order-1102.

8. Clean Air Act, 42 U.S.C. §7401 *et seq.* (1970).

9. Federal Water Pollution Control Act, 33 U.S.C. §1251 *et seq.* (1972).

10. Resource Conservation and Recovery Act, 42 U.S.C. §6901 *et seq.* (1976).

11. Endangered Species Act, 16 U.S.C. §1531 *et seq.* (1973).

12. Toxic Substances Control Act, 15 U.S.C. §2601 *et seq.* (1976).

13. Safe Drinking Water Act, 42 U.S.C. §3007 *et seq.* (1974).

14. Occupational Safety and Health Act, 29 U.S.C. §651 *et seq.* (1970).

15. Comprehensive Environmental Response, Compensation, and Liability Act, 42 U.S.C. §9601 *et seq.* (1980).

16. See United Nations Environment Programme, *About UNEP, available at* http://www.unep.org/About/ (accessed January 17, 2014).

17. United Nations Conference on the Human Environment, *Declaration of the United Nations Conference on the Human Environment* (Stockholm, Sweden, June 16, 1972), available at http://www.unep.org/Documents.Multilingual/Default.asp?DocumentID=97&ArticleID=1503.

18. Among the documents generated at the Rio Conference were the *Rio Declaration on Environment and Development*, *Agenda 21*, the *United Nations Framework Convention on Climate Change*, and *the United Nations Convention on Biological Diversity*. Information about the Rio Conference and the texts of these documents is available at http://www.unep.org (accessed January 16, 2014).

19. Pope Paul VI, *Octogesima Adveniens*, ¶21 (May 14, 1971).

20. As this new attention has increased, a number of useful reference sources have been compiled to offer background on Catholic teaching on ecological matters. *See, e.g.*, Drew

Christiansen and Walter Grazer, eds., *And God Saw That It Was Good: Catholic Theology and the Environment* (United States Catholic Conference, 1996); Marjorie Keenan, *From Stockholm to Johannesburg: An Historical Overview of the Concern of the Holy See for the Environment 1972–2002* (Vatican Press, 2002); Marjorie Keenan, *Care for Creation: Human Activity and the Environment* (Vatican Press, 2001), Charles M. Murphy, *At Home on Earth: Foundations for a Catholic Ethic of the Environment* (Crossroad Publishing Co., 1989); Kevin W. Irwin and Edmund D. Pellegrino, eds., *Preserving the Creation: Environmental Theology and Ethics* (Georgetown University Press, 1994); and Robert W. Lannan, *Catholic Tradition and the New Catholic Theology and Social Teaching on the Environment*, 39 Cath. Law. 353 (2000). Perhaps most accessible is the *Compendium of the Social Doctrine of the Church* (2004), available at http://www.vatican.va/roman_curia/pontifical_councils/justpeace/documents/rc_pc_justpeace_doc_20060526_compendio-dott-soc_en.html [hereinafter *Compendium*] which devotes ¶¶451–87 to ecological questions. In addition, the U.S. Catholic bishops have also contributed several documents to the discussion, including United States Catholic Conference, *Renewing the Earth: An Invitation to Reflection and Action on the Environment in Light of Catholic Social Teaching* (November 14, 1991), available at http://www.usccb.org/issues-and-actions/human-life-and-dignity/environment/renewing-the-earth.cfm and United States Catholic Conference, *Global Climate Change: A Plea for Dialogue, Prudence, and the Common Good* (June 15, 2001), available at http://www.usccb.org/issues-and-action/human-life-and-dignity/environment/global-climate-change-a-plea-for-dialogue-prudence-and-the-common-good.cfm. Rather than breaking new ground, these documents provide restatements of the traditional principles as applied to modern situations.

   21. Pope John Paul II, *Message of His Holiness Pope John Paul II for the Celebration of the World Day of Peace: Peace with God the Creator, Peace with All Creation*, January 1, 1990 [hereinafter *Peace with God the Creator*].

   22. Pope Benedict XVI, *Message of His Holiness Pope Benedict XVI for the Celebration of the World Day of Peace: If You Want to Cultivate Peace, Protect Creation*, January 1, 2010 [hereinafter *Protect Creation*]. The attention Pope Benedict XVI paid to environmental questions took many by surprise and was the subject of commentary. See, e.g., Pope Benedict XVI, *The Environment* (Our Sunday Visitor, 2012) (collection of Pope Benedict's writings on ecological questions); Jame Schaefer and Tobias Winright, eds., *Environmental Justice and Climate Change: Assessing Pope Benedict XVI's Ecological Vision for the Catholic Church in the United States* (Lexington Books, 2013); Pope Benedict XVI and Woodeene Koenig-Bricker, *Ten Commandments for the Environment: Pope Benedict XVI Speaks Out for Creation and Justice* (Ave Maria Press, 2009); and Lucia A. Silecchia, "Discerning the Environmental Perspective of Pope Benedict XVI," 4 *J. Cath. Soc. Thought* 227 (2007).

   23. I have written about these six principles in Lucia A. Silecchia, *Environmental Ethics from the Perspectives of NEPA and Catholic Social Teaching: Ecological Guidance for the 21st Century*, 28 William & Mary L. Rev. 659 (2004).

   24. *Peace with God the Creator, supra* note 21, ¶3. See also *Compendium*, ¶451 ("At the summit of this creation . . . God placed man").

   25. As Pope John Paul II warned:

> The most profound and serious indication of the moral implications underlying the ecological problem is the lack of respect for life evident in many of the patterns of environmental pollution. Often, the interests of production prevail over concern for the dignity of workers, while economic interests take priority over the good of individuals and even entire peoples. In these cases, pollution or environmental destruction is the result of an unnatural and reductionist vision which at times leads to a genuine contempt for man. . . . Respect for life, and above all for the dignity of the human person is the ultimate guiding norm for any sound economic, industrial or scientific progress.

Peace with God the Creator, supra note 21, ¶7.

26. See e.g., Exec. Order No. 12898, 59 FR 7629 (February 16, 1994), available at http://www.archives.gov/federal-register/executive-orders/1994.html#12898.

27. For example, the EPA's own program for Children's Health Protection urges that "childhood should be viewed as a sequence of life stages, from conception through fetal development, infancy, and adolescence." See "Lifestage Versus Subpopulation," U.S. Environmental Protection Agency, http://Yosemite.Epa.gov/ochp/ochp/ochpweb.nsf/content/lifestage.htm (accessed January 17, 2014).

28. See *Protect Creation, supra* note 22, ¶8 (urging a "renewed sense of intergenerational solidarity, especially in relationships between developing countries and highly industrialized countries"). A full discussion of solidarity can be found in the *Compendium*, at ¶¶192–196.

29. I have explored this link between environmental responsibility and the preferential option for the poor more fully in Lucia A. Silecchia, *The "Preferential Option for the Poor": An Opportunity and a Challenge for Environmental Decision-Making*, 5 U. St. Thomas L. J. 87 (2008). For a fuller discussion of the preferential option, see generally *Compendium* at ¶¶182–84.

30. Pope Benedict XVI was particularly critical of this aspect of modern environmentalism. He wrote:

[A] correct understanding of the relationship between man and the environment will not end by absolutizing nature or by considering it more important than the human person. If the Church's magisterium expresses grave misgivings about notions of the environment inspired by ecocentrism and biocentrism, it is because such notions eliminate the difference of identity and worth between the human person and other living things. In the name of a supposedly egalitarian vision of the "dignity" of all living creatures, such notions end up abolishing the distinctiveness and superior role of human beings.

Protect Creation, supra note 22, ¶13.

31. *Peace with God the Creator, supra* note 21, ¶3. A similar theme is developed more fully in *Compendium*, ¶¶456–57 and 460.

32. Pope John Paul II, *Tertio Millenio Adveniente* ¶13 (Nov. 10, 1994).

33. *Protect Creation, supra* note 22, ¶8. While he was still Jorge Cardinal Bergoglio, now-Pope Francis wrote about this role as steward and the delicate balance it requires. He said:

We receive creation in our hands as a gift. God gives it to us, but at the same time He gives us a task: that we subdue the Earth. This is the first form of non-culture: what man receives, the raw material that ought to be subdued to make culture—like the log that is transformed into a table. But there is a moment when man goes too far in this task; he gets overly zealous and loses respect for nature. Then, ecological problems arise, like global warming, which are new forms of non-culture. The work of man before God and himself must maintain a constant balance between the gift and the task. When man keeps the gift alone and does not do the work, he does not complete his mission and remains primitive; when man becomes overly zealous with his work, he forgets about the gift, creating a constructivist ethic: he thinks that everything is the fruit of his labor and that there is no gift.

Jorge Mario Bergoglio and Abraham Skorka, *On Heaven and Earth: Pope Francis on Faith, Family and the Church in the 21st Century*, (Image, 2013), 5. See also Pope Francis, *General Audience* 1 (May 1, 2013), available at http://www.vatican.va/holy-father/francesco/audiences/2013/documents/papa-francesco_20130501_udienza-generale_en.html:

The Book of Genesis tells us that God created man and woman entrusting them with the task of filling the earth and subduing it, which does not mean exploiting it but nurturing and protecting it, caring for it through their work. . . . [W]e are called

to cultivate and care for all the goods of creation and in this way share in the work
of creation!

See also Pope Francis, *General Audience* (June 5, 2013), available at http://
www.vatican.va/holy-father/francesco/audiences/2013/documents/papa-frances-
co_20130605_udienza-generale_en.html.
34. Pope Francis, *Mass, Imposition of the Pallium and Bestowal of the Fisherman's Ring for
the Beginning of the Petrine Ministry of the Bishop of Rome, Homily of Pope Francis* (March
19, 2013), available at http://www.vatican.va/holy-father/francesco/homilies/2013/documents/
papa-francesco_20130319_omelia-inizio-pontificato_en.html:

> The vocation of being a "protector," however, is not just something involving us
> Christians alone; it also has a prior dimension which is simply human, involving
> everyone. It means protecting all creation, the beauty of the created world. . . . It
> means respecting each of God's creatures and respecting the environment in which
> we live. . . . In the end, everything has been entrusted to our protection, and all of us
> are responsible for it. Be protectors of God's gifts! Whenever human beings fail to
> live up to this responsibility, whenever we fail to care for creation and for our
> brothers and sisters, the way is opened to destruction and hearts are hardened. . . .
> [L]et us be "protectors" of creation, protectors of God's plan inscribed in nature,
> protectors of one another and of the environment.

Since this inaugural homily, Pope Francis has indicated, in many public statements, that he
will continue to explore ecological issues during his papacy with a particular emphasis on the
impact of environmental degradation on the poor.
35. See, e.g., Alyson C. Flouroy, *In Search of an Environmental Ethic*, 28 Colum. J. Envtl.
L. 63, 64 (2003) (describing the legal response to various high-profile environmental events).
36. See generally National Park Service, *History of the NPS*, http://www.cr.nps.gov/history/
(accessed January 16, 2014).
37. See, e.g., *Peace with God the Creator, supra* note 21, ¶6 ("We cannot interfere in one
area of the ecosystem without paying due attention both to the consequences of such interference in other areas and to the well-being of future generations"); *Protect Creation, supra* note
22, ¶7 ("[T]he current pace of environmental exploitation is seriously endangering the supply
of certain natural resources not only for the present generation, but above all for generations yet
to come"). See also *Compendium*, ¶459.
38. Pope Benedict XVI describes an analogous virtue of prudence, "the virtue which tells us
what needs to be done today in view of what might happen tomorrow." *Protect Creation, supra*
note 22, at ¶9.
39. One of the most popular articulations of the precautionary principle, as a scientific
principle, is fully explored in United Nations Educational, Scientific and Cultural Organization
and World Commission on the Ethics of Scientific Knowledge and Technology, *The Precautionary Principle* (UNESCO, March 2005), available at http://unesdoc.unesco.org/images/
0013/001395/139578e.pdf (accessed July 9, 2014).
40. In the environmental context, Pope Benedict XVI urged that "[i]n accordance with the
principle of subsidiarity it is important for everyone to be committed at his or her proper level,
working to overcome the prevalence of particular interests." *Protect Creation, supra* note 22,
¶11. For excellent discussions of the interplay between subsidiarity and environmental regulation, see, e.g., Gregory R. Beabout, *Challenges to Using the Principle of Subsidiarity for
Environmental Policy*, 5. U. St. Thomas L. J. 210 (2008) and Jerome M. Organ, *Subsidiarity
and Solidarity: Lenses for Assessing the Appropriate Locus for Environmental Regulation and
Enforcement*, 5 U. St. Thomas L. J. 262 (2008). See also *Compendium*, ¶¶185–89.
41. Pope Pius XI, *Quadragesimo Anno*, ¶79 (May 15, 1931).
42. U.S. Const. amend. X. ("The powers not delegated to the United States by the Constitution, nor prohibited by it to the States, are reserved to the States respectively, or to the people.")

43. In one of the most significant early decisions to do so, *NLRB v. Jones & Laughlin Steel Corp.*, 301 U.S. 1 (1937), allowed use of the commerce clause to regulate manufacturing activity with a significant impact on interstate commerce.

44. Pope John Paul II said this explicitly when he commented, "In many cases, the effects of ecological problems transcend the borders of individual states; hence their solution cannot be found solely on the national level." *Peace with God the Creator, supra* note 21, ¶9. This doctrine was explained further as he emphasized "the need for concerted efforts aimed at establishing the duties and obligations that belong to individuals, peoples, States and the international community." *Peace with God the Creator,* ¶15.

45. See, e.g., Beabout, *supra* note 40, at 230–31:

> [S]ubsidiarity is more than a rule for determining which level of government should set policy. Granted, subsidiarity has implications for task allocations among levels of government. But subsidiarity says more than this. . . . Policy makers can recognize that there is a great deal that can be done to improve the environment in the individual choices we make and in the habits that we cultivate at the levels of our families and through the various groups in which we participate. Subsidiarity encourages higher and larger groups to recognize the importance of a participatory approach for cultivating responsible habits among individual persons and smaller, more personal groups along with local communities.

46. Pope Leo XIII, *Rerum Novarum,* ¶8:

> God has given the earth to the use and enjoyment of the whole human race. . . . Not in the sense that all without distinction can deal with it as they like, but rather that no part of it has been assigned to any one in particular, and that the limits of private possession have been left to be fixed by man's own industry and by the laws of individual races. Moreover, the earth, even though apportioned divided among private owners, ceases not thereby to minister to the needs of all, inasmuch as there is not one who does not sustain life from what the land produces.

This dual teaching with respect to private property is explicated more fully in *Compendium,* ¶¶ 171–81.

47. *Peace with God the Creator, supra* note 21, ¶7. See also ¶8: "It is manifestly unjust that a privileged few should continue to amass excess goods, squandering available resources, while masses of people are living in conditions of misery at the very lowest level of subsistence."

48. *Protect Creation, supra* note 22, ¶5 ("Our present crises . . . are ultimately moral crises, and all of them are interrelated. They require us to rethink the path which we are travelling together. Specifically, they call for a lifestyle marked by sobriety and solidarity"). See also ¶9 ("[T]echnologically advanced societies must be prepared to encourage more sober lifestyles, while reducing their energy consumption and improving its efficiency"); and ¶11 ("[T]he issue of environmental degradation challenges us to examine our life-style and the prevailing models of consumption and production, which are often unsustainable from a social, environmental and even economic point of view").

49. *Peace with God the Creator, supra* note 21, ¶5.

50. *Peace with God the Creator, supra* note 21, ¶13. Modern society will find no solution to the ecological problem until it takes a serious look at its lifestyle. In many parts of the world, society is given to instant gratification and consumerism while remaining indifferent to the damage which these cause. . . . [T]he seriousness of the ecological issue lays bare the depth of man's moral crisis. If an appreciation of the value of the human person and of human life is lacking, we will also lose interest in others and in the earth itself.

51. *Compendium,* ¶487.

Chapter Eighteen

American Bankruptcy Law and Catholic Social Theory

John M. Czarnetzky

The most ancient form of bankruptcy, found in American and many nations' laws, is the liquidation bankruptcy. This simple model originated as a remedy for creditors collecting debts from an insolvent debtor. In a liquidation bankruptcy, the debtor turns over all of his/her assets to a bankruptcy trustee who must liquidate the assets and distribute them to the debtor's creditors. This is the debt collection aspect of the liquidation. However, in an innovation of English law adopted early by American law, the debtor receives a significant benefit in exchange for the pain of financial liquidation—a discharge of pre-bankruptcy debts. The discharge means that the debtor is no longer personally liable for the debts, and his creditors may not attempt to collect them.[1]

Though many of the technical aspects of American bankruptcy law are explained by practical considerations of efficiency, incentives, etc., there nevertheless is a mystery at its core. Why did bankruptcy law, an ancient method of debt collection wholly oriented to the interests of creditors, embrace a discharge of a debtor's debts? Catholic social theory ("CST") offers a sophisticated and nuanced answer to this question, which has bedeviled bankruptcy scholars for decades.

THE NATURE OF THE DEBATE

Scholars of American bankruptcy law have offered numerous theories of the bankruptcy discharge. One school of thought connects the discharge with the traditional bankruptcy goal of an orderly distribution to creditors.[2] The discharge is the carrot that the law dangles in front of debtors to foster cooperation with the distribution to creditors. Others, including scholars working in the Catholic tradition, assert the discharge is the result of mercy and forgiveness.[3] The "honest but unfortunate debtor,"[4] in the words of the United States Supreme Court, is not blameworthy and therefore deserves forgiveness when unable to pay debts. Others view bankruptcy law as a type of social welfare scheme, through which society apportions losses attributable to either bad fortune[5] or bad decisions.[6]

These theories of the discharge all contribute to an understanding of its purpose; however, none is entirely satisfactory. Can it truly be the case that creditors, given their lobbying power, exercise altruistic mercy and restorative justice by acquiescing in the Code's discharge of debts? Are all debtors truly in financial difficulty because of some cognitive failing or lack of impulse control? Is it true that a promise—even one memorialized in a contract—is sacrosanct and must never be abrogated by the law?

The purpose of this chapter is to replace the anthropology underlying these and other incomplete theories of the discharge with the view of the human person in CST. The goal is a more satisfactory explanation for the bankruptcy discharge and why it persists in the law despite the losses creditors suffer as a result.

CAPITAL AND HUMAN CAPITAL IN CST

The Church in CST has devoted much effort to developing a theory of human work which flows from the nature of the human person. The human person is an unrepeatable unity of spirit and body, created in the image of God and entitled to inherent dignity. Human beings are social creatures in the sense that they require interaction with other humans to achieve their highest aim, which is to develop their inherent talents in service to the common good. It is the human individual, not the community, who is the object of all social life. Importantly, however, by striving for the common good the individual will realize his/her own potential. Thus, all social institutions—from schools, to bowling leagues, to local, state, and federal governments, etc.—are legitimate to the extent they permit individuals to develop their own talents and abilities while serving the common good through the licit goals of the institution.

In CST, human work is crucial to the development of the person. Work is an "*actus personae*" or "an essential expression of the person."[7] Work has both an objective and subjective dimension. In the objective sense, human beings through work exercise dominion over created things. In the subjective dimension, it is through work that a person is "capable of acting in a planned and rational way, capable of deciding about himself, and with a tendency to self-realization."[8]

At birth a human being possesses certain aptitudes and abilities in germinal form, and these qualities are to be cultivated so that they may bear fruit. By developing these traits through formal education of personal effort, the individual works his way toward the goal set for him by the Creator. Endowed with intellect and free will, each man is responsible for his self-fulfillment even as he is for his salvation. He is helped, and sometimes hindered, by his teachers and those around him; yet whatever be the outside influences exerted on him, he is the chief architect of his own success or failure. Utilizing only his talent and willpower, each man can grow in humanity, enhance his personal worth, and perfect himself.[9]

As a person, man is therefore the subject, not the object of work. It is the integrated human development of each person that is the purpose of work. This means that it is no less than the human person that is the measure of the dignity of human work.[10]

Human work not only proceeds from the person, but it is also essentially ordered to and has its final goal in the human person. Independently of its objective content, work must be oriented to the subject who performs it, because the end of work, any work whatsoever, always remains man. Even if one cannot ignore the objective component of work with regard to its quality, **this component must nonetheless be subordinated to the self-realization of the person**, and therefore to the subjective dimension, thanks to which it is possible to affirm that work is for man and not man for work. It is always man who is the purpose of work, whatever work it is that is done by man—even if the common scale of values rates it as the merest "service," as the most monotonous, even the most alienating work.[11]

The dignity of human work, derived from its subjective dimension, means that the subject fruit of work—sometimes labeled "human capital"[12]—takes priority over material capital.[13] Given the dignity of work and human capital, CST also holds that the right of economic initiative must be given "ample leeway."[14] Any curtailment of economic initiative is an attack on the creative subjectivity of the person. It is only in cases of "incompatibility between the pursuit of common good and the type of economic activity proposed or the way it is undertaken" that the individual's right to economic initiative should be curtailed.[15]

Thus, the human being serves the common good by developing his/her capabilities to the extent possible, in service to, but not subordinated to, the common good. The dignity of work, it must be repeated, does not depend upon the level of contribution or creativity or individual talents possessed by any individual. Each person is entitled to dignity not in proportion to his contribution to the common good, but precisely because through work each person's "human capital," in all its forms, increases and flourishes. Work increases human capital by the person's exercise or development of inherent qualities or acquired virtues. Whether through an increase in knowledge, exercise of entrepreneurial creativity, or development of virtues associated with work such as diligence, organization, prudence, etc., work operates to qualitatively change the person performing the labor. Crucially, therefore, an individual may never be particularly distinguished in his vocation, or may never make a valuable economic contribution to the common good. Nevertheless, the value of that humble person's work is entitled to dignity and "ample leeway" precisely because it is that individual who is the subject of her own work. Put directly, the subjective aspects of human capital—exercise of creativity, dedication to excellence, courage, diligence, virtuous work habits, prudence, etc.—are inalienable and entitled to the same dignity to which the human being who possesses them are entitled. It is this sense in which "human capital" is always superior to capital in the material or financial sense.

CST AND THE BANKRUPTCY DISCHARGE

A Brief Summary of the Bankruptcy Discharge

Absent the Code and its bankruptcy discharge, the law gives creditors substantial leverage over their debtors. If a debtor fails to pay a debt, the creditor must sue him in court and obtain a judgment. Once a creditor obtains a judgment against the debtor, the creditor then seeks to enforce it. The first step to enforcing a judgment is for the creditor to register the judgment in a location where the debtor has or may have assets. Having registered the judgment, the creditor then requests the state, generally in the form of the sheriff, to levy or execute the judgment.[16] Once enrolled, a judgment will be valid for ten to twenty years, renewable potentially *ad infinitum*.[17] A creditor may employ any of a variety of powerful remedies to collect the debt, including seizure of the debtor's property, or garnishment of wages and bank accounts. A debtor who is insolvent might have one or more judgments against him, with others looming. This is the context in which debtors turn to the bankruptcy discharge for relief from their debts and a fresh start.

The discharge comes with a price, however. The debtor—at least in a liquidation case—loses all of his nonexempt assets.[18] The debtor's assets make up the bankruptcy estate, which the bankruptcy trustee administers for the benefit of the debtor's creditors. The estate is liquidated and distributed to creditors, subject to the rule of "bankruptcy justice" that when the estate cannot pay off creditors in full, each creditor receives the same pro rata share of the estate. Thus, if the estate has $100 in assets and the claims of creditors total $1,000, each of those creditors will receive 10¢ per dollar of the claim.[19]

An insolvent debtor, therefore, faces two unpalatable options. If the debtor does not file bankruptcy, the creditors will seize his financial assets. Until the debtor satisfies all judgments against him, his creditors may continue to seize his property as he earns it, potentially forever. On the other hand, if the debtor does file a bankruptcy case, the bankruptcy trustee will seize all of the property that his creditors could seize outside of bankruptcy. The immediate effect on the debtor's finances will, therefore, be the same. The difference between the choices boils down to the discharge—at the end of the case, the debtor will no longer have the potentially permanent threat of debt collection hanging over his head. Why should this be so?

The Discharge Codifies CST's Prioritization of Human Capital

The answer to the apparent riddle of the bankruptcy discharge lies in CST's insight that human capital is superior to physical or financial capital. Human work leads to the accumulation of human capital. Such capital is not limited to the traditional economic sense of education, knowledge, experience, tacit knowledge, etc. Rather, human capital encompasses all of these things, but also includes the virtues and other qualitative changes that are gained by the individual through work. In other words, human capital, properly understood, includes the subjective changes in the human person which are the fruits of work virtuously undertaken and performed. CST teaches that development of human capital is the means by which human work serves the common good by fostering the integral development of the human individual. Moreover, such human capital is superior to physical capital because, as a part of the essence of the human person, it is unique, unrepeatable, and inalienable. In short, CST recognizes that a person's material goods are alienable, and therefore subject to the claims of creditors, but the person himself is not.

The bankruptcy discharge elegantly captures this precise distinction between capital and human capital. In a liquidation bankruptcy case, the debtor loses all of his physical capital immediately, just as the insolvent debtor would outside of bankruptcy.[20] By discharging the unpaid portion of a debtor's debts, the Code frees what otherwise would be a charge on the *human* capital of the debtor. The nearly permanent ability to collect debts would mean that the individual's future labor would be subject to the will of creditors, thus preventing the free development of human capital. The creditors essentially would have a permanent lien on the debtor's human capital. Because human capital is inalienable in CST, such a charge or lien is impermissible.[21] The discharge of debts frees the individual to exercise his human capital going forward through the removal of this *de facto* lien.

American Bankruptcy Law and CST

What evidence exists in the American experience to indicate that CST's insights explain the introduction and continuing vitality of the bankruptcy discharge? First, strikingly, some Congressional supporters spoke in terms very nearly the same as CST when justifying the introduction of the discharge in the face of creditor opposition. Typical is a statement by Senator Henry Clay:

> The right of the State (I use the term in its broadest sense), to the use of the unimpaired faculties of its citizens as producers, as consumers, and as defenders of the commonwealth, is paramount to any rights or relations which can be created between citizen and citizen. But an honest and unfortunate debtor, borne down by a hopeless mass of debt from beneath which he can never rise, is prostrated and paralyzed, and rendered utterly incapable of performing his duties to his family or his country. To say nothing of the dictates of humanity . . . I maintain that the public right of the State, in all the faculties of its members, moral and physical, is paramount to any supposed rights which appertain to a private creditor. This is the great principle which lies at the bottom of all bankrupt laws, and it is this which gives to the States the right to demand the passage, and imposes upon congress the duty of enacting a bankrupt system.[22]

Senator Clay makes the same point, phrased in slightly different terms, as CST regarding human work. An individual's human capital—"their unimpaired faculties"—are at the service of the State "in its broadest sense"—that is, the common good of society, not just the government. Therefore, the common good of society requires the human capital of its members to be dedicated to the common good, not subjugated to the will of a "private creditor."

Equally striking is the persistent explanation from supporters such as Henry Clay and, later, the Supreme Court itself, that the bankruptcy discharge is available to the "honest but unfortunate" debtor. This recognizes that along with rights of a debtor to exercise his/her human capital, there comes a duty to do so in a manner consistent with CST. Nobody would argue, for example, that the right to the exercise of human capital is without exception, and thus it is illicit to incarcerate a criminal. In such a case, the right gives way to a duty to act virtuously. Thus, the discharge frees the human capital of debtors who act in a virtuous manner, consistent with CST, to develop human capital through work. A person is entitled to "ample leeway" in developing his human capital because such leeway is necessary for the person to achieve his earthly and eternal ends. However, if the individual is not acting virtuously, the justification for freeing human capital from claims of creditors disappears. In other words, if the debtor is not serving the common good through self-development, the rights of the private creditor do trump that of the polity.

Even so, the Code provides a nuanced solution to the problem of the debtor who is not "honest, but unfortunate." The Code completely denies a discharge of debts where the debtor has done something in connection with the bankruptcy case itself which is dishonest.[23] For example, if a debtor bribes the bankruptcy trustee or hides assets from the estate, the court denies him a discharge of *any* debt.

The Code is more forgiving of a debtor who is dishonest in a way that does not threaten to undermine the bankruptcy system itself.[24] A debt that arises from such behavior is non-dischargeable, but all other debts are dischargeable. For example, debts attributable to the debtor's fraud, operation of vehicles while intoxicated, larceny, or embezzlement are non-dischargeable individually, but all other debts would be discharged. Interestingly, the list of non-dischargeable debts includes several that are not attributable to dishonest or sinful behavior, but which implicate directly the common good of society. For example, most debts for taxes, alimony, maintenance, child support, or government-guaranteed student loans are also non-dischargeable. These provisions represent a legislative judgment that the common good is sometimes better served through collection of such debt, even at the cost of a charge on a debtor's human capital.

In short, both in justification and in structure, the Code seems to embody the insights of CST. The honest but unfortunate debtor is afforded a discharge of his debts in order to free his human capital from continuing claims of his creditors. The discharge is therefore not based on mercy or charity, as important as those traits are in CST. Rather, the discharge is necessary to foster the common good through the debtor's continuing development of his human capital. The individual's development serves the common good as long as it is virtuous, and the discharge codifies CST's assertion that this is more important than the claims of private creditors.

Implications: Bankruptcy Reform

The application of CST to American bankruptcy discharge is useful not just in explaining the discharge, but in examining proposals to reform the Code. A particularly relevant example is the 2005 Bankruptcy Abuse Prevention and Consumer Protection Act ("BAPCPA"),[25] which limits access to Chapter 7 liquidation cases based upon a debtor's income. To boil complicated legislation down to its essence, if a debtor makes too much money, he is not permitted to get an immediate discharge through a Chapter 7 liquidation. Rather, he must file a reorganization case in which the debtor makes payments to creditors for several years in exchange for keeping his property. At the end of the reorganization, the debtor receives a discharge. The justification for this aspect of BAPCPA is the congressional judgment that a nontrivial number of bankruptcy debtors have been abusing Chapter 7's immediate discharge because they have the ability to repay a significant portion of their debts in a reorganization case.

BAPCPA does not deprive debtors of a discharge entirely; rather, the discharge is merely delayed while the debtor is subject to federal court jurisdiction for several years in the reorganization case. During that time the debtor must pay all of her income over to a trustee who distributes those funds to creditors. Putting aside empirical questions of whether BAPCPA actually yields greater returns to creditors, is there a CST argument for or against these revisions to the Code?

On the one hand, the debtor's discharge is delayed, but not eliminated. So, although CST holds that human capital is inalienable, it is clear from examples *supra* that American bankruptcy law does permit charges on human capital in some circumstances. A debtor's human capital remains subject to claims of creditors based upon the debtor's dishonesty or considerations of the common good. Therefore, a delay in a debtor's discharge might be defended if such a delay would serve the common good.

On the other hand, such an argument arguably runs afoul of CST. An individual's right to a discharge is true for all human beings or it is true for none.[26] More accurately, for the person acting virtuously in the economic sphere, his freedom in the exercise of his human capital applies to all. A utilitarian balancing of the benefit to society through repayment of private creditors versus the benefit to the common good of individual development is impermissible. Human persons are not mere instruments to be valued like physical capital. Human capital, as an expression of the human person, therefore may not be indentured as an instrument to repay creditors. Such restrictions are only permissible when a debtor is not fulfilling a concomitant duty under CST; making a higher-than-average wage does not fit that criterion.

CONCLUSION

The contribution of Catholic Social Doctrine to the debate over the nature of the bankruptcy discharge lies in CST's insistence that the human being can never be a mere instrument of another. Therefore, although a person's capital is subject to charges by creditors, the human person is not. Human capital is at the core of the human person, and therefore cannot be alienated, voluntarily or involuntarily. The bankruptcy discharge enforces this understanding of the human person, to the benefit of the individuals who receive it, and thus to the common good of society in general.

NOTES

1. The second form of bankruptcy, reorganization, involves a debtor retaining assets in exchange for presenting a plan of reorganization whereby the debtor pays his creditors, over time, an amount equal at least to the amount the creditors would receive in a liquidation. Although there are slightly different considerations concerning the discharge in a reorganization, this chapter only treats the discharge in the classic liquidation case.

2. Charles Jordan Tabb, *The Scope of the Fresh Start in Bankruptcy: Collateral Conversions and the Dischargeability Debate*, 59 Geo. Wash. L. Rev. 56, 63 (1990).

3. Veryl Victoria Miles, *Assessing Modern Bankruptcy Law: An Example of Justice*, 36 Santa Clara L. Rev. 1025, 1054 (1996) (Aristotelian and Thomist notions of social or general justice explain the mercy and forgiveness embodied in the bankruptcy discharge).

4. One of the primary purposes of the Bankruptcy Act is to "relieve the honest debtor from the weight of oppressive indebtedness, and permit him to start afresh free from the obligations and responsibilities consequent upon business misfortunes." This purpose of the act has been again and again emphasized by the courts as being of public as well as private interest, in that it gives to the honest but unfortunate debtor who surrenders for distribution the property which he owns at the time of bankruptcy, a new opportunity in life and a clear field for future effort, unhampered by the pressure and discouragement of preexisting debt. *Local Loan Co. v. Hunt*, 292 U.S. 234, 244 (1934) (citations omitted).

5. See, e.g., Karen Gross, *Failure and Forgiveness. Rebalancing the Bankruptcy System* (Yale University Press, 1999), 15. (Discharge provides a restorative function once debtor admits, through filing, the harm he/she has caused creditors.)

6. See, e.g., Thomas H. Jackson, *The Fresh-Start Policy in Bankruptcy Law*, 98 Harv. L. Rev. 1393 (1985) (debtors unable to control their impulse toward gratification, thus requiring a discharge of debts to deal with the inevitable result).

7. Pontifical Council for Justice and Peace, *Compendium of the Social Doctrine of the Church*, ¶271 [hereinafter *Compendium*].

8. *Compendium*, ¶271.

9. Pope Paul VI, *Populorum Progressio*, ¶15.

10. *Compendium*, ¶271.

11. *Compendium*, ¶272 (citations, italics omitted; emphasis added).

12. "One can also speak of 'human capital' to refer to human resources, that is, to man himself in his capacity to engage in labour, to make use of knowledge and creativity, to sense the needs of his fellow workers and a mutual understanding with other members of an organization." *Compendium*, ¶276. This definition is not entirely consistent with non-CST uses of the phrase. This chapter uses the phrase "human capital" in the same way it is defined in the *Compendium*—the human resources, whether innate or developed through work, which permit a person to engage in work.

13. *Compendium*, ¶336.

14. *Compendium*, ¶336.

15. *Compendium*, ¶336.

16. The purpose of government involvement is presumably to minimize the threat of violence that might inhere in private debt collection.

17. In fairness, creditors often lose track of judgments and fail to renew them. Nevertheless, the point remains that a judgment is potentially a permanent sword of Damocles hanging over a debtor.

18. Inside or outside of bankruptcy, states and the federal government provide that a debtor may keep certain assets necessary for a debtor to maintain a minimum subsistence. Common exemptions include clothing, household implements such as cooking utensils, and tools of a trade. Exemption law often also permits a debtor to keep items of deep significance to the debtor but much less value to creditors, such as wedding rings and family Bibles. That such laws are recognized both in state law and the Code indicates that in the debtor–creditor context some values are, and always have been, more important than full performance of a contract. Of course, the most prominent example of this point is the bankruptcy discharge itself.

19. It is this aspect of bankruptcy law that the Oxford legal philosopher discussed in his seminal philosophical work as an example of the interplay between general, commutative, and distributive justice. John Finnis, *Natural Law and Natural Rights* (Clarendon Press, 1980), 188–93.

20. In distributing assets of the debtor to creditors, the Code provides an orderly, pro rata distribution to creditors, which replaces the nonbankruptcy rule of "winner take all." That is, rather than the richest or strongest creditor being paid in full because they have the wherewithal to sue first, the creditors in a bankruptcy case share and share alike. In this sense, there certainly are interesting implications regarding justice raised by the bankruptcy distribution scheme. Those implications, however, could and did exist in American bankruptcy law without the bankruptcy discharge. Therefore, the justification for the bankruptcy discharge must lie elsewhere.

21. States long have codified this very point by deeming unenforceable a consensual security interest in future wages. Such security interests are best understood as a charge on human capital because future wages are the fruit of human capital. Though there is no problem in granting a security interest in a debtor's existing material or financial capital when the debtor borrows money because such capital *is* alienable under CST, a charge on human capital is not permissible because human capital is inalienable under CST.

22. 26th Cong., 1st Sess., Cong. Globe 816 (June 4, 1840 App.).

23. 11 U.S.C. § 727 (a) (1978).

24. 11 U.S.C. § 523 (a) (1978).

25. Bankruptcy Abuse Prevention and Consumer Protection Act of 2005, Pub. L. 109–8, 119 Stat. 23 (April 20, 2005).

26. In fairness, despite the Constitution's grant to Congress the power to pass uniform bankruptcy laws in article I, section 8, American law has never recognized the bankruptcy discharge as a constitutional right. See *United States v. Kras*, 409 U.S. 434 (1973).

Chapter Nineteen

Intellectual Property

Thomas C. Berg

In today's high-tech world, hardly a day passes without news of some dispute over intellectual property ("IP"): patent, copyright, and trademark rights. Many disputes are ordinary struggles between business competitors in technology or media industries. But some IP disputes plainly implicate questions of morality and social justice. Should a developing nation ravaged by disease be able to import cheap generic versions of essential medicines in violation of drug manufacturers' patents? Should biotech companies be able to patent human genes or genetically modified ("GM") crops, own the codes for various characteristics of living things, and control uses such as genetic testing for disease or farmers' replanting of seeds?

To have property is to have a bundle of rights in a thing, including the right to exclude others. IP gives exclusive rights for set times in the intangible intellectual components of products: twenty years for a novel, useful invention under patent, seventy years from the author's death for a creative work under copyright. These laws rest on Congress's constitutional power "to promote the progress of science and the useful arts, by securing for limited times to authors and inventors the exclusive rights to their respective writings and discoveries."[1] IP has also become a priority in U.S. international economic policy. Treaties such as the 1994 Trade-Related Aspects of Intellectual Property Rights ("TRIPS") agreement have pushed other nations to strengthen their protection of IP, expanding overseas markets for America's high-tech and creative industries.

The Catholic Church has periodically weighed in on IP matters. When affordability of medicines in poor nations became a pressing global issue in the early 2000s, Pope John Paul II and Vatican diplomats argued that under Catholic teaching, patent rights should give way to the fulfillment of essential human needs. More recently, Latin American bishops opposed trade

agreements with the United States that would boost patent rights on medicines and GM crops.[2] Benedict XVI's encyclical *Caritas in Veritate*, in
surveying the obstacles to "authentic human development," complained that
"[o]n the part of rich countries there is excessive zeal for protecting knowledge through an unduly rigid assertion of the right to intellectual property,
especially in the field of health care."[3]

These statements have not articulated a full Catholic account of IP, but
such an account can be developed and make a meaningful contribution to IP
law and policy. For many years, analysis of the proper scope of IP has been
dominated by economic, instrumentalist approaches. Under these the sole
inquiry is how to strike the right balance between (a) encouraging the production and distribution of creative or innovative goods through ownership
and (b) preserving room for further creation through a public domain of
freely accessible information. But the recent high-profile disputes have made
clear that IP is also a morally fraught subject. IP holders call the infringement
of their rights "stealing" or "theft," whether it is the avoidance of drug
patents by developing nations or the sharing of digital music files by college
students.[4] In turn, critics of broad IP rights have attacked them on various
ethical grounds, most notably the human right to health care and other basic
needs.[5] "[T]he accessibility, affordability, and widespread diffusion of the
goods regulated by [IP] have tangible effects upon human beings"; in cases
such as affordability of medicines, IP can be "a matter of life and death."[6]
When IP discourse implicates morality, the thought of Catholicism (and other religious traditions) can participate and contribute.

Under Catholic thought, private property, including IP, is a vital institution grounded in human dignity and the resources given by the Creator, but
these same grounds impose limits on property rights and obligations on owners to vindicate the dignity of others. This chapter sketches Catholic thought
on property and its application in light of IP's distinctive features, then
briefly explores some implications of Catholic thought in two major areas:
(1) the relation of IP to human creativity, the natural world, and morality in
the context of patents on living things; and (2) how to structure (and appropriately limit) IP rights to promote social justice, especially in meeting the
needs of, and empowering, the poor.

PROPERTY, IP, AND CATHOLIC THOUGHT: FOUNDATIONS

Property and Catholic Thought

A Catholic approach to IP begins with Catholicism's longstanding, distinctive tradition of thought on property rights in general.[7] Private property is an
important institution, a corollary of human dignity that recognizes the value
of individuals' work, encourages their productive effort, and "by stimulating

[the] exercise of responsibility[,] . . . constitutes one of the conditions for civil liberty."[8] But the equal dignity of human persons also means that property rights are qualified. Pope John Paul II summarized the teaching:

> [T]he goods of this world are originally meant [by God the Creator] for all. The right to private property is valid and necessary, but it . . . is under a "social mortgage," which means that it has an intrinsically social function, based upon and justified precisely by the principle of the universal destination of goods.[9]

Private property may typically be the best means of generating these goods, but it should give way if necessary to ensure others' basic needs.

The notion that property comes with social obligations finds expression in several other concepts. One is the biblical theme of stewardship. Just as the master in Jesus' parables directs his servants, God directs us to both use and care for the resources He has given us. This includes our own creativity, which is likewise a gift. Gratitude plays a role here: If we recognize resources and talents as significant parts of a gift, it naturally follows that we should be generous in sharing them with others. Notions of gift and stewardship are not limited to religious doctrine; they also appear in secular thought.[10]

The ultimately social nature of goods implies a duty to seek the common good, which the Second Vatican Council defines as "the sum total of social conditions which allow social groups and their individual members relatively thorough and ready access to their own fulfillment."[11] This in turn implicates the virtue of solidarity with others. Catholic social thought asserts that because human beings can only find fulfillment "'with' others and 'for' others," both individuals and society have the responsibility to seek others' well-being, in every "expression of social life": families, associations, businesses, and governments.[12] Solidarity requires that a person, in appropriate ways and in her particular location, give up her "desire for profit [and] thirst for power" and "lose [her]self for the sake of the other instead of exploiting him."[13]

The duty to ensure others' access to goods requires specification and limitation, of course, since Catholic thought is far from communistic. One component is an obligation to provide "essential goods," those that are indispensable if people are to "succeed in realizing their basic human vocation."[14] God calls people to work, use their gifts, associate with each other, and respond to him; Catholic thought focuses on the poor because people are severely hampered in these activities if they lack basics such as nourishment, shelter, and health care.[15] Beyond essential goods, Catholic thought focuses fundamentally on empowerment: on enabling people, particularly through education, "to acquire expertise, to enter the circle of exchange, and . . . make the best use of their capacities and resources" so as to "contribut[e] to [c]ultural, economic, political and social life."[16] There is a strong emphasis, especially in John Paul II's encyclicals, on empowering the poor to become producers and creators themselves.

Although solidarity and common good are often best pursued through voluntary activity, they can also justify legal limits on property rights. State rules are no substitute for the direct connections with others that tend to come more easily through voluntary activity: this fact among others animates the Catholic doctrine of subsidiarity, the preference for smaller, voluntary institutions.[17] But law is also relevant because solidarity, especially with the vulnerable, "must be translated at all levels into concrete actions," in John Paul II's words, in both "[o]ur daily life and our decisions in the political and economic fields."[18]

Intellectual Property

Intellectual property shares many features with tangible property, and the case for a basic level of protection is strong. As John Paul II recognizes in *Centesimus Annus* (1991), increasingly "[t]he decisive factor" in economic activity is not land or physical equipment, but "*man himself*, that is, his knowledge, especially his scientific knowledge"; thus "the possession of know-how, knowledge, and skill" is a crucial form of ownership.[19] All human productivity reflects the image of God, as humans mirror "the very action of the Creator" and "shar[e] in the work of creation."[20] But authorship and invention (the subjects of IP law) parallel divine creativity in a special way, since God the Creator conceives and designs and does not only build. Basic IP rights are supported by arguments of both social utility and moral desert. The first emphasizes that economic incentives are typically necessary to enable people to devote their full energy to producing works or inventions and bringing them to distribution. Thus IP rights, in the Constitution's words, "promote the progress of" knowledge. The second argument, hearkening back to John Locke's justifications for property rights, emphasizes that creators have a right to reward for advances they have made through their talents and labor.[21]

At the same time, however, IP rights have always been subject to significant limits not applicable to tangible property. Most obviously, a copyright or patent lasts for only a "limited tim[e]," as the Constitution requires. Moreover, each right is qualified by a series of statutory exceptions (some of which the next section will discuss in greater detail). Because traditional IP law explicitly strikes such balances between private ownership and public access, it fits especially well with the Catholic conception of property as an important but limited right instrumental to broader goals.

A chief reason for greater limits on IP is that information, unlike physical goods, is typically "nonrivalrous": another person's use of it does not interfere with the owner's use. As Thomas Jefferson wrote:

He who receives an idea from me, receives instruction himself without lessening mine; as he who lites his taper at mine, receives light without darkening me. That ideas should freely spread from one to another over the globe, for the . . . improvement of his condition, seems to have been . . . designed by nature."[22]

Since sharing of information has *prima facie* benefits and usually does not prevent the creator's use, restrictions on sharing may impose unnecessary costs—unless the restrictions are necessary to encourage the production and distribution of information in the first place. And although IP rights can encourage creation and innovation, they can also discourage it by increasing the costs of building blocks for future creation. For example, overly broad patents may deter innovation by conferring market power on the patent holder; but narrower patents, issued in larger numbers, can create a so-called thicket of rights that boosts the cost of transacting for licenses for further use.

On balance, then, even the goal of encouraging creation justifies only qualified IP rights. Moreover, IP is surely subject to the demands of stewardship and the social mortgage: As a Vatican statement on the provision of essential medicines put it, "the very creative and innovative impetus" that IP rights provide "is there to serve the common good of the [entire] human community," so its benefits should be "sprea[d] as widely as possible."[23] As the following section discusses, many traditional limits on IP rights strike this balance, but some have been threatened by recent pressures to expand IP rights. Catholic thought cannot specify precisely how to respond to these pressures and challenges; but detailed below are some considerations for maintaining the general nature of IP as a limited, instrumental right.

CURRENT IP ISSUES AND CATHOLIC THOUGHT

Divine and Human Creation, Morality, and Patents on Living Things

The biotechnology revolution of the last forty years has been accompanied by thousands of U.S. patents on living things and their parts: patents on genetically engineered crops, microorganisms, and even some higher animals, as well as on human gene sequences and related genetic material. These give the patent holder a monopoly over the manufacture, sale, or use not just of individual organisms or genetic sample, but of any others with the same features. Such ownership rights trigger religious concerns about excessive human control over the natural order, God's creation—and in the case of human gene patents, concerns about compromising the unique status and dignity of human beings. The Supreme Court opened the door in 1980, in *Diamond v. Chakrabarty*,[24] by upholding a patent on a bacterium not occurring in nature, genetically engineered to clean up oil spills. The Patent Office and the courts extended the principle to permit patents on GM crops, on human stem cells and genetic material, and on complete, genetically engineered animals from oysters to mice—but both legislation and regulations forbid any patent "on a claim directed to or encompassing a human organism."[25]

Gene Patents, Creativity, and Morality

In 1995, a "joint appeal" by nearly two hundred religious leaders from eighty religious bodies opposed the patenting of genetically engineered animals and human genes, cells, and body parts on the ground that "humans and animals are creations of God, not [of] humans."[26] But religious opinions on the issue have been divided and religious interventions sporadic. In any event, gene patents went forward: The Patent Office granted thousands of patents, covering at least 20 percent, and probably much more, of the human genome.[27]

When the Supreme Court revisited the issue in 2013 in a case involving Myriad Genetics' patents on the genes for breast cancer, the sole brief filed by a religious organization (the Southern Baptist Convention) attacked the patents on two grounds. The first, echoing the 1995 Joint Appeal, was that DNA "is a divine creation, not a human one"—a "divine gift"—and Myriad had "merely removed the DNA from the body."[28] U.S. law holds that "laws of nature, natural phenomena, and abstract ideas" are unpatentable, "free to all men and reserved exclusively to none," because they "are not created."[29] Under Catholic thought, it is vital to maintain this principle, which reflects humility toward the natural order (as well as valid fears that ownership of natural phenomena will block too much beneficial activity: Myriad used its patents to claim exclusivity over all breast-cancer genetic testing and charged $3,000 per test, triple the price of tests in Canada that were free of patent[30]).

The unanimous Court in *Myriad* reaffirmed the product-of-nature exclusion by invalidating patents on the DNA sequences that Myriad simply isolated from the body. Conversely, however, the Court upheld the patents on "complementary DNA" ("cDNA"), a substance with a different, nonnaturally-occurring chemical structure that excludes regions of the genome that do not generate, or "code for," proteins and resulting human characteristics.[31] Indeed, the Court indicated the product-of-nature exclusion would not bar any patent on "[s]cientific alteration of the genetic code."[32] Some such alterations (eugenic creations, human–animal hybrids) would plainly transgress human dignity; the product-of-nature exclusion alone cannot handle the moral concerns.

The second argument against the patents in *Myriad* invoked morality and human dignity, arguing that patenting any part of the body, including genes, "degrades humanity, dropping it from its special role in creation to a mere species of property" and opening the door to further commodification of body parts.[33] U.S. patent law long had a test of "moral utility," under which courts denied applications for inventions such as gambling machines.[34] But this limit has significantly waned. The Supreme Court in the *Chakrabarty* case reasoned that to reject patents on living things on moral grounds would require Congress to amend the statute; the Patent Office went forward paying little attention to moral concerns in granting gene patents.[35] This contrasts with both European law and international treaties, which require or at least permit denial of patents whose exploitation would violate "public order and morality." Indeed, the U.S. office has cultivated such an image of "scientific neutrality" that even pro-life groups have not seriously scrutinized it when it has granted patents on abortifacient drugs and devices.[36]

It is surely important, from a Catholic standpoint, to question the premise of value neutrality, and to preserve the notion that an invention's morality is relevant to whether granting a patent on it serves the social purposes of patent law. However, as a matter of institutional reality, it is questionable whether courts and patent examiners can make such determinations under a general doctrine of morality, except in the most egregious cases. Congress should take a role, and it occasionally has done so by barring human-organism patents (as already noted) and exempting doctors and hospitals from suit when they use patented processes in medical treatments.[37]

As some theologians and ethicists have pointed out, certain arguments against gene patents are too simplistic.[38] The notion of stewardship does not call solely for humility toward nature; it also affirms human creativity in refashioning nature for the good of others (which some biotechnology clearly does). Moreover, a patent does not directly commodify individuals or body parts, since it does not actually confer ownership over a physical thing such as an organ, let alone a human individual. But moral concerns should in no way disappear from consideration of life patents. Public morals aimed at legislation can identify those genetic manipulations that are degrading to humans and forbid them as well as exclude them from patentability. Improper uses of genetic tests—for abortive or eugenic purposes—likewise should be independently prohibited (although some such prohibitions would face constitutional challenge). Finally, concerns about patent holders' monopolization of genetic technology might be addressed in various ways: shortened patent terms or an exemption from suit for research uses of patented technology (since U.S. patent law currently makes little or no exception for fair uses or research).

Agricultural Patents

Patents on genetically modified plants, most notably agricultural crops, raise different issues. A crop such as Monsanto's Roundup Ready soybeans—

genetically manipulated to be resistant to herbicides intended to kill weeds—
is a nonnaturally occurring product under *Chakrabarty*, and patenting it does
not directly implicate humans' special dignity as do human-gene patents. But
such patents still affect people dramatically: They may increase farmers'
yield, but they also change centuries-old farming practices, such as replanting seeds for the next year's crop. The farmers become licensees of Monsanto, which dominates GM-crop markets: Monsanto limits the farmers to planting one generation of seeds then subjects them to ongoing supervision of
their behavior.

In the recent Supreme Court case of *Bowman v. Monsanto Co.*,[39] a farmer
bought a late-season second batch of soybeans, tested them for the herbicide-
resistant characteristic, and replanted them. When Monsanto sued, Bowman
invoked the patent exhaustion doctrine, under which the purchaser of a particular physical copy of a patented invention may use or resell it. The doctrine does not permit the buyer to make further copies, but Bowman argued
that the replanted beans were "self-replicating": the first generation may have
been created nonnaturally, but its progeny germinated naturally (by divine
rather than human acts, theologically speaking). The Court, however, unanimously rejected the exhaustion defense under these facts, finding that Bowman had made copies by strategically culling seeds for replanting and that
Monsanto's rewards and incentives from its patent would be eviscerated by
the farmer's "reproduction (unto the eighth generation) of [the] invention."[40]

Bowman shows again the difficulty of drawing the line between natural
processes and human intervention so as to undercut patent protection altogether. But given the significant potential effects from the patenting of GM
crops, courts and legislatures should consider ways of mitigating them. "Religious leaders are likely to make a more substantive contribution to debates
about agricultural biotechnology by addressing these life patents than by
speculating that genetic engineering is playing God."[41] American critics of
GM foods—paralleling stronger movements in Europe—have suggested returning seeds to the public domain or retaining only the more limited protection of the 1970 Plant Variety Protection Act, which allows replanting and
seed research.[42]

IP, the Social Mortgage, and the Needs of the Poor

As has already been noted, since creativity is a gift, the property rights that
recognize it should be subject to obligations to others, whether that is expressed in terms of stewardship or "social mortgage." This section briefly
sketches the implications of this approach. The principles have relevance to
domestic law, but even more to the effects of IP on people in developing
nations. Such effects are highly relevant to U.S. policy, since the United

States pushes repeatedly for broad IP rights overseas through multilateral, regional, and bilateral trade agreements.

Basic Needs

As already noted, one ground for limiting IP rights is to ensure the poor have access to necessities—food, water, basic health care—since these are preconditions both for life itself and for further empowerment. That tailored limits on IP can be necessary was dramatized by the crisis over essential medicines: in the early 2000s a year's supply of AIDS drugs cost more than $10,000 in the United States under patent, but less than $400 in generic batches from Indian manufacturers, yet patent holders tried to block the least developed countries ("LDCs") from importing generics. Even prominent pro-globalization economists, such as Columbia's Jagdish Bhagwati, concluded that patent enforcement was "[c]learly . . . unnecessarily harmful to the poor countries" because it inflated drug prices while failing to incentivize research and development directed at epidemics in LDCs.[43] There was thus ample warrant for the Doha world-trade declarations of the 2000s, which—in response to pressure from developing nations, relief organizations, and the Vatican—allowed LDCs to delay implementation of global patent requirements and to create exceptions to patent rights, such as compulsory licenses at more affordable prices, in public-health crises. Catholic thought cannot specify precisely when such state measures are necessary; in recent years voluntary arrangements among drug companies, LDCs, and relief organizations have increased the distribution of affordable medicines. But massive challenges remain. The solution should include flexibility for LDCs to legislate and put immediate needs above the speculative promises of long-term benefits from full patent enforcement.

Empowerment and IP Limitations

Recall that in situations beyond basic necessities, the key question is whether IP will empower others to create, to become participants in economic and cultural life. On that score, the prospects are again mixed. IP can encourage the creativity of people on the economic margins by offering them rewards (through copyright or patent) and helping them market their products (through trademark).[44] However, because developing countries often lack the capacity to absorb and benefit from new technology, strong IP rights may act primarily to "retard diffusion of new products (because of high prices)" while doing little to promote "access by local firms to foreign technologies."[45]

The poor can be empowered in part by certain traditional limits on IP, especially in copyright, that encourage new creativity by users directly or (through educational uses) indirectly. In U.S. copyright law, the fair use defense favors "transformative uses," those that build upon the copyrighted work to add "new meaning, expression, or message," as well as uses for "teaching, scholarship, or research."[46] Other provisions promote empowerment through education by explicitly protecting certain copying by libraries and archives and performances and displays of works in classroom teaching or distance education.[47] And the Copyright Act exempts multiple nonprofit uses—by religious groups, agricultural organizations, veterans' and fraternal organizations, and groups transmitting information to the blind or deaf[48] — which as a class are not particularly remunerative even though they "serve important social purposes."[49] Although these exceptions limit property rights, they create nothing like the dependency and bureaucracy that John Paul II once criticized the welfare state for encouraging.[50] Instead they encourage new creativity and benefit the sort of intermediate, charitable associations commended by the doctrine of subsidiarity.

Reasonable limitations of this sort, reducing the costs of education and of charitable assistance, may be particularly beneficial for developing countries to enact. (The implication for American law is that the United States should not seek to bar such enactments through trade agreements.) But the limitations in U.S. law itself should also be preserved and strengthened. As noted, patent law should make more room for fair-use arguments. And copyright fair use is under pressure from copyright owners who argue that the defense should be inapplicable whenever a use might cause even the most speculative harm to license fees or other sources of revenue. Such claims should be resisted.

Empowerment: Technology Transfer and Training

Finally, if IP is to empower the poor to create and innovate, there must be enforceable obligations on developed nations to transfer technology and training to developing nations. Vatican references to IP have, correctly, emphasized this as crucial, unfinished business in the implementation of the TRIPs agreement.[51] In the 1990s, the United States assured developing nations that strengthening their IP laws would not only encourage their citizens' innovation but "attract foreign investment and spur technology transfer."[52] But while TRIPS made increased IP protection a "bound obligation" on developing nations, it created no mechanism to force developed nations to reciprocate with technology transfers and training. As a result, "the grand bargain has been ephemeral" or even "a major disappointment" for developing nations; "most studies show that there is no direct influence of [IP] protection on the promotion of transfer of technology [to] LDCs."[53] Effective enforcement mechanisms are necessary "because the private sector does not have automatic incentives to transfer technology."[54] Whether to tie enforcement mechanisms directly to the IP system (by conditioning IP protection on technology transfer and training), or impose separate requirements, is a matter for prudential judgment.

CONCLUSION

Intellectual property, like other property rights, is important and valuable. But is also "socially contingen[t]": it "exists for certain social purposes, and it must be structured [by policy makers] with reference to those purposes."[55] Catholic thought can contribute to orienting IP toward its proper purposes.

NOTES

1. U.S. Const., art. I, § 8, cl. 8.

2. For summaries of these statements, see Thomas C. Berg, "Intellectual Property and the Preferential Option for the Poor," *Journal of Catholic Social Thought* 5 (2008): 193, 197–98.

3. Pope Benedict XVI, *Caritas in Veritate*, ¶22 (2009).

4. See, e.g., Recording Industry of America, "Who Music Theft Hurts," http://www.riaa.com/physicalpiracy.php?content_selector=piracy_details_online.

5. See, e.g., Lawrence R. Helfer and Graeme W. Austin, *Human Rights and Intellectual Property: Mapping the Global Interface* (Cambridge University Press, 2011); Margaret Chon, *Intellectual Property and the Development Divide*, 27 Cardozo Law Review 2821 (2006).

6. Gabriel J. Michael, *Catholic Thought and Intellectual Property: Learning from the Ethics of Obligation*, 25 Journal of Law and Religion 415, 418 (2009–2010) (*quoting* Christopher May and Susan K. Sell, *Intellectual Property Rights: A Critical History* [Lynne Rienner Publishing, 2006], 7).

7. This article draws on more extensive discussions of IP and Christian social thought, including, e.g., David Carey, *The Social Mortgage on Intellectual Property* (Acton Institute, 2009); Berg, "Intellectual Property," *supra* note 2; Roman Cholij, "IP in Christian Law," *Intellectual Property Quarterly* 17 (2012): 137; and Michael, *Catholic Thought and Intellectual Property*, *supra* note 6.

8. *Pastoral Constitution on the Church in the Modern World: Gaudium et Spes*, ¶71 (December 7, 1965) [hereinafter *GS*], http://www.vatican.va/archive/hist_councils/ii_vatican_council/documents/vat-ii_cons_19651207_gaudium-et-spes_en.html; Pontifical Council for Justice and Peace, *Compendium of Social Doctrine of the Church*, ¶176 at 77 (English trans. USCCB, 2004) [hereinafter *Compendium*].

9. John Paul II, *Sollicitudo Rei Socialis*, ¶42 (1987) [hereinafter *SRS*].

10. Lewis Hyde, *The Gift: Imagination and the Erotic Life of Property* (Vintage Books, 1983); Helena Howe, "Copyright Limitations and the Stewardship Model of Property," *Intellectual Property Quarterly* 16 (2011): 183 (applying stewardship concepts from environmental law to copyright).

11. *GS*, ¶26.

12. *Compendium*, ¶165, at 73.

13. *SRS*, ¶¶37–38.

14. *SRS*, ¶28.

15. Berg, "Intellectual Property," *supra* note 2, at 199–200 (*citing SRS* and *Compendium*).

16. John Paul II, *Centesimus Annus*, ¶34 (1991) [hereinafter *CA*]; *Compendium*, ¶189 at 83.

17. See *Compendium*, ¶419 at 180 (commending "volunteer organizations and cooperative endeavors in the private-social sector" that "create new areas for the active presence and direct actions of citizens"); Ronald J. Rychlak and John M. Czarnetzky, *The International Criminal Court and the Questions of Subsidiarity*, Third World Legal Studies, Vol. 16 (2003), 115.

18. *SRS*, ¶43, ¶42.

19. *CA*, ¶32.

20. Pope John Paul II, *Laborem Exercens*, ¶4, ¶25 (1981); see Roberta Rosenthal Kwall, *Inspiration and Innovation: The Intrinsic Dimension of the Artistic Soul*, 81 Notre Dame Law Review 1945, 1951–58 (2006) (exploring these themes, in both Judaism and Christianity, with respect to artistic creativity).

21. See, e.g., *Mazer v. Stein*, 347 U.S. 201, 219 (1954) (justifying copyright on both rationales—that "encouragement of individual effort by personal gain is the best way to advance public welfare," and that "such creative activities deserve rewards commensurate with the services rendered"—but calling the latter "a secondary consideration").

22. Letter from Thomas Jefferson to Isaac McPherson (August 13, 1813), in thirteen *Writings of Thomas Jefferson*, ed., Albert E. Bergh (Thomas Jefferson Memorial Association, 1905), 333–35.

23. Address of H.E. Msgr. Diarmuid Martin, "Intervention by the Holy See at the World Trade Organization" (December 20, 2002), available at http://www.vatican.va/roman_curia/secretariat_state/documents/rc_seg-st_doc_20021220_martin-wto_en.html (emphasis in original).

24. *Diamond v. Chakrabarty*, 447 U.S. 303 (1980).

25. America Invents Act, § 33(a) (2011), 35 U.S.C. § 101(a); see Manual of Patent Examining Procedure § 2105, http://www.uspto.gov/web/offices/pac/mpep/s2105.html.

26. General Board of Church and Society of the United Methodist Church, "Joint Appeal Against Human and Animal Patenting" (May 17, 1995), *quoted in* Audrey Chapman, *Unprecedented Choices: Religious Ethics at the Frontiers of Genetic Science* (Fortress Press, 1999), 146.

27. American Civil Liberties Union, "BRCA FAQs" (June 2013), https://www.aclu.org/free-speech/brca-faqs. The ACLU brought the *AMP v. Myriad* case, discussed *infra*, challenging gene patents.

28. "Brief for *Amici Curiae* Ethics and Religious Liberty Commission of the Southern Baptist Convention and Prof. D. Brian Scarnecchia," at 4–5 [hereinafter "*Myriad* Amicus Brief"], available at http://www.americanbar.org/content/dam/aba/publications/supreme_court_preview/briefs-v2/12-398_pet_amcu_southernbaptist.authcheck dam.pdf.

29. *Association for Molecular Pathology v. Myriad Genetics*, 133 S. Ct. 2107, 2116 (2013) (*quoting Chakrabarty*, 447 U.S. at 309).

30. *Association for Molecular Pathology v. U.S. PTO*, 702 F. Supp. 181, 203 (S.D.N.Y., 2010).

31. *Myriad*, 133 S. Ct. at 2119.

32. *Myriad*, 133 S. Ct. at 2119.

33. *Myriad* Amicus Brief, *supra* note 28, at 6, 17.

34. See Margo A. Bagley, *Patent First, Ask Questions Later: Morality and Biotechnology in Patent Law*, 45 William and Mary Law Review 469, 489 (2003).

35. *Chakrabarty*, 447 U.S. at 316–17.

36. See Kara W. Swanson, "Patents, Politics, and Abortion," in *Intellectual Property Law in Context: Law and Society Perspectives on IP*, William T. Gallagher and Debora J. Halbert, eds., forthcoming, available at http://papers.ssrn.com/sol3/papers.cfm?abstract_id=2337062.

37. See America Invents Act, § 33(a) (2011), 35 U.S.C. § 101(a), *supra* note 25 (ban on patenting human beings); 35 U.S.C. § 287(c) (medical-treatment exception). The matter is complicated by the fact that a patent monopoly can be used to confine rather than facilitate an objectionable invention. For example, pro-life groups were able to focus pressure on the sole manufacturer, the patent holder, of the abortion drug RU-486; and anti-biotech activist Jeremy Rifkin (unsuccessfully) filed for a patent on human–animal combinations in order to prevent anyone else from making them. Swanson, "Patents, Politics, and Abortion," *supra* note 36.

38. For detailed presentation of the following arguments, see, e.g., Chapman, *Unprecedented Choices, supra* note 26, ch. 4; Michael J. Hanson, "Religious Voices in Biotechnology: The Case of Human Gene Patenting," 27:6 *Hastings Center Report* 1 (November/December, 1997).

39. *Bowman v. Monsanto Co.*, 133 S. Ct. 1761 (2013).

40. *Bowman* at 1769.

41. Keith Douglass Warner, "Are Life Patents Ethical? Conflict Between Catholic Social Thought and Agricultural Biotechnology's Patent Regime," 14 *Journal of Agricultural and Environmental Ethics* 14 (2001): 301.

42. Center for Food Safety and Save Our Seeds, *Seed Farmers vs. U.S. Giants*, 36–38 (2013), available at http://www.centerforfoodsafety.org/files/seed-giants_final_04424.pdf ("CFS Report").

43. Jagdish Bhagwati, *In Defense of Globalization* (Oxford University Press, 2004), 184–85 (concluding that diseases limited to poor countries, like malaria, generated minimal R&D, and for diseases present in both rich and poor countries, like AIDS, drug patents simply forced relief organizations "to give money to the poor countries to buy the drugs at [the higher] prices").

44. Berg, "Intellectual Property," *supra* note 2 at 216 (describing organizations aiming to "mak[e] IP laws work for the poor").

45. Carlos M. Correa, "Pro-Competitive Measures Under TRIPS to Promote Technology Diffusion in Developing Countries," in *Global Intellectual Property Rights*, Peter Drahos and Ruth Mayne, eds. (Palgrave, 2002), 40, 42.

46. *Campbell v. Acuff-Rose Music*, 510 U.S. 569, 579 (1994); 17 U.S.C. § 107.

47. 17 U.S.C. §§ 108, 110(1), (2).

48. 17 U.S.C. § 110(3), (4), (6), (8)–(10).

49. Molly Shaffer Van Houweling, *Distributive Values in Copyright*, 83 Texas Law Review 1535, 1545 (2005).

50. *CA*, ¶32 (criticizing the "social assistance state" on this ground).

51. Martin Address, *supra* note 23. ("Improved technology and know-how transfer from the developed countries is necessary so the less-developed countries can catch up and gain international trade competitiveness.")

52. E. Anthony Wayne, "Why Protecting Intellectual Property Rights Matters," *Focus on Intellectual Property Rights* (U.S. Dept. of State, Bureau of International Information Programs, January 2006): 10 (article by Assistant Secretary of State for Economic and Business Affairs).

53. Gehl Sampath and Pedro Roffe, "Unpacking the International Technology Transfer Debate: Fifty Years and Beyond," ICTSD Issue Paper 36, (ICTSD, November 22, 2012) at 26, 25, available at http://papers.ssrn.com/sol3/papers.cfm?abstract_id=2268529.

54. Sampath and Roffe at 33.

55. Michael, *Catholic Thought and Intellectual Property, supra* note 6 at 451.

Chapter Twenty

Labor and Employment Law

David L. Gregory

INTRODUCTION

Come to me all you who labor and are burdened, and I will give you rest. Take up my yoke, and learn from me, for I am meek and humble of heart, *and you shall have your rest*, for my yoke is easy and my burden light. [1]

The great danger in today's world, pervaded as it is by consumerism, is the desolation and anguish born of a complacent and covetous heart, the feverish pursuit of frivolous pleasures, and the blunted conscience. Whenever our interior life becomes caught up in its own interest, and concerns, there is no longer room for others, no place for the poor. [2]

When Pope Leo XIII promulgated the Church's first encyclical on labor, *Rerum Novarum* in 1891, it would have been difficult for him to imagine that his successor, Pope Francis, would be *Time* magazine's Person of the Year. Pope Leo, however, would no doubt be utterly sanguine in his core belief that the truth is timeless and can simultaneously be profoundly timely.

Over the course of the past thirty years, much of my academic scholarship has been devoted to exploring the implications of Catholic social teaching for the rights of workers and the dignity of work. This chapter further advances that larger project and focuses on the truth as both Alpha and Omega. The most efficient way of doing so is to examine the story of creation in Genesis, the life of Jesus as carpenter, priest, prophet, and King and then briefly assess the influence of Benedict XVI and Francis on furthering the dignity of work and of workers.

LABOR IN SCRIPTURE

Throughout Scripture, workers have been chosen to be lifted up. God chose to make a king out of a shepherd and chose to first announce the birth of Jesus to shepherds working in the fields. Jesus lived the skilled trade, blue-collar life of a carpenter in the family business. He performed his public life doing white-collar intellectual work as a teacher and rabbi. He thus had distinctive roles as priest, prophet, and ultimately as King. Workers received a great deal of favorable attention in the Gospel parables. Work is the most basic of human activities and reflects an exalted nature. Work is so fundamentally important, it is central to the very notion of humanity.

Labor is a common theme throughout Scripture. It first appears in the book of Genesis.[3] Work is God's first action. God begins creation by the act of work. God works for six days in the creation of all things but rests on the seventh day. By working in the act of creation, God deems the results of work to be inherently good. Thus, work done by humans also holds a special, exalted place.

Not only is work an action taken by God, it is the first command that God gives to Adam. This makes work an integral part of human existence. In Genesis 2:15, God places Adam in the Garden of Eden with the command to "cultivate and care" for the land. From that moment on, humans have worked. The work that God gives to Adam is a good thing. It only becomes toil after Adam and Eve sin. Without sin, humans are meant to work. With sin, humans toil. When humans live good holy lives they experience work as God intended.

God asks those whom he favors to work. When He speaks to Noah, God orders him to work in building an ark.[4] God saves Noah and his family from the flood, but on the condition that Noah work. Noah's salvation from the flood comes at the price of his work.

After the flood, the centrality of work in human existence is reaffirmed when God makes a covenant with Noah. This covenant is very similar to the command to work given to Adam. God tells Noah to subdue the earth. Thus, even after humanity ends and restarts, work still holds an exalted place because it is what God wants.

Throughout the Old Testament, there are examples of God choosing those He wants to act for Him from among the workers. For example, when God calls Gideon to lead the people, Gideon is "beating out wheat in the wine press."[5] When it is revealed to Samuel that Saul would be the first king of Israel, Saul is searching for the lost asses that belong to his father.[6] God chooses to make a king out of a shepherd. These are examples of God choosing those who work to be His servants. It is the workers that God chooses to bless and perform His work.

Work is also a key feature in many of the love stories in the Old Testament. It is through her work in giving water to the servant and camels of Isaac that Rebekah is chosen to be his wife.[7] It is through seven years of hard work that Jacob is able to marry Leah and another seven years of hard work to marry Rachel.[8] It is through working in his fields and caring for Naomi that Ruth wins the love of Boaz.[9] These examples show that it is work that is valued. Work is the way to win a beloved spouse.

This exaltation of workers and work continues in the New Testament. It begins with the angels announcing to the shepherds that the Messiah has been born.[10] God does not announce the birth of Christ to priests or wealthy men. He chooses to make the announcement to those who are hard at work. Work is valued from the very beginning of Jesus' time on Earth. Some of the best examples of the value of work can be found in the parables of Jesus.

The first parable that shows the exalted nature of work is that of the Prodigal Son.[11] A father has two sons. One of the sons requests that his father give him his inheritance. After receiving it, the son squanders it and is left with nothing. When the son eventually returns home, the father celebrates his return. The son who did not squander his inheritance is upset that his father is rejoicing over his brother when he is the better son who stayed and worked. The father reminds his good son that even though they are celebrating the son who was lost, the good son will still get what is owed to him. The good son still inherits his full share from his father.

While this parable seems to be celebrating the prodigal son's failure, it is also a commentary on the rewards that come from work. The prodigal son has made his father happy by returning even though he has nothing left; however, the good son has earned his future reward by staying with his father and working.

The second parable continues on the theme of brothers, with the parable of the two sons ordered to work in the vineyard by their father.[12] The first son initially refuses, but then repents and goes to the vineyard to work. The second son says he will work, but does not ever go to the vineyard. It is not words and promises that are pleasing to their father. Their father is pleased with work. It is by actually working that humans give value to their promises.

In the Parable of the Talents, a man gave talents to each of his servants before he left on a journey.[13] To the first servant, he gave five talents. The second servant received two talents. The third servant only received one talent. The servant who received five used those five to trade and doubled his money. The servant who had two also doubled his money. But, the servant who had one buried the talent and earned nothing. When the master returned, he was pleased with the first two because of the work they had done. The master was displeased with the third because he was lazy.

This parable reflects on the expectation that humans do work. It is the duty of those who have been entrusted with goods and skills to use them.

When a person has the ability to work, he is expected to work. It is the basic expectation of human existence.

In the parable of the Workers in the Vineyard, a landowner makes agreements with individual workers to pay them the value of their work at the end of the day. He makes agreements with some of the workers at the beginning of the day. He makes agreements with other workers late in the day. When it comes time to pay out the wages, the landowner pays all the workers the same amount even though some of them worked longer than the others.

This parable reflects on the nature of work to human life because it shows the importance of paying fair wages to workers. When the master is confronted by the laborers who worked all day, but for no greater pay, he reminds them that he did not cheat them. He has treated them fairly and has given them the wages to which they agreed. While some laborers receive more money per hours worked, none of them receives less than what is owed to him. The master's actions are an example of how work is to be justly compensated. While the wages are not equal, no one receives less than what is fair. If the master feels that the work deserves to be compensated at a higher rate, he does so without harming those who work for a longer time. While all of the laborers worked, none of them left with less than what was agreed.

JESUS CHRIST, THE APOSTLES, AND THE MAGISTERIUM: REGARDING LABOR

There are three salient themes that define the social teachings of the Church regarding labor. In the Papal encyclical *Rerum Novarum* promulgated by Pope Leo XIII in 1891, capital serves labor; people are inherently superior to material things. Everyone should have the opportunity for dignified work and a just wage: Work has inherent value and can be the means for a sanctification and salvation.

He called them. They were fishermen. Jesus invited them to become fishers *of* men. This was somewhat like a "promotion." From that moment onward, the Apostles (at least Peter and Andrew) left the grunt work of hauling, cleaning, and catching, and entered the supervisory/managerial work of leading, guiding, and teaching the people.[14] Much later, James and John attempted to acquire a special promotion by requesting that they sit at the immediate right and left of Jesus. But this, Jesus indicated, required much in the way of labor. And even so, such a promotion Christ declared is "not [his] to give," highlighting the hierarchical nature of the Church (the workplace).[15] Moreover, Jesus commanded that the greatest shall be employed in roles of service. How fitting, because those with the capital (the greatest) are meant to conduct their business in service to their laborers. The economy is merely a construct in which man can grow and earn his keep.

When commissioning his Apostles to preach the good news of the kingdom of heaven, Jesus sent them without cash, and with no extra resources for the journey. The Apostles had one task: to preach the good news. No food was necessary to this task; neither was money, nor clothing. But, of course, these things were necessary for the well-being of any human person. Would Jesus leave his Apostles so empty-handed? No. Jesus understood that "the laborer deserves his wages."[16] Rather than have the Apostles provide their own sustenance, Jesus had them receive it as payment from the people they were to serve. Jesus, in other words, provided the Apostles access to employment. Perhaps too often these days, the laborer is not given his just deserts, and must provide for himself from resources which are not the fruit of his labor.[17]

In commissioning the Twelve, Jesus told them to expect persecution because "no slave is above his master. . . . [but] it is enough for the slave that he becomes like his master."[18] It is a bit awkward in American culture today to hear Jesus Christ speak of slavery with no mention of its dastardly nature. Of course, Christ was neither speaking of, nor presciently aware of (at least not in his human nature) American chattel slavery. Fledgling America received immense economic support from Africa by its slave trade and its usage of slaves as machinery in agricultural industry. There are two things to consider here, one more cynical than the other. The cynical: If the slave is expected to rise to no greater level than his master, does that mean that the foundation of labor and economic theory in America is inherently flawed, founded upon the misunderstanding of the white slave masters of (not so) old? The less-cynical: Those who were slaves, or at least their descendants, have achieved their masters' roles; that is, at long last they are industrious, enterprising capital earners.

Once, when Jesus' disciples were hungry on a Sabbath, they began to pick the grain from the nearby stalks in the field. The hypocrites complained of this action as an unlawful offense against the Sabbath. Jesus replied, "The Sabbath was made for man, not man for the Sabbath." This loudly sounds the theme of man's primacy over other created things. God's interest is in man, not in the tangents that keep man alive.[19]

Among the radical good news that Jesus preaches: "Blessed are the poor." What makes poverty such a blessing? He completes it for us: "Theirs is the kingdom of heaven."[20] The poor are poor for either of two main reasons. Either they cannot find employment; or else they are underpaid in the employment they do have. In revealing that the poor belong to the kingdom of heaven, Jesus Christ sheds light on the reality of poverty. First, poverty is not the miserable end; there awaits a glory to be had. Second, poverty can and should be overcome. And indeed, the Lord consistently rehearses this theme in his ministry as he continues to open the eyes of the blind, or heal the leper. Poverty, an illness in itself, gives way to the weight of healing charity. Jesus reminds us, though, that there will always be poverty.[21] The best bet is not to pour resources into the hands of the poor, but to allow the poor a chance to engage in meaningful employment.

When Judas betrays Jesus for thirty silver coins, he commits the sin of all sins in handing the Lord God over to death; however, he commits another fundamentally grave sin by reducing a person, a man (although, also God) to a value less than that of capital. Judas chooses money over his fellow man. In today's highly financially driven globe, money makes the world go round. But it should not. The worker is demoted to a class below the dollar. It seems that the dollar does not so much serve man, as man serves the dollar. Jesus' words are apropos here: The Sabbath was made for man, not man for the Sabbath.[22]

At another moment, Jesus noted how Judas (by no specific mention of his name) was plotting to betray him. "He who has dipped his hand into the dish with me is the one who will betray me."[23] Perhaps one is too imaginative by considering the "dish" full of economic benefits. For one to greedily reach into the dish on his own gumption, not allowing Jesus (the natural economic movement) to dispense its contents justly around the table of society, is to act against the will of God who desires that all his children be provided for.

In fact, adhering to this metaphor, the story of the feeding of the five thousand illustrates just what God prefers in every way. He prefers the fruits of the economic environment to be dispensed evenly and justly, no single person reaching in to grab what he desires. (Rejecting the idea that the people go off to find food each on their own, Jesus told his Apostles, "Give them some food yourselves.") None took what he greedily desired, but accepted what he naturally needed. "They all ate and were satisfied." Moreover, this action of feeding the masses accords with the will of God because of Jesus Christ's well-known association with the poor. "The poor you will always have with you; you do not always have me."[24] This admonition does not remove the divine spotlight from the poor. Rather it draws our attention to the urgency of the poor because in it, Jesus likens himself to the poor. Once Jesus has gone, what we have done for Him we presumably must do for the poor.

A woman who suffered years of hemorrhages came to Jesus and touched his robes. In America today, the national discussion is focused on Obama-care. That health care policy is one which widely distributes access to medi-cine and medical care. This woman went from doctor to doctor fruitlessly seeking a cure. She was out of money. On this fortuitous day, when she meets the Lord, she receives medical care for free. "Power had gone out from [Jesus]." So he definitely *gave* something, but only without receiving in return. Rather, he blessed the woman and bid her well.[25]

Commonly, the boat in Christian art is seen as the haven called the Church of Christ. May we liken the boat to a large company or plant today? The Apostles (employees) are in this plant with Jesus (employer). Jesus is fast asleep while the storm rages and causes much havoc among the employees in the plant. They awaken the employer. "Teacher, do you not care that we are perishing?" Jesus swiftly quells their concerns by quelling the storm.[26] This is entirely reminiscent of protected concerted activity as described in the National Labor Relations Act. The workers go to the master with a common concern, and the employer acts (we hope) to assuage their concerns.[27]

POPE BENEDICT XVI ON LABOR

Pope Benedict XVI's major contribution to Catholic social justice is *Caritas in Veritate*. This encyclical, promulgated in 2009, addresses a world that has just been through the collapse of the subprime mortgage market and an economy that nearly failed in the Great Recession of 2008.[28]

Caritas in Veritate was originally scheduled for the fortieth anniversary of Pope Paul VI's *Populorum Progressio* but was delayed in publication because of the financial crisis.[29] In *Populorum Progressio*, Pope Paul VI calls for development of more than wealth: the development of the person.[30] The ultimate goal is not increased possession but instead it is "good and genuine" development of individuals.[31] The goal of development is to "promote the good of every man, and of the whole man."[32] *Caritas in Veritate* is a fresh look at human development.[33]

In this encyclical, Pope Benedict XVI contributes to the corpus of papal commentary on the economic, political, and cultural problems of the day. Pope Benedict XVI makes his commentary on these three areas by the development of two key themes in *Caritas in Veritate*. First is the theme of truth and love. Second is the idea of gift.

The first key theme in *Caritas in Veritate* is the integration of truth and love. Love and truth complement one another. They build off of one another in human life because "only in truth does charity shine forth, [and] only in truth can charity be authentically lived."[34] Truth and love are both given to human beings, and they are both in turn shared by human beings.[35] Truth is further illuminated and experienced by love. Love on the other hand is given meaning by truth that allows it to be true charity and not just sentimentality.[36] Truth and love intermix and interplay with one another so that the more true a person is, the more they can love. Yet the more a person can love, the more they can have truth.

Through the proper understanding of truth and love, there can be just politics, economics, and a good culture. Without proper intermixing of truth and love, truth will be "blind" and love will be "sterile."[37] Love allows truth to be properly understood and expressed.[38] Truth allows love to be pure and not distorted.[39]

Both love and justice are necessary for true human development.[40] These two gifts are not identical but they are inseparable.

The gift of justice is giving to another that which is his or her due. In order for someone to be owed something there must be a debt. Justice is the repayment of a debt. On the other hand, the gift of love is giving that is not based on debt. It is a gift purely as an expression of will.[41] Love is beyond justice. Love is giving what is "mine" to someone else.[42] Before love (or charity) can be given to someone, he must first receive justice[43]; however, justice without love would not be sufficient for a good society. If a person only ever got what was due to them and nothing more, human need and want would persist.[44] Love is what would take a society from being just to being good.

A key to authentic development is in "the logic of gift" or gratuitousness. The logic of gift is the giving out of love. It is opposed to the principle of "equivalence" or "the logic of exchange."[45] In both of those the giving is out of obligation or through duty. Gift is a giving of superabundance. It is a gift where nothing is expected in return and is given out of a free choice, not obligation.[46]

If Pope Benedict XVI's two themes were to be distilled into a single sentence, it would be: Charity and truth drive authentic human development.

Caritas in Veritate adds to the previous social justice encyclicals by focusing on the relationships between society and labor unions. The two key sections in which Benedict XVI reflects on labor unions are Sections 25 and 64. In Section 25, Benedict XVI looks at the decline of labor conditions as states race to the bottom.[47] States compete with one another to draw in producers and manufacturers by deregulating the labor market. This has created a "downsizing of social security systems" such as the rights of labor and labor unions.[48] Labor unions have previously been a social security system that helped to achieve social justice; however, with competition between nations to be the most attractive for producers, labor unions have lost much of their ability to aid and assist workers.[49]

As Benedict XVI puts it, the "price to be paid for seeking greater competitive advantage in the global market [is the] consequent grave danger for the rights of workers."[50] Workers are being left powerless against the wrongs done to them. As one commentator explains, "Wealth creation and development have too often been at the expense of the poor."[51] Pope Benedict also notes that governments are making it more difficult for labor unions to protect and serve the workers. While he is calling for unions to regain their power, he finds his solution on the local level.

In Section 64, Benedict XVI suggests that changes are needed in labor unions. He focuses on changing the relationship between the union and society. Specifically, the unions could assist the workers by aiding in the relationship between the worker and the consumer. Now that there is global context for business, labor unions can no longer limit themselves to their members.[52] They should be working for the benefit of all labor. The proper role for unions is "defending and promoting [labor], especially on behalf of exploited and unrepresented workers, whose woeful rendition is often ignored by the distracted eye of society."[53] The role of the unions is not just to protect labor from the wrongs of employers but also from society. The best way for unions to right these wrongs is to aid in the social changes that Benedict is calling for in his main themes of charity and justice.

The real power to improve the treatment of workers lies not with the employers but with the ability to lead cultural changes that lies with the unions and society as the customers. The Pope seems to be saying that reform and change will come through social changes. He does not address changes in corporations or businesses. Unions can address more than just the conflicts between unionized workers and the employers or capital. Unions could also act for the benefit of those in society at large. They could help protect more than just their members' rights but also the rights of individuals who are being harmed. Unions could assist these countries in developing in ways that are authentic so that ethical and social concerns are met. Unions would be able to protect and defend employees in ways that society has failed and continues to fail. In a society of truth and love, unions would be better able to protect workers. Therefore, the changes that Pope Benedict XVI is seeking are not changes in corporations but changes in society. Those changes would create a way for workers to gain authentic development. By focusing on unions and society, Benedict XVI seems to be implying that it is through them that the changes can happen, not through the employer.

Caritas in Veritate urges labor unions to take up new points of view in their duty to protect workers. Specifically, the Pope encourages them to be creative and explore new areas in which to act. Benedict XVI also encourages unions to be open to "new perspectives."[54] He also seems to suggest that the unions could aid in the recovery from the recent economic crisis.[55] Labor unions have a special role in the economy that makes them able to aid in the recovery of workers' rights if they encourage a society of truth and love.

By reminding them to serve not only their members but all workers, Benedict is reminding union leaders to serve the common good. Unions must not focus solely on their own good. Benedict XVI fully supports unions, and he also encourages them to mend their former mistaken ways in order to truly be able to encourage authentic development.

On his first Sunday after being elected Pope, Benedict XVI gave a public blessing and reflected on the roles of solidarity, justice, and peace in the workplace.[56] These comments were made to the representatives of Italian labor unions who were celebrating the feast of St. Joseph the Worker. From the very beginning of his pontificate to the legacy he left in the corpus of social justice writings, Pope Benedict XVI supported the role that unions should play in authentic human development.

POPE FRANCIS

Pope Francis chose to begin his Petrine ministry on March 19, the Feast of St. Joseph, Husband of Mary. Joseph is, of course, known as a worker, the humble carpenter of Nazareth.[57] In his homily to the people of God's Church that day, Francis said, "lowly, concrete, and faithful service . . . marked Saint Joseph," and the Pontiff's ministerial goal as Shepherd of the Church is to "protect all of God's people and embrace with tender affection the whole of humanity, especially the poorest, the weakest. . . ."[58] Later, on the feast day of Joseph the Worker proper, Francis spoke of the Church's never-dying call for human solidarity. He called attention to employment issues and the crisis of slave labor.[59]

The first explicit Church teaching regarding the labor of humankind was *Rerum Novarum*, in which Pope Leo XIII proclaimed the natural rights of the working man. Five subsequent Popes promulgated on the dignity of human labor and the rights of man therein.[60] The question is, will Francis add more to the full century of Catholic social teaching, and, if so, what is he likely to say?

Pope Francis, on November 24, 2013, promulgated the apostolic exhortation *Evangelii Gaudium*, calling the entire Church to a renewal of the Church's fundamental social mission on earth. Pope Francis will be sure to "preach the Gospel of God to all men."[61] No small part, in fact perhaps the entirety, of this Gospel involves the social teaching of Christ and the Church. Thus, this teaching quite obviously includes an expounder on humanity's effort in labor.

CONCLUSION

"Conclusion" is exquisitely ironic, although following academic protocol, for the very reason that the work of evangelizing has been renewed and reenergized through the wonderful work of Pope John XXIII, Pope Paul VI, Pope John Paul II, Pope Benedict XVI, and, looking ever forward, Pope Francis. There may be nothing in the world today more important than addressing the pressing needs of the poor, of the young, and of all those who seek the truth.

The obvious panorama of desperate conditions can be substantially alleviated as the plight of the poor may be structurally ameliorated through many initiatives of both the private and public sectors. These may range from the proliferation of living-wage initiatives to a full-scale assault on the deeply embedded problem of catastrophically high, long-term unemployment. The history of the applications of Catholic social teaching has been very promising, however, the stratification of society between the very rich and the very poor adds meaning to the essential point of social justice: failing or refusing to pay the workers just wages is one of the four sins that cries out to Heaven.

NOTES

1. Matthew 11:28–30 (New American Bible).
2. Pope Francis, *Evangelii Gaudium* (November 24, 2013).
3. Genesis 1:1–2:4.
4. Genesis 6:5–9:17.
5. Judges 6:11.
6. See First Samuel 9:3.
7. Genesis 24:1–66.
8. Genesis 29:14–30.
9. Ruth 1:1–4:22.
10. Luke 2:15–20.
11. Luke 15:11–32.
12. Matthew 21:28–32.
13. Matthew 25:14–30; Luke 19:12–27.
14. Mark 1:16.
15. Mark 10:37.
16. Matthew 10:10.
17. Matthew 10:10; Mark 3:13–19; Luke 6:12–16.
18. Matthew 10:25.
19. Luke 6:1; Matthew 12:1; Mark 2:23.
20. Matthew 5:3; Luke 6:20.
21. Matthew 26:11.
22. Matthew 26:14–16.
23. Matthew 26:20–25.
24. John 12:8.
25. Mark 5:25–34.
26. Mark 4:35–41.
27. Mark 4:35–41; Mathew 8:23–27; Luke 8:22–25.
28. John M. Breen, *Love, Truth, and the Economy: A Reflection on Benedict XVI's Caritas in Veritate*, 33 Harv. J. L. & Pub. Pol'y 987 (2010).
29. Breen, *Love, Truth* at 989. Since *Populorum Progressio* was published in 1967, the fortieth anniversary would have been in 2007, but due to the financial crisis, the publication of *Caritas in Veritate* was delayed by two years to 2009. Twenty years after *Populorum Progressio*, Pope John Paul II published his encyclical *Sollicitudeo Rei Socialis*.
30. Breen, *Love, Truth* at 991.
31. Breen, *Love, Truth* at 991.
32. Breen, *Love, Truth* at 991.
33. Thomas J. Molony, *Charity, Truth, and Corporate Governance*, 56 Loy. L. Rev. 825, 839 (2010).
34. Breen, *Love, Truth* at 992.
35. Breen, *Love, Truth* at 1004.

36. Breen, *Love, Truth* at 1004.

37. Breen, *Love, Truth* at 1005–6.

38. Molony, *Charity, Truth, supra* note 33, at 840.

39. Molony, *Charity, Truth* at 840.

40. Breen, *Love, Truth* at 1007.

41. Breen, *Love, Truth* at 1007.

42. Breen, *Love, Truth* at 1008.

43. Breen, *Love, Truth* at 1008 ("[C]harity demands justice: recognition and respect for the legitimate rights of individuals and peoples").

44. Breen, *Love, Truth* at 1008.

45. Breen, *Love, Truth* at 1016.

46. Breen, *Love, Truth* at 1016–17.

47. Benedict XVI, *Caritas in Veritate*, ¶25 (2009).

48. *Caritas in Veritate*, ¶25.

49. *Caritas in Veritate*, ¶25.

50. *Caritas in Veritate*, ¶25.

51. Rev. Patrick Flanagan, *Sustaining the Import of Labor Unions: A Common Good Approach*, 50 J. Cath. Legal Stud. 205, 224 (2011).

52. *Caritas in Veritate*, ¶64.

53. *Caritas in Veritate*, ¶64.

54. Flanagan, *Sustaining the Import of Labor Unions, supra* note 51, at 224.

55. Chaz Muth, "Pope Urges Workers' Voices Be Heard, Unions Adapt to Global Economy," Catholic News Service (July 20, 2009), available at http://www. catholicnews.com/data/stories/cns/090.3304.htm; See also, Tim Newman, "Pope: Unions Can Help Resolve Financial Crisis," *International Labor Rights Forum* (February 4, 2009), available at http://laborrights-blog.typepad.com/internationallabor_right/2009/02/pope-unions-can-help-resolve-financial-crisis.html (accessed March 18, 2014) ("Recently Pope Benedict XVI told the Confederation of Italian Labor Unions that labor unions have a very important role to play in resolving the global economic crisis").

56. Elein E. Dimmler, "Pope Stresses Peace, Workers' Rights, Unity in First Sunday Blessing," *American Catholic*, https://www.americancatholic.org/News/BenedictXVI/PopeBlessing.asp (accessed October 19, 2013).

57. See Matthew 13:55.

58. Francis, *Homily of Pope Francis* (March 19, 2013).

59. See Francis, *General Audience*, (May 1, 2013).

60. See generally Pius XI, *Quadragesimo Anno* (1931); John XXIII, *Mater et Magistra* (1961) and *Pacem in Terris* (1963); Paul VI, *Populorum Progressio* (1967) and *Octogesima Adveniens* (1971); John Paul II, *Laborem Exercens* (1981), *Sollicitudo Rei Socialis* (1987), and *Centesimus Annus* (1991); Benedict XVI, *Deus Caritas Est* (2005) and *Caritas in Veritate* (2009).

61. Mark 16:15. See *Catechism of Catholic Church*, ¶888.

Chapter Twenty-One

International Human Rights, Catholic Social Teaching, and American Practice

The Case of Human Rights Treaty Committees

William L. Saunders

INTRODUCTION

At the beginning of February 2014, a United Nations human rights body (the Convention on the Rights of the Child) released a report sharply critical of the Catholic Church on issues affecting children (hereinafter, the "Report").[1] The Report criticized the Church on a number of matters, including abortion,[2] contraception,[3] corporal punishment,[4] homosexuality,[5] parental rights,[6] and "barriers and taboos concerning adolescent sexuality."[7] It expressed "regret" for the Church's continued "emphasis on the promotion of complementarity and equality in dignity" of males and females.[8] It told the Catholic Church to "ensure its interpretation of scripture" was in line with the UN body's views,[9] and it told the Church to change its internal laws and practices to ensure conformity.[10]

The release of the Report—which assumes that the Catholic Church is obligated to respect "human rights" that are directly contrary to its moral teaching on issues such as abortion—raises a host of questions. For instance, what are "human rights"? How do we know what they are? Do "human rights" include abortion and contraception and the other matters? Which ones? All identified by the report? It also raises the closely related question of whether "human rights" are directly opposed to Catholic social teaching ("CST").[11] This chapter examines those questions and considers whether American law and practice are in conformity with CST.

INTERNATIONAL HUMAN RIGHTS

America—and much of the world—is obsessed with "rights talk."[12] Often, this functions as coded language for "something I dearly want"; however, merely wishing to be able to do or have something does not give one a "right," at least from a legal perspective. In fact, from a lawyer's perspective, one does not have a "right" to do (or have) something unless there is a corresponding and enforceable obligation on some person or entity to respect, or grant, it. For example, consider private property. Ordinarily, I do not have a "right" to cross your property; however, I may gain that right through your actions and/or my own, perhaps through a prescriptive easement. A prescriptive easement grants me a legally enforceable right to cross your land, and you have a legally binding obligation to permit me to do so. If I have a "right" to cross your land, your "rights" are not infringed by my crossing your land, even though you dearly desire that I would not do so.

Thus, "rights," as I am using the term, are legally enforceable entitlements. "International" rights are simply those secured by international agreements, and "human rights" are, correspondingly, the rights secured for human beings by those international agreements.

There is a series of international agreements intended to secure human rights. Their origin is, paradoxically, in the brutality and degradation of World War II. This was a truly worldwide war in which, in addition to all the combatants who died, millions of innocent people were tortured and killed in concentration camps, through the direct targeting of noncombatants and by inhumane experimentation on human beings.

In 1948, a scant three years after the end of that war, the nations of the world gathered at the United Nations headquarters in New York and issued the Universal Declaration of Human Rights (hereinafter, the "Declaration"). They stated several reasons why it was important, even necessary, to issue the Declaration. Among these are three that I want to emphasize. First, "disregard and contempt for human rights have resulted in barbarous acts which have outraged the conscience of mankind. . . ."[13] Second, "recognition of the inherent dignity and of the equal and inalienable rights of all members of the human family is the foundation of freedom, justice and peace. . . ."[14] Third, "if man is not to be compelled to have recourse . . . to rebellion . . . human rights should be protected by the rule of law."[15] It can be said that these are really three ways of making the same point: In order to avoid another world war, human rights—which reflect the inherent worth and dignity of every human being—must be recognized and respected.

While the Declaration set the stage for the recognition and protection of human rights, it imposed no binding legal obligations. It was not a treaty that was binding on whatever sovereigns ratified it (whether nation-states or international legal personalities such as the Holy See). Rather the Declaration was simply a statement of what the nations believed to be, and were committed to recognize as, human rights. Still, it was always envisioned that the rights would be realized in law through a series of treaties designed to protect those rights by imposing legal obligations upon the nations who ratified the treaties. The two primary treaties were the International Covenant on Civil and Political Rights ("ICCPR")[16] and the International Covenant on Economic, Social, and Cultural Rights ("ICESCR"). Treaties do not come into legal effect until they are ratified by a sufficient number of nations, as specified in each treaty.[17] Both the ICCPR and ICESCR were submitted to the nations of the world for ratification in 1966 and came into force and effect in 1976. The ICCPR, the ICESCR, and the Declaration are so closely related that they are sometimes referred to collectively as the "international bill of rights."

Nonetheless, there are many human rights treaties in addition to the ICCPR and the ICESCR. One of those is the Convention on the Rights of the Child ("CRC"). Even though many of its provisions track the rights of adults,[18] it is in many ways a unique treaty since it deals with the rights of those who are not of the age of majority, i.e., children. Hence, it reasonably makes provision for the rights of parents to be respected.[19]

The CRC came into force and effect in 1990 in record time, within a year of its submission to the nations. In fact, by 2013, the CRC had been ratified by every nation in the world except three—including the United States. Nor has the United States ratified the ICESCR. The United States has received heavy criticism for failing to ratify various human rights treaties.

A treaty binds a nation that ratifies it much as a contract that an individual signs binds him/her by its written terms. Just as when an individual buys a car, his obligations are limited to those within the four corners of the contract, a nation is bound only to those of the treaty. (And if a nation has not ratified a treaty, it is not bound by that treaty at all.) In other words, it is the written words that sets the binding obligations. Thus, it is important to examine the actual words of each treaty.

What human rights are protected in these treaties? The ICCPR protects, *inter alia*, (1) "the inherent right to life,"[20] (2) the right not to be tortured or subject to coercive "medical or scientific experimentation,"[21] (3) the right not to be enslaved,[22] (4) the right not to be arrested or detained arbitrarily,[23] (5) the right to a fair trial,[24] (6) "the right to freedom of thought, conscience and religion,"[25] (7) "the right to freedom of expression,"[26] (8) "the right to peaceful assembly,"[27] (9) "the right to freedom of association,"[28] (10) "the right of men and women of marriageable age to marry and to found a family,"[29] and (11) equality and "the equal protection of the law."[30]

The ICESCR obligates nations "progressively" to realize, "to the maximum of its available resources,"[31] various rights, including: (1) "the right to work,"[32] (2) the right to "just and favourable conditions of work,"[33] (3) "the right . . . to form trade unions,"[34] (4) the right of the family to protection by, and assistance from, the state,[35] (5) the right to "the highest attainable standard of physical and mental health,"[36] (6) "the right . . . to education,"[37] and (7) "the right . . . to take part in cultural life . . . and to enjoy the benefits of scientific progress. . . ."[38]

From this recitation of just a few provisions of these two treaties, some things are obvious. First, the two treaties aim at protecting very different things, as captured by their titles—one being on "civil and political rights," and the other being about "economic, social, and cultural rights." Second, one might wonder whether the "rights" secured by the ICESCR are really "rights" at all. For instance, a group of scholars and intellectuals, gathered by Richard John Neuhaus as the Ramsey Colloquium upon the fiftieth anniversary of the Declaration in 1998, was critical of the concept of economic, social, and cultural rights: "In retrospect, it would have been better if the human goods specified [as economic, cultural and social "rights"] . . . had been described as our duties of solidarity rather than as the rights of others."[39] Still, two things should be noted. First, those economic, social, and cultural rights in the ICESCR *do* echo rights recognized in the Declaration.[40] Second, if any nation has ratified the ICESCR—as over 150 nations have—it is legally bound to implement it (as its resources permit).

Every human rights treaty has provisions for the election of a committee. For instance, in the ICCPR, an entire section—Part IV—is devoted to details about the committee.[41] Most of Part IV is devoted to the procedural details of elections[42] and to the special situation where one nation complains that another is not fulfilling its obligations.[43] Only one article concerns the actual, ordinary duties of the committee—article 40. It states the extent of the committee's powers: "The Committee shall study the reports submitted by the States Parties. . . . It shall transmit its report, and such general comments as it may consider appropriate, to the States Parties"[44]

While it is clear that the committee is intended to play an important role, it is equally clear, from the fact that only one single article concerns the substantive duties of the committee, that its role is limited. It is less of an "enforcer" than it is a "facilitator." It is not like a court that makes binding "adjudications." Rather it is a body that enters into a kind of conversation with the ratifying nation (or State Party). The committee receives and "studies" reports from States Parties as to how they are implanting the terms of the treaty,[45] makes comments to the States Parties in response, and receives a reply from State Parties that choose to reply.[46] In other words, since ratifying states have undertaken to implement the terms of the treaty,[47] and are "submit[ing] reports on the measures they have adopted which give effect to the rights recognized herein,"[48] the committee assists them in doing so. Nowhere does the ICCPR suggest that the committee may oblige a ratifying state to adopt the committee's views on the meaning of treaty provisions.

This is the pattern of the other human rights treaties—committees are created to receive and review reports from ratifying states. These are limited powers. And yet, it was one of these committees that issued the stinging criticism, and rather bizarre demands, to the Holy See described in the introduction to this chapter.

CATHOLIC SOCIAL TEACHING

In the first year of his pontificate, John Paul II in his first encyclical, *Redemptor Hominis* (*Redeemer of Man*), spoke of "the magnificent effort made to give life to the United Nations Organization, an effort conducive to the definition and establishment of man's objective and inviolable rights."[49] Recognition of these rights is essential because "peace comes down to respect for man's inviolable rights . . . while war springs from the violation of these rights."[50] The Pope elaborated the point:

> The common good that authority in the state serves is brought to full realization only when all the citizens are sure of their rights. The lack of this leads to the dissolution of society, opposition by citizens to authority or a situation of oppression, intimidation, violence, and terrorism, of which many examples have been provided by the totalitarianisms of [the 20th] century. Thus the principle of human rights is of profound concern to the area of social justice and is the measure by which it can be tested in the life of political bodies.[51]

As John Paul noted, "The [Universal] Declaration of Human Rights linked with the setting up of the United Nations Organization certainly had as its aim not only to depart from the horrible experiences of the last World War, but also to create the basis for the continual revision of programmes, systems, and regimes" in light of whether they respect human rights.[52]

Examples could be multiplied,[53] but the foregoing represents the Catholic Church's view on human rights. What the Church means by "human rights" are man's "objective" rights, rights that reflect his (human) nature, and, hence, may not be violated. As John Paul II wrote, "The theory of human rights is based precisely on the affirmation that the human person, unlike animals or things, cannot be subjected to domination by others."[54]

The Church supports the Declaration and the various rights listed therein. Three rights in particular—the right to life, religious freedom, and family life—are rights which the Church considers the foundation stones of CST and each of which is closely intertwined with the others.

Religious freedom was, of course, treated extensively in *Dignitatis Humanae* (*Declaration on Religious Liberty*), at Vatican Ecumenical Council II. Subsequently, John Paul II called religious freedom "the premise and guarantee of all freedoms that ensure the common good."[55] "Actuation of this right is one of the fundamental tests of man's authentic progress in any regime, in any society, system or milieu."[56] Religious freedom can, thus, rightly be called the "first"—i.e., the most basic or fundamental—freedom.

In 1995, John Paul II devoted his encyclical *Evangelium Vitae* to building a culture of life. There, and elsewhere, he called the right to life "the fundamental right and the source of all other rights."[57] The right to life is, therefore, literally the "first right."

In *Evangelium Vitae*, John Paul II also underscores the importance of the family to recognizing and protecting human life: "In the face of the so-called culture of death, the family is the heart of the culture of life."[58] Thus he concludes: "A family policy must be the basis and the driving force of all social policies."[59] That is, all—every, each—social policy undertaken by a state should be based upon how it impacts the family.

At Vatican II, in the document, *Gaudium et Spes* (*Pastoral Constitution of the Church in the Modern World*), the Church elaborated on the vital role the family plays in society and the reason why the state must support it:

> The family is the place where different generations come together and help one another to grow wiser and harmonize the rights of individuals with other demands of social life: as such it constitutes the basis of society. . . . Civil authority should consider it a sacred duty to acknowledge the true nature of marriage and the family, to protect and foster them.[60]

Subsequently, the importance of the family was addressed in many documents, receiving its most extensive treatment in *Familiaris Consortio*, wherein John Paul II developed themes from Vatican II. In that document, he also announced the forthcoming release by the Church of its own declaration of human rights, this time concerning the family.[61] On October 22, 1983, the Charter of the Rights of the Family was released.[62]

It might at first seem that recognizing "group rights" (i.e., family rights) is somewhat contradictory to "human rights," which one tends to think of as individual rights, but that is a misconception. Human rights formulations have always recognized the importance of the family and its right to support and protection by the state. For instance, the Declaration notes that "the family is the natural and fundamental group unit of society and is entitled to protection by society and the state."[63] The principle is reflected in the basic human rights treaties.[64] It is not surprising, therefore, that the Charter of the Rights of the Family makes frequent reference to the Declaration.[65]

The emphasis of CST on life and religious freedom is also reflected in international human rights laws and principles as noted previously in the section on international human rights law.[66]

This too-brief review should help the reader to see that there are many commonalities and points of convergence between international human rights law and CST and a fruitful interplay between them.

THE MISUSE OF HUMAN RIGHTS TREATIES

Few thoughtful people are unaware that some things are asserted to be "human rights" today which are not. An obvious example (and the one that illustrates this general problem) is abortion. It has even been claimed that abortion is protected under treaties that do not mention the word. [67]

The CRC committee's report, discussed in the introduction, is a paradigmatic case. [68] In the report, the committee, which lacks authority to go beyond the words of the treaty, and despite the fact abortion is not mentioned in the CRC, called upon the Holy See to change its law and practice (and doctrine) to permit at least some abortions. In doing so, the committee ignored the plain meaning of several articles of the CRC—(a) "the child, by reason of his physical and mental immaturity, needs special safeguards and care, including appropriate legal protection, before as well as after birth," [69] (b) "a child means every human being below the age of eighteen years," [70] and (c) "States Parties recognize that every child has the inherent right to life. . . . States Parties shall ensure to the maximum extent possible the survival and development of the child." [71]

Instead, the CRC committee makes vague reference to several articles—6 (the right to life!), 18-3 (children of working parents), 23 (disabled children), 24 (right to health), 26 (right to social security), 27 (right to adequate standard of living), 33 (protecting children from drugs)—in asserting that the Church's "position on abortion . . . places obvious risks to the life and health of pregnant girls." Such an interpretation of these articles is clearly unreasonable. One can only conclude the CRC committee issued this report to embarrass the Holy See and, perhaps, to pressure other nations to recognize abortion. [72]

While it is true that a nation may ignore committee recommendations (since they are nonbinding), doing so may expose the nation to various informal sanctions from the UN and international lending agencies. It subjects the nation to international "peer pressure" to conform. But, perhaps more importantly, it provides an item of "evidence" that can be used against nations who do not provide for abortion. In lawsuits around the world, abortion advocates claim comments of treaty committees, such as that issued by the CRC committee to the Holy See, constitute evidence of international law binding on nations.

The Holy See is not a party to every international treaty. For instance, it has not ratified the ICESCR. But it has ratified the CRC, and, as a result, it suffers the indignities of the recent CRC report, despite the absolutely certain fact that the Holy See would have never ratified a treaty that even arguably provided for abortion. ("Abortion . . . [is a] crime which no human law can claim to legitimize."[73])

U.S. PRACTICE

Today there is a widespread, and tragic, misunderstanding of "human rights." Certain things are asserted to be human rights which simply are not mentioned in the documents,[74] while other things that are expressly mentioned are ignored or diminished. It is a misunderstanding that threatens the entire effort to secure protection for inalienable (or, as the Church says, "inviolable") human rights. John Paul II addressed the problem in *Evangelium Vitae*, an analysis that merits repeating:

> [A] long historical process is reaching a turning-point. The process which once led to discovering the idea of "human rights"—rights inherent in every person and prior to any constitution and state legislation—is today marked by a surprising contradiction. Precisely in an age when the inviolable rights of the person are solemnly proclaimed and the value of life publicly affirmed, the very right to life is being denied or trampled upon, especially at the more significant moments of existence: the moment of birth and the moment of death. . . . How can these repeated affirmations of principle be reconciled with the continual increase and wide-spread justification of attacks on human life? . . . These attacks go directly against respect for life and they represent a direct threat to the entire culture of human rights.[75]

The United States, like the Holy See, has not ratified all human rights treaties. When it has done so, as with the ICCPR, it has often attached reservations that limit the legal effect of those treaties in the United States.[76] (Of course, most of the civil and political rights protected by the ICCPR were protected by the U.S. Constitution long before the Declaration was issued in 1948; for instance, freedom of religion, speech, assembly, petition, and the press in the First Amendment and the right to a fair trial in the Fifth and Sixth Amendments.)

It is fair to say the United States has, historically, taken a skeptical attitude toward such treaties. Considering examples such as the recent critique of the Holy See by the CRC committee as well as the crisis in understanding what constitutes human rights, it is difficult to avoid the conclusion that the United States has been right to be skeptical. While Catholic social teaching recognizes human rights and is supportive of the Declaration and, in general, of treaties that secure such rights (by holding states to legal obligations to do so), the misuse of human rights treaties by committees creates a situation where it would be imprudent to ratify such a treaty. And prudence is a virtue under CST.[77]

NOTES

1. United Nations Convention on the Rights of the Child, *Concluding Observations on the Second Periodic Report of the Holy See* (January 31, 2014), available at http://tbinternet.ohchr.org/Treaties/CRC/Shared%20Documents/VAT/CRC_C_VAT_CO_2_16302_E.pdf [hereinafter *Report*].

2. *Report*, ¶55.

3. *Report*, ¶56.

4. *Report*, ¶¶39 & 40.

5. *Report*, ¶25.

6. *Report*, ¶¶31 & 41.

7. *Report*, ¶57(a).

8. *Report*, ¶27.

9. *Report*, ¶40(d).

10. *E.g.*, *Report*, ¶55.

11. "Catholic Social Teaching" refers to teachings of the Magisterium of the Catholic Church, whether in papal encyclicals or in Conciliar documents, and reflected in various compilations such as the *Catechism of the Catholic Church*.

12. See generally, Mary Ann Glendon, *Rights Talk: The Impoverishment of Political Discourse* (The Free Press, 1991).

13. United Nations Office of the High Commissioner for Human Rights, *Universal Declaration of Human Rights* (December 1948) [hereinafter *Declaration*], Preamble, ¶2. Available at http://www.ohchr.org/EN/UDHR/Pages/Language.aspx?LangID=eng.

14. *Report*, Preamble, ¶1.

15. *Report*, Preamble, ¶3.

16. The ICCPR echoes the reasons from the *Declaration* why human rights must be protected, i.e., that "recognition of the inherent dignity and the equal and inalienable rights of all members of the human family is the foundation of freedom, justice and peace in the world." See *Report*, Preamble, ¶1.

17. *E.g.*, article 49-1 of the ICCPR states: "The present Covenant shall enter into force three months after the date of the deposit with the Secretary-General of the United Nations of the thirty-fifth instrument of ratification. . . ."

18. *E.g.*, ICCPR article 13 on freedom of expression.

19. United Nations Office of High Commissioner for Human Rights *Convention on the Rights of the Child* (September 1990), article 5: "States Parties shall respect the responsibilities; rights and duties of parents . . . to provide . . . appropriate direction and guidance in the exercise by the child of the rights recognized in the present Convention" [hereinafter CRC], available at http://www.ohchr.org/en/professionalinterest/pages/crc.aspx.

20. ICCPR, article 6. This is the right of "every human being." "This right shall be protected by law. No one shall be arbitrarily deprived of his life."

21. ICCPR, article 7.

22. ICCPR, article 8.

23. ICCPR, article 9.

24. ICCPR, article 14.

25. ICCPR, article 18.

26. ICCPR, article 19.

27. ICCPR, article 21.

28. ICCPR, article 22.

29. ICCPR, article 23.

30. ICCPR, article 26.

31. ICESCR, article 2-1.

32. ICESCR, article 6.

33. ICESCR, article 7.

34. ICESCR, article 8.

35. ICESCR, article 10.

36. ICESCR, article 12.

37. ICESCR, article 13.

38. ICESCR, article 15.

39. "On Human Rights—the Universal Declaration of Human Rights Fifty Years Later: A Statement of the Ramsey Colloquium," *First Things*, April 1998. (The author was a member of the Colloquium and signed the statement.)

40. See *Declaration*, articles 22–27 covering rights, *inter alia*, to work, just wage, form trade unions, rest and leisure, education, and cultural life.

41. ICCPR, Part IV comprises articles 28–45 (eighteen out of fifty-three articles).

42. ICCPR, articles 28–39.

43. ICCPR, articles 41–45.

44. ICCPR, article 40-4.

45. ICCPR, article 40-1.

46. ICCPR, article 40-5.

47. ICCPR, article 2-2: "Where not already provided for by existing legislative or other measures, each State Party to the present Covenant undertakes to take the necessary steps, in accordance with its constitutional processes and with the provisions of the present Covenant, to adopt such legislative or other measures as may be necessary to give effect to the rights recognized in the present Covenant."

48. ICCPR, article 40-1.

49. John Paul II, *Redemptor Hominis* (1979), ¶17.

50. *Redemptor Hominis*, ¶17.

51. *Redemptor Hominis*, ¶17.

52. *Redemptor Hominis*, ¶17.

53. E.g., *Catechism of the Catholic Church*, ¶1930 citing as an example John XXIII in *Pacem in Terres*, puts it: "Respect for the human person entails respect for the rights that flow from his dignity as a creature. These rights are prior to society and must be recognized by it. They are the basis of the moral legitimacy of every authority. . . ."

54. John Paul II, *Evangelium Vitae* (1995), ¶18.

55. John Paul II, *Redemptor Missio* (1990), ¶39.

56. *Redemptor Hominis*, ¶17.

57. *Evangelium Vitae*, ¶72.

58. *Evangelium Vitae*, ¶39.

59. *Evangelium Vitae*, ¶90.

60. Paul VI, *Gaudium et Spes* (1965), ¶52.

61. John Paul II, *Familiaris Consortio* (1981), ¶46.

62. Holy See, *Charter of the Rights of the Family* (October 22, 1983) [hereinafter Charter] available at http://www.vatican.va/roman_curia/pontifical_councils/family/documents/rc_pc_family_doc_19831022_family-rights_en.html.

63. *Declaration*, article 16-3.

64. ICCPR, article 23 repeats the formulation of the *Declaration* exactly. Likewise, the ICESCR, in article 10-1, states: "The widest possible protection and assistance should be accorded to the family, which is the natural and fundamental group unit of society. . . ."

65. For instance, Charter, article 1 cites the *Declaration*, article 16 as one of its sources.

66. Life and religious freedom are protected, respectively, in articles 3 & 18 of the *Declaration* and in articles 6 & 18 of the ICCPR.

67. For instance, in *ABC v. Ireland* in the European Court of Human Rights, a right to abortion was claimed to exist under the European Convention on Human Rights under articles dealing with torture (7) and private life (8).

68. For a discussion of other examples, see, William L. Saunders, "The Family and Parental Rights in Light of Catholic Social Teaching and International Human Rights Law: A Conver-

gence," in *Child Abuse, Family Rights and the Child Protective System*, Stephen Krason, ed., (Scarecrow Press, 2013).

69. *Report*, Preamble, ¶9.

70. CRC, article 1.

71. CRC, article 6.

72. As can be seen by reviewing other aspects of the report noted in the introduction, the committee also criticized the Church on topics related to the other two foundation stones of CST that have been identified, *i.e.*, the family and religious freedom.

73. *Evangelium Vitae*, ¶73.

74. The United States is as guilty of this error as any other nation. For instance, in connection with the release of the 2014 State Department "country reports" on human rights, Secretary John Kerry equated the right not to be enslaved, which is guaranteed in several human rights treaties such as article 8 of the ICCPR, with homosexual rights, which are not mentioned in any treaty. See http://www.state.gov/secretary/remarks/2014/02/222645.htm.

75. *Evangelium Vitae*, ¶18 (original emphasis omitted).

76. Senate Committee on Foreign Relations, International Covenant on Civil and Political Rights, S. Exec. Rep. No. 102-23 (1992).

77. "Prudence is the virtue that disposes practical reason to discern our true good in every circumstance and to choose the right means of achieving it." *Catechism of the Catholic Church*, ¶1806.

Chapter Twenty-Two

Looking Back, Looking Ahead

A Strategy for the Pro-Life Movement

Hadley Arkes

At the end of June 2000 I was in the courtroom of the Supreme Court as the closely divided Court struck down the legislation in Nebraska that barred that grisly procedure of partial-birth abortion.[1] That was the "procedure" in which 70 percent of the body of child is dangling from the birth canal, the head of the child is punctured, and the brains sucked out so that the child can be removed, one could say, intact. That decision was rather jolting, and it was jolting enough to my friends at National Right to Life that they backed the bill I had been pushing for several years, the most modest bill of all, to protect the child who *survived* an abortion. For in one notable case, in 1977, in Tennessee, a child had survived an abortion for about twenty days, undergone a surgery, and died.[2] The question was raised as to whether there had been an obligation to preserve the life of that child. The answer given by Judge Clement Haynsworth was "no." The pregnant woman had decided on abortion, and therefore, he said, "the fetus in this case was not a person whose life state law could protect."[3] It was not a child; it was a fetus marked for termination. In other words the right to abortion became the right to an "effective abortion" or a dead child.

The measure I had been pushing was called, in that awful legislative language, the "Born-Alive Infants' Protection Act." Most people did not know that under the rulings in *Roe v. Wade*[4] and *Doe v. Bolton*,[5] abortions could be performed during the entire length of the pregnancy and even when the child came out alive. Those of us who supported the bill felt that even those people who were pro-choice would join us in protecting the child who survived, and that could be the beginning of a conversation. For as we made clear, we would be raising the question of what was different about that same child five minutes earlier, five days, five weeks, five months earlier. Step by step we would try to convince the other side, and if we failed, well at least from that vast volume of 1.2 million abortions each year we would have rescued a handful of lives, and that, to us, was no trifling matter.[6]

We also thought that our position was critical in putting some anchoring premises in place. During the litigation over partial-birth abortion in the states, Judge Richard Posner, dissenting on a case from Wisconsin, said that we had never claimed the authority to protect the child in the womb, and so why would the state have any compelling interest in shifting the killing of that child back from the birth canal to the uterus.[7] In his typically uncharming way, he had a point: Our friends had never put in place this premise that our own bill could supply—that even the child marked for abortion may have a claim to the protection of the law. So we drew upon that line attributed to Andrew Jackson at the Battle of New Orleans: "Boys, I want you to elevate them guns a little lower." Let's take things back to the simplest point, start planting premises there, and work forward.

The pro-life side lost that key case on partial-birth abortion in 2000 because of the presence on the Court of Sandra Day O'Connor. By the time the federal bill on partial-birth abortion came to the Court, in 2007, Sandra O'Connor had been replaced by Samuel Alito, and a pro-life side, fortified now by John Roberts and Alito, sustained the federal bill on partial-birth abortion.[8] What I took the Court to be saying with that decision was that there were five justices now ready to start sustaining a stream of legislative restrictions emanating from the states, and that stream has been coming. There have been measures on "waiting periods," "informed consent," giving information on fetal heartbeats, and bills predicated on fetal pain. Some of these measures seem to have taken their model from a bill in the U.S. House to bar abortions after twenty weeks.[9] They had been attended by reports from doctors and researchers that unborn children, or fetuses, at a gestation of twenty weeks, are perfectly capable of feeling pain, especially when they are being surgically dismembered. It surely had to be one of those arresting, notable moments during the litigation over partial-birth abortion in New York, when Judge Richard Casey Conway asked Dr. Kanwaljeet S. Anand, a professor who specialized in pediatrics and anesthesiology—whether Dr. Anand had ever thought of administering an anesthetic to the child, dangling from the birth canal, before the protocol prescribed the puncturing of the child's head. Dr. Anand was taken aback by the question: No, it had not occurred to him, and why should it? The decision had already been made, after all, either explicitly or implicitly, that the child simply did not count, and neither then did the pains suffered by that being they were now "removing."[10]

The bills proscribing abortions at twenty weeks were brought forth to elicit the recognition of the public that we were not dealing here with mere clumps of cells but with small humans who could feel intense pain. The awareness of that kind of pain has inspired many restrictions on the research done on animals, along with provisions for humane treatment and slaughtering. The point was to spark a recognition on the part of people like Dr. Anand along with many ordinary folks who had never been bothered to think about the problem.

As it turns out, that period of twenty weeks was remarkably conservative. Nearly thirty years ago, in 1985, the Senate Committee on the Judiciary held hearings on the matter. The committee had been inspired by President Reagan's remark on an article reporting that fetuses feel pain. That comment led to a rash of arguments on late-night shows. Finally, the Senate committee held hearings, and in the course of those hearings Professor Daniel Robinson forced a doctor on the other side, a professor from Yale, to back away from his claim that the fetus at twelve weeks could not yet feel pain. As Robinson pointed out, the receptors of pain did not depend on a highly developed cerebral cortex. The reaction to pain depended, rather, on the most primitive sensory receptors, the kind we associate with reflexive actions, not syllogisms and arguments. [11]

We felt that the twenty-week limitation bills had a fair chance of being sustained, for Justice Kennedy had provided the fifth vote to sustain the federal bill on partial-birth abortion. He seemed willing to sustain discrete, precise restrictions on abortion. His hesitation seemed related to a leap or dramatic movement by the Court that seemed to dispossess people in a single stroke of that right to abortion.

It was disappointing when the Supreme Court declined to hear the case from Arizona that overturned a bill barring abortions at twenty weeks, but it was a telling moment. It takes only four votes of the Supreme Court to grant certiorari. We have on the Court now at least four solid pro-life votes. So, it seems that one or more of the pro-life justices was telling us that this legislation was not likely to be sustained. The thought may have been that if the purpose was to avert fetal pain, it could be done by insisting on the provision of an anesthetic. Even more to the point, it could be done without forbidding the abortion itself. If that were a likely result, perhaps it was better that the Court did not take the case.

This predicament shows itself on many other bills that offer, on their face, the most plausible and appealing measures to restrict abortion. We could command considerable support in the country for measures restricting abortion late in pregnancy because so many people, in the most common reaction, finally see in the womb something they recognize as a human being.

The surveys of the public show that a clear majority—about 62 percent—would forbid an abortion when there is awareness of a heart beating in the womb, but most people don't know how early the fetal heartbeat can be detected. In fact, a heartbeat can be heard with a simple stethoscope between

18 and 20 weeks. [12] With echograms, there have been readings as early as 6-1/2 to 7 weeks, and by vaginal sonogram, the heartbeat can be heard as early as 5 weeks after the last menstrual period or about 22 days after conception. Which is to say, the beating of that heart can be noticed before a woman may even know that she is pregnant.

The critical point, so obvious that it is so persistently overlooked, is that the advent of the heartbeat cannot mark the beginning of life. The heartbeat comes into being in the course of development *of a life already in being*; a life that is powering its own development and integrating its own functions and parts as they take form and become more visible.

Now these are all measures worth pressing—they make important points, and they may jar certain people who have not thought overly long or deeply on the matter. But they are not likely to generate any tension for the most committed partisans of abortion, for these people have shown levels of shamelessness that allow them to brush away these vexing facts about the beings they are content to see destroyed. One notable example here tells all, the example of federal Judge Mary Ann Trump Barry, when she was faced years ago with the bill on partial abortion in New Jersey. Judge Barry expressed her contempt for the effort to draw a line between the child in the womb and the child at the point of birth. That distinction has been known to common sense for millennia, but the application of that distinction in these cases, she thought, involved "semantic machinations, irrational line-drawing, and an obvious attempt to inflame public opinion":

> The Legislature would have us accept, and the public believe, [she said] that during a partial-birth abortion, the fetus is in the process of being born at the time of its demise. It is not. A woman seeking an abortion is plainly not seeking to give birth. [13]

This was post-modernist jurisprudence—with a vengeance. It was all a matter of perception. There were no objective facts—no birth, no "child" being killed at the point of birth, because the mother, after all, had elected an abortion. Once she had made that fateful choice, there was no child to be killed, no birth to take place.

I would not discount then the capacity of the other side to treat all of these pro-life measures as something struck from an ideology of the hard right, with its view of the world; and the media, for their part, will be content mainly to look the other way. Or, the media will not be deflected from what they usually seek to do: foster a minor civil war in the pro-life party by persistently asking politicians whether they really want to talk about these issues that most people would rather not talk about, and which the media are quite willing to treat plausibly as a "war on women."

There is another approach, another strategy that the party of abortion will not be able to avoid or deflect, and the media will find in it no lever they can use in embarrassing a pro-life candidate and fanning conflicts within the pro-life party. Once again it's a matter of "elevating them guns a bit lower"—a matter of returning to that issue that is most disarming, less subject to distraction, and an issue that has 80 percent of the public on our side. For that reason it is also the most distressing and politically costly for the pro-abortion party. This is the issue we could have engaged already if the pro-lifers in Congress had been agile enough to recognize the new moment suddenly before them. That moment was supplied by the trial of Kermit Gosnell, the abortionist in Philadelphia. Gosnell was indeed engaging in the live-birth abortion by killing babies who had survived the abortion—and drawing members of his staff into complicity with the killing. The surveys showed about 80 percent of the public in favor of the prosecution of Gosnell. Many people were of course surprised to learn that babies can survive abortions—and that others would think that the right to kill the child inside the womb carries over to the same child outside the womb. It is quite clear that the abhorrence at killing the born child is shared massively even by people who regard themselves as pro-choice.

In other words, the experience confirmed precisely the effect that we had expected from the Born-Alive Infants' Protection Act; the effect that we might have produced if the media had not gone along with the strategy of the Democrats in Congress by muffling the news—not giving the bill the coverage that would draw attention and produce the effect we were seeing now with the Gosnell case.

The muffling was so effective that even now people who had supported the Born-Alive Infants' Protection Act had not noticed the way in which that act could have been brought powerfully into play in the Gosnell case. Gosnell was being prosecuted under the homicide laws of Pennsylvania, but what about a federal prosecution? A federal prosecution would have brought the issue into our national politics. But there could not be a federal prosecution because the penalties contained in the original bill, the Born-Alive Infants' Protection Act, had been stripped from the bill for the purpose of averting a veto from President Clinton. It was decided to make the bill into an almost pure "teaching bill," a bill that would plant premises that could be drawn on later. Just a year or two later a case arose on a live-birth abortion in Morristown, New Jersey, but the most that could be done would have been the removal of federal funds from the hospital, and that turned out to be a complicated, difficult business.

When the scandal over Dr. Gosnell broke through to the public, it was a moment when we could have dropped everything else and introduced a bill to restore the penalties for something that people in the country emphatically thought should be punished. Even if we could not enact that bill, it would have created the occasion for the hearings at which the nurses could tell their stories.[14] That would be a hard story for the media to refuse to cover.

The problem is sharpened because the bill would raise a piercing problem for the Democrats. For this is not a matter of avoiding *new legislation* or pretending that this is just another show brought by the pro-lifers. This is a return to a bill that passed the Congress by voice vote, *with no congressman or Senator in opposition*. The Democrats had agreed once that the kinds of acts performed by Dr. Gosnell were reprehensible and that they should be forbidden by federal law. So now here is the question posed directly to the party that has been adamant in defending the right to abortion as something close to a "first freedom," more fundamental, apparently, than the freedom of speech or religion: "You voted to condemn these acts and stamp them as *wrong*. If you were serious when you said that these acts were wrong, then what kind of a punishment would show how wrong they were? Is it as grave as a moving violation in traffic, or a speeding ticket? Or would it be truly worse than that?" We really must put the question to the Democrats and let them reveal just how serious they were when they voted to ban this kind of killing. At the same time, this focus would bring out the fact that the only Democrat of national visibility who had opposed the Born-Alive Act was a certain Senator from Illinois, one Barack Obama, who had managed, as the chairman of a key committee, to kill that bill.[15] It is not merely a delicious sport, but a point with a serious lesson, to put the question of whether the Democrats really stand now with the president they feel obliged to defend.

When it comes to the Republicans, my strategic plan would be to make this quite simple and tightly confined: that all we wish to talk about is adding the penalties to the Born-Alive Infants' Protection Act; to hear the stories of the nurses; to gauge how extensive this practice of killing the babies who survive abortions really is.

If that is all we wish to talk about, I don't think that the people in the media are going to be running to interview so-called Republican moderates, asking them if they really want to keep their tie to "extremists" who do such illiberal things as vote punishments for people who kill babies born alive. It would be slightly harder to paint as "extremist" a bill punishing what 80 percent and more in the country regard as an egregious wrong. Could the willingness to punish the Gosnells of the world be translated to mean a "war on women"? It took, of course, nothing less than an inversion of moral sensibility for the public to be lulled even for a moment into the notion that women were being oppressed and diminished when they were simply barred from killing their young. To suggest that the Gosnells of the country stand as revered figures liberating women, even for the modern liberal sensibility, that may be a stretch too far.

Everyone understands, of course, that this simple measure is part of a larger, principled package. If we manage to elect a Congress in control of the pro-life party, there will be a whole train of measures, springing from the same core, served up and enacted. If this simple strategy helps to elect a pro-life president, we would have someone in office then to sign these measures into law.

Folded into this simple measure is a constitutional argument, simple in its own way but running deep, an argument we sought to make at the same time we were enacting the Born-Alive Infants' Protection Act. It is a simple point, drawn from an understanding running back to Chief Justice John Marshall, and if it had been in place—if it had been understood by our political class when *Roe v. Wade* was decided—there would have been no need to have vast throngs gathering in Washington every January to seek the overturning of *Roe v. Wade*. For there would have been no need to seek the overruling of *Roe*; no need then to keep affirming anew the supremacy of the Supreme Court in reshaping our lives and our institutions.

In the case of *Cohens v. Virginia* (1821),[16] Chief Justice Marshall observed that "the judicial power of every well constituted government must be co-extensive with the legislative, and must be capable of deciding every judicial question which grows out of the constitution and laws."[17] To put it another way, virtually any issue that arose under the Constitution and laws of the United States had to come within the jurisdiction of the federal courts. Yet, even jurists are persistently taken by surprise by the corollary of that axiom: Any issue that comes within the competence of the judicial branch must come, presumptively at least, within the reach of the legislative and executive branches as well. So when we drafted the bill for the Born-Alive Infants' Protection Act we sought to add a preamble, setting out the purposes of the bill and its constitutional ground. We offered the proposition: That if the Supreme Court can articulate new rights under the Constitution—if it can discover a "right to abortion" lurking somehow in a clause in the Fourteenth Amendment, then the legislative branch—the Congress—should be able to vindicate those constitutional rights on precisely the same ground on which the Court professes to find them, and in filling them out, marking their limits. One thing that should not be tenable under the logic of this Constitution is that the Court can articulate new rights—and then assign to itself a monopoly of the legislative power in shaping those rights.[18]

We could bring that sense of things instantly into play in explaining the move to add the penalties to that bill that the Congress had already enacted, the Born-Alive Infants' Protection Act, and say, "Whatever the Court established in a right to abortion, it could not have meant the right to kill a child who survived an abortion." Of course once this is in place, the Congress could move with additional, discrete steps, each drawing, as we know, on wide assent in the public, on the part even of many people who call themselves pro-choice. It could be said then with ample support from the public, that "whatever else the right to abortion meant, it could not mean the right to kill a child because she might be afflicted with deafness." Or with Down syndrome, or other disabilities, in the same way that the law could hardly stand by while other people were killed, or had their lives ended, solely because their lives, with disabilities, were not thought worth living.

What a profound difference it would have made if at the time that *Roe v. Wade* was announced the members of the Court had understood that once they introduced this new "right" into our law, they could not have control of it—they could not control the task of working out its shape, its reach, its conditions, the grounds on which it could be rightly restricted. If judges had been aware of that point from the outset, it might have given them a strong infusion of sobriety and caution. They would have been even more alert that any novel right of this kind, suddenly introduced into the work of Congress, could convulse our politics and matters would run well beyond their control.

We would have had every reason to suspect that, if Congress had been brought into this matter of abortion on the day that the "right to abortion" was announced, *Roe v. Wade* would have been scaled down instantly to accord with the state of opinion on this matter in the country. The surveys have been remarkably stable here for years: That most people in the country do not think that abortions should be performed because of financial strain, because a child would interfere with the education or prospects of the mother, or because the child is not wanted. Most people continue to think that the corrective for a child thought to be unwanted is an adoption, not a lethal surgery. Richard Doerflinger, of the Conference of Catholic Bishops, who has been tracking these polls for years, pointed out a long time ago that about 60 percent of people in the country would reject about 90 percent of the abortions that are performed under the authority of *Roe v. Wade* and *Doe v Bolton*. If the matter were in the hands of Congress from the beginning, there would have been no need to overrule *Roe*, because *Roe* probably would have been scaled down to the state of the law in most places at the time *Roe* was decided—which is to say, that abortions would have been accepted mainly when they were thought to be necessary to that condition, exceedingly rare these days, where the life of the pregnant woman would be in danger. Of course we would argue over that minuscule portion of cases involving rape and incest.

If we installed—or restored—this understanding, bound up with the logic of the Constitution, we would gently transform both the legal and the political structure in which the most vexing issues in our law and politics have come to us. For along with the dose of sobriety and caution administered to the judges, there would be a severe test of the seriousness of our political class. For many years we had congressmen proclaiming they were pro-life, while at the same time they were safely insulated from any expectation that they had the power actually to do anything about it.

Edmund Burke said that "refined policy is ever the parent of confusion." So my advice to the pro-life party is to keep the focus simple and confined: Let us keep it on the proposal to restore the penalties for killing children who survive abortions—that this is all we wish to talk about on our agenda, the thing most urgent to be done. From the logic of that bill—and from the constitutional argument that comes along with it—everything else will radiate. If this simple, disarming approach helps elect a pro-life president and Congress, other good things will come in time.

I was making a visit to the Holocaust Museum in Washington, and as I moved through the halls with a friend, I suddenly came upon a scene that has been encountered by many visitors to the museum: a vast vat filled with shoes. They were the shoes of the victims, as the Nazis sought to extract anything they could use again or sell. What came flashing back instantly were those searing lines of Justice McLean, in his dissenting opinion in the Dred Scott case: You may think that the black man is merely chattel, but "He bears the impress of his Maker, and is amenable to the laws of God and man; and he is destined to an endless existence." He has, in other words, a soul, which is imperishable; it will not decompose when his material existence comes to an end. The sufficient measure of things here is that the Nazis looked at their victims and thought that the shoes were the real *durables*.

My colleagues back in Amherst are people of large liberal sympathies, who have taken as their signature tune that that line from Nietzsche, amplified by Dostoyevsky—that "God is dead," and everything is permitted. They have sympathies for the hurts of body and mind suffered by the mass of mankind, but even they will concede that they cannot give the same account of the wrong of the Holocaust or the wrong of slavery that someone like McLean was in a position to give. For McLean speaks for those of us who would say that, as diminished as that character in the gutter may be, he is made in the image of something higher. My colleagues could not exactly move themselves to say, as Lincoln said, that "nothing stamped with the Divine image and likeness was sent into the world to be trodden on, and degraded, and imbruted by its fellows." [19]

The question is whether there is, in any of us, an intrinsic dignity, which becomes in turn the source of rights that others would be obliged to respect. That sense of the problem would be conveyed in Brookline, Massachusetts, just after a shooting that took place at an abortion clinic there, a shooting that took the lives of two women on the staff. The gunman, a young man crazed, eventually took his own life while in jail. A couple of nights after the shooting, there was a candlelight vigil. One young woman was there holding her daughter, born only about two weeks earlier. She explained to the interviewer that she was there for the sake of preserving, for her daughter, the same "reproductive rights" that she had enjoyed—meaning, of course, the right to have destroyed that child right up through the time of birth.

If her daughter possessed those reproductive rights as rights that were part of "women's rights," it becomes apt to ask: What was the source of those rights, and when did she acquire them? Were they a species of "natural rights"? If so, they flowed to her as a human being, or as a woman, and those rights would have come into existence as soon as she herself began to be, or began her existence as a female. With this understanding of "natural rights," as James Wilson has pointed out, the common law cast its protection over human life from the moment "when the infant is first able to stir in the womb."[20] If we have natural rights, they begin *as soon as we begin to be*. In that event, this new daughter would have been the bearer of those rights when she was in her mother's womb, and her mother could not have held a franchise then to sweep away all of her rights through the simple device of removing, in a stroke, the bearer of those rights. In short, if that child possessed "rights," her mother could not have possessed an unrestricted right to abortion.

No logic of natural rights can be squared with that right to abortion. So even if there is something called a "right to abortion," what would that mean? That right cannot begin with the sense that there is, in any of us, from the very beginning, an intrinsic dignity, the source in turn of rights with an intrinsic dignity. Rights are conferred by the powerful, so long as they are seen as consistent with the interests of those who confer them, and they may be withdrawn when they no longer seem to be in accord with those interests.

When we come through this chain of steps, the right to an abortion would have no more significance than attaches to a "right to use the squash courts" at the college. It is a right that will always be contingent, always dependent on its acceptance by those with power, always open to repeal at any point. It would bear no resemblance to what the partisans of abortion refer to these days as "abortion rights."

When I wrote *Natural Rights and the Right to Choose*, I was feeling my frustration with George W. Bush and many old-line Republicans who kept shying away from the need to shape the public discourse by talking about this issue of abortion in public. That problem is still with us, and it has become even sharper of late, for the same people who feared talking about these issues before are ever more spooked about the prospect that Republicans who speak about abortion will be accused of carrying on a "war against women." The same people, already slouching toward a terminal timidity, would avoid saying anything critical now about same-sex marriage, lest they be painted as bigots in a "public discourse" that has driven out any patience, or wit, in the exchange and testing of reasons. The public at large has been very much on our side on these issues, and the evidence shows these questions have been net winners for the conservatives in elections. Yet, in the face of the evidence some of the most seasoned hands among Republican consultants keep advising us not to talk about these issues that ordinary people truly care about, and which run to the core. A political class that has confidence in itself as a political class would not be spooked by the media but use its arts and its skills to provide the storylines for the media.

Aristotle observed that if the art were in the material, then ships would be springing, fully crafted, from trees [Physics, 199b 28]. But ships were not part of the world of "causation," produced through the workings of the laws of nature. Ships were part of a world governed by design, by the awareness of ends, and the shaping of reasons. We may be bringing forth now a political class more and more detached from the sense that there is any particular importance in compelling the other side to come out with their reasons and claim them as their own. To a political class molding itself in that way, we may not only ask, where is the reason that gives meaning to political life, but where, in all of that, is the *art*? Where do we find the distinctive hand that shows your work? Where do we find the design that marked your understanding, the touch that reflected the experience you had cultivated? And where, finally, do we find the impression, lingering through time, that you were here?

NOTES

1. *Stenberg v. Carhart*, 530 U.S. 914 (2000).
2. *Floyd v. Anders*, 444 F. Supp. 535 (D.S.C. 1977).
3. *Floyd v. Anders*, at 539.
4. *Roe v. Wade*, 410 U.S. 113 (1973).
5. *Doe v. Bolton*, 410 U.S. 179 (1973).
6. The story of that bill—the understanding behind it, the strategy behind it, and the travails of moving it through Congress is told as part of my book *Natural Rights and the Right to Choose* (Cambridge University Press, 2002).
7. See *Planned Parenthood of Wisconsin v. Doyle*, 162 F. 3d 463, at 470 (7th Cir. 1998).
8. *Gonzales v. Carhart*, 550 U.S. 124 (2007).
9. See H.R. 1797, Pain-Capable Unborn Child Protection Act, 113th Congress (2013–2015) available at https://www.govtrack.us/congress/bills/113/hr1797/text.
10. See Hadley Arkes, "Empathy and the Law," *First Things* (August/September 2009), at 12–14.
11. Hearings on "The Medical Evidence Concerning Fetal Pain," Subcommittee on the Constitution, U.S. Senate, Committee on the Judiciary, 99th Cong., 1st Session, May 21, 1985, at 28–32, 35–36, 38.
12. Hadley Arkes, *First Things* (Princeton University Press, 1986). See chapters XVI and XVII, and p. 365.
13. Quoted in Arkes, *Natural Rights and the Right to Choose, supra* note 6, at 275–77.
14. When we had done that earlier bill I was joined by Jill Stanek, a brave nurse who had blown the whistle on the live-birth abortions performed at the Christ Hospital in Oak Lawn, Illinois: the child was delivered and then simply put in the refuse room, uncovered, to die. See *Natural Rights and the Right to Choose, supra* note 6, at 251–52, 267, 277. This was the safest abortion at all—no instruments introduced into the body of the mother, no parts of the child left in the body to cause infection. As Jill Stanek went on the radio to talk about our bill, nurses were calling in from different parts of the country, saying that "we've performed that procedure for years in our hospital." This chilling business happened far more often, and in far larger numbers, than even we had realized.

15. See my column in the web journal *The Catholic Thing*: "The Born-Alive Act and the Undoing of Obama" (August 18, 2008), available at http://www.thecatholicthing.org/columns/2008/the-born-alive-act-and-the-undoing-of-obama.html.

16. *Cohens v. Virginia*, 6 Wheaton 264 (1821).

17. *Cohens*, at 384.

18. For the account of this move with the Born-Alive Act, see Arkes, *Natural Rights and the Right to Choose, supra* note 6 at 250–51, 262–71, 278–80.

19. Abraham Lincoln, "Speech at Lewistown, Illinois," in *The Collected Works of Abraham Lincoln, Vol. 2,* ed. Roy P. Basler (Rutgers University Press, 1953), 546.

20. James Wilson, "Of the Natural Rights of Individuals," in *The Works of James Wilson* (Harvard University Press, 1967) (originally published in 1804), II, 585, 591. Wilson went on to say that "by the law, life is protected not only from immediate destruction, but from every degree of actual violence, and, in some cases, from every degree of danger."

Index

About the Contributors

Robert John Araujo, S.J., John Courtney Murray, S.J. University Professor, Emeritus, Loyola University, Chicago. Formerly, Professor Ordinarius, Pontificial Gregorian University and Bellarmine University Professor of Public and International Law, Gonzaga University. Academic Degrees: A.B., J.D., Georgetown University; M.Div., S.T.L., Weston School of Theology; B.C.L., Oxford University; LL.M., J.S.D., Columbia University. Active military service, United States Army, 1973. Past work experience: Office of the Solicitor, United States Department of the Interior, 1974–1979. Law Department, The Standard Oil Company of Ohio, 1979–1985. Entered the Society of Jesus, 1986. Legal Consultant to the Holy See, 1997 to the present: representative assignments include Preparatory Committee for the International Criminal Court; Preparatory Commission for the International Criminal Court; Diplomatic Conference of Plenipotentiaries, International Criminal Court; United Nations, General Assemblies 57, 58, and 59.

Michael Ariens is professor of law and director of Faculty Scholarship at St. Mary's University School of Law, San Antonio, Texas, where he has taught since 1987. He teaches constitutional law, American legal history, evidence, and other courses. He is the author of four books, including *Lone Star Law: A Legal History of Texas* (2011), which was awarded the 2012 Coral Horton Tullis Memorial Prize by the Texas State Historical Association for best 2011 book on Texas history and the Ray and Pat Browne Award for Best Reference/Primary Source Book in 2011 by the Popular Culture Association/ American Culture Association. His writing focuses on the American legal profession and constitutional law, the latter focusing particularly on issues of law and religion. He has been a visiting professor at the Columbus School of

Law of Catholic University of America, Southern Methodist University Dedman School of Law, and the University of Innsbruck.

Hadley Arkes is the Edward N. Ney Professor of Jurisprudence and American Institutions at Amherst College, where he has taught since 1966. He received a B.A. degree at the University of Illinois and a Ph.D. from the University of Chicago. In a series of books and articles dating from the mid-1980s, Arkes has written on *a priori* moral principles and advocated for their impact on constitutional interpretation. His works draw on political philosophers from Aristotle through the U.S. Founding Fathers, Lincoln, and contemporary authors and jurists. Arkes is founder and a member of the Committee for the American Founding, a group of Amherst alumni and students seeking to preserve the doctrines of "natural rights" exposited by some American Founders and Lincoln through the Colloquium on the American Founding at Amherst and in Washington, D.C. In 2010 Arkes, born and raised a Jew, converted to Catholicism, which he described as a fulfillment of his Jewish faith. Arkes serves on the advisory board and writes for *First Things*.

Thomas C. Berg is the James L. Oberstar Professor of Law and Public Policy at the University of St. Thomas School of Law, Minnesota, where he teaches constitutional law, law and religion, intellectual property, and religious liberty. He is the author of four books, dozens of scholarly and popular articles, and numerous briefs in the U.S. Supreme Court and lower courts on law and religion issues. His scholarship has also examined intellectual property in light of Christian thought (*see, e.g.*, "Intellectual Property and the Preferential Option for the Poor," *Journal of Catholic Social Thought* [2008]). He has served as codirector of the law school's Murphy Institute for Catholic Thought, Law, and Public Policy and on boards for the Democrats for Life of America and several law and religion organizations. He has degrees from the University of Chicago, in both law and religious studies; from Oxford University, in philosophy and politics (as a Rhodes Scholar); and from Northwestern University, in journalism.

Gerard V. Bradley is professor of law at the University of Notre Dame, where he teaches legal ethics and constitutional law. At Notre Dame he directs (with John Finnis) the Natural Law Institute and coedits *The American Journal of Jurisprudence*, an international forum for legal philosophy. Bradley has been a Visiting Fellow at the Hoover Institution of Stanford University and a Senior Fellow of the Witherspoon Institute in Princeton, New Jersey. He has published over one hundred scholarly articles and reviews.His most recent books are an edited collection of essays entitled *Challenges to Religious Liberty in the Twenty-First Century* (Cambridge University Press, 2012), *Essays on Law, Religion, and Morality* (St. Augustine's Press, 2014), and *Unquiet Americans: U.S. Catholics and the Common Good* (St. Augustine's Press, 2015).

John M. Breen is a professor of law at Loyola University Chicago School of Law. As an undergraduate, Professor Breen studied the "Great Books" while majoring in Liberal Studies at the University of Notre Dame. He graduated from Notre Dame in 1985 with highest honors. He then attended Harvard Law School where he was a member of the Board of Student Advisors, teaching research and writing to first-year law students. Following his graduation from Harvard in 1988, Professor Breen clerked for Hon. Boyce F. Martin, Jr., of the United States Court of Appeals for the Sixth Circuit. He then practiced law at Sidley & Austin in Chicago where he specialized in commercial litigation. Professor Breen served as an associate visiting professor of law at the Detroit College of Law at Michigan State University from 1994 to 1996. He joined the Loyola faculty in 1996. At Loyola, he teaches or has taught courses in contracts, professional responsibility, sales, negotiable snstruments, jurisprudence, and Catholic social thought. He has published numerous articles in law journals including the *University of Miami Law Review*, the *Connecticut Law Review*, and the *Harvard Journal of Law and Public Policy*. His scholarly writings have addressed a wide variety of topics including commercial law, statutory interpretation, abortion, law and religion, professional responsibility, and legal education.

John M. Czarnetzky is professor and Mitchell McNutt and Jessie Puckett Lecturer in Law at the University of Mississippi School of Law. He earned his B.S. at the Massachusetts Institute of Technology and his J.D. at the University of Virginia, School of Law. Professor Czarnetzky is an advisor to the Holy See's delegation to the United Nations and a former member of the Mississippi Advisory Committee to the U.S. Civil Rights Commission. He teaches and writes on bankruptcy, corporate, and commercial law. Professor Czarnetzky also has taught a freshman seminar on Catholic social doctrine, and has applied its tenets in his scholarship.

Robert A. Destro is professor of law and founding director of the Interdisciplinary Program in Law and Religion at The Catholic University of America's Columbus School of Law. He has been a member of the faculty since 1982 and served as interim dean from 1999 to 2001. From 1983 to 1989, Destro served as a Commissioner on the United States Commission on Civil Rights and led the Commission's discussions in the areas of discrimination on the basis of disability, national origin, and religion. He has served as Special Counsel to the Ohio Attorney General and the Ohio Secretary of State on election law matters from 2004 to 2006; as General Counsel to the

Catholic League for Religious and Civil Rights from 1977 to 1982; and as an adjunct associate professor of law at Marquette University from 1978 to 1982.

Robert P. George is McCormick Professor of Jurisprudence at Princeton University, where he lectures on constitutional interpretation, civil liberties, and philosophy of law. He also serves as the director of the James Madison Program in American Ideals and Institutions. George has been called America's "most influential conservative Christian thinker." He is a Senior Fellow at Stanford University's Hoover Institution and the Herbert W. Vaughan Senior Fellow of the Witherspoon Institute. He is also a visiting professor at Harvard Law School. He was awarded the Presidential Citizens Medal by President George W. Bush, and in Warsaw he received the Honorific Medal for the Defense of Human Rights of the Republic of Poland. He is a recipient of the Canterbury Medal of the Becket Fund for Religious Liberty, and he was one of four winners of the 2005 Bradley Awards for Civic and Intellectual Achievement.

Kevin H. Govern is associate professor at the Ave Maria School of Law. He began his legal career as an Army Judge Advocate, serving twenty years at every echelon during peacetime and war in worldwide assignments involving every legal discipline. He has also served as an assistant professor of law at the United States Military Academy and has taught at California University of Pennsylvania and John Jay College. He has published widely and spoken frequently on international and comparative law, national security and homeland security law, military operations, and professional ethics. The views expressed in his chapter are those of the author and do not reflect the official policy or position of Ave Maria School of Law or of any other institution or entity. Substantial portions of this chapter have been previously published under a nonexclusive right of publication as Kevin H. Govern, "Fidelity and Fairness: *Mulieris Dignitatem*'s Wisdom Relating to Marital Commitments, Contractual Relationships and the Roman Catholic Church©" *Rutgers Journal of Law and Religion* JO.Part 2 (2009): 1–17.

David L. Gregory is the Dorothy Day Professor of Law and the executive director of the St. John's University Center for Labor and Employment Law. He has taught at St. John's since August 1982 and has visited at the Colorado, Brooklyn, Hofstra, and New York Law Schools. He was appointed the Kenneth Wang Research Professor of Law for the 1987–1988 academic year. General Counsel pro bono for the Catholic League for Religious and Civil Rights, 2000–2012, he is also an active member of the Catholic Lawyers Guild for the Archdiocese of New York. In 2006, he was named the inaugural chair holder of the Dorothy Day Professorship. In 2008, he received the

Faculty Outstanding Achievement Award from the president of St. John's. In August 2009, he was appointed the inaugural executive director of the Center for Labor and Employment Law. At Professor Gregory's invitation, His Eminence Edward Cardinal Egan became the inaugural Honorary Chairman of the Center. They have convened major symposia on the Theology of Work and the Dignity of Workers and on Employment Dispute Resolution Across the Globe. He is a member of the National Academy of Arbitrators and author of more than two hundred academic and professional articles and papers,—including the first major law review articles on Catholic social thought on labor and employment, Dorothy Day, and Frederic Ozanam. Dave was a Basselin Scholar in the Honors Program of the School of Philosophy of The Catholic University of America, B.A. *cum laude* 1973; Wayne State University, M.B.A. 1977; University of Detroit, J.D. *magna cum laude* 1977. His LL.M. and J.S.D. degrees, 1982 and 1987, are from the Yale University Law School. He most recently coauthored a major case book, *Modern Labor Law in the Public and Private Sectors* (LexisNexis, 2013). Josephine McGrath and Gene Ubawike, St. John's Law Class of 2015 faculty research assistants, brought extraordinarily astute insights into our continuing conversations.

Dorie Klein is a professor at St. Mary's University School of Law, where she teaches criminal law, evidence, and mental health law. She graduated in 2002 from Vanderbilt University Law School, where she was an articles editor for the Vanderbilt Law Review. She also holds a B.A. from Swarthmore College and an M.A. in psychology from the University of Pennsylvania. Her scholarship focuses on the intersection of law and psychology and examines such topics as the competency of criminal defendants to stand trial, the competency of people who are mentally ill to make medical treatment decisions, and the reliability of expert psychiatric testimony.

Stephen M. Krason is professor of political science and legal studies, director of the Political Science Program, and associate director of the Veritas Center for Ethics in Public Life at Franciscan University of Steubenville. He is also cofounder and president of the Society of Catholic Social Scientists. He earned his J.D. and Ph.D. (political science) from the State University of New York at Buffalo. He is admitted to several bars, including the U.S. Supreme Court. His books include *Abortion: Politics, Morality, and the Constitution*; *Liberalism, Conservatism, and Catholicism*; *The Public Order and the Sacred Order*; and *The Transformation of the American Democratic Republic.* He is a member of the James Madison Society, a group of distinguished scholars affiliated with the James Madison Program in American Ideals and Institutions at Princeton University. He writes a monthly column for *Crisismagazine.com* and other publications entitled "Neither Left nor Right, but Catholic."

Richard V. Meyer is the director of the LL.M. Program at Mississippi College School of Law. He writes and teaches in the areas of humanitarian law, military justice, international criminal law, comparative criminal law, contracts, and torts. Professor Meyer's recent publications concern targeted killing, The Military Commissions Act of 2006, and humanitarian interventions. He has presented on these topics at law schools and cities around the country and the globe, including Brasilia, Yale, Columbia, Pennsylvania, West Point, Amsterdam, Beijing, Chongqing, Monrovia, Munich, Wuerzburg, Nuremberg, ChengDu, and Washington, D.C. Prior to joining the faculty of Mississippi College, Professor Meyer served as an associate professor of law at the United States Military Academy at West Point and also taught at Columbia Law School. He holds an LL.M. from Columbia, an LL.M. from the Judge Advocate General's School, a J.D. from Northern Illinois, and a B.A. from Illinois State. He is completing his J.S.D. at Columbia studying the future of the military jurisdiction. Professor Meyer is a retired Army Judge Advocate who practiced in the United States, Europe, and Asia in the fields of military justice, international law, administrative law, intelligence law, humanitarian law, and environmental law, among others. He is married to his wife of twenty-five years, Melissa, and they have five children ages five to eighteen.

Richard S. Myers is professor of law at Ave Maria School of Law. He is a graduate of Kenyon College and Notre Dame Law School. He taught at Case Western Reserve University School of Law and the University of Detroit Mercy School of Law before moving to Ann Arbor, Michigan, to help start Ave Maria School of Law. He has also taught as a visitor at Notre Dame Law School. His courses have included constitutional law and first amendment, in addition to antitrust, civil procedure, and conflict of laws. He has published extensively on constitutional law in the law reviews of Catholic University, Case Western Reserve University, Notre Dame University, and Washington and Lee University. Professor Myers is the coeditor of *St. Thomas Aquinas and the Natural Law Tradition: Contemporary Perspectives* (2004). He is also the coeditor of the *Encyclopedia of Catholic Social Thought, Social Science, and Social Policy* (original two volumes, 2007; third volume, 2012). He was the president of University Faculty for Life (2004–2011) and is now its vice president. He is the executive secretary of the Society of Catholic Social Scientists.

Bill Piatt is the former Dean (1998–2007) and currently a professor of law at St. Mary's University School of Law. He is the author of numerous books and articles including *Catholic Legal Perspectives* published in 2012 by the Carolina Academic Press. His writings have received international human rights awards. Bill previously served on the law faculty at the University of Oklahoma, Washburn, Southern Illinois, and Texas Tech. Bill is Hispanic, fluent in Spanish, and has taught and lectured in Mexico, Spain, Chile, Argentina, Austria, and China.

Ronald J. Rychlak is the Butler, Snow, O'Mara, Stevens and Cannada Lecturer and Professor of Law at the University of Mississippi. He also serves as the university's Faculty Athletic Representative and is the former associate dean for Academic Affairs. He is a graduate of Wabash College (B.A., *cum laude*) and Vanderbilt University (J.D., Order of the Coif). Prior to joining the faculty, he practiced law with Jenner & Block in Chicago, and he served as a clerk to Hon. Harry W. Wellford of the U.S. Sixth Circuit Court of Appeals. Professor Rychlak is an advisor to the Holy See's delegation to the United Nations and a member of the Mississippi Advisory Committee to the U.S. Civil Rights Commission. He is on the committee appointed by the Mississippi Supreme Court to revise the state's criminal code, the Southeastern Conference Executive Committee, and he serves on advisory boards for the Catholic League for Religious and Civil Rights, Ave Maria School of Law, and the International Solidarity and Human Rights Institute.

William L. Saunders is senior vice president for Legal Affairs and Senior Counsel at Americans United for Life ("AUL"). He directs AUL's international project and writes and speaks on a wide range of life-related and human rights topics, though the opinions expressed in his chapter are his alone. Before joining AUL, William served for ten years as Senior Fellow in Bioethics and Human Rights Counsel at the Family Research Council. A graduate of the Harvard Law School and the University of North Carolina, he has written widely on human rights and on Catholic topics. He was a private-sector member of the United States delegation to the United Nations Special Session on Children in 2001–2002.

Michael A. Scaperlanda holds the Gene and Elaine Edward Chair in Law and serves as associate dean for Academic Affairs at the University of Oklahoma College of Law where he has taught since 1989. He teaches in the areas of Catholic legal theory, constitutional law, immigration law, and professional responsibility. Scaperlanda's scholarship centers on two areas: the intersection of immigration law and constitutional law and Catholic perspectives on law. His books include *Immigration Law: A Primer* (Federal Judicial Center, 2009); *Recovering Self-Evident Truths: Catholic Perspectives on American Law* (CUA Press, 2007 coedited with Teresa Collett); and *The Journey: A Guide for the Modern Pilgrim* (Loyola, 2004 coauthored with

María Ruiz Scaperlanda). His articles have been published in the *Connecticut Law Review*, the *Georgetown Immigration Law Journal*, the *Iowa Law Review*, the *Stanford Review of Law and Policy*, the *Texas Law Review*, and the *Wisconsin Law Review*, among others.

D. Brian Scarnecchia, M.Div., J.D., is an associate professor of law at Ave Maria School of Law in Naples, Florida, where he teaches property law, origin of the United States Constitution, criminal law, and bioethics. He is also an associate professor and the director of the Legal Studies Program and the Human Life Studies Program at Franciscan University of Steubenville in Steubenville, Ohio. He is the founding president of International Solidarity and Human Rights Institute, a non-governmental organization ("NGO") in consultative status with the United Nations. He serves on the Board of Directors for the Society of Catholic Social Scientists and is their main NGO representative to the United Nations. He has also served as an assistant County Prosecutor for Jefferson County, Ohio. He is the author of *Bioethics, Law, and Human Life Issues: A Catholic Perspective on Marriage, Family, Contraception, Abortion, Reproductive Technology, and Death and Dying* (Scarecrow Press, 2010) and coauthor of *The Millennium Development Goals in Light of Catholic Social Teaching* (C-Fam, 2009). He is a founding member and an expert on family and social issues for the Catholic Inspired NGO Forum working in association with the Pontifical Council for the Family and Secretariat of the Holy See.

Lucia A. Silecchia received her B.A. from Queens College (CUNY) and her J.D. from Yale Law School, where she was a senior editor of *The Yale Law Journal*, a current topics editor of *The Yale Law and Policy Review*, and a Francis Coker Teaching Fellow. After working in the litigation department of Rogers & Wells, she joined the faculty of Catholic University's Columbus School of Law in 1991. She served as associate dean for Academic Affairs in 2004 and 2005, and she directs Catholic University's International Human Rights Summer Law Program in Rome. In April 2007, Professor Silecchia was one of nine Americans to participate in a Vatican conference on Climate Change and Development, organized by the Pontifical Council for Justice and Peace. She has also participated in the Association of Religiously Affiliated Law Schools and was the 2008–2009 chair of the Conference on Catholic Legal Thought. Professor Silecchia has written and lectured in the areas of environmental law and ethics, elder law and estate planning, Catholic social thought, legal education, law and literature, and legal writing. She has taught in Catholic University's cooperative programs at Jagiellonian University in Cracow, Poland, and lectured in Portugal as part of Catholic University's U.S.–Portuguese Law Initiative at the University of Lisbon. Professor Silecchia is admitted to the bars of New York, Connecticut, the District of Columbia, and the Supreme Court of the United States.

Lee J. Strang is a graduate of the University of Iowa, where he was Articles Editor of the *Iowa Law Review* and Order of the Coif. Professor Strang also holds an LL.M. degree from Harvard Law School. Prior to joining the faculty at the University of Toledo College of Law, Professor Strang served as a judicial clerk for Chief Judge Alice M. Batchelder of the U.S. Court of Appeals for the Sixth Circuit. He was also an associate for Jenner & Block LLP in Chicago. Professor Strang has published in the fields of constitutional law and interpretation, property law, and religion and the First Amendment. He is currently editing a case book on constitutional law for LexisNexis, drafting a book proposal tentatively titled *Originalism: Its Promise and Limits*, and writing a book on the history of Catholic legal education. Professor Strang's course offerings include constitutional law, constitutional interpretation, jurisprudence, property law, administrative law, business associations, federal courts, and appellate practice.

Timothy J. Tracey serves as associate professor of law at Ave Maria School of Law in Naples, Florida. His publications include the "Demise of Equal Access and a Return to the Early-American Understanding of Student Rights" and "*Christian Legal Society v. Martinez*: In Hindsight." He teaches numerous subjects including constitutional law and first amendment. He studied at Wake Forest University School of Law and Grove City College, and practiced law with the Christian Legal Society's Center for Law and Religious Freedom and the Alliance Defending Freedom. He lives with his wife and two children in Fort Myers, Florida.